# The Soviet Union and Social Science Theory

*Russian Research Center Studies, 77*

# The Soviet Union and Social Science Theory

## Jerry F. Hough

Harvard University Press
Cambridge, Massachusetts
and London, England
1977

**Library of Congress Cataloging in Publication Data**

Hough, Jerry F        1935-
  The Soviet Union and social science theory.

  (Russian Research Center studies; 77)
  Includes index.
  1. Communist state.   2. Russia—Politics
and government—1917-   3. Social sciences.
I. Title.   II. Series: Harvard University.
Russian Research Center.   Studies; 77.
JC474.H58        321.9'2        77-1545
ISBN 0-674-82980-8

*To Denis Sullivan*

# Preface

A collection of essays can be seen from many perspectives. As the two part titles suggest, this book seeks to demonstrate why many of our fundamental assumptions about the Soviet Union need rethinking, and then explores some of the implications this reconceptualization poses for democratic theory in contemporary political science. For the layman, however, the major significance of the book lies in another direction. Although these chapters were written as part of a scholarly debate on how best to understand the Soviet Union, today they can also be considered commentaries on the basic assumptions of American foreign policy.

Despite the stated desire of each new administration in the United States to concentrate its attention upon Western Europe, Japan, and the Third World, competition with the Soviet Union always becomes the fulcrum of foreign policy—and rightly so because of the nuclear aspect of Soviet-American relations. Questions relating to other parts of the world come to be interpreted in relation to this competition or struggle, and policy toward the Soviet Union—regardless of its nature—inevitably becomes the subject of major public debate.

A number of factors affect one's opinions about the proper policy to follow toward the Soviet Union, but the most important is one's view of the nature of the Soviet political system. If one sees the top Soviet leadership and the party apparatus as essentially united on major questions, if one sees the prime concern of the bureaucracy as preservation of its privilege and therefore united on this basic level, if one sees power as residing almost exclusively among top political and governmental officials, above all if one sees the political system as being a real "system" which flows from ideological commitments and then evolves in line with its inner dynamics, one is likely to have little sense of a political process on important questions and little sense that individual actions might affect this process. If one sees the Soviet leaders becoming more repressive and alien, then peaceful coexistence and detente are likely to be viewed as counterproductive in terms of human rights and meaningless at best in terms of the achievement of American foreign policy goals.

If this view is coupled with the belief that the Soviet leaders are essentially hostile to the West, the natural conclusion is that almost nothing, short of the collapse of the Soviet system, will produce change of importance to the United States. The Soviet-American relationship becomes a contest pure and simple—some would say an ideological war pure and simple—and a plus for one side must be a minus for the other and vice versa. The job for the United States must be to hold firm, to advance our position aggressively, to try to score points. Not only might this posture help in the struggle for allies in the world arena, but also a Soviet system without elementary legitimacy may prove to be more fragile than expected and may crack under the pressure.

There is, however, another image of the Soviet Union—the one advanced in this book. It does emphasize that the Soviet Union is a repressive state in which many individual rights are not guaranteed and in which the Marxist ideals of full equality have not been achieved. Yet it recognizes that a great deal of debate is permitted on most policy questions in the Soviet Union and that, within the framework of the basic authoritarianism, an increased tendency to tolerate individual differences is observable. It sees the Brezhnev era—even in comparison with the Khrushchev era—as featuring less repression of individual freedom, more egalitarianism in its social policy, a far greater dispersion of actual power (but not, of course, final authority) from the top political leadership, and greater caution in foreign policy. It insists that there is a politics in the Soviet Union, even on the most important questions, and suggests that the multiplicity of forces struggling to shape the Soviet Union could produce change either for the better or for the worse from an American point of view.

Perhaps most basic of all, this image of the Soviet Union is based on a rather different view of the relationship of the party and society in the Soviet Union. The word "legitimacy" is a fuzzy term in any discussion of any political system, but this image contends that the Soviet system has had a broad range of societal supports from its earliest days—perhaps even a very basic legitimacy developing among large segments of the Russian urban population and even those peasants aspiring to move to the city. It treats the Soviet system as a very participatory one, with many societal inputs in the decision-making process and considerable societal influence upon many decisions. It treats even the much-criticized "bureaucrats" of the Soviet Union as, in large part, trained specialists who usually advocate various types of policy change and whose political role must at least in part be understood as analogous to certain kinds of political participation and interest group activity in the West.

In this view, the legitimacy of the system might well be eroding among key elements of the population (not because of excessive benefits to the bureaucratic and professional personnel of the New Class but because of insufficient benefits accorded them), but the system remains deeply rooted in Russian nationalism. There has been a strong strain in Russian intellectual history that has seen Moscow as a Third Rome and that has insisted that Russian development could and should take a different path from the Western one. The Communist regime in a sense has been a compromise between Western and Slavophil tendencies. It brought Western industrial development, but it did so under new organizational forms—forms that a number of other countries emulated and that were associated with the achievement of historic Russian national goals and a great increase in Russian power.

A public opinion poll in the Soviet Union might well show considerable dissatisfaction with the political system or certain aspects of it, but to speak about any system being illegitimate in a real sense, one must be able, I think, to say that the population believes that another type of system is better or at least no worse than the present one. We should never forget that for a Russian, the establishment of competitive elections and a multiparty system would mean the abandonment of a system Russians had created and its replacement by a system created in the West. Since democratization would inevitably be extended to the non-Russian republics and the countries of East Europe, it would also mean the loss of Russian control over most, if not all, of these territories. Faced with these choices, many Russians may feel that—to paraphrase Winston Churchill's statement about democracy—the Soviet system is the worst in the world except for all the others.

If one holds this view of the Soviet Union, it too has foreign policy implications. If the Brezhnev era is seen as one more liberal and egalitarian than the Khrushchev era, one is likely to be more optimistic about the impact of detente on the evolution of the Soviet system and the state of human rights within it. (Indeed, if there has been liberalization, it is much easier to understand the Soviet reaction to President Carter's emphasis on human rights in the formulation of foreign policy, for improvement has only produced an escalation in American criticism.) If one sees evolution in the system in the last ten to fifteen years, one is more likely to see the possibility of evolution in the future.

More important, if one sees the party-society relationship as much more than the imposition of an alien ideology and system of controls by a group largely divorced from society, one is far more likely to feel the need to take Soviet sensitivities into account in American efforts to affect the evolution of the Soviet system—sensitivities not only of top officialdom but also of major elements of the population as a whole. Persons holding this view of the Soviet Union generally assume that the Soviet future will be shaped largely by internal Soviet forces, but they also usually believe that the international atmosphere may have some impact on the course of developments. They are likely to feel strongly that a confrontation posture, an emphasis upon ideological differences, a we-or-they mentality will deepen Soviet suspicions and will strengthen the position of those in the Soviet Union who think in similar terms. They assume that overt Western pressure to change in Western directions will put Soviet liberals in the position of serving Western power aims and seeming "soft" to foreign pressure and will undercut them in their political struggles.

Not surprisingly, the logical corollary of this view has been that the United States, while maintaining its defense forces and the willingness to use them, should act in such a way as to try to relax the atmosphere and to encourage the Soviet Union to think less in an ideological manner and more in terms of mutual interests. Such a view clearly underlay Secretary of State Kissinger's Soviet policy, but it was expressed most eloquently by President Kennedy in his American University speech less than five months before his death:

> Let us re-examine our attitude toward the Soviet Union. It is sad to read . . . Soviet statements—to realize the extent of the gulf between us. But it is also a warning—a warning to the American people not to fall into the same trap as the Soviets, not to see only a distorted and desperate view of the other side, not to see conflict as inevitable, accommodation as impossible and communication as nothing more than an exchange of threats . . . Let us re-examine our attitude towards the cold war, remembering we are not engaged in a debate, seeking to pile up debating points. We are not here distributing blame or pointing the finger of judgment. We must deal with the world as it is, and not as it might have been . . . Let us not be blind to our differences—but let us direct attention to our common interests and the means by which these differences can be resolved. And if we cannot end now our differences, at least we can help make the world safe for diversity.

This is not, of course, a book that focuses directly on foreign policy questions. It is concerned with the way we understand the Soviet Union. It is based on the assumption that the tendency to talk about *the* party, *the* system, *the* ideology, and so forth in a general and sweeping manner has been one of the major causes of our misunderstanding. It is based on the assumption that there is an enormous amount to gain from sorting out what we mean—or should mean—when we use words like "the bureaucracy," "the party," "the party apparatus," "power," and the like.

This book is further based on the assumption that there is even more

to gain from looking at reality and data closely rather than simply generalizing in an abstract manner. If we understand, for example, that more
than half of the men over 30 with college degrees are party members, that
"ideological" party secretaries have major responsibility for seeking
health-education-welfare appropriations in the budgetary process, that
city party leaders are usually engineers with managerial experience, that
the percentage of women among speakers to the regional soviets varies
greatly from region to region, that governmental services such as day-care
centers and hospital beds per capita also vary greatly from region to
region and that there is some statistical association between the level of
these services and political factors such as the percentage of women speakers, the old clichés about party, ideology, red vs. expert, and total direction from the center rapidly lose much of their meaning. And if these
clichés lose their meaning, we most urgently come face to face with the
crucial questions: what are the motivating factors behind Soviet policy,
what are the social forces working for change within the Establishment as
well as among the dissidents, how are Soviet goals and perceptions vis-à-
vis the outside world formed and how do they evolve?

These are the most important questions for American foreign policy,
but there is no way to discuss them meaningfully until we begin to get a
sense of real officials rather than of a faceless bureaucracy, a sense of the
reality of great participation rather than the myth of an apolitical Soviet
population, a sense of the richness of Soviet within-systems politics instead of an abstract frozen system. That is what this book is about, and, as
such, it relates most directly to the question of the type of policy toward
the Soviet Union that this country should pursue.

J.F.H.

# Acknowledgments

The older a scholar becomes, the greater difficulty he has in acknowledging his intellectual debts. The number of such debts multiplies over the years, and one's memory undoubtedly manages to forget many of the most important. The problem is particularly great for a collection of essays written at different times. For this reason it seems most appropriate to mention several people whose general impact over time seems to have been the greatest and to hope that many of the more specific intellectual debts are at least partially acknowledged in the notes.

Certainly I could not have been more fortunate than in having had the opportunity to attend Harvard University and the Russian Research Center in the middle and late 1950s when Merle Fainsod and Barrington Moore were actively leading Soviet studies in political science and when the results of the Harvard Refugee Project were still creating fresh intellectual excitement. To some extent, much of my work can probably be seen as an unconscious attempt to reconcile tensions in my own mind produced by the rather different insights and perspectives of Fainsod and Moore, with the former shaping my sense of how the Soviet system works and the latter having a major impact upon my comparative perspective.

A second great influence on this book has been Zbigniew Brzezinski and Samuel Huntington, *Political Power USA/USSR.* When that book appears in the notes—as it frequently does—the reference is usually to a statement with which I disagree. However, *Political Power USA/USSR* was the first major attempt to discuss a policy process in the Soviet Union, and it did so in comparative terms at that. Even when it aroused disagreement, it presented innumerable new hypotheses and to a very considerable extent it has shaped in a fundamental way the questions I have asked.

A third influence has been that of colleagues who are not specialists on the Soviet Union. The number is so large that it probably is wrong to mention any names at all, but I cannot bring myself to leave several persons unmentioned: Philip Monypenny of the University of Illinois, Denis Sullivan of Dartmouth College (formerly of the University of Illinois), H. Donald Forbes of the University of Toronto, and Ronald Rogowski and

David Price of Duke University. One year of intense discussions with
Denis Sullivan was so important in the development of many of the
themes of this book that I am dedicating the book to him.

My wife, Sheila Fitzpatrick, bore the brunt of the creation of the
book itself and provided many valuable suggestions.

Finally, two grants were extremely useful in the preparation of the
book—and indispensable so far as several of the chapters are concerned.
One grant, the Social Science Research Council retraining fellowship at
the University of Michigan, was crucial in my acquiring some capability to
use quantitative techniques and in deepening my exposure to empirical
political science theory. A second was awarded by the Policy Sciences
Institute of Duke University and was vital for the collection and analysis
of the regional data on hospital beds in chapter 7.

A number of the chapters in this book appeared elsewhere first, and
I would like to thank the publishers for permission to reprint them. "The
Bureaucratic Model and the Nature of the Soviet System" is reprinted
from *Journal of Comparative Administration,* 2 (August 1973), 134-168,
by permission of the publisher, Sage Publications, Inc. "The Soviet
System: Petrification or Pluralism?" first appeared in *Problems of Communism* (March-April 1972). "The Party Apparatchiki," in H. Gordon
Skilling and Franklyn Griffiths, eds., *Interest Groups in Soviet Politics*
(copyright © 1971 by Princeton University Press), pp. 47-92, is reprinted
by permission of Princeton University Press. "The Soviet Experience and
the Measurement of Power" is reprinted from the *Journal of Politics,* 37
(1975), 685-710. "Political Participation in the Soviet Union" first
appeared in *Soviet Studies* (January 1976).

# Contents

Introduction                                                          1

## I Reconceptualization of the Soviet System

1  The Soviet System: Petrification or Pluralism?            19
2  The Bureaucratic Model and the Nature of the Soviet
     System                                                            49
3  The Party Apparatchiki and Interest Group Theory       71
4  Political Participation in the Soviet Union              109
5  Party Saturation in the Soviet Union                     125
6  The Impact of Participation: Women and the
     Women's Issue in Soviet Policy Debates                 140
7  Centralization and Decentralization in the Soviet
     Administrative System                                   159

## II Implications for Social Science Theory

8  Inputs and Responsiveness in American Political
     Science                                                          173
9  Communications and Persuasion in the Analysis of
     Inputs                                                            190
10 The Soviet Experience and the Measurement of
     Power                                                             203
11 The Comparative Approach and the Study of the
     Soviet Union                                                     222
   Notes                                                               241
   Index                                                               273

# The Soviet Union and
# Social Science Theory

# Introduction

To a very considerable extent, Soviet studies in the United States—indeed, Communist studies as a whole—have been confined to a ghetto within the social sciences. In part it has been a self-created ghetto, for most American scholars working on the Soviet Union have come to a study of that country either out of a conscious or unconscious search for their personal roots or out of an interest in understanding America's major adversary in the postwar period. As a result, these scholars have generally been happy to be trained as area specialists, and their concern with social science theory has tended to be limited to those modernization theories that might illuminate the course of evolution of Soviet society. Moreover, in their frequent insistence upon the primacy of politics in the Soviet case or, in some instances, of Russian historical traditions, they often have been more concerned with denying the relevance of that modernization theory than with trying to employ and modify it.

Nevertheless, the ghettoization of Soviet studies is not the fault only of those in the ghetto. Over the last two decades, leading figures in the social sciences have condemned area studies and have demanded that area specialists become main-line social scientists, but in practice they themselves have shown little interest in bringing Communist world studies into the discipline. In their books, comparative theorists have tended to analyze the Soviet Union in black-and-white, ideal-type terms that emphasize the distinctive character of the Soviet Union both empirically and normatively. They generally have used the Soviet system for little more than a foil against which to highlight the virtues of Western political systems or non-Communist models of development. Even scholars like Joseph LaPalombara, who reject "the tendency of Western comparativists' to treat Communist systems as historical and developmental aberrations," often also reject the use of Western concepts in discussions of the Soviet Union and thereby unintentionally leave that country described in ways that make it seem aberrant.[1]

The following assertion by Alfred G. Meyer is directed at the work of specialists on the Soviet Union, but it applies even more to the work of comparative theorists:

In dealing with the Communist world, our notions of what a political system is or does have been suspended. For describing that world we have used concepts and models reserved for it alone or for it and a few other systems considered inimical. Thus one might almost say that the Communist world was analyzed outside the framework of comparative political science. Or else we used one set of concepts for Communist countries and another for the rest of the world. Most American political scientists would reject the elitist models of Pareto, Mosca, and Michels and would criticize a sociologist like Mills for seeking to apply them to the United States. Yet have not most studies of the Communist world described Communist states in the crudest Paretan terms as the rule of self-appointed elites striving to perpetuate themselves and structuring the entire system to this purpose? And I stress the crudeness of these interpretations, which neglect most of the subtleties and sophistication of both Mosca and Pareto.[2]

From many points of view, the ghettoization of Soviet studies has been quite convenient for everyone directly involved. Graduate students already burdened with learning a strange culture and language have been spared the task of mastering a vast social science literature. Social science theorists have been spared the effort of testing their theories against the experience of one third of the world's population. And in particular, they have been spared the task of facing up to phenomena that challenge many of their fundamental ideological and empirical assumptions about the sources and exercise of power.

It is only our understanding of the Soviet political system and the development of social science theory that has not benefited from the ghettoization of Soviet studies. The essays included in this volume have been written in the conviction that a policy of integration and assimilation, while perhaps discomforting at first, is vital for achieving these aims. This book, notably in the first seven chapters, attempts to illuminate the Soviet political system by looking at it in terms of "our notions of what a political system is or does," to use Meyer's words, and by utilizing quantitative and analytical techniques that have been developed in the social sciences in recent decades. The book further attempts, particularly in the concluding four chapters, to indicate certain modifications in social science theory that seem to be dictated or at least suggested by the Soviet experience, when it is properly understood.

The decade of work embodied in this book can be summarized in a number of ways, and it may well be that the reader has a better perspective on this question than the author. Certainly, it would be wrong to imply that these essays result from some conscious five-year or ten-year plan that was set out in the mid-1960s and carried through to completion. Indeed, several of the articles would not even have been written had there not been a specific invitation.

In retrospect, however, these essays do seem to have a common core: they represent an attempt to rethink what political scientists of the past would have called the state-society relationship in the Soviet Union. The essence of the totalitarian model was a passive society dominated by an elite that was determined to maximize its own power and to transform society on the basis of its own ideological perceptions. When the to-talitarian model began to fall into disrepute during the Khrushchev years, it was replaced by a series of "directed society" models that largely retained this view of the state-society (really party-society) relationship. Allen Kassof spoke of an "administered society" ("totalitarianism with-out terror");[3] T. H. Rigby of an "organizational society" (a "command-dominated society" in which command is defined as "a relationship in which one party is active and the other is passive in the determination of what is done");[4] Zbigniew Brzezinski and Samuel Huntington of an "ideological system" (one in which "the [political] system is used by the political leaders to create a new society along the lines of their own beliefs and aspirations"),[5] and so forth. There was some tendency to recognize that, in the words of Brzezinski and Huntington, "the Soviet system has lost some of its freedom to mold society,"[6] but that system was still defined basically in terms of the models described.

In the course of a long and intensive study of the Soviet political-administrative system, *The Soviet Prefects,* I came to the conclusion that this way of visualizing the Soviet political process has grave shortcom-ings.[7] Although the local party first secretaries have been directly respon-sible to higher party officials and have served as their representatives in the locality, the local party organs turned out to function less as the direc-tors of the region in some active sense than as the arbiters for disputes and problems brought to them by other agencies in the region. These dis-putes were frequently as technical and minor as the priority to be given various recipients in the delivery of supplies or the production of orders. As one Soviet article explained, "It is not the party obkom which makes demands on the oblast [regional] organizations, but, on the contrary, the leaders of these organizations which present their endless demands to the obkom: do this, interfere in this, give such an instruction."[8] Indeed, the central thesis of *The Soviet Prefects* was that the local party organs have not been an intrusive and parasitical element in Soviet industrial admin-istration but, given the general structure of the governmental and plan-ning system, have been indispensable for its successful operation pre-cisely because they have been the local "common boss" to which the subordinates of all ministries and other organizations can take their conflicts for resolution.

In my view, this coordinating role assigned the local Party organs has had a number of important consequences. First, the party secretaries called upon to play this role generally have behaved in ways that correspond less to the stereotype of a rigid ideologue than to that of a bargainer imbued with the values of the civic culture. Second, the responsibility of the local party organs for economic performance in the region has made them especially dependent upon the record of the region's most important economic producers in the shaping of their own record. Consequently, it has often been in the party officials' own interest to support proposals and priority demands that are in the interest of the major economic producers. Third, because technical expertise is often required for judging the relative priorities in production scheduling and supplies procurement, not to mention for participating in the planning process, engineers with managerial experience—including that of plant manager—have been drawn into party work in urban areas. Thus, the general tendency for the party organs to support industry out of self-interest has been reinforced by the fact that their decisions are often being made by persons with an industrialist's background and perspectives.

When the relationship between the local party organs and economic managers is seen in this light, the state-society relationship seems far different from what was described in the totalitarian or directed society models. The local party organs may have supreme legal authority, but they often are timid in putting pressure on the "rich uncles" of the region or city—those who have the economic base in their hands.[9] As William Taubman argues, the Soviet city often takes on the appearance of a company town in which the political leaders are dominated by the major industry, that is, in which the state is dominated by one segment of society.[10]

It might be argued that generalizations about political relationships at the local level relate only to the process by which the center's policy is administered and that they are not relevant to the process by which the center determines policy and to the relationship of the party leadership to society. However, in practice, most of those who come to sit in the Party Politburo have risen through the party apparatus and have in a long career proved successful in the brokering role associated with it, and it would not be surprising if they retained some of the habits of a lifetime as they come to the top. It is the central argument of this book that—for whatever reason—the national leaders have, in fact, begun to function more according to the norms of the regional party officials.

There are many ways in which the party-society relationship in the

Soviet Union has come to deviate—or has always deviated—from the directed society models, and a number of them are discussed here. In the image of the Soviet Union that emerges, society is not inert and passive but participatory in almost all senses of the term. Indeed, even the form of participation that is thought to be most exclusive—membership in the Communist Party—engages approximately 22 percent of all men between the ages of thirty and sixty—a broader group than the "attentive public" as usually defined in the United States on the basis of survey research. Participation in various commissions and committees at the place of work (groups that deal with housing distribution, passes to resorts, dismissal of personnel, planning of social-cultural affairs, and so forth) is even wider.

Despite censorship against the expression of certain types of ideas (especially against the expression of them in "improper" ways), and the prohibition against confrontation politics and nearly all types of dramatization of demands, Soviet citizens are permitted to advocate not only change in the behavior of local administrators, but incremental change in national policy in most policy areas. Moreover, the multiplicity of cleavages within Soviet society guarantees that a broad range of views is expressed and a broad range of interests represented, even in print. Societal interests become embodied in state, party, and public institutions—for example, those of the doctors and to a lesser extent of the patients in the Ministry of Health, the public health sector of the Central Committee apparatus, and the Medical Workers Trade Union; those of the steel industry and to some extent the steel workers in a similar ferrous metallurgy complex.

These pluralistic aspects of the Soviet political system are the product of many forces. To some extent they stem from the ideology itself. In our absorption with the authoritarian aspects of Lenin's image of a political system as a whole, we have overlooked the particularly strong emphasis that he always placed on citizen involvement in public administration, and we have forgotten that in a country that is one "bureaucracy writ large," public administration embraces much that would be city and state politics in the United States.

To some extent, these pluralistic aspects of the system also flow from the irrepressible characteristics of human nature. Students of Western bureaucracy have repeatedly noted an almost invariable tendency for these "executive agents" to suggest plans of action, to press for more money, to represent at least some of the interests of the clientele they serve. As the early Bolshevik leaders discovered to their surprise after the revolution, Communists are no different in this respect.[11] Even if the Komsomol organization had been established solely to shape the world-view of the youth rather than to represent youth, its officials would soon have been advocating more leisure facilities for youth as a way of combating "unhealthy" attitudes among them. Even if a Communist is named ideological secretary of a party committee and is put in charge of propaganda, education, and culture as an ideological watchdog, the nature of his responsibilities would soon lead him to fight the bureaucratic battles for funds for his branches and in a Soviet-type economic system even to "beat out" supplies for school construction "with all truths and half-truths."

But to a considerable extent the phenomena that we are discussing are also inherent in the assumptions of those who have developed the directed society models. The very drive to rule and control that is posited as the central element of the Soviet system has implications that make any simplistic directed-society model quite unrealistic. For example, if the leadership wants a check on the work of bureaucrats, it must encourage a good deal of citizen participation on the local level, and if this participation is to have the effect the regime wants, then there must be citizen input into the type of decisions that are at the heart of local politics in the West. If the leadership fears becoming dependent on the advice of the ministries, establishes an overlapping system of hierarchies to check upon the ministries and to provide alternate channels of information, and encourages the population to use these various channels, citizen input again becomes inevitable if the system of competing bureaucracies that is defined as the essence of totalitarian administration is to function effectively.

The logic of rule has also affected the basic nature of the Communist party itself. If the leadership wants to limit party membership to those who are willing to devote their lives to the fulfillment of the party's goals, if for a series of reasons (including the hope that the regime will be more secure if the fate of the administrative-professional stratum is more directly tied to the fate of the party) it wants to require party membership for all important administrative posts, then it faces several very real dangers. Foremost is the danger that many persons will proclaim total loyalty to the party's cause and will pretend ideological orthodoxy simply to obtain the jobs and material advantages associated with membership. If, as a consequence, the party becomes filled with people with little talent (except perhaps in acting ability), the policy of reserving administrative posts for members could lead to a most ineffective administrative system.

The obvious solution to this dilemma of party membership is to deny people the right to enter it until they demonstrate "dedication to the building of Communism" in their daily work—that is, to deny them admission until they are in their mid-to-late twenties and have had some opportunity to develop a proven record of accomplishment. This is precisely the policy the leadership has followed since the end of World War II. The average age of admission in 1966 was thirty-one, while in 1975 it was twenty-seven. As a consequence, those who enter the party and the administrative elite come in large part to be the same type of persons who would be successful in any country, except for the difference in their ideology. The old dichotomy between "Red" and "expert" becomes meaningless as the elite becomes Red *and* expert, with its expertise being established before membership in the party is permitted.

The other major danger flowing from the leadership's membership goals is that the legitimacy of the party as an instrument of the proletariat will be undermined. If a broad range of posts is going to be limited to party members and if a broad selection of candidates is desired, then large numbers of trained specialists must be admitted into the party. And, in practice, approximately 30 percent of all citizens with completed higher education in 1973 were Party members, over 50 percent of the men with such education.

Given the enormous expansion in the number both of specialists and skilled workers during the course of the industrialization drive, the large scale enrollment of those with higher education in the party further necessitates the admission of a large number of workers into the party if the proletariat representation within it is to be meaningful.[12] The result, if the leadership finds this logic compelling, must be a party which, while selective in its admission policies, is still a mass one by any reasonable definition. The percentage of women in the party remains low (some 5-6 percent of those between the ages of thirty and sixty), but at least if one thinks in terms of representation and involvement of family units, the figure of 22 percent of all men in this age group being in the party is the crucial one. It is totally impossible for such a party to be some kind of priesthood that stands outside of society; rather, virtually all societal interests have penetrated into the party to some extent.

Finally, as mentioned earlier, the logic of rule has also affected the staff of the party apparatus itself. In order to strengthen the ability of the party organs to understand and control the technical decisions being taken by governmental and economic administrators, the leadership has recruited many party officials—in fact, most of them—from among those with specialized knowledge and experience. This policy undoubtedly has had a number of the consequences desired, but it has also meant that the controllers in the center, as well as those in the localities, have often come from the agencies being controlled. For example, the head of the transportation-communications department of the Party Central Committee is a former head of the Gorki Railroad and thus a former subordinate of the present Minister of Railroads. This penetration of the party apparatus by the diversity of views and interests represented in the Soviet professional and administrative stratum means that the phenomena that led Taubman to speak of a company town in many Soviet cities can exist in the central policy making process as well.

There are, of course, scholars who would suggest that political participation in the Soviet Union is somehow not real; that there are no interest groups in the Soviet Union, despite the obvious correspondence of Soviet political phenomena to Arthur Bentley's and David Truman's definitions of interest groups; that the word "pluralism" can never be used even in a qualified sense to describe the Soviet Union because groups and persons in a condition of bureaucratic subordination can never be autonomous political actors, despite the experience of the military in innumerable countries. However, such assertions do not seem to me to be worth prolonged and serious discussion. If they do not flow from mere ideological reluctance to admit that the Soviet and Western political systems might be comparable in some senses, they rest on legalistic and formalistic definitions derived from Western institutional experience rather than on definitions based upon processes at work.

The question that does seem worth discussing is the relationship of the multiplicity of societal inputs in the Soviet Union to the structure of power in that country. One could describe the inputs simply as the result of the leadership's encouragement of information feedback for its own purposes, of its wish to be exposed to a broad range of policy alternatives in order to avoid dependence upon a single source of advice, of its desire for checks upon performance of lower bureaucrats. Such an image could save the directed society model (and give it more sophisticated form), for the leadership could be said to retain total power to make the final decision and could be seen as directing society along lines that its interpretation of incoming information and its choice among proposed policy alternatives suggested. But the question remains: is this really a reasonable way to conceptualize the Soviet political system, or is it simply the product of the same type of deep identification with ideology that compels many Soviet intellectuals to explain everything in the United States in crude ("vulgar") Marxist terms? The second crucial question is: how do we determine which method of conceptualization is the more reasonable?

The central concern of this volume is to attempt to come to grip with these questions. We see a very wide range of inputs in the Soviet Union and the United States; we see people in both countries striving to push through their pet policy alternatives (and generally they are people of similar occupations and backgrounds in both countries); we see policy decisions and outcomes that inevitably correspond to some of the societal input. How do we judge that the input has produced or influenced the decision in the United States and that the successful input in the Soviet Union has just chanced to correspond with the leadership's or the elite's preference? How does the Soviet Marxist justify a similar judgment, which, it turns out, is diametrically opposite in its conclusions so far as the United States and the Soviet Union are concerned? Is there any more empirical basis for our judgment that input does not equal power in the Soviet Union than for the Marxist's judgment that of course American political participation cannot be real or meaningful because of the dominance of the political system by the owners of the means of production? Almost every essay in this book either concludes with this methodological question or is focused in large part upon it.

The problem, however, is even deeper than the questions of the last paragraph suggest. The major American pluralist scholars of the 1950s and 1960s described both the American political system and the normatively good political system in terms that deemphasized the importance of majority rule, of confrontation politics, and even, at times, of elections. This literature focused on such phenomena as a bargaining culture, a population that was socialized into accepting the necessity of moderation in political participation and in the type of political demands that should be made, comprehensive interest group representation by figures in the "leadership echelon," political leaders that function as brokers and that introduce policy change in an accommodating and incremental manner, and policy outcomes that are largely determined by those with specialized knowledge and interests in the respective policy areas ("minorities rule," Robert Dahl called it; "interest group liberalism" in the phrase of Theodore Lowi). Whatever may have been the classic British definition of pluralism, these features became the defining core of the pluralist political system against which the Soviet Union has been compared in the last quarter of a century.

To a careful student of the Soviet political process, however, the most striking characteristic of this American pluralist literature of the 1950s and the 1960s is the extent to which many of the phenomena it highlighted seem to have their counterparts in the Soviet political system during the Brezhnev era. The political leadership has not been intervening against the interests of major groups in the system; decisions do largely seem to be those that the respective specialized ministerial-party-scientific complexes could be expected to favor in the various policy areas; a wide range of proposals for incremental change are observable in the press, as is a great deal of interest representation by specialized figures within a broadly defined "leadership echelon;" the bargaining mentality seems deeply imbedded in the political and administrative actors. In-deed, in its insistence that the population make moderate demands and avoid confrontation politics, in its open acknowledgment that (in Charles Lindblom's description of the American political system) the "real engine" of interest group power is persuasion, the Soviet leadership almost seems to have made the Soviet Union closer to the spirit of the pluralist model of American political science than is the United States. Whatever the nature of behind-the-scene decision making, the open political process in the United States has little of the moderation of the pluralist model, for the media's definition of news pushes political actors towards confrontation, dramatic and extreme presentation of demands, and personal attacks upon opponents if they want publicity for their demands.

If the similarities between the Soviet political system and the plural-ist model of American political science are taken seriously, they obviously raise fundamental questions both about the actual nature of the state-society relationship in the Soviet Union and about the proper way of characterizing the Soviet Union in comparative terms. It has been my basic contention that these similarities should be taken seriously. Our understanding of the Soviet political system, and of Western political systems, is too uncertain for any definitive judgments about the distribu-tion of power, but in advancing the model of institutional pluralism, I have been arguing that it is worthwhile—as a scholarly exercise, if nothing else—to make a clean break with the directed society models and to see what the results are if we look at the Soviet Union with different eyes.

The model of institutional pluralism does not simply point to diversity in Soviet society or to the existence of societal inputs into Soviet political decision making. It hypothesizes that the power relationships between party and society in the Soviet Union have some things in common with the power relationships more usually associated with a pluralist political system. In the Soviet Union, as in all modern political systems that are stable, the political authorities have the ultimate power to decide almost anything if a sufficient number of them are in agree-ment, but it is being suggested that thus far the regime has been moving towards a diffusion of real political power.

The chapter on "The Soviet Experience and the Measurement of Power" even raises the question about the relative power of the masses in the Soviet Union, but the diffusion that is being emphasized in the model of institutional pluralism is to the administrative-professional stratum. A 1976 article not included in this volume describes this type of diffusion as follows:

If an attempt has been made to introduce a more constitutional system in the Soviet Union [in recent years], then the de facto definition of that system, at least as it has appeared thus far, must include many elements of the model of institutional pluralism that this author presented earlier. In this definition, decisions should be based on specialized knowledge; hence, those with such knowledge should have a major role in decision-making process. Ministerial officials should not be permitted to make decisions unchecked. But the various control agencies—the Central Committee apparatus, Gosplan, the trade unions, the Komsomol, the People's Control Committee—have all been structured internally along branch lines, and the officials in the different subdivisions usually have specialized knowledge and experience in the area they are supervising in order to facilitate their work. Indeed, they often come from the ministries they control.

As a result, the specialized controllers, inevitably have much in common with the controlled, and one can speak of ''complexes'' (in the sense of a military-industrial complex) and of ''whirlpools'' (to use the term of Ernest S. Griffith) of specialized Party, state, ''public,'' and scientific personnel working within the respective policy areas. The definition of goals formally remains the responsibility of the Party leadership, but except for ensuring that Marxist goals in social policy are pursued, the leadership is not to act with ''voluntarism''—that is, it generally should follow the advice of the specialized ''complexes'' or ''whirlpools'' in their respective policy areas, limiting itself to a mediation of the conflicts that arise among them. In practice, policymaking power informally comes to be delegated to these complexes.

The degree of individual freedom to be permitted within a system of institutional pluralism is a problem with which the Party leadership has been uneasily grappling. Clearly, it feels that advocacy of incremental change in policy should be permitted on most questions if phrased carefully (particularly in media aimed at those in the appropriate whirlpool), but that such advocacy should not be accompanied by the type of confrontation politics, dramatization of demands, and public criticism of the leadership found in the West—let alone by negative moralizing about the system as a whole or about the past. There also seems to be a growing sense of the need for some rule of law, at least in the sense of a guarantee against punishment for dissent that is applied without warning. Such innovations as the introduction of some possibility for emigration, the liberalization of the divorce laws, and the relaxation of Khrushchev's overt pressure on religion suggest a lessening of the determination to interfere in people's private lives and to throttle all iconoclasm. [13]

This long quotation explicitly refers to a system that the Soviet leadership—or some of its members—may be trying to imbed in constitutional restraints on the leader. It is meant to suggest an ideal type toward which the actual political system of the Brezhnev years seems to have moved, and I have repeatedly insisted (most recently and forcefully in the article just quoted) that the changes are not necessarily permanent. Yet while the model of institutional pluralism is explicitly focused on the Brezhnev period and all the essays in this volume were essentially written in present tense, one could of course go much further in questioning the traditional image of the party-state relationship in the Soviet Union. Obviously neither Stalin nor Khrushchev can be described as brokers who never challenged major groups in society, but one could follow Adam Ulam's insight that successful Communist revolutions have always occurred at the early rather than the late stages of industrialization and suggest that in broader terms the Communist leadership of the Soviet Union was always to some extent the representative of the industrializing, modernizing forces in society rather than being a self-appointed usurping elite.

The Bolshevik Revolution in November 1917 might be dismissed as an accidental or Jacobin coup d'etat in a period of war-produced anarchy, but the Bolshevik victory in a long Civil War can not be explained in these terms. Above all, Stalin's success in carrying through his collectivization program cannot be so explained. Bitter experience has demonstrated the difficulty that regimes can face in herding peasants into strategic hamlets or the like, in controlling peasant guerilla movements, in providing safety for its officials stationed in the villages, in preventing largely peasant armies from dissolving in the face of rebel action. Collectivization did produce guerilla action, but the fact that it was overcome in a few years indicates clearly the existence of societal forces, even in the countryside, on which Bolshevik policy at least partially rested.

The relationship of Stalin to society was different from Brezhnev's in the 1970s, but even Stalin must be understood partly in terms of the societal forces he often represented—forces for whose benefit he often adjusted policy. As suggested briefly in Chapter 10, even the peasants should not be seen as powerless in the 1930s, and the position of skilled labor and the new technical intelligentsia was much stronger. The totalitarian model's suggestion of a constant assault upon society and societal values, of a constant effort to transform society, has considerable relevance to the policies of the First Five-Year plan, but very little to the Stalin period after 1932—except to the extent that industrialization should be visualized in this manner in every country.[14]

For all these reasons it seems to me almost incontestable that the power relationship between the party leadership and the rest of society, including the professional-administrative stratum, is now and always has been far more complex than the directed society models have indicated. However, any hypotheses about the exact nature of that distribution of power should be advanced hesitantly and tentatively, as they should with respect to any country. Earlier I betrayed real impatience with the notion that concepts such as "political participation" and "interest groups" cannot properly be used in discussions of the Soviet scene, and I hold a similar attitude toward statements about the Soviets elite's alleged monopoly of power that seem to have little relationship to insights of political science about the ambivalence of power. Nevertheless, it should be absolutely clear to any reader that propositions about the actual structure of power have been presented in quite a different spirit. The repeated acknowledgment—in fact, the insistence—that we do not know and the repeated raising of the methodological question result from my conviction that our understanding of how to measure power in any broad societal sense is extremely weak, and that the conclusions drawn from existing methodologies have very little claim to validity.

Ultimately of course a confession of ignorance is not a sufficient answer, particularly when made in conjunction with the argument that differences in political phenomena in the Soviet Union and the West make the use of similar concepts impossible. We are then left with little more than the comfortable conclusion that there are, after all, similarities and differences between the political systems of the Soviet Union and the West. Having rejected the totalitarian model with proper righteousness, we still have a deep sense that the differences are so essential that we are not required to rethink our fundamental assumptions about anything.

These essays suggest, however, that theoretical advance depends upon rethinking a number of our fundamental assumptions. The reasons for the extreme reluctance of political scientists to admit that there have been societal inputs, let alone societal power, in the Soviet political system lie deep in Western social science theory. That theory has assumed that the existence of Western-type institutions and the right of citizens freely to organize Western-type associations are an indispensable pre-condition for a broader distribution of power. Yet, is it really reasonable that, in the words of Peter Wiles, "[no] country can show a more rapid and sweeping progress towards equality" than the Soviet Union in the quarter of a century since Stalin's death, and that mass power is totally unrelated to that development?[15] Is it reasonable to say that the Soviet political system has developed many of the characteristics that Western political scientists have associated with a broad distribution of power and that no such dispersion has occurred? Or, if we do say that the absence of the right to dramatize demands, to express frontal attacks on the system and leadership, and to form issue interest groups—as well, of course, as the absence of competitive elections—in the Soviet Union are all that are crucial, how do we demonstrate this fact conclusively?

The concluding chapters in the book raise and discuss these questions, but unfortunately they do not provide definitive answers. Yet it seems to me an advance toward understanding to recognize that they do require an answer. It also seems to me an advance towards understanding if we recognize that our long-time concern with classifying and labeling political systems has contributed much more to our efforts to make normative evaluations of systems than it has to our efforts to understand them. Biology began to make major progress when it moved beyond a concern with classification of different species to an interest in processes that would be found in many species, and I think that progress in political science lies in an analogous direction.

It is for this reason more than any other that the break with the directed society models seems vital to me. In some sense there may not be much difference between stating that the Soviet Union is basically a directed society with a number of pluralistic or semi-pluralistic elements and stating that the Soviet Union is a kind of pluralist society with certain types of restrictions. It is perhaps the difference between saying that the bottle is 55 percent full or that it is 55 percent empty: the difference in tone is greater than the difference in substance.

Where the difference is critical is in determining the questions we ask and the subjects that we study. If we look upon the Soviet Union as essentially a directed society, we are inexorably drawn to the old questions —how do the leaders still maintain control? Are there indications (such as dissent) that some of society is breaking away from the control? What sort of deviations (alcoholism, crime, juvenile delinquency) are produced by popular frustrations at the control? More important, we seem inexorably led to explore mobilization rather than participation, what is censored rather than what can be said, the regime's policy rather than the policies pushed by societal forces, and so forth. Most important, we are not really driven to think about the theoretical implications of the nondirected political phenomena.

I would not deny the legitimacy of the control or mobilization questions as research topics, but it seems to me that they seldom get us out of the ghetto (unless done comparatively with very sophisticated systems-control research in the West). Above all, just as it is difficult to do biochemical studies of cell division if one is doing classification-oriented biology, so the control questions distract us from the work that a tentative acceptance of some pluralist model for the Soviet Union would stimulate. In particular, if the Soviet and Western political systems are each visualized as types of pluralist systems, then we are led to explore the respective impact of those aspects of pluralism which they have in common and those on which they differ. We are led to ask what difference the differences make and then are driven to ask methodological questions in an attempt to answer this question. And these questions may lead in turn to fundamental questions about basic assumptions.

As argued earlier, the Soviet studies ghetto has had many comfortable aspects to it, both for those within it and for the comparative theorists outside. But there is also an excitement in breaking out of a ghetto. The political theory relating to the industrial world has primarily been the theory of American area studies and to a lesser extent of Western area studies. If the experience of one-third of the world is integrated into it, many changes will be required, and those who are studying the Soviet Union should not shy away from the responsibility and the excitement of tackling this task.

# I

## Reconceptualization of the Soviet System

# 1

# The Soviet System Petrification or Pluralism?

During the last year of the Khrushchev era, scholars vigorously debated the nature of the power relationships within the Soviet Communist Party Presidium, but their images of the relationship between the leadership —however defined—and the rest of society were usually quite similar. Whether the scholar spoke of an "administered society," an "organizational society," or an "ideological system," he summarized the Soviet system as "a command-dominated society," as one in which there is "totalitarianism without terror," as one in which the political system is "used by the political leaders to create a new society along the lines of their own beliefs and aspirations."

Even iconoclastic models were not very iconoclastic on this point. The "conflict model" focused almost exclusively upon conflicts within the leadership and, in so doing, created the strong impression that all persons below the top were acted upon rather than having any impact on the resolution of conflicts. Similarly, Alfred Meyer's "bureaucratic model" presented an image of modern bureaucratic society very similar to that of Herbert Marcuse and Barrington Moore. Such a society, he argued, "is characterized [in all countries] by the prevalence of certain totalitarian features," including "the imposition of ceaseless social change unwanted by the constituents."[1]

Since the fall of Khrushchev, the situation has changed drastically. Although thus far there is wide agreement about the collective nature of the leadership within the Politburo, the basic concensus about the nature of the political system as a whole has disappeared. Now there are competing images or models of the system, and scholarly uncertainty is further reflected in the fact that these images themselves are often quite ambiguous.

*A Directed Society.* One group of scholars still emphasizes the directed nature of Soviet society and the political leaders' "determination . . .to make a 'new man,' without regard for the individual or social costs."[2] Or at least they emphasized this view in 1966-67 when the articles most clearly expressing it were written. A succinct summary of this position is provided by Jeremy Azrael:

> While the ouster of Khrushchev has inevitably resulted in more open access to the political arena for other elite groups, it has not seriously weakened the political-power position of the party *apparat* . . . If the growth of ideological agnosticism is apt to be a relatively slow process among all convinced Communists, it is likely to be particularly slow among the *apparatchiki* . . . It is precisely by stressing the continuing need to remold society and to juxtapose consciousness to spontaneity that the *apparatchiki* can best hope to legitimate their political sovereignty and the hegemony that they exercise over all facets of Soviet life . . . [Even among the] young men [in] the manpower pool from which the apparatus has been and is being replenished . . . [there] is unlikely to [be] a rapid erosion of the authoritarian-mobilization impulses that their world view implies . . . The final demise of the "permanent revolution" is many years away.[3]

*Oligarchic Petrification.* A second group of scholars presents a model that retains much of the traditional image of a directed society: the dominant role of the officials at the top of the hierarchy, the flow of power from the top down, and the continued importance of ideology. In this view, however, the men at the top are not a dynamic political leadership determined to transform society, but rather a "government of clerks" anxious only to preserve their power and perquisites of office.

The word "ideology' is no longer defined as it once was by the theorists of totalitarianism ("a reasonably coherent body of ideas concerning practical means of how to change and reform a society"),[4] but has reverted to the meaning used by Karl Mannheim and many others: the rationalizations that legitimate and support the dominant interests in a society.[5] Since the Soviet Union is still directed from the top and since the top leaders have lost their will to change society, the Soviet system is described as being in a state of stagnation, decay, immobilism, or petrification. To quote Zbigniew Brzezinski:

> Oligarchic petrification would involve the maintenance of the dominant role of the party and the retention of the essentially dogmatic character of the ideology. In effect, more of the same. Neither the party nor the ideology would be in a particularly revolutionary relationship to society; instead, the main thrust of the relationship would be for the party to retain political control over society without attempting to impose major innovations. Strong emphasis would be placed on ideological indoctrination and the confinement of ideological deviations. Political leadership could remain collective, for the absence of deliberately imposed change would not re-

quire major choices. The domestic result would be rule by an ossified bureaucracy that would pursue a conservative policy masked by revolutionary slogans.[6]

Unfortunately, the model of oligarchic petrification can be quite ambiguous. Brzezinski's reference to "the maintenance of the dominant role of the party and the retention of the essentially dogmatic character of the ideology"—which he sums up as "in effect, more of the same" —clearly suggests continuity with the Soviet past; yet these terms have different meanings than they did in the past. The end of "deliberately imposed change" means that the party is not, in fact, dominant over society and the bureaucracy in the same sense that it was previously depicted to be. In the language of Friedrich and Brzezinski, the Soviet Union has changed from a totalitarian dictatorship into an authoritarian dictatorship or even an oligarchy.

There are several possible variants of the petrification model that would render it less ambiguous. One such variant would specifically identify the party with the party apparatus, depicting the latter as the central bureaucracy in the Soviet system. This image of a petrified system would be particularly neat if coupled with Leonard Schapiro's view of the policy position of the party apparatus: "By and large, the views that favor discipline, centralized controls, and absolute priority for heavy industry can be regarded as those of the party apparatus, while the views that look toward greater reliance on material incentives, increased application of market principles, decentralization of industrial controls, and higher priority for consumer goods can be identified with the government apparatus, including the planners and managers."[7] There is, however, not the slightest evidence to support the hypothesis of a party apparatus united on a conservative policy position—and a great deal of evidence to indicate that the hypothesis is wrong.[8] Nor is there any evidence that there is a simple power relationship between the party and state hierarchies.

A second and far more defensible variant of the petrification model would feature rule by an inherently conservative bureaucracy, an "ossified bureaucracy" in Brzezinski's phrase. The party apparatus would certainly be included as an important component of the bureaucratic system, but it would only be one component. One could use the language of Milovan Djilas and speak of rule by a "new class" embracing all "those who have special privileges and economic preference because of the administrative monopoly they hold."[9] Or one could—and perhaps should—emphasize the relative supremacy of the defense and heavy-industry bureaucracies over the others, as evidenced by the fact that men with experience in these two areas have come to occupy a very large number of key positions in the party and state machinery of the Soviet Union.[10]

*Institutional Pluralism.* A third group of scholars has been moving toward a model of the Soviet system that represents a far more drastic break with the traditional images—a model that will be termed "institutional pluralism." Like the adherents of the petrification model, these scholars accept Alfred Meyer's insight that the Soviet Union is a giant bureaucracy, but they have a quite different conception of the nature of bureaucracy. They do not believe that either Soviet society or bureaucracy is inert. Soviet society is viewed as undergoing dynamic changes produced by industrialization, and Soviet professional-administrative personnel are seen more as the sort of functional specialists who are considered to be a major source of innovation in the West than as the conservative bureaucrats of the petrification model.[11] The scholars of this group believe that ideas and power flow up the administrative hierarchies as well as down, and they do not see immobilism in the process of policy formation. In the words of Robert Daniels, "What appears to be evolving in the Soviet Union is a new kind of politics, participatory bureaucracy. . . . In any complex modern bureaucratic organization, it is impossible to function purely from the top down: all manner of influences—information, advice, recommendations, problems, complaints—must flow upwards. . . . The problems of managing a complex economy and technology have made it abundantly clear to the Soviet leadership that they must allow this reverse stream of influence to flow freely, and their main concern is that the flow be kept within the organizational structure of the Communist Party."[12]

Daniels heavily qualifies this image by emphasizing "the power of the party and its monopoly position in the Soviet power structure" and by treating the admission of "segments of the administrative and intellectual class into the decision-making and controlling process" as a future possibility rather than as a present fact. In this respect, he seems to have moved only partially away from the earlier image of "policy groups" whose members come from a very narrow elite and who are "careful not to cross the shadowy line between advocacy and pressure."[13] Other scholars, however, have gone further, emphasizing the existence of group activity "outside the formal system of political authority"[14] or the role of "intermediate actors" and "intermediate participation."[15] Still others have been willing to assert that "Soviet interest groupings . . . share political power in the Soviet policy process."[16]

Like the petrification model, this third construct of the Soviet system is not without its ambiguity. No one is yet willing to equate pluralism of the Soviet type with that in the West. If compelled to characterize the

Soviet system as either a dictatorship or a democracy, the third group of scholars would vehemently protest the choice but would ultimately join the others in electing the former term. At most, in Skilling's words, the Soviet Union is viewed as "a 'pluralism of elites,' or to borrow Robert Dahl's expressive term, a 'polyarchical' system, but oligarchical rather than democratic in character."[17] One receives the clear impression of far less direction and control from above than in other images of the Soviet system, but the amount remains far greater than in the classic pluralist model. This intermediate stage has not been defined very precisely. One senses what Daniels means when he speaks both of influence flowing upwards and of the "monopoly position" of the party in the "Soviet power structure." But the concepts are by no means clear.

Perhaps the difficulty is the absence of a generally accepted model (or, more precisely, an ideal type) for a political system that is somewhere in between a directed society and classical pluralism. Such a model —which I call "institutional pluralism"—would certainly contain a number of the features of the conventional American model of pluralism:

(1) There exists in society a multiplicity of interests: nothing is monolithic about society or the political system, and no single interest dominates either.

(2) The political process revolves around conflict among a complex set of crosscutting and shifting alliances of persons with divergent interests.

(3) Citizens and officials usually treat politics as "the art of the possible" and see it "as a set of give-and-take interactions in which each side bargains for a set of more or less limited objectives."[18] So long as they stay strictly within this framework, they are free to express their views.

(4) Political leaders serve essentially as mediators or brokers in the political process, their "most universal function" being to bring "men together in masses on some middle ground where they can combine to carry out a common policy."[19]

(5) Governmental decisions on various questions are most heavily influenced by those especially affected by them and especially knowledgeable about them. In short, the government process is one of "minorities rule," featuring "the steady appeasement of relatively small groups."[20]

(6) To the extent that accommodation of the demands of some groups requires restrictions upon other groups, the changes are undertaken gradually and in a way that is accommodating to the disadvantaged group. Incrementalism is thus the hallmark of the system.[21]

The differences between institutional pluralism and classical pluralism center on the framework in which the political process takes place and on the types of political behavior that are tolerated. The model of classical pluralism allows all citizens to choose between the programs of competing elites in elections and to form new pressure groups or parties to advance their political interests. Indeed, the contention that a pluralist system is the most equitable possible rests on the assumption that the disadvantaged and the dissatisfied will regularly use such political mechanisms to seek redress of their grievances. In the model of institutional pluralism on the other hand, those who want to effect political change must, with a few exceptions, work within the official institutional framework. Those who fail to do so run the danger of severe repression, especially when they call for nonincremental change in the fundamentals of the system. Although any citizen can make appeals or suggestions for incremental change through official channels, the leading political participants will almost always be "establishment" figures—usually civil servants and political figures, but also policy-oriented scholars and educators. However, the model assumes that the institutional forces are at least somewhat responsive to broader societal forces. It includes an image of bureaucratic officials as men who are driven to represent many interests of their clientele and low-level subordinates, as well as an image of politicians as men who take the danger of popular unrest into account as they mediate conflicts among the political participants.

The model of institutional pluralism is an ideal type that is meant to conform to Inkeles' usage of the term "model"—an abstraction, a set of "ideas or concepts which have a certain unity."[22] No scholar believes that it accurately summarizes the situation in the Soviet Union today; at most, it could be claimed that the Soviet Union is moving in the direction of the model. Indeed, since past Soviet policy has made the specialized elites associated with heavy and defense industry far stronger in numbers, talent, and power than other members of the upper stratum, the model itself suggests that current Soviet policy will reflect this imbalance for some time to come, and that the dominance of heavy industry will disappear only incrementally.

The crucial question is—how are post-Khrushchev developments in the Soviet Union best summarized? Does the Soviet Union still correspond most closely to a model of a command-dominated society, or has it moved substantially in the direction either of the petrification model or the model of institutional pluralism? Is the Soviet political system one in which power—whether used for change or for the prevention of change—is still concentrated in the party leadership, or has there been a diffusion of power to other elements of Soviet society?

Seven-and-a-half years passed between Khrushchev's fall and the Twenty-Fourth CPSU Congress. The republic party congresses that preceded it, the subsequent five-year plan, and elections to the republic supreme soviets and councils of ministers provided a wealth of new policy and elite data, giving us the opportunity to explore the relevance of the three models for the early years of the Brezhnev regime.

Any reasonably relevant model is likely to illuminate some aspects of a political system. But while the first model—that of a political leadership which actively strives to transform society in accordance with its ideological preconceptions—may help to explain a number of Soviet phenomena rooted in an earlier period, it seems of very little use in explaining the dynamics of the last dozen years. Indeed, whatever the future may bring, events of the Brezhnev period make this model appear as anachronistic as the image of a system based primarily on arbitrary terror came to appear in the Khrushchev era.

One of the key elements of any model of an ideological system is a political leadership that has beliefs and aspirations on the basis of which it seeks to remold society. Classically, this image of Soviet society has pictured it as a system in which the leadership endeavors to transform society along the lines of the guiding Marxist-Leninist ideology. Increasingly in the post-Stalin period, however, and especially in the post-Khrushchev period, the leadership has given the impression that it is far from certain about the solution of society's problems. Increasingly, it has been willing to listen to policy advice from "society" and to permit far-ranging public discussion of policy questions.

To be sure, not all Soviet specialists agree that the last twelve years have witnessed a freer flow of information in the Soviet Union; indeed, many would speak of a reverse tendency toward greater repression of criticism and iconoclastic thought. For example, Brzezinski speaks of a "movement in the opposite direction" between 1964 and 1969 and predicts that "in the short run, development toward a pluralist, ideologically more tolerant system does not seem likely."[23] In my view, however, there is in the West more misunderstanding on this subject than on any other development in recent Soviet history.

The contention that the present Soviet leadership is less tolerant of critical ideas rests on three pieces of evidence. The first has been the repression of well-known intellectual dissenters who have dared to criticize the fundamentals of the system. The second has been the renewed sensitivity of the leadership to moralizing about the past, especially the Stalin era. On this question, censorship clearly has been more repressive under Brezhnev than it was under Khrushchev. The third bit of evidence has been some slight increase in the political weight of the secret police. The Chairman of the KGB, Yuri Andropov, was elected to candidate and then full membership on the enlarged Politburo, while the representation of the KGB in the republic party bureaus rose from one full member and three candidate members in 1966 to three full members and four candidates in 1971.[24] The election of Andropov to the Politburo eventually was replicated in nearly all the republics, and by 1976, five of the bureaus had KGB chairmen among their full members and seven among their candidate members.

None of this evidence, however—and particularly the last—seems conclusive. Even if we accept an increase in the representation of the KGB in the republic party bureaus as a reliable indicator of the degree of repression in the system, the number of full members in 1976 was not much more than it was in 1961 (five full members and two candidate members), and Andropov's election to the Politburo may owe as much to his responsibilities in the foreign policy field as to his police role (he had fourteen years of foreign policy experience before becoming KGB chairman).

More important than status indicators, however, is the actual repression of ideas, and the contents of the published media, which are quick to reflect changes in policy affecting the flow of information, certainly provide little evidence of an increased sway of "police mentality." The republic newspapers, for example, now contain more articles about victims of Stalin's purges than they did in late 1965 and early 1966. The press also reflects less official sensitivity on a number of topics that used to be considered security matters. The large aviation plants in Tashkent, Tbilisi, and Kiev, which were never mentioned in the newspapers before late 1966, are now discussed quite frequently, and press reports identify by name such holders of security-sensitive positions as border-guard officials and directors of titanium and computer plants.

Even more important is the increasing extent to which policy questions are now debated in the newspapers, periodicals, and books. To speak of "the retention of the essentially dogmatic character of the ideology" and to state that the years since 1964 have seen movement away from "an ideologically more tolerant system" is to overlook the crucial fact that on all but the most central questions, party policy is less and less incorporated into clearcut, undebatable ideology, with a consequent widening of the areas open to public discussion. In almost every policy sphere ideology is ambiguous and ill-defined; and in almost every policy sphere, the published debate is now freer and more wide-ranging than it was under Khrushchev.

In the last ten years virtually all conceivable proposals for incremental change in party policy have been aired in the Soviet press.[25] The proposals must sometimes be carefully phrased, and the more radical ones often have to be published in scholarly journals and books rather than in the pages of *Pravda,* but hardly any official policy is immune from questioning. Even in the sensitive areas of foreign and nationalities policy, where advocacy of change is permitted only in the most veiled terms, lively debate still goes on in the guise of discussions on the nature of the prevailing factual situation.[26]

Certainly the party leadership tolerates no direct challenge to the basic legitimacy of one-party rule or to its own ultimate authority. It still restricts the flow of information severely by comparison with Western countries, particularly in the media that reach the largest audiences, and as Brzezinski correctly emphasizes, it remains inflexible in its rejection of "alien" world views and its determination to combat their dissemination. Those dissenters who try to circulate forbidden ideas can testify eloquently that neither the KGB nor the labor camps have withered away.

Yet even in those areas, the present regime seems more tolerant than that of Khrushchev. The myth has arisen that Khrushchev merely "relied on verbal chastisement," whereas "the Brezhnev leadership has put writers and other dissidents in jail or insane asylums."[27] However, a look at the past experiences of dissenters like Brodsky, Bukovsky, Dobrovolsky, Galanskov, Grigorenko, and Tarsis indicates very clearly that their suppression did not begin with the advent of the present regime, but rather under Khrushchev.[28] One cannot be certain how the late First Secretary would have reacted to the increase in open dissent and the circulation of documents such as the *Khronika tekushchikh sobytii* (Chronicle of Current Events) on the scale seen since 1964—and especially to the transmission of such materials to Western newsmen. There is, however, good reason to doubt that Khrushchev would have been more liberal than the present leadership, and to suspect that dissent, rather than being more rigorously suppressed, is now enjoying increased publicity.

A willingness to tolerate a freer flow of information and to hear advice does not correspond to traditional Western images of the ideological mind, but it is not incompatible with a political leadership that strives to transform society. Indeed, if the party leadership were to act upon some of the advice that has been publicly expressed, it would transform Soviet society as radically as Stalin did in 1928-29. On the other hand, it the leadership prefers to follow the advice of those who insist upon maintenance of the status quo, there can be little change. The question is: what sort of advice does the present leadership seem to be following? Or, to put it in broader terms, what is the leadership's relationship to the rest of society?

Looking at the last twelve years of Soviet political evolution in historical perspective, the overwhelming impression is that this period has witnessed a major change in the relationship of the leadership to the key segments of the Soviet establishment. Whereas Stalin in his last years ignored the policy suggestions of the institutional centers of power, and whereas Khrushchev challenged the basic interests of almost every one of these centers (and with some success), the present leadership has not done major battle with any important segment of the establishment and seems, on the contrary, to have acceded to the most central desires of each.

One clear-cut piece of evidence is found in the realm of personnel selection. At the end of the Stalin period Brzezinski could speak of a "permanent purge" in the Soviet Union: he saw its purposes as "many and varied" and the need for it as "ever-present" and not diminishing "with the growing stability of the totalitarian regime."[29] Under Khrushchev, indeed, the purge did seem as permanent as ever, but after his fall the turnover rates among top officials—whatever may have been the cause—took a sharp downturn. For certain categories of officials, the turnover for the *ten* years between 1961 and 1971 has proven considerably lower than it was for the *five* years between 1956 and 1961, and in some cases it was unbelievably low between 1966 and 1971 (see table 1.1). For example, not one of the 11 first deputy or deputy chairmen of the USSR Council of Ministers was replaced between the Twenty-Third and the Twenty-Fourth Congress, and only four of the 57 ministers and state committee chairmen that sat on the Council of Ministers were removed in the same period (another three died).

Khrushchev's successors have seemed especially reluctant to demote anyone who has reached the level of full membership in the Central Committee or higher—or perhaps they have found it difficult to do so. All of the members or candidate members of the Politburo elected in 1966 were renamed to this body in 1971, while 81 percent of the living full members of the 1966 Central Committee retained their membership in 1971 (82 percent, if we exclude the three workers and peasants on the committee, all of whom were replaced). The reelection rate among the voting members of the Central Committee exceeded 87 percent among the living officials who were still sixty years of age or younger in 1971. The fate of the 1966 obkom first secretaries is quite instructive. Twenty-one of the 44 obkom first secretaries with voting membership on the

**Table 1.1.** Turnover of leading personnel (in percent)[a]

| Position | 1956-61 | 1961-71 | 1966-71 | 1971-76 |
|---|---|---|---|---|
| Full members, Politburo | 70 | 36 | 0 | 27 |
| Full members, Central Committee | 50 | 39 | 24 | 16 |
| Secretaries, Central Committee | 75 | 67 | 27 | 20 |
| Members, USSR Council of Ministers[b] | 67 | 45 | 10 | 17 |
| Republic first secretaries | 79 | 43 | 21 | 29 |
| Obkom first secretaries (RSFSR) | 86 | 67 | 43 | 21 |

[a]The figures in each column are the percentages of officials who were not in the same position in the terminal year of the period specified as they were at the beginning of the period. The figures are based on the situation immediately after the Party Congress in each of the years indicated. Turnover is considered to have occurred if the incumbent died as well as if he retired or moved to another job.

[b]Excluding chairmen of the republic Councils of Ministers, who are ex-officio members of the all-Union body.

CPSU Central Committee were replaced between congresses, but fifteen of these 21 were named to other posts that resulted in their reelection to the 1971 Central Committee, and a sixteenth had been appointed to such a post and subsequently died. The same pattern occurred in 1976, for an incredible 89 percent of the living full members of the 1971 Central Committee were reelected at the Twenty-Fifth Congress in 1976.

The unwillingness or inability of the present leadership to remove the members of the administrative elite has been matched by its abstention from imposing any major policy change that would seriously diminish the status of any important institutional group. The policy decisions of the last dozen years, unlike those of the Khrushchev period, have been such as would be expected from committee decision making in which the leadership assumes the role not of the major policy initiator but of a broker mediating competing claims of powerful interests. Khrushchev's unpopular initiatives were quickly reversed, and subsequent Soviet policy in any particular area has remained close to what the relevant segment of the specialized elite could be predicted to favor (at least, given the limitations imposed by the prevailing distribution of funds). Certainly this seems to be true of policy with respect to education, agriculture, military affairs, industrial organization, and party structure. On questions involving the relative priority to be given to the interests of different institutional centers of power, any changes that have occurred have been slow and incremental.

The leadership's deference to the top specialized officials seems so apparent that it need not be documented at length. This deference may now even be increasingly extended to the top elite of the major regional centers as well. The evidence is not certain on this point, but there are a number of evidences that seem to point in this direction.

First, the regional representation on the Politburo has been gradually increasing. When the voting membership of this body was increased by four at the Twenty-Fourth Party Congress, three of the added full members were regional representatives: Shcherbitsky (Ukraine), Kunaev (Kazakhstan), and Grishin (Moscow), and in 1975 the Leningrad leader (Romanov) was named to full membership. The five large republics, as well as Azerbaidzhan in the Transcaucasus, now have officials on the ruling Politburo, while the Baltic states have de facto representation in the person of the Latvian, Arvid Pelshe, Chairman of the Party Control Commission.[30] An analogous development has occurred in the republics. The number of first secretaries of outlying oblasts and cities named to republic party bureaus rose from none in 1956 to two in 1961, six in 1966 (two full members and four candidates), seven in 1971 (four full members and three candidates), and nine in 1976 (five full members and four candidates).

Second, there has been a change in the pattern of selection of obkom first secretaries, at least in the Russian Republic. Brezhnev has announced a policy "of promoting local officials [to the post of obkom first secretary],[31] sending people from the center to these posts only in exceptional cases," and this policy has generally been followed in the RSFSR. In the 1957-61 period, only 26 percent of new obkom first secretaries in the republic had worked for more than five years in their respective oblasts before their appointment, while 64 percent came directly from the outside. (In earlier periods the percentage of outsiders seems to have been even higher.) Between the Twenty-Third and Twenty-Fourth Congresses, on the other hand, 75 percent of new obkom first secretaries in the RSFSR had at least five years of past service within their oblasts, and most had spent their entire careers there.[32]

Since the center has a wide range of choice among officials living in any given oblast, it is possible that the new personnel policy has not appreciably altered the relationship between the party leadership (specifically the General Secretary) and the obkom first secretaries. However, internal promotion is at least consistent with the possibility that local party establishments have increasingly been allowed to determine their own leadership succession.

Third, a few signs have appeared of greater policy autonomy for the republic leaders, at least on a few issues. On one question—the newspaper treatment of local victims of the Stalin purges—the partial autonomy is readily observable. Biographies of purge victims have been published frequently, but the republics do not follow a uniform policy in this matter. At one extreme, the Ukraine in 1970 erected monuments to S. V. Kossior and V. Y. Chubar (both "liquidated" in 1937-38),[33] while Uzbekistan has published a biography of Akmal Ikramov and the collected works of Faizulla Khodzhaev, both of whom were major republic leaders purged by Stalin.[34] (Khodzhaev remained under a shadow throughout the Khrushchev period because of his inclusion among the "Right Oppositionists" prosecuted with Bukharin.) At the other extreme, Kazakhstan appears not to have published any biography of a purge victim. Even the seventieth birth anniversary of Levon Mirzoian, Kazakhstan's initial party First Secretary after the republic's formation, was not mentioned in *Kazakhstanskaia pravda* in 1967, despite the fact that a commemorative article about him appeared at that time in Azerbaidzhan, where he had previously served as republic party secretary during the 1920s.[35]

The press in the individual republics today gives an impression of greater variation on other questions as well, but it is possible that this is more a change in the eye of the beholder than in the actual situation. It would require a comprehensive study of economic, educational, and cultural developments in the republics to determine the extent of any trend toward greater autonomy for the regional elite. As John Armstrong has pointed out, however, the treatment of the union republics by the central Soviet authorities has for some time been much more differentiated and subtle than most of our conceptions of the Soviet federal system would suggest.[36] As a rule, the more industrialized republics appear to have been granted somewhat more autonomy than those in Central Asia in particular, and this would logically seem to imply some increase in authority for all republics as they become more industrialized.

Whatever devolution of authority to the leading regional officials has occurred, it is clear that in the Soviet Union the vertical administrative units—the ministries and state committees (together with associated educational-scientific personnel and specialized party officials)—remain much stronger than the horizontal or regional ones. (Comparison with Yugoslavia is instructive on this point.) Rather than the regional political leaders, the leading specialized establishments seem to have been the main beneficiaries of the diffusion of power from the top party leadership.

Even within the regions, the administrative subordinates of the central ministries (particularly the subordinates of the heavy-industry ministries) have often had a key role in local decision making. In drawing an analogy between Soviet regional party organs and the French prefectural authorities, I have tried to suggest that the leading party officials in the regions have been granted the great legal authority of the prefect but have had their real influence limited by the same factors that have weakened such officials throughout the world.[37] The enormous range of responsibilities placed on the shoulders of party officials, the superior knowledge of the specialized administrators, and the administrators' ties with powerful central ministries have all combined to bring about a situation in which the local party first secretaries often function more as broker politicians vis-à-vis local specialized officials than as the source of policy guidance for the officials' specialized decisions.

In at least one respect, the developments of recent years may have pushed the local party organs even more strongly toward the broker role. For the first time, party theorists have been strongly emphasizing the coordinating function of the party organs, and the leadership has continued the practice of gradually building up the state apparatus in policy areas where the party organs had previously assumed (or, perhaps, been compelled to assume) a major operational role. The creation of the State Supply Committee and of republic state committees for labor resources (both with offices in the localities) may have reduced the considerable burdens on the party organs in these realms. Similarly, the resubordination of the *raion* (county) argicultural administrations to the raion soviets after nearly a decade of independence, together with the new decrees purporting to give the soviets new powers, may imply the beginnings of a policy of significantly increasing what is now the virtually nonexistent ability of local soviets to engage in meaningful regional and urban planning.[38] In the ideological (the educational-cultural-publishing) realm, the creation of new governmental committees was largely the product of the last years of the Khrushchev period, but the status of these bodies rose significantly after 1964.[39] Whereas 31 officials attached to such committees were elected full members of the republic party central committees in 1961, their number rose to 38 in 1966, and 45 in 1971. (This is one of the most noticeable changes to take place in the republic central committees in that decade.)

In view of these developments, the image of an "ideological system" hardly seems appropriate to the Soviet Union of recent years. How, then, should we characterize the present Soviet political system? Has it petrified, or has it been evolving towards the model of institutional pluralism? Have the frequent reorganizations, striking policy innovations, and permanent purge of the Khrushchev era been replaced by immobilism or by a Western type of incrementalism in policy change?

These are extremely difficult questions to answer, for there are few clear-cut criteria by which one can easily distinguish between immobilism and institutional pluralism. If either model were firmly linked with the power position of a specific institution, such as the party apparatus, then incremental changes in the status of that institution might provide a reliable indicator.[40] But this is hardly the case. Moreover, the crucial consideration is the *nature* of the party and the party apparatus, not their continued dominance.

Nor does the relative degree of freedom to advocate incremental policy change serve as a convincing criterion by which to judge the degree to which Soviet society corresponds to either model. The important thing is not simply the flow of ideas but rather what practical force these ideas have, and—even more—their content. The basic problem is the nature of the ''new class''—that is, the upper five-to-ten percent of Soviet society in socioeconomic terms. Does the fact that almost all its members are employed in bureaucratic institutions of one sort or another and are almost all required to be members of the Communist party ensure that the ideas flowing from them will be conservative rather than innovative? Does the fact that almost all the major political actors are senior bureaucrats (or civil servants, to use a more neutral term) who supervise state, economic, party, or educational-scientific institutions of one type or another mean that ideas challenging the status quo will be filtered out before they reach the political decision makers?

Ultimately, the test of the direction in which the Soviet political system is evolving must be the nature of the policies that emerge from the system. But here, too, evaluation is by no means simple. There are elements of both change and continuity in the life of every country, and unless the former are very dramatic, we face great problems when we try to decide which merit greater emphasis. If changes are less than dramatic, are they the kind of incremental changes that, taken individually, appear insignificant but which cumulatively transform society and the political system in a fundamental way? Or do they constitute merely the sort of minor tinkering that would not invalidate the judgment that the system is immobilized?

In trying to differentiate between immobilism and incrementalism, we essentially are making a judgment as to whether changes are or are not important or significant. As the debate over the New Left's charge of immobilism in the American political system demonstrates, however, any evaluation of this type rests essentially upon a subjective value judgment or on an unprovable assumption about what is required at a particular stage of history. In practice, there is a real tendency for such judgments to vary according to one's view of the status quo. If the status quo is considered fundamentally unjust, then no change short of the most drastic transformation of the system will be considered significant. If, on the other hand, the status quo is considered more or less tolerable, then incremental change seems much more important—and, in fact, desirable. Judgments of this type must remain basically nonscientific in nature.

Certainly the patterns of change and continuity in the Soviet Union since 1964 have been sufficiently ambiguous to prevent a definitive choice between incrementalism and immobilism as the proper label to apply to this period. On the one hand, there have been a number of evidences that might be cited in support of the thesis of immobilism in the Soviet political system. One such evidence surely would be the turnover rates in top administrative positions. Not only do these rates tend to suggest that there have been few "losers" such as are often produced by the resolution of great policy conflicts, but they have, in themselves, led to a significant aging of the top elite. The voting members of the first Central Committee elected after the 1917 Revolution averaged 36 years of age, and the average age thereafter rose quite slowly in both the Stalin and Khrushchev periods: it still was under 45 in 1934, dropped perhaps a year or two by 1939, then increased only to 49 in 1952, to 51 in 1956, and to 52 in 1961. In 1966, however, the average age of voting members jumped to 56, and from there it rose to 58 in 1971 and to 60 in 1976.[41] These figures are, of course, a reflection of the average age of the categories of officials from whom Central Committee members are usually drawn, and it is easy to argue that the increase in average age is likely associated with an increase in conservatism among these officials.

From many points of view, indeed, the policies of the Soviet leadership have been as conservative as the aging might lead one to expect. If the Soviet system is viewed as one committed to certain ideological goals, then the failure of the leaders to carry on the transformation of society prescribed by the ideology logically suggests a loss of dynamism, a petrification of the system. Or if the system is viewed as one in which the party has played out its historical role and the present stage of technological development of Soviet society dictates evolution toward constitutional democracy and market socialism, then the painfully slow pace of change along those lines is equally suggestive of immobilism. Whatever the long-term impact of the Soviet program of economic reform may be, the organization and operating principles of the economy (both in industry and agriculture) remain at present much more similar to those of the Stalin era than to those now in force in Yugoslavia. Similarly, much as public debate may have broadened in the USSR, there is still no evidence of the type of political liberalization that was seen in Czechoslovakia or the kind of devolution of authority from the center to the republics that is found in Yugoslavia. The continued prosecution of dissidents suggests an unwillingness on the part of the Soviet regime to accept ideological deviation that formally challenges the fundamentals of the system.

Moreover, despite some signs of change, the highest rewards and prestige are still accorded to those in the heavy-industry and defense sectors. These sectors continue to receive priority in such matters as material deliveries and housing allocations, and recent party elections revealed little decline in the status accorded them. It is true that agriculture has experienced some increase in its representation both on the all-Union and republic central committees, but no change has occurred within the urban sector.[42] Even the workers named to these bodies come overwhelmingly from heavy industry—nine of the ten workers on the all-Union Central Committee and 78 of the 115 identified workers on the republic committees in 1971.[43]

But while this evidence does point to a certain immobilism in the system, changes of some significance have, in fact, occurred. The devolution of power to the major institutional centers is a very important change indeed—especially if it should turn out to be more or less permanent. Of equal importance are the growing ambiguity of Soviet ideology and the increased vitality of public policy debate. In addition, there have been developments that are not consonant with any petrification model, especially one emphasizing bureaucratic ossification and preservation of the privileges and power of a narrow economic-social elite.

First, the bureaucracy itself has undergone a number of changes that do not suggest ossification. While, as pointed out earlier, the turnover rates of top officials have dropped markedly in comparison with the Khrushchev years, those at the middle levels of the bureaucracy remain substantial (see table 1.2). Moreover, the age of officials at the intermediate levels is considerably lower than that of their superiors (see table 1.3). Age is by no means a clear indicator of attitudes, but the relative youth of lower party officials is well worth noting, especially in view of the significant role of the party apparatus as a source of policy initiation. If present trends continue, the apparatus will within a few years be staffed predominantly by men whose entire work experience has fallen in the post-Stalin period.

Moreover, while it is admittedly difficult to ascertain how a bureaucracy actually operates in practice, such evidence as is available on the

Table 1.2. Rates of personnel turnover, 1966-71 (percentages of 1966 officials not in the same positions in 1971)[a]

| Party apparatus | | State apparatus | |
|---|---|---|---|
| Position | Turnover | Position | Turnover |
| Full members, CPSU Politburo | 0 | Deputy chairmen, USSR Council of Ministers | 0 |
| Full members, CPSU Central Committee | 24 | Ministers and chairmen of state committees sitting on the USSR Council of Ministers | 12 |
| Full members, CPSU Central Committee (party and government officials only)[b] | 19 | USSR deputy ministers of defense | 55 |
| CPSU Central Committee secretaries | 27 | Commanders, military districts | 100 |
| CPSU Central Committee department heads[c] | 46 | USSR deputy ministers[d] | 35 |
| Republic party first secretaries | 14 | Chairmen, republic Councils of Ministers | 60 |
| Full members, republic party bureaus | 37 | Deputy chairmen, republic Councils of Ministers | 45 |
| Full members, republic party CC | 41 | Republic ministers and chairmen of state committees | 41 |
| Full members, republic party CC (party and government officials only) | 33 | Oblispolkom chairmen[e] | 56 |
| Republic CC secretaries (except first secretaries) | 58 | Directors, 170 largest factories[e] | 44 |
| Republic CC department heads | 65 | | |
| Obkom first secretaries | 44 | | |
| Obkom second secretaries[e] | 67 | | |
| Gorkom first secretaries (50 largest cities)[e] | 61 | | |
| Raikom first secretaries (in 10 republics) | 57 | | |

aThe percentages of turnover shown for members of the CPSU Politburo and Central Committee, CPSU and republic Central Committee secretaries, CPSU Central Committee department heads, republic and obkom party first secretaries, deputy chairmen of the USSR Council of Ministers, Ministers and Chairmen of state committees sitting on the USSR Council of Ministers, and factory directors represent turnover between the 23rd (1966) and 24th (1971) CPSU Congresses (excluding several changes that occurred a few days after the 23rd Congress). The percentages given for all other categories of officials represent turnover between September 1, 1966, and September 1, 1971, these dates having been chosen to permit the utilization of data on republic government officials designated during the summer of 1971.

bThis excludes military officers (except the Minister of Defense), diplomats, scholars, and factory managers who are full CC members.

cIn the five cases in which a Central Committee secretary heads the department, the first deputy head is included in the calculation in order to avoid duplication.

dAs complete informaion is not available for all categories of officials, the turnover percentages given for USSR deputy ministers are only approximate.

eThe figures given for obkom second secretaries, oblispolkom chairmen, gorkom and raikom first secretaries are based on identification of 95 percent of the total number in each case; and for factory directors, on identification of 67 percent of the total number.

Table 1.3. Average ages of republic and RSFSR oblast officials, 1967 and 1971

| Position | 20 Oblasts 1967 | 5 Republics 1971 | 44 Oblasts 1973 |
|---|---|---|---|
| First secretaries, republic CCs or obkoms | 52 | 57[a] | 55 |
| Second secretaries, republic CCs or obkoms | 49 | 51[a] | 51 |
| Other secretaries, republic CCs or obkoms | 47 | 49 | 49 |
| Department heads, republic CCs or obkoms | 44 | 46 | 47 |
| Gorkom first secretaries | 44 | 44 | 46 |
| Raikom first secretaries | 44 | 44 | 44 |
| Chairmen, republic Councils of Ministers or oblispolkoms | 47 | 52[a] | 51 |
| Deputy chairmen, republic COMs or oblispolkoms | 50 | 52 | 51 |
| Republic ministers or heads of oblast administrations | 49 | 51 | 50 |

*Source:* The average age of oblast officials was calculated from lists of deputies to the oblast soviets, published in the respective oblast newspapers at the time. They were examined in the Lenin Library in Moscow.

The information on republic officials comes from lists of deputies to the republic supreme soviets elected in 1971. The five republics (the only ones where the lists gave the year of birth) were Estonia, Kirgizia, Latvia, Lithuania, and Tadzhikistan.

[a]Based on data for all republics rather than five.

functioning of Soviet officialdom does not suggest petrification. One of the major Soviet campaigns of recent years has focused on the "scientific organization of labor" (*nauchnaia organizatsiia truda,* or NOT), which has as its goals not only the rationalization of work at the factory-bench level but also "scientific" administration at the middle levels of the bureaucracy. This effort has been characterized by a preoccupation not so much with structural details (as under Khrushchev) as with the development of sophisticated managerial techniques, improved organization of information flow, and the like. One important by-product of this has been the recent renaissance of sociology in the USSR, with the regime itself now placing special emphasis on applied sociological research of potential use to party and governmental administrators. One cannot be certain about the end results of this new preoccupation with "scientific management," but it does suggest that what Peter Solomon has termed "a new administrative ethos" may be in the making.[44]

A second type of change that has been observable in the last dozen years is a very gradual erosion of those forces—surely the dominant forces of recent decades—that emphasize priority for industrial growth over other interests. These forces (except for the military) are no longer exempt from attack in the widening public debate. Many economists have advocated a change in the ratio of investments between Group A (heavy industry) and Group B (light and consumer industry) as well as institutional changes that would increase the sensitivity of the economy to consumer demands. The dominance of heavy industry is indirectly challenged by the mounting press criticisms of unsatisfactory conditions of life in the countryside, by the growing attention to environmental issues (a proconservationist film on Lake Baikal was the most popular Soviet film in 1970), and by repeated appeals for the transfer of housing and municipal services to the complete control of the local soviets. Although the results of the challenge to heavy industry have thus far undoubtedly been disappointing from the critics' standpoint, they have not been inconsequential.

The third type of change—and perhaps the most important of all—has been in the realm of social policy. It is curious that American specialists writing on the Soviet Union, though usually liberal in their domestic politics and inclined to judge American political leaders by their activism on social welfare issues, seldom consider such issues in evaluating the Soviet leadership. Yet, it must be recognized that the post-Khrushchev leadership has in fact initiated major steps toward greater egalitarianism that amount to a veritable war on poverty affecting millions of low-income citizens.

The most striking evidence of this is the progress made in recent years toward a narrowing of inequalities in income. Although comprehensive wage data are not published in the Soviet Union—a fact which suggests that considerable inequalities still exist—all the available evidence suggests that the pattern of income distribution has been changing quite substantially in the direction of greater equality. From 1966 to 1971 the minimum wage for wage earners (collective farmers excluded) rose 50 percent to 60 rubles a month, and during the 1971-75 Five-Year Plan it has risen to 70 rubles. Since large amounts of persons have been at minimum wage levels, according to an authoritative analyst, "the resulting very substantial reduction in the spread in basic wage rates must have meant a substantial narrowing in differentials in earnings."[45] The minimum pensions have also increased.

The assault on inequality of income has resulted in even more significant gains for the nation's collective farmers, who have long been at the bottom of the income ladder. Average kolkhoznik income (excluding income from private plots) rose 42 percent in the 1966-70 plan period compared with 26 percent for all wage earners, and it was scheduled to increase another 30-35 percent during the 1971-75 Five-Year Plan compared with a 20-22 percent rise for wage earners. The inherent uncertainty of collective farm incomes has also been reduced by the introduction of a guaranteed payment plan. In addition, the collective farmers have for the first time been included in the national pension system.[46]

The precise impact of Brezhnev's "war on poverty" will not be clear until Moscow decides to publish fuller income data, but it may well be that the Soviet Union in recent years has seen a shift in income distribution that is quite striking by Western standards, and that the pattern of income distribution in the Soviet Union today is substantially more egalitarian than it is in the advanced Western countries, particularly if income from property is taken into account. In any case, if it is true, as many contend, that the entrenched ruling elite in the Soviet Union has been gaining in power since Khrushchev's fall, at least its allegedly augmented authority does not appear to be reflected in a larger share of the national income.

The types of change observable in the Soviet Union do not, of course, demonstrate conclusively the absence of immobilism in the system, but they should give reason for pause. This is particularly true if we examine the Soviet Union in a comparative framework. In any assessment of what some see as petrification of the Soviet system, it is, for example, worth remembering that President Lyndon Johnson was considered a dynamic innovator in American domestic policy. Johnson initiated forward-looking legislation in the realms of medical care, education, civil rights, and social welfare. Yet he was able to produce only minor institutional change, and his education, fair housing, and War on Poverty programs can scarcely be said to have changed American reality in a major way. Probably his most important innovation—the Medicare program— was limited to those over sixty-five years of age and was financed through the most regressive of American taxes, the social security tax.

Notwithstanding these qualifications, it still seems fair to credit President Johnson with having been a major policy innovator. Then do the programs of the present Soviet leadership really seem like immobilism by comparison? We have already cited evidence showing the results of the steps taken by Brezhnev to reduce inequalities in income in the USSR. Certainly these steps have had a greater impact on the income levels of the poor than has President Johnson's War on Poverty.

A comparative framework may also be of use in analyzing other data that seem to provide clearcut evidence of petrification. The rate of turn-over among the top Soviet elite has unquestionably declined, and their average age has increased. But does this apparent desuetude of the per-manent purge mean that its many and varied purposes are not being served and that the system has ipso facto become immobilized? Or do the new turnover rates mean that the Soviet Union has adopted a pattern of personnel selection that is more normal for an advanced industrial coun-try?

To delve into such questions in a comprehensive way would require a comparative examination going well beyond the scope of this chapter. However, there is one comparison that is feasible and may also be useful in putting this whole problem in clearer perspective. That is a comparison of the average ages of various categories of Soviet officials with those of their closest American counterparts. At the time of the Twenty-Fourth Congress, the average age of Soviet obkom first secretaries was fifty-two as compared with fifty-one for state governors in the United States; industrial ministers in the Soviet Union averaged sixty years of age as compared with fifty-nine for the chief operating officers of the 50 largest American corporations (who are, in fact, the United States' top industrial administrators);[47] the average age of the party first secretaries of the capital cities of 13 out of the 15 Soviet republics (the ages of the other two are not ascertainable) was forty-seven, as compared with fifty-two for the mayors of the 25 largest American cities.

Moving toward the higher levels, one of course finds no American equivalent of the Soviet Central Committee, but for purposes of compari-son one can construct a hypothetical American "Central Committee" of 200 members, composed as follows: the members of the Cabinet, the governors of the states, the Congressional leadership, the chairmen of the Congressional committees, the justices of the Supreme Court, the chief executives of the 50 largest corporations, the members of the Armed Forces Policy Council, an additional five military officers, and 30 sub-cabinet officials from the White House staff, the executive departments and the independent agencies. Doing this, we arrive at an average of fifty-eight for this body in the spring of 1971, which interestingly enough is exactly the average age of the membership of the CPSU Central Com-mittee elected at that time.

Naturally, a comparative perspective—particularly one based on a two-country comparison—provides no final standard for judging petrification. One might argue that the standard of reference (in this case, the United States) is also afflicted with immobilism, that the Soviet system is so anachronistic that it requires more radical change than the American, or that the Soviet leadership must be more innovative to compensate for the weakness of innovative forces in the social and economic systems. However, if we do speak of a petrification of the Soviet system, let us recognize quite frankly the assumptions we are employing.

The contention that the Soviet Union petrified during the Brezhnev era—especially the first decade of that era—must rest on one of two possible lines of argument. One is that a few nonpluralist developments (notably the renewed restrictions on freedom to condemn Stalin's repressive actions) should outweigh all other developments in any assessment of the direction in which the Soviet system is moving. The second is that the Soviet Union has indeed been moving in the direction of institutional pluralism, but that the pace of change is so slow in comparison with societal requirements that the system must be called immobilized. (One might further argue that the impetus for further change is disappearing.)

To this observer at least, the first line of argument is very unconvincing. It seems to reflect no more than the "group bias" of Western social scientists—namely the unspoken and perhaps unconscious belief that a policial system should be judged solely on the basis of how it treats intellectuals who share Western values.

The second line of argument is more difficult to either prove or refute. Ultimately the question is not susceptible of a definitive answer, except perhaps by a future historian who will have the advantage of knowing what has occurred during the rest of this century. But if this line of argument is to be made, let it be made explicitly. Let the movement in the direction of institutional pluralism be acknowledged, and then let the precise nature of the argument for immobilism be spelled out.

For this purpose, it seems far more illuminating to begin, not with a petrification model that prejudges the analysis, but with an abstract or idealtype model such as institutional pluralism. Such a model is much easier to use as a model should be used (to "ask how far reality fits" it),[48] and there is less temptation to confuse the model with reality. One can easily and naturally speak of the movement of a system *either* toward the model or away from it. Moreover, with an abstract model that contains elements of similarity to classical pluralism (notably pluralism of elites and some elite representation of mass interests) as well as elements of divergence from it, it is also much easier to go on to raise a series of important comparative questions that tend to be foreclosed by models based on "good-evil" dichotomies.[49]

Clearly the operation of the Soviet political system in the twelve years since Khrushchev's removal seems significantly different from what it was during the twelve years prior to that event, but the interpretation of the differences is not an easy matter. Is the permanent revolution really dead, or is it only hibernating? Have the political leaders forever lost the ability or the will to challenge the major institutional centers of power, or are the developments of the last dozen years simply the product of a rather protracted succession crisis? In short, will historians of the future look back at 1964 as a major turning point in Soviet history or merely as the beginning point of one of a large number of cycles in a Soviet political tradition characterized by basic continuity?

If movement toward institutional pluralism is to be reversed, four possible alternatives suggest themselves. First, a strong leader might emerge—either through a military coup or, more likely, through a consolidation of power by the General Secretary—and initiate drastic political action. Second, one might see the emergence of a strong leader who would base his policy almost entirely on the narrow interests of the military/heavy-industrial elite. Third, a stalemate might develop within the leadership if the low rate of turnover among top officials were to continue so long as to result in a leadership old and rigid by anyone's definition. Fourth, institutional pluralism might prove an unsatisfactory compromise, generating inexorable pressures on the system to move toward classic pluralism.

A comprehensive discussion of the various factors that might lead to or foreclose all these alternatives would far exceed the limits of this chapter. The burden of proof, however, rests upon those who would prophesy drastic change away from institutional pluralism in any of the alternative directions just indicated.

A prediction of full pluralism, for example, must face the fact that political institutions associated with economic growth, social mobility for the ambitious, representation of the economic elite in the political process, and the achievement of nationalist goals normally are able to defend themselves quite well against frontal attack. Moreover, as Brzezinski emphasizes, such a prediction must also reckon with the multinational nature of the Soviet system.[50] The profound consequences that full or classic pluralism would have for the relationship of the Russians to the other nationalities in the USSR is likely to make that alternative quite unattractive to most Russians, except perhaps as a last resort. Movement toward classic pluralism in the near term would therefore seem unlikely except in the event of major and persistent unrest among the nationalities or a zero-growth kind of crisis in the economic system.

A prediction of clear stalemate, on the other hand, overlooks the fact that the leading party bodies are broadly representative of the different institutional forces in Soviet society, and that the basic political institutions are arranged in a way that is quite conducive to the rise of strong leadership. Given these institutional arrangements as well as the historical commitment of the Communist party to industrial development and to the enhancement of the USSR's position in the world arena, everything that we have learned about the behavior of elite groups and about committee decision making suggests that a coalition would form to overcome any stalemate that might begin to have obviously harmful consequences in terms of governmental functioning.

Compared to the possibilities of classic pluralism or stalemate, the likelihood of a strong leader emerging in the Soviet Union is much greater. Indeed, Myron Rush has argued that the late 1960s actually were a period of succession crises,[51] and there are several reasons to suspect that he may be right.

The basic Western explanation for the dominance of the General Secretary over other members of the Soviet Politburo in the past has been a theory that Robert Daniels calls "the circular flow of power." According to this theory, the General Secretary derives his great power primarily from his responsibility for supervising the party apparatus throughout the country and from his ability to appoint and remove the provincial party secretaries. Since the provincial secretaries in turn control the selection of delegates to the all-Union Party Congress, and since the Congress names (or at least ratifies) the members of the Central Committee, to which both the Politburo and the Secretariat are responsible, "the circuit is closed: The [General] Secretary is confirmed in office by a circular process that ultimately he himself controls—or can control."[52]

Assuming that the provincial party secretaries and the delegates to the all-Union Party Congress are still selected in the ways suggested by the circular-flow-of-power theory, one could well expect Khrushchev's fall to be followed by an especially slow consolidation of power in the hands of the succeeding General Secretary. To an extent that is not fully appreciated by many scholars (and is completely unappreciated by most journalists), the CPSU Congress is the key institution in the process of the circular flow of power. Even when there is no contest at the Congress, the loyalty of the bulk of the delegates to the regional party secretaries and ultimately to the General Secretary is a decisive factor preventing the old Politburo members from challenging the list of new Central Committee members prepared by the General Secretary.

When viewed from this perspective, the fact that the Twenty-Third CPSU Congress came so soon after Khrushchev's removal, and that the next Congress was not held for five years, could have seriously interfered with Brezhnev's ability to undermine the independence of the Central Committee and quickly consolidate his power. By the spring of 1966, when the Congress met, changes of first secretary had taken place in oblasts and small republics accounting for only 13 percent of the delegates to the Congress.[53] The Twenty-Fourth Congress, however, should have marked a very important stage in the unfolding of the circular-flow-of-power process, for in the period between the two congresses new first secretaries had been selected in oblasts and small republics commanding 50 percent of the delegates.[54] In all, the proportion of delegates to the Twenty-Fourth Congress politically indebted to post-1964 first secretaries stood at 63 percent, and of course the proportion would be considerably higher if one were to include in it delegates from the small non-Russian republics on the assumption that they owe their party positions wholly or in part to the Russian second secretaries of these republics.[55]

On the basis of the Stalin and Khrushchev experiences, the circular-flow-of-power theory would have predicted that Brezhnev could force through a substantial expansion in the size of the Central Committee elected at the Twenty-Fourth Congress and in the size of the Politburo elected by the new Central Committee; and that he would then be able to remove his major Politburo rivals by the end of 1972. The Twenty-Fourth Congress did ratify an increase in the number of voting members of the Central Committee from 195 to 241 and in the number of voting members of the Politburo from 11 to 15. While 82 percent of the still-living members of the 1966 Central Committee were reelected in 1971, proponents of the circular-flow-of-power theory would consider it more significant that 38 percent of the 1971 voting members had reached this status since 1966 and 55 percent since Brezhnev's assumption of the party leadership in 1964. And, in fact, some presumed rivals—Shelepin, Shelest and Voronov—were removed in subsequent years.

Relationships within the Politburo today may or may not still be shaped by the factors suggested by the circular-flow-of-power theory.[56] In any case, it should not be assumed that a return to "limited personal rule" (to use Rush's phrase) automatically implies a return to the relationships that formerly existed between the political leadership and the societal centers of power. Much, of course, depends on the type of limited personal rule that emerges. If one accepts Rush's citation of Lenin between 1917 and 1922 and Stalin between 1928 and 1937 as typical examples of such rule,[57] and if Brezhnev or anyone else were to succeed in acquiring a similar position, then movement toward institutional pluralism would scarcely seem likely. Lenin and Stalin had the most clear-cut ability as well as determination to force through change of enormous magnitude in the periods in question.

Yet it is possible for a leader to have a dominant political position, to have the final say on policy questions if he wishes, and still to fulfill, usually, a broker-like role. In short, there must be some category (or categories) between the "limited personal rule" of a Lenin or an early Stalin on the one hand and pure oligarchy on the other, and the term "political boss" may have the proper connotations for such an intermediate type. (Some term such as "limited dictator" might be applied to a leader in the position of Lenin and the early Stalin, and some term such as "full dictator" to one in the position of the post-1937 Stalin.)

Whatever label is employed for the intermediate category between limited dictator and oligarchy, a political boss of the type indicated is not only compatible with the model of institutional pluralism but perhaps a significant component of it. Change in a classic pluralist system often requires political leadership and governmental action to overcome the entrenched resistance of those who benefit from the status quo, and at times very strong leadership may be required in a system of institutional pluralism, particularly in a country where one group has the superior political weight possessed by the elite associated with defense and heavy industry in the Soviet Union.

Compatibility between institutional pluralism and one type of personal rule does not, of course, guarantee that a strong General Secretary would assume such a role. There are, however, many reasons to doubt that any General Secretary in the near future will become more than a political boss as defined here. If the last twelve years have been a succession crisis, they certainly have been much less dramatic than either 1924-29 or 1953-57, and it is most probable that the movement toward institutional pluralism has been more the product of fundamental, long-term changes in the Soviet political and social system than simply of a temporary configuration of forces in the Politburo.

One change of long-term significance is the background of those from whom the leadership is selected. While Brzezinski's phrase "a government of clerks" seems unnecessarily pejorative, the Soviet leaders now are, in fact, recruited from among persons who have risen through the ranks of bureaucratic organizations rather than from among men with the very different experience and perspectives of the revolutionary. Today eleven of the fifteen voting members of the Politburo have been successful republic, obkom, or gorkom first secretaries—positions that require the abilities and frame of mind of the broker politician. Such men, when they reach the top, certainly may have ideas and ambitions of their own, but it would be surprising if the instincts of the broker did not remain.

A second change is the precedent of Khrushchev's removal. As Daniels emphasizes, "This was the first time in the history of Russia since Riurik that the established leader of the country was removed by the rules of representative procedure. Since the leader was removed, it follows naturally that he was and had been removable. It follows equally that the successor leadership is removable in the same way."[58] Under the circular-flow-of-power theory, the power of the General Secretary depends upon the same factors that solidify the position of the leader of any political machine—the gratitude, loyalty, and especially the self-interest of subordinates. The memory of Khrushchev's removal will remind any successor that there can be circumstances in which these factors cease to be decisive, and it is hard to believe—barring a major crisis—that a General Secretary will soon choose to challenge the fundamental interests of as many different institutional groups as Khrushchev did.

Most important, however, are the changes of a gradual and subtle nature that have been taking place throughout the Soviet political and social system. Obviously the structure of material and psychological rewards has over time resulted in the flow of a large number of the most talented people into the "military/heavy-industrial complex" very broadly defined, and just as obviously these people will long remain a powerful political force. Yet there are many forces at work within and outside Soviet society that are beginning to undermine the dominance of this complex. They are: (1) the creation in large numbers of new types of personnel with perspectives and backgrounds quite different from the prodution-oriented, heavy-industrial-engineer types who had been the dominating political force in recent years; (2) the tendency of the children of the top and middle elite to enter occupations less clearly associated with the administration and development of heavy industry; (3) the impact of constant press criticism of poverty problems on the legitimacy of heavy-industry and military expenditures; (4) the egalitarian aspects of the ideology, especially those calling for the elimination of urban-rural differences; (5) the assignment of responsibility for health-education-welfare functions (and of seeking appropriations for them) to the "guardians of the ideology"—the ideological party secretaries; (6) elite fear of popular unrest, reinforced by the memory of events in Eastern Europe, most recently in Poland; and (7) developments abroad, such as the reduction of United States overseas military commitments and evidences of a possible return to more normal conditions in China—both of which might tend to diminish the Soviet inclination to stress defense and heavy industry.

There are also forces at work that tend, more generally, to undermine the authoritarian features of the system: (1) the rising educational level of the Soviet elite; (2) the gradual disappearance of the economic-

social forces that generate a propensity toward authoritarianism (as discussed in Erich Fromm's *Escape from Freedom*);[59] (3) the erosion of
ideological certainty under the impact of events in the outside world and
the expanding scope of sociological research at home; and (4) the tendency for dissenters to come from the upper stratum of Soviet society, in
conjunction with the fact that it is difficult for an elite to ruthlessly suppress its own.

It is possible to imagine a Soviet political leader or a group of leaders
becoming alarmed at these developments and deciding to seek a return
either to revolutionary ideological purity or to a more single-minded
dedication to building Soviet military strength. But possibilities are not
necessarily probabilities. The usual reaction of a political leader attempting to consolidate his position is to adapt himself to major societal forces
rather than to try to combat them. If we are inclined to predict that a
Soviet leader will behave differently, we should ask ourselves the reasons
for such a prediction. Is it based upon our observations of the Soviet
experience of the last two decades, upon "our notions of what a political
system is and does,"[60] or upon the lingering impact of the totalitarian
model on our thinking about the Soviet Union?

Predicting the future development of any political system is, of
course, even more hazardous than trying to describe an existing one in
capsule form. If we are to judge by the evidence of both Soviet and
Western experience, the Soviet future will be far more inconsistent than
any theory suggests. There will be developments that indicate movement
toward institutional pluralism and others that seem inconsistent with
such movement. The mixture of continuity and change will likely continue to be ambiguous enough to provoke countless more arguments
about whether the Soviet Union is or is not petrifying. Only a man who is
totally committed to some theory of societal development and who believes that the future is predetermined can predict with a sense of complete confidence.

What is needed as we look at the future of the Soviet system—and at
its recent past as well—is not certainty in our judgments, but openness in
our approach. We must recognize that, even when we have consciously
rejected the totalitarian model, it continues to color many of our assumptions about the rationale and dynamics of Soviet behavior. What is
needed is a willingness—indeed, a determination—to subject our
assumptions to searching examination and to separate our distaste for the
Soviet system from our descriptive analysis of it. Nothing will serve these
purposes better than a rigorous comparative approach in the choice of the
standards that we apply and strict comparability in the definitions of the
concepts we employ.

# 2

# The Bureaucratic Model
# and the Nature
# of the Soviet System

During the past fifty years, many observers have noted the looming presence of large-scale organizations in the Soviet Union and decided to place bureaucracy at the center of their analysis of the present and the future. In the early years of the Soviet regime, Lenin had worried about the dangers of bureaucratization, and Trotsky had asserted that the bureaucracy had become the ruling element in Soviet society.[1] Just prior to World War II, James Burnham developed the Trotsky analysis further, asserting that a "managerial revolution" had occurred in the Soviet Union and was spreading throughout the world.[2] Shortly after the death of Stalin, Barrington Moore relied heavily upon Max Weber's theory of bureaucracy in developing a model of "rational-technical society" which he believed provided the best clue to the future evolution of Soviet society.[3] Six years later Alfred Meyer agrued that "the whole [Soviet] society is a bureaucratic command structure, with all of the features familiar to students of bureaucracy" and that the bureaucratic model should form the basis for our understanding of Soviet society.[4] When Khrushchev was replaced, Zbigniew Brzezinski labeled his fall a "victory of the clerks," suggesting that it resulted from a tendency of "bureaucratic politics . . . to elevate non-entities" and contending that "bureaucratic conservatism is now dominant."[5]

That scholars have turned to the concept of bureaucracy in trying to understand the nature of the Soviet system is not at all surprising. Even in the West,

> Most people spend much of their time as small cogs in the machinery of large impersonal bureaucracies. It is through these structures that they must find success, that they must find their livelihood. The demands of bureaucracy govern them during most of their waking moments. The influence of bureaucracy is felt in nearly all aspects of life . . . Modern man's life is organized for him. His education, his livelihood, his recreation, and even his religion are products of the planned and coordinated activities of great numbers of people, most of whom he has never met and never will.[6]

This assessment obviously fits the Soviet Union, and must be accentuated by the fact that Soviet society quite literally is a "bureaucracy writ large" with all large-scale organizations ultimately being subordinate to a single political institution.

Nevertheless the diversity in the views of the scholars who employ some type of bureaucratic model suggests that the popularity of the model owes something to its elasticity. Large-scale organizations have many characteristics, and there are many conflicting images of their inner nature. When Alfred Meyer, for example, speaks of the USSR as a "large complex bureaucracy," he basically has in mind a hierarchical image of bureaucracy—one with "a thoroughly authoritarian political structure [with] centralized control [and] homogenized patterns of organization."

> In all bureaucratic systems the basic aims are given. They have been defined by those who make all the final decisions . . . The system remains unified under one command, coordinated by one universally binding set of goals, guided and controlled by one central hierarchy . . . The elite is independent of control by the lower ranking members of the organization . . . The individual finds himself thrown into a situation in which unseen and uncontrollable authorities ceaselessly impose social change unwanted by the constituents.[7]

A similar conception of bureaucracy is embodied in the models of an "administered society" and an "organizational society" advanced by Allen Kassof and T.H. Rigby, respectively.[8]

On the other hand, when Barrington Moore depicts the Soviet society that "industrialization exerts very strong pressures towards creating," he does not see a bureaucracy that is a tool of those who make all the final decisions, but one staffed by "technocrats" who make their decisions on the basis of technical and rational criteria. His image of bureaucracy emphasizes predictability and rationality: "conformity to a code of legality," "conformity with objective rules and objectively appraised performance," "an emphasis on merit as the criterion for retaining any status," "a firm allocation of rights and duties for each post in a well-defined chain of command," rather then unseen and uncontrollable authorities and the imposition of ceaseless change. As a consequence, Moore, unlike Meyer, foresees "a limitation on the arbitrary power of the center" and "a heavy reduction of emphasis in the power of the dictator." The "rules, necessary to give a bureaucracy its qualities of regularity and precision, also serve to inhibit the leader from exercising his power fully."[9]

Trotsky and Brzezinski also conceive of bureaucracy as more than the executor of central policy, but they view it as a self-interested and power-seeking institution rather than the technocratic representation of rationality. They argue that the bureaucracy has already come to dominate Soviet policy formation—and with unpleasant consequences for the Soviet population. Trotsky insisted that as early as the 1920s the bureaucracy "conquered the Bolshevik party . . . [and] defeated the program of Lenin." In his opinion, Stalin was the servant of the bureaucracy, not its master. "The success which fell upon him was a surprise at first to Stalin himself. It was the friendly vote of the new ruling group, trying to free itself from the old principles and from the control of the masses and having need of a reliable arbiter in its internal affairs."[10] Brzezinski dates the triumph of bureaucracy forty years later with the fall of Khrushchev, but his conception of a post-Khrushchev "government of clerks"—of rule by an "ossified bureaucracy"—has many similarities to Trotsky's image of the Soviet political leadership.[11]

The great diversity in the analyses of the Soviet Union that accompany an emphasis upon the role or impact of bureaucracy demonstrates one point very clearly: there is no single bureaucratic model.[12] Indeed, the number of models exceeds that already implied in the foregoing discussion, for, as will be argued in this chapter, none of the authors cited employs the implicit bureaucratic model most widely accepted by recent students of administrative organizations in the West. If we are to use the bureaucratic model in illuminating the Soviet system, we must define our terms precisely and must specify the model or conception of bureaucracy we are using. Moreover, the multiplicity of models suggests the need to explore more seriously the general question, what *is* the political significance of the fact that the Soviet Union is a large complex bureaucracy?

The first issue that must be clarified is the definition of the terms "bureaucracy" and "bureaucrat." Nearly all Western discussions of the Soviet policy process list the bureaucrats as one—but only one—of the participants. One classic line of analysis has distinguished between the party apparatus and the state bureaucracy,[13] between the politicians and the bureaucrats,[14] between the political professionals of the party apparatus and the claimants and advisors who constitute the policy groups— "the military, the heavy-industry and light-industry managers, the agricultural experts, and finally the state bureaucrats."[15]

As specialists on the Soviet Union have come to adopt more of a group approach, they named many of the same groups that Brzezinski and Huntington did—ones that invariably included bureaucrats among them. In a later article discussing the policy views of groups more explicitly, Brzezinski spoke of the "ministerial bureaucrats" instead of "state bureaucrats," moved the party apparatus (now divided into central apparatus and regional apparatus) onto his list of groups, and added the following to it: heavy industry, secret police, light industry, agronomists, and consumers' goods industry.[16] Similarly, Vernon Aspaturian thinks the major groups in Soviet politics to be "(1) the party apparatus, (2) the professional military, (3) the state bureaucracy, and (4) the managerial-technical bureaucracy or economic bureaucracy,"[17] while H. Gordon Skilling places "party apparatchiki, state bureaucrats and managers, police officials, and the military" on his abbreviated list of groups.[18]

However, while the various distinctions reflect differences of actual significance in Soviet society, they tend to obscure one basic fact: the party apparatchiki, the military, the heavy or light industry managers, the agronomists or agricultural experts in high positions, and the police are bureaucrats just as much as the officials actually given this label by Western scholars. All these persons—definitely including the politicians of the party apparatus—have worked and risen within a centralized hierarchy, learning to operate successfully within the framework of superiors' rules and instructions, achieving many of their aims through the medium of "committee politics," knowing that promotion to significant administrative posts depends on the judgments of those above them in the hierarchy.

Moreover, all these groups, again including the party apparatchiki, are composed of officials who have had orderly, Weberian career patterns. Nearly all significant Soviet officials are college graduates, generally with specialized training appropriate for the post they hold.[19] Promotion seems based primarily upon performance, and, except for those at the very highest political levels, honest officials are usually assured of tenure with good performance. They usually are not demoted more than one level in the hierarchy even with unsatisfactory performance. While membership in the Communist party is almost always required for appointment to a significant administrative position, college-educated citizens generally are not permitted to join the party until they have reached their late twenties and have demonstrated their dedication to the party's cause through performance on the job. Hence, for those who accept the fundamentals of society or are willing to act as if they do, party membership becomes less an independent requirement for promotion than a sign that the person is seen as having the technocratic criteria for it.[20]

Consider, for example, the biography of Boris Korotkov, the former first secretary of the Perm obkom. Born in 1927, Korotkov attended the Kuibyshev Industry Institute and, upon graduation in 1950, worked for two years as a foreman, a technologist, and then the deputy head of a shop at a major defense industry plant in Perm. In 1952 he was named secretary of the Young Communist (Komsomol) organization at the plant, a fact that surely indicated he had been politically very active as a student and an engineer. Soon Korotkov became first secretary of the Perm city Komsomol committee, then first secretary of the Perm oblast Komsomol committee. In 1958, he was transferred to party work —initially as first secretary of the Dzerzhinsky *raikom* (borough) in Perm, then as first secretary of the city Party committee in Berezniki, the second largest city in Perm oblast. In 1963 Korotkov was moved to work in the Perm obkom, first as the secretary in charge of industrial construction questions, then in 1968 as its first secretary.[21]

If the process of working within a large-scale hierarchical organization with professionalized career patterns has some inherent impact upon a person, then a party official— a politician—like Korotkov surely has had this type of bureaucratic experience just as much as if he had worked within a state institution.[22] Whatever else may be said about Brzezinski's image of a government of clerks in the Soviet Union, he is absolutely and indisputably correct in pointing to this central fact about the major political as well as administrative actors in the Soviet political system.

As pronounced as is the blurring of the distinction between politician and bureaucrat in the Soviet Union, any distinction between state bureaucrats or ministerial bureaucrats on the one hand and economic managers, heavy industry, light industry, and agronomists on the other hand is even more difficult to defend, unless the former are simply shorthand residual categories for those officials not involved in economic management. However, it certainly should be understood that, among the 82 ministries, state committees, and other central agencies represented on the USSR Council of Ministers in 1973, 36 were responsible for a branch of industry, 9 for a branch of construction, 4 for agriculture, and 4 for transportation or communications. The other 29 central institutions represented on the Council of Ministers, excluding the military and the police, were a most diverse lot: the Ministries of Culture, Education, Finance, Foreign Affairs, Foreign Trade, Geology, Health, Higher and Specialized Secondary Education, Justice, and Trade; the State Committees for Foreign Economic Ties, Forestry, Labor and Wages, Movies, Peoples' Control, Planning, Prices, Publishing, Science and Technology, Standards, Supply, Television and Radio, and Vocational-Technical Education; and, finally, the Central Statistical Administration and the State Bank.

Not only do the economic ministries and committees, the police, and the military comprise 70 percent of the central institutions on the

Council of Ministers (78 percent if we include seven state committees whose work is primarily directed toward economic management: Forestry, Inventions and Discoveries, Labor and Wages, Planning, Prices, Standards, and Supply), but the career patterns of their officials have great similarity to those labeled bureaucrats, at least in terms of their professional nature and their regularity. Consider, for example, the biographies of the following representatives of the military, agronomists, heavy industry, and light industry.[23]

*Andrei A. Grechko, late Minister of Defense,* born in 1903. 1919 —Soldier in the Red Army, then commander of a platoon, then of a squadron. 1936—Graduated from the Frunze Military Academy and became commander of a squadron. From 1938 to 1939—Commander of a regiment, then chief of staff of a cavalry division. 1941—Graduated from the Military Academy of the General Staff. During World War II—Commander of a division, then of a corps, then of an army. First deputy commander of the First Ukrainian Front. 1945—Commander of the Kiev Military District. 1953—Commander-in-chief of Soviet troops in Germany. 1957—Commander-in-chief of Soviet infantry. 1958—First Deputy Minister of Defense (and later, simultaneously, Commander of the Warsaw Pact Troops). 1967—Minister of Defense, USSR.

*Vladimir V. Matskevich, former Minister of Agriculture,* born in 1909. 1930—Graduated from the Kharkov Zootechnical Institute. 1930 —Teacher, then director of an agricultural secondary school, then director of a zoological institute. 1946—Deputy Minister of Livestock of the Ukraine, then Ukrainian Minister of Livestock, then Ukrainian Minister of Agriculture. 1950—First Deputy Chairman of the Ukrainian Council of Ministers in charge of agriculture. 1953—First Deputy Minister of Agriculture of the USSR. 1955—Minister of Agriculture, then Deputy Chairman of the Council of Ministers in charge of agriculture, then Deputy Chairman of the Gosplan (in charge of agriculture). From 1960 to 1965—Chairman of the Executive Committee of the Virgin Lands Regional Soviet (a form of political exile). 1965—Minister of Agriculture.

*Ivan F. Sinitsyn, Minister of the Tractor and Agricultural Machinery Industry,* born in 1911. 1929—A draftsman, then the head of a sector, then a senior technologist at the Gorki Auto Works. 1936—Senior inspector of the technical control department, then shop head, then chief mechanic, then chief engineer of the Red Etna Works in Gorki. Meanwhile, in 1937, Sinitsyn had graduated from the evening division of the Gorki Industrial Institute. 1944—Director of the Red Etna Works. 1946 —Director of the Ural Truck Works. 1950—Director of the Stalingrad Tractor Works. 1957—Chairman of the Stalingrad, then the Lower Volga Regional Economic Council. 1965—Minister of the Tractor and Agricultural Machinery Industry.

*Nikolai N. Tarasov, Minister of Light Industry,* born in 1911. 1935 —After graduation from the Moscow Textile Institute worked at the Orekhovo-Zuevo cotton combine as shift foreman, then deputy head of a shop, then shop head, then head of a spinning factory, then head of a department. 1942—In the Soviet army. 1945—Chief engineer of a spinning-weaving factory, then chief engineer of the Cotton Textile Administration of the USSR Ministry of Light Industry, then head of this administration. 1952—Deputy Minister of Light Industry. 1953—Responsible work in the apparatus of the USSR Council of Ministers (probably head of the light industry department). 1955—Deputy Chairman for light industry of the State Committee for Long-Term Planning. From 1957 to 1960—Work in the USSR Gosplan and the Vladimir regional economic council. 1960—Deputy Chairman of the All-Union Economic Council (for light industry). 1962—Chairman of the State Committee for Light Industry. 1965—Minister of Light Industry.

On the whole, the economic managers and the military acutally have more specialized bureaucratic career patterns than the twenty-five ministers and chairmen who are labeled bureaucrats in the West. Thus, as of August 1973, four of the latter (those in charge of health, higher education, geology, and science and technology) were men with a background in scientific research and college teaching, while another fourteen came to their posts with a career background outside the policy area of their present ministry or state committee. In contrast, 82 percent of the economic ministers rose essentially within the hierarchy they now head (at least given the limitations imposed on career regularity by the frequent industrial reorganizations of recent years).

A similar difficulty is encountered if one attempts to define the state bureaucrats as a distinctive group of officials who supervise the provincial soviets.[24] The specialized officials of the soviet, who are in dual subordination to a ministry as well as to the soviet, tend to be persons with specialized career patterns within their ministerial hierarchy—or, in the case of a few leading officials, with substantial experience in the party apparatus. Those officials in general positions in the soviets, however, are never promoted along a career ladder of such posts, from the chairmanship of the executive committee of one soviet to the chairmanship of others at progressively higher territorial levels. For example, in the summer of 1970, 73 percent of the chairmen of the republican councils of ministers had come to their position directly from a position in the party apparatus as had 69 percent of the forty-two chairmen of regional soviets who were elected deputies to the Supreme Soviet in that year. In addition, another 17 percent of the latter group had been employed in the party apparatus in the next-to-last job they had held before becoming soviet chairman.[25]

For these reasons, while specific groups of state officials may be associated with specific interests and policy proposals (for example, the chairmen of regional soviets with the demand that the financing and control of housing and communal services be taken from industrial enterprises and given entirely to the soviets), any effort to analyze the Soviet Union in terms of a bureaucratic model must encompass all of the bureaucracies in the Soviet Union—the ministerial hierarchies (including those dealing with the economy, military affairs, and law and order), the party apparatus, the educational-scientific establishment, the mass media, and the public organizations. All these institutions are controlled from above, all are subject to directives emanating from the same political institution or institutions, all have their key officials in the *nomenklatura* of higher Party officials, and all have developed many of the characteristics associated with bureaucratization. Moreover, now that the prerevolutionary and civil war generation has (with a few exceptions in the Baltic republics) passed almost completely from the political scene, the top political leaders in the Soviet Union—indeed, the entire political echelon—have had the socialization experiences associated with rising through such hierarchies. This is the essence of Meyer's insight about the applicability of a bureaucratic model to the Soviet Union; this is the essence of Brzezinski's insight about a government of clerks.

But if we assume that the Soviet Union is a corporation writ large and that it has a government of clerks, what implications should be drawn from this assumption?

The articles on the Soviet Union written in the 1960s (excluding those written by Brzezinski after the fall of Khrushchev) emphasized that a bureaucratized society is particularly susceptible to being directed, organized, or mobilized. Indeed, this aspect of bureaucracy probably explains much of the popularity of the bureaucratic model in its various guises, for it has permitted Western scholars to retain many of the traditional notions of totalitarian control in the face of the disappearance of many of the "elements of gross irrationality . . . that we have come to associate with totalitarian systems in recent decades."[26] And surely the hierarchical nature of bureaucracy is a fact that does have relevance for an understanding of Soviet society.

Yet to say that bureaucracies are supposed to execute their leaders' policies scarcely says everything about the nature of an actual bureaucracy or of its role in an actual society.

In the first place, of course, the formal organizational structures and operating rules of bureaucracies do not guarantee that they will always carry out the policies they are given. On the simplest level, lower officials may consciously or unconsciously pursue their interest or may follow the advice to reject immoral orders. But the basic problem is a far deeper one.

The conception of duty upon which the modern bureaucracy is built assumes that the official should carry out orders faithfully, observe the rules strictly, and perform the job according to the best professional standards. We all take these responsibilities for granted, but, in reality, they can be so mutually contradictory in their implications that bureaucracy simply cannot function as some automatic executive instrument.

The most obvious potential conflict in bureaucratic responsibilities is that between the acceptance of superior orders and adherence to professional standards or long-standing rules. In fact this possibility is so great that Blau and Meyer are driven to suggest that "If trained experts perform tasks within the limits set by the technology and administrative framework, resort to strict command authority is unnecessary and, indeed, must be eschewed lest it interfere with the exercise of discretion in making expert judgments . . . The advanced technology of the twentieth century necessitates information feedback and specialized skills, which are incompatible with an authority structure resting on blind obedience to orders issued through a chain of command."[27] Similarly, strict observance of all the rules governing any bureaucrat is so dysfunctional for the performance of the basic mission that the threat to "work to rule" is akin to a threat to strike.[28] But problems remain if rule evasion for the sake of performance is legitimated—and Dalton insists that "the iron law of American bureaucratic practice echoes in the refrain, 'There's always a way to get around the rule—look for it.'"[29] What, for example, is to happen when the professional judgment of the police on the best way of preventing crime is inconsistent with the formal rules of procedure designed to protect the rights of the accused and the suspected?[30]

The second problem with any model which focuses exclusively on the administrative functions of bureaucracy is that it essentially ignores a critical question that certainly should be illuminated by any model of society as a whole: how is the policy that is being executed by the bureaucracy actually determined?

Western scholars on the Soviet Union who have retained the executive instrument concept of bureaucracy have dealt with policy formation simply by agreeing with Weber that "at the top of a bureaucratic organization, there is necessarily an element which is at least not purely bureaucratic."[31] They have quickly identified this element as the Party leadership. Like George Fischer (whose "monist model" is very much a bureaucratic model), they argue that "politicians [the Party's full-time executives] are the main leaders of a monist society . . . [Their] power stands over the specialized 'strategic elites' near the top." They acknowledge that "politicians may have learned a good deal from work in . . . a bureaucratic organization," but still believe that "this does not at all mean they remain bureaucrats."[32]

Classically, those specialists on the Soviet Union who emphasize the executive role of bureaucracy have pointed to the impact of Marxism-Leninism—or at least the leadership's perception of Marxism-Leninism—as a major source of the policy that is adopted by the political leaders:

> The administered society can be defined as one in which an en-trenched and extraordinarily powerful ruling group lays claim to ultimate and exclusive scientific knowledge of social and historical laws and is im-pelled by a belief not only in the practical desirability, but the moral neces-sity of planning, direction, and coordination from above in the name of human welfare and progress . . . The technicians and experts operate only under license of the political elite and in terms of the latter's self-pro-claimed ultimate knowledge of the proper uses of science and technology in the larger socio-historical setting. [33]

Yet whatever the actual role of the bureaucracy in the Soviet political system, there certainly is no a priori reason to assume that administrative organs are always limited to an administrative role alone. Indeed, one of the most insistent spokesmen for specific policies (in many parts of the world to the point of overthrowing established authority) is the military—precisely the institution from which Weber's ideal type was largely drawn, precisely the institution that is one of the first to take on the characteristics of a modern bureaucracy in a developing nation.

The military is scarcely the only bureaucractic institution that becomes involved in policy making. In many parliamentary systems, the civil service frequently formulates the policy that the cabinet formally adopts, a point made by Max Weber, among others. "Generally speak-ing, the trained permanent official is more likely to get his way in the long run than his nominal superior, the Cabinet minister, who is not a specialist." [34] For similar reasons, the American bureaucracy has been referred to as "the fourth branch of government." [35] Weber and his fol-lowers have insisted that "the primary source of the superiority of bureaucratic administration" is its ability to utilize in coordinated fashion the technical knowledge possessed by diversely trained specialists. They have contended that the inevitable consequence of the superior's relative lack of expertise is that his "right to decide, which is authority" is coupled with a loss of "the power to do, which is specialized ability" and with a loss "to experts [of] the ability to command." [36]

If we are going to try to understand the Soviet Union in terms of a bureaucratic model, we need to move well beyond any conception that depicts bureaucracy solely as a passive instrument. We need a model, an ideal type, a set of assumptions that incorporates the conflicts in our conceptions of bureaucratic duty and the bureaucratic impact on policy

making. Fortunately, such a model or set of assumptions has been implicitly developed by mainline American theorists on bureaucracy, and it
would usually include the following points:

1. The bureaucratic form of organization does not result merely from
the need to coordinate the type of specialization of *task* found on the
assembly line. It also reflects the advantages to be gained from using
specialized *personnel* in concerted action. Industry, for example, hires
not only the proverbial worker who tightens the same kind of nut every
day, but also "experts in purchasing, transportation, finance, law, engineering, personnel, and many [other fields]." "The specialists who have
mastered these new specialties are not lesser men who perform fewer and
simpler programs than the former managers. Their preparation for their
functions takes longer."[37]

In practice, therefore, the vast majority of bureaucratic employees
with any input into decision making are not clerks, but trained specialists.

> The functions performed by civil servants [suggest] the inaccuracy of
> the common stereotype of "the bureaucrat." There is no "typical govern-
> ment employee," for the civil service is little less diversified than society
> itself. Every sort of work, every type of skill, every level of technical and
> professional specialization is represented. Included in 1964, for example,
> were not only the tens of thousands of lawyers, accountants, and adminis-
> trative specialists of whom everyone knows, but literally thousands of
> engineers, doctors, dentists, nurses, biological and physical and social
> scientists, mathematicians, statisticians, librarians, archivists, veterinaries,
> and many others.[38]

2. Some officials do correspond to the popular conception of the
bureaucrat who is interested primarily in security, income, or prestige
—"conservers" or "climbers," Anthony Downs calls them.[39] Basically,
however, "the members of the organization act as human beings—often
friendly and sometimes disgruntled—rather than like dehumanized,
impersonal machines."[40] Their values may differ, but perhaps of greatest
importance for the policy process is that most identify with professional
standards and with the program they administer. "A man who has spent
many years working in, say, the natural resources area can be expected to
believe that his programs are immensely worthy of support . . . Indeed,
he would hardly be worth having as a governmental employee if he did
not feel this way in his position."[41]

The administrator—and, consequently, the organization as a whole
—is also likely to identify with the interests of those the organization
serves. Thus, even though "migrant laborers . . . do not vote and are not

organized . . . the situation is not quite as bad as it might be [for] the
Department of Labor has to some extent constituted itself as a guardian
of the interests of migrant laborers."[42] Or, at least, the administrators are
likely to identify with the interests of the clientele as the administrators
perceive them—a qualification which, as Patrick Moynihan has bitterly
suggested with respect to the welfare bureaucracy, may sometimes be of
great importance.[43]

   3. The structure of power and influence in an organization is very
complex. As Max Weber and early American administrative theorists
both emphasized, the employees of a bureaucracy are organized, first and
foremost, in hierarchical relationships. "Although many spontaneous,
nonhierarchical, informal group discussions constantly take place in
organizations, the decisions which commit the organization, the official
decisions, take place in hierarchically structured groups. Though attempts are often made to hide the hierarchical structure in the formal
group-decision process and to pretend that it is not there, the hierarchy is
*in fact* present and all group participants know it."[44]

   Yet whatever the impact of hierarchy, policy making is not simply
the province of those at the top of the organization. As Harold Laski
noted thirty-five years ago, "You cannot ask an able man to concern
himself with questions like education, public health, factory legislation,
safety in mines, without two consequences following. To ask him to discover facts is to ask him indicate conclusions; and the very fact that he
reports conclusions necessarily indicates a theory of action."[45] As a consequence, in Galbraith's words, "Effective participation is not closely
related to rank in the formal hierarchy of the organization . . . [Any sig-
nificant] decision will require information . . . Some power will then pass
to the person or persons who have this information. If this knowledge is
highly particular to themselves, then their power becomes very great."[46]
Given the diffusion of many kinds of specialized knowledge through the
organization, power and influence also become diffused.

   Indeed, the pressures that lead to the utilization of specialists in the
first place, and that have given them power or influence, may also lead
inexorably to a type of collective decision making. "Specialized decisions
must be group decisions if the solution of the problem at hand requires
more than one kind of specialized competence."[47] Since the major
decisions in large organizations are often of this character (according to
Galbraith, "*all* that are important" in modern industry), decisions in
practice are usually made not by individuals, but by a collective entity
that Galbraith calls the technostructure—everyone in the bureaucracy
with "specialized knowledge, talent, or experience."[48]

One can do worse than think of a business organization as a hierarchy of committees . . . Decision in the modern business enterprise is the product not of individuals but of groups. The groups are numerous, as often informal as formal, and subject to constant change in composition. Each contains the men possessed of the information, or with access to the information, that bears on the particular decision together with those whose skill consists in extracting and testing this information and obtaining a conclusion. This is how men act successfully on matters where no single one, however exalted or intelligent, has more than a fraction of the necessary knowledge. It is what makes modern business possible, and *in other contexts it is what makes modern government possible.*[49]

Even the establishment of the most basic goals of a bureaucracy may be the product of a process in which administrative personnel are involved. Instead of accepting the official image of bureaucracy as a hierarchy responsive to its leaders, one may "view the organization as . . . a coalition of individuals, some of them organized into subcoalitions."

Basic to the idea of a coalition is the expectation that the individual participants in the organization may have substantially different preference orderings (i.e., individual goals) . . . [and] any theory of organizational goals must deal successfully with the obvious potential for internal goal conflict inherent in a coalition of diverse individuals and groups.

Studies of organizational objectives suggest that agreement on objectives is usually agreement on highly ambiguous goals . . . The studies suggest further that behind this agreement on rather vague objectives there is considerable disagreement and uncertainty about subgoals, that organizations appear to be pursuing different goals at the same time . . . As a result, recent theories of organization objectives describe goals as the result of a continuous bargaining-learning process.[50]

Some scholars may reject these views of coalition or technostructure dominance of bureaucratic policy making as exaggerated, but at a minimum, agency advocacy is an accepted part of organizational life. It is an "apparently invariable law" that if you "get a group of people together who are professionally interested in a subject, no matter how conservative or frugal they might otherwise be . . . they are certain to find additional ways in which money could be spent."[51] At a minimum, the formal policy makers' recognition of the specialists' greater knowledge means that they will often defer to specialist advocacy.

4. The impact of bureaucratic participation on policy making varies, but there is general agreement that modern decision making in large-scale organizations tends to be incremental in nature, that it is largely

limited to efforts to "satisfice."[52] To a considerable extent, this phenomenon may result from the basic difficulty that any decision maker faces in comprehending the consequences of radical change, but the need for higher officials in a bureaucracy to deal with and to budget for a large number of diversely specialized subordinates intensifies the tendency towards incrementalism. "The number of policies that a modern government must carry out is vast and their nature extremely complex. There is an enormous disparity between the complexity of bureau operations and the limited information-absorbing capacity of any individual or small group. This disparity lies at the heart of the budgetary process."[53] In addition, the likelihood that the bureaucracy itself will push for more than incremental change is reduced by the practice of gradual promotion within the bureaucracy and by the natural tendency for specialists to fear change that would make their specialized knowledge and experience outmoded.

A strong tradition—going back at least to Michels and Weber—suggests that incrementalism is too kind a word to use in describing bureaucratic operations and that conservatism would be much more appropriate. Yet, while acknowledging the possibility of conservatism, especially when the self-interest of officials becomes embodied in previous policies, most scholars believe that this development is not inevitable. In the developing nations, for example,

> It is possible to envisage a continuum in which bureaucracies at one end of the scale seek to safeguard the traditional structure of society in all its aspects, while bureaucracies at the other end operate as spearheads of fundamental social, economic, and political transformation. In between one can identify many variants. There are conservative bureaucracies which try to protect the political and social status quo, while undertaking to modernize their armed forces and the parts of the economy which support them in order to ward off external military threats. There are modernizing bureaucracies which are hospitable to Western administrative and political practices, but resist innovation in the economic and social realm. There are still others which turn their backs on the Western political practices and confine their borrowings to the area of technology and advanced industrial practice. Even among bureaucracies which accept the goals of modernization, however interpreted, there may be sharp differences in the extent to which they are able to translate aspirations into action.[54]

Despite variations from bureaucracy to bureaucracy, however, allegations of bureaucratic conservatism should be kept in comparative perspective. "Resistance to change . . . is not uniquely related to bureaucratic organizations but is a characteristic of all institutions . . . [From this perspective] excessive bureaucratic inertia is much less widespread than is supposed."[55] "In an era of ever more rapid change, it seems unlikely that man has evolved a kind of organization which is particularly resistive to innovation. The traditionalistic organization was the kind most resistive, and in many places it had to be blasted off the scene by revolutionary action. The bureaucratic form replaced it, partly because it was able to accomodate to a changing world."[56]

5. Advanced industrial societies, and most notably the United States, are particularly likely to be postbureaucratic,[57] at least in the sense that "certain 'bureaucratic' traits were more likely to appear in earlier organizations than in those of today."[58] The difference is strikingly apparent if one compares "the quasi-monarchal type that seemingly was necessary for maintaining large-scale organizations at the beginning of the capitalist era with the relatively easy-going and tolerant corporation of the affluent society. But even during the last thirty years, there has been a not insignificant change throughout the Western world."[59]

> Perhaps nineteenth-century technology made the most impersonal and efficient method of exercising authority a rigid hierarchical structure in which communication comprised mostly commands and orders from superiors that subordinates were required to obey. But the advanced technology of the twentieth century necessitates information feedback and specialized skills, which are incompatible with an authority structure resting on blind obedience to orders issued through a chain of command. As a result, authority becomes depersonalized, and impersonal mechanisms of control displace old-fashioned discipline and command authority.
>
> The trend toward depersonalization of authority in organizations is still in its early stages and one may anticipate that it will progress much further in the future. The grounds for this prediction are that reliance on impersonal control mechanisms rather than command authority is most evident today in those organizations that have the most advanced technology and the most highly skilled personnel, such as research laboratories. One can expect technological progress and rising levels of education to make other organizations in the future more similar to these than they are now. If trained experts perform tasks within the limits set by the technology and the administrative framework, resort to strict command authority is unnecessary and, indeed, must be eschewed lest it interfere with the exercise of discretion in making expert judgments. Competent specialists tend to be consulted by colleagues and superiors, and the resulting greater frequency of social interaction concerning the work contributes to coordination, further reducing the need for commands.[60]

It goes without saying that the foregoing statements about the nature of modern bureaucracy are not universally accepted. Even the scholars cited would not necessarily agree with all the propositions, and there are other scholars whose view is quite different.[61] There also is disagreement about terminology, and some would suggest that this section describes a model of postbureaucratic large organizations, not bureaucratic ones.[62] If the bureaucratic model of Soviet society really is a large-organization model, however, then the nomenclature is not a crucial question, and at a minimum there is no doubt that most American specialists on large organizations would tend to describe modern American organizations in the terms indicated.

Of course, even if the judgments are generally valid so far as American organizations are concerned, there is no guarantee that they also apply to the Soviet Union. For example, Brzezinski and Huntington suggest that European middle-level officials in general take less initiative in the policy process, and they argue that this is also true of Soviet administrators.[63] Others insist even more strongly that Soviet officials are inherently cautious and conservative and that the operation of the bureaucracy is marked by red tape, formalism, and inefficiency. Thus, Downs asserts that because of "weaker feedbacks" and "absolute size," "the rigidity cycle is much more likely to appear in communist countries than in most western nations,"[64] while Crozier emphasizes dysfunctional consequences he believes to be inherent in the system of "checking and counter-checking relationships."

> Subordinates have had to internalize the autocratic rule to the point where they accept favor and arbitrariness as givens one does not discuss. But they cannot help protecting themselves. They do so in two ways: on the one hand, they remain passive, slow, apathetic . . . on the other hand, they constantly build informal groups that traditionally have served as protective networks.
>
> People in this type of system, where no consensus independent of the power structure can develop, cannot, however, be trusted. There is no way of ending suspicion, and on this point the all-powerful state remains helpless . . . When the whole productive apparatus has been pervaded by this pattern of suspicion, bureaucratic vicious circles of a type more rigid than those we have analyzed will develop.[65]

While this image of the Soviet bureaucracy is rather widespread, we should, nevertheless, keep one fact firmly in mind: our data base for generalization about the operation of the Soviet administrative system is really limited. Very few Soviet hierarchies have been subjected to detailed Western analysis, particularly analysis that shares the interests of Western administrative science. Typically, books are written on policy areas such as education and health, but little is said about the bureaucracies that administer these fields.

With the exception of the party apparatus, studied in a small number of rather specialized books, the only Soviet administrative hierarchy examined in great detail has been that supervising industry, especially heavy industry. On this hierarchy we have two exhaustive studies of the plant manager: one based on the Soviet press of the 1930s, including that of the Purge period, and the other based on refugee testimony about the late 1930s.[66] We have a comprehensive survey of the plant manager—party secretary relationship as portrayed in the Soviet literature of the late 1940s,[67] a detailed study of relations between the industrial administrators and the provincial party organs that contains a good deal of career data both on industrial ministers and plant managers,[68] a book-length history of the relationship of the top industrial administrators to the political leader from 1917 through the early 1960s,[69] an attempt to summarize the system of industrial management of the 1960s,[70] and innumerable articles and book chapters on some phase of the behavior of this hierarchy at different periods of Soviet history.

The conclusions about this well-studied section of the Soviet bureaucracy point in quite a different direction than Downs and Crozier indicate. Scholars generally agree that the existing incentive system has pushed the plant manager toward conservatism in technological and particularly product innovation, but they do not suggest that Soviet industry has been administered with rigidity and inflexibility. Indeed, in the one book that makes an explicit attempt to analyze the manager in light of Weber's ideal type (a book that surprisingly is almost never cited by political scientists studying or commenting on Soviet bureaucracy), David Granick explicitly asserts, "Soviet administration has sharply deviated from the behavior patterns idealized by Weber . . . Throughout this study, we have seen the great powers granted to directors and the considerable autonomy left to them. From the point of view of practical independence in making concrete decisions, the Soviet director may be conceived of as an entrepreneur."[71] Similarly, the Soviet planning appropriation process, as described by Berliner, does not feature a passive, withdrawn manager (even during the Purge period), but instead is strikingly similar to Wildavsky's description of the American budgetary process seven years later.[72]

It may be, of course, that the industrial bureaucracy is an atypical Soviet administrative hierarchy, and, in fact, such a possibility has been suggested by John Armstrong on the basis of his interviews with Western

European industrial and welfare officials.[73] Those European officials in
the welfare area, Armstrong reports, found lower career motivation and
greater doctrinal concern among their Soviet counterparts than did those
in industry, as well as greater departure from hierarchical principles in
administrative structure in this realm.

Yet testimony of this nature about the nonindustrial hierarchies in
the Soviet Union must be treated with great caution. The performance
record of Soviet health and education officials has been impressive, and
Western scholars studying Soviet medicine and education have not been
sufficiently struck by indications of bureaucratic pathology to give it
much emphasis in their books. Moreover, the many articles on the politics
of education during the Khrushchev era do not depict a group of officials
who passively accepted central directivees, but rather an interest group
that actively fought against the Khrushchev reforms both before and
after they were instituted—and that succeeded in gutting them to a considerable extent.[74]

Similarly, while the interpretation of the party apparatus has been a
more controversial subject, this hierarchy too seems to have much in
common with the industrial administration. The Smolensk party officials
of the 1930s, as I read Merle Fainsod's book, do not seem to have been
rigid bureaucrats, but men who creatively struggled to juggle and reconcile a multiplicity of conflicting pressures both from above and below. My
book on the participation of urban party organs in industrial decision
making, admittedly not an independent source of support for the argument of this article, likewise concludes:

> The Party secretaries described in this book do not emerge as men
> whose decision-making "tends to be relatively rigid," as men with "an
> ideological form of political calculation and analysis" and a "rigid and
> closed set of rules of conduct spelled out by the ideology." Rather, they
> emerge (at least in the role we have been studying) as men "increasingly
> rational, analytical, and empirical in their political action," men with a
> "pragmatic, instrumental style" and "the open, bargaining attitudes
> associated with full secularization."
> The assignment of the prefectoral role to the local Party organs . . . has
> virtually required the first secretaries in the republics, oblasts, and cities—
> even those of the Stalin period—to acquire a balancing, incremental per-
> spective on many issues and to develop bargaining techniques. Or, at least,
> this role has meant that those without these perspectives surely have soon
> been selected out of these key positions. The fact that the republican and
> obkom first secretaries have been the major group from which the Soviet
> leadership has been chosen in the post-Stalin period (they constitute, for
> example, nine of the eleven voting members of the 1967 Politburo) may be
> quite important in explaining the political changes that have taken place.

As these men moved into the central leadership posts, it would have been surprising if they had shed completely the habits and attitudes of a long career.[75]

Moreover, even if the industrial hierarchies are somewhat atypical, they may be more relevant for an understanding of the Soviet system than the welfare bureaucracies. In the first place, they have been a far more important source of recruitment for the top political leadership. Nine of the fifteen voting members of the Politburo in 1973, seven of the ten secretaries of the Central Committee, and nine of the eleven members of the Presidium of the Council of Ministers (the Chairman and the Deputy Chairmen) were engineers. The only officials among these groups who might be considered welfare administrators were several former ideological secretaries in the party apparatus, and they were quite without experience in the corresponding state ministries. Many of the engineers on the Politburo and the Secretariat rose to the top primarily through posts in the party apparatus, but four of the Politburo members, two of the secretaries, and eight of the top Council of Ministers officials once held industrial posts at the level of plant manager or higher. If there is a diversity of bureaucratic ethoses among the various administrative hierarchies, then that in industrial administration is likely to have had a profound impact on the political system as a whole.

In the second place, to the extent that the industrial bureaucracies have been atypical, they may have represented the wave of the future (and, increasingly, the present) in the Soviet administrative system. If other hierarchies seem to correspond more to Crozier's line of analysis, these differences may result not from the basic Soviet system of checking and counter-checking, but from the fact that the enormous preference given heavy industry "inevitably results in less capable people being drawn" into other hierarchies.[76] These bureaucratic characteristics, especially those reflected in relationships with clientele, may simply represent defenses against the types of demands which cannot be met because of the regime's priorities. Churchward is quite right to remind us that "the very understaffing of bureaucratic structures, both party and state, frequently produces the appearance of excess bureaucracy.[77]

As the general education level of all officials rises, as the party becomes less onesided in the preference it gives to heavy industry, as advanced managerial techniques are developed and the white-collar staffs like secretarial help and sales force are increased to the point where the needs of information flow and of clientele can be better served, the discrepancies among the administrative hierarchies, to the degree they actually exist, may tend to disappear. Indeed, as the level of economic development in the Soviet Union continues to rise, one should suspect that the postbureaucratic model derived from the experience of Western bureaucracies may become even more relevant for an understanding of the Soviet Union.

If we accept the relevance of the prevailing Western model of bureaucracy for Soviet studies, what are the implications that follow?

First, we should recognize that in the Soviet Union, even more than in the West, the bureaucracy is far more than a collection of line administrative officials and clerks. As Meyer emphasizes, "every citizen is a civil servant; and many if not all of them belong to a number of bureaucratic agencies."[78] The Soviet administrative hierarchies have staff officials with the widest range of specialties, and, in addition, science and education have been organized in such a way as to expand the expertise at the disposal of the administrators. Specialized scientific research and higher educational institutions have been subordinated directly to the various ministries and state committees, and have been instructed to assist in the solution of the problems for which these bureaucracies have responsibility.[79]

Second, if we view the Soviet Union as a bureaucratic system in Brzezinski's terms rather than Meyer's, that is, as a total bureaucratic system in which the leaders themselves rose through the bureaucracy and are part of it rather than as a parliamentary system in which a cabinet of generalist political leaders gives direction to a pliable bureaucracy, then we must take seriously the questions raised by Cyert and March:

> Once we drop the concept of a single, universal, organizational goal (e.g., profit maximization) and look instead at the process for defining objectives in organizations, we need some propositions about the development of goals. What is the effect of departmental structure on the goals actually pursued in an organization? It is commonly alleged that one of the most frequent phenomena in an organization is the differentiation of sub-unit goals and the identification of individuals with the goals of the sub-units, independently of the contribution of that goal to the organization as a whole. What difference does this make for a business firm and its decisions on such matters as resource allocation? . . . How do objectives change?[80]

The Soviet administrative theorist, V. G. Afanasev, may assert that "the party" determines goals, and he may view communications upward simply as feedback which permits "the party" to adjust policy to achieve its goals more fully.[81] However, David Easton's demands and feedback are virtually indistinguishable to an observer looking at real political behavior, and we should not forget the possibility that what Afanasev describes as a feedback process may actually be the process of goal and policy formation. The party led by Brzezinski's bureaucrats, the party led by men with the broker experiences gained while regional first secretaries, may have a far less clear sense of its "ultimate and exclusive scientific knowledge of social and historical laws" than a single leader whose early experience was that of a revolutionist.

Third, we must accept the possibility that raising Cyert and March's questions and acknowledging the relevance of the Western model of bureaucracy may lead us into quite different ways of conceptualizing the Soviet political system. In recent years, many new models of the Soviet system have been proposed, but, with a few exceptions, the basic paradigm for understanding the Soviet Union—essentially the directed society paradigm—has remained largely unchanged. We have recognized that irrational terror is not necessary for such a society, that industrialization has certain consequences for a society regardless of its political system, that the leaders of a directed system require information feedback, and that the encouragement of this feedback inevitably means the open emergence of group phenomena. But except for a few scholars, these points are made as qualifications to or elaborations of the directed society paradigm. Daniels is typical when he couples his assertions about "a new kind of politics, participatory bureaucracy" in the Soviet Union with a continued emphasis upon "the power of the party and its monopoly position in the Soviet power structure" and with a continued belief that the admission of "segments of the administrative and intellectual class into the decision-making and controlling process" is a future possibility rather than a present fact.[82] Inkeles is typical when he qualifies his statement that "we need a model different from that developed to deal with totalitarianism" by asserting, "This is not to say we must entirely abandon the models we have been using . . . The totalitarian model is still highly relevant."[83]

The Western model of bureaucracy may suggest a more drastic break with the directed society paradigm. I already argued that, since the removal of Khrushchev, the Soviet political system has come to develop a number of characteristics associated by American political scientists of the 1960s with the essence of pluralism and that there is a need for a model of institutional pluralism or the like to highlight this fact. However, my purpose here has not been to present a single controversial image of the Soviet system as being inherent in the use of the bureaucratic model; rather, it has been to emphasize that the dominant bureaucratic model implicit in American political science has not been used by those talking about bureaucracy in the Soviet Union and that that model is far indeed from the old line-of-command images prevalent in the past.

In acknowledging the bureaucratic nature of the Soviet system, we most of all should be aware of the diversity and complexity of large-scale organizations, and be at least willing to consider Soviet data in the light of more pluralistic images of bureaucracy and bureaucratic policy making. We should recognize that many Soviet complaints about such phenomena as departmentalism or localism are evidence not simply of bureaucratic pathology, but also possibly of the politics of goal and policy formation. We should understand that the complex system of checking and counter-checking involves a good deal of citizen participation in administrative life. We should at least entertain the possibility that this participation has the consequences hypothesized by Western theorists on participation in administration rather than simply those suggested by Crozier. Willingness to see Soviet data in a new perspective is the greatest potential benefit of employing the bureaucratic model. It should greatly enrich both our understanding of the Soviet Union and the development of Western theory about large-scale organizations.

# 3

# The Party Apparatchiki
# and Interest Group Theory

As scholars began to speak of the existence of interest groups in the Soviet Union, they have invariably pointed to the party apparatchiki as one of the key groups in the political process. Implicitly or explicitly, most would follow the lead of Zbigniew Brzezinski and Samuel Huntington in describing the apparatchiki as men with a "highly professionalized career pattern"—with loyalties "more exclusive" and a commitment "more intense" than Western politicians. In this view of the party apparatus, the commitment of party officials to it has important consequences for the apparatus as a group: "The organizational tradition and discipline of the Party inhibit the formation of a narrow, specialized outlook among the Presidium and Secretariat members. Like the cardinals on the Vatican Curia, they are predominantly professional politicians, sharing a common organizational outlook, common interests, and increasingly a common background."[1]

Although this image of the party apparatus is often retained by those moving toward an interest group interpretation of Soviet politics, it is in fact far more the product of a different approach to the study of political systems—one concentrating on the nature of the elite in a given country. This is particularly true if one accepts Brzezinski's and Huntington's broad definition of the apparatchiki: not only full-time party officials, but also those who have passed through the party apparatus into governmental posts. The correct use of the interest group approach would suggest quite a different image of the party apparatus, one which would correspond much more closely to Soviet reality.

What does an interest group approach to politics entail? What are its implications for the study of the party apparatus? There are, of course, a number of different interest group theories and approaches, and many are of little relevance to the study of the Soviet Union. However, that presented by Arthur Bentley a half-century ago does embody some concrete propositions which can be used to illuminate the role of the party apparatus in the Soviet political system:

1. Political life can never be fruitfully analyzed in terms of a striving

for the national interest. In the words of Arthur Bentley, "On any political question which we would study . . . we should never be justified in treating the interests of the whole nation as decisive. There are always some parts of the nation to be found arrayed against other parts."[2]

2. Political life can seldom be fruitfully analyzed in terms of the interests of a unified elite or unified classes. Indeed, Bentley, unlike many of his followers, cautioned against using such broad categories as "race, various economic interests, religion, or language." He asserted that "in practice we shall have to do mainly with much more specialized groupings than these."[3]

3. Persons engaged in similar activities, particularly of an economic-professional nature, tend to have similar attitudes on key political issues. However, all men have a multiplicity of interests (or group memberships —to phrase the identical point in different language) which destroy the possibility of "hard and fast" groups and which involve each man in a complex set of crosscutting alliances with a variety of different persons.

4. Every government, every policy, inevitably must reflect some interest or set of interests within society—or to put the same point in different words, some group or set of groups within society. While Bentley insisted that any stable government has to be somewhat responsive to the aspirations of broad groups in the population, he recognized that a government might provide "wretched mediation" to the various interests in society and might in practice be responsive to the interests of a relatively few. (He explicitly discussed the tsarist regime in these terms.)

5. The most useful approach to the study of the political process is to look for the way in which interests clash and coalesce and to ascertain which interests are expressed in the policy that emerges. This is true if we are analyzing the formation of specific policies within a country: "If a law is in question, we find that our statement of it in terms of the groups of men it affects—the group or set of groups directly insisting on it, those directly opposing it, and those more indirectly concerned in it—is much more complete than any statement in terms of self-interest, theories, or ideologies." It is also true if we are comparing entire political systems.[4]

Even if the five propositions only approximate the conclusions of the group approach—or, perhaps better, the interest approach—they still suggest a far different analysis of the party and the party apparatus than that customarily found in Western studies. Given the distribution of party members throughout the administrative hierarchy, Bentley would surely react to statements about "the party's point of view," "the party's goals," "the party's hierarchy of values," "the party's distrust of all officials"[5] in the same way that he reacted to talk about "the" national interest. If he was doubtful about an analysis focusing on broad occupational groups, he would be even more dubious about the "common interests" of 100,000 "politicians" working in all territorial units of the country, many in specialized positions with responsibility for one sector of economic life.[6]

Even if we were to discover that officials of the party apparatus hold certain interests in common, the group approach would deny the possibility that they share many common interests. A proponent of the Bentley approach would take for granted that Soviet politics features a broad and shifting variety of alliances, with any official of the apparatus being allied with some party officials on one issue in opposition to a group containing other party officials, while being allied with other party officials on another issue, and so forth. If we examine the actual participation of party officials in the political process from this perspective, we find support for an image of the apparatus characterized by many sources of cleavage, which moreover are reflected in political behavior.

Even a cursory examination of the officials of the party apparatus reveals a number of potential sources of cleavage among them. In terms of their age distribution, for example, the officials of the lower levels of the apparatus are quite different from those in higher positions.

The significance of these patterns of age distribution is difficult to judge, but the quarter of a century range in table 3.1 covers a wide variety of experience. Early political socialization, nature of education, participation in the Great Purge, involvement in World War II—these can be strikingly different for Soviet citizens born in 1910 and 1920, let alone in 1905 and 1930. For example, 95 percent of the RSFSR obkom first secretaries born after 1914 had graduated from a regular university or institute early in their career as compared with 44 percent of those born prior to that time.[7]

Another potential source of cleavage within the party apparatus is the considerable ethnic diversity among the party officials. The top officials of the Central Committee secretariat—the secretaries and the heads of the departments—have been almost exclusively Russians in recent years. Between the removal of Podgorny in 1965 and the election of Zimianin in 1976, not a single one of the ten or eleven Central Committee secretaries was a non-Russian. Of the seven nonsecretarial heads of department elected to the Supreme Soviet in 1966, all were Russians except for the head of the culture department—V. F. Shauro, a Belorussian. The background of other department heads suggests that one at most is non-Russian.[8]

The Russian domination of the Central Committee secretariat does

**Table 3.1.** Percentages of party officials by year of birth in 1966-67

| | | RSRSR[a] | | | | | |
| Year of birth | CC secretaries and department heads | Obkom first secretaries[b] | Obkom second secretaries | Other obkom secretaries | Obkom department heads | Gorkom first secretaries | Raikom first secretaries |
|---|---|---|---|---|---|---|---|
| Pre-1905 | 4 | – | – | – | – | – | – |
| 1905-09 | 25 | 15 | 4 | – | – | – | 3 |
| 1910-14 | 38 | 51 | 35 | 27 | 5 | 7 | 3 |
| 1915-19 | 33 | 25 | 22 | 20 | 22 | 18 | 16 |
| 1920-24 | – | 7 | 26 | 29 | 34 | 33 | 31 |
| 1925-29 | – | 2 | 13 | 23 | 31 | 38 | 36 |
| 1930- | – | – | – | 2 | 7 | 7 | 10 |
| Average year of birth | 1912 | 1914 | 1918 | 1920 | 1923 | 1923 | 1923 |
| Total number | 24 | 55 | 23 | 56 | 82 | 62 | 92 |

*Sources:* Information on the Central Committee officials and obkom first secretaries was drawn from biographies published in the 1966 yearbook of the *Bol. sov. entsik,* pp. 574-621, and in *Deputaty Verkhovnovo Soveta SSSR, Sedmoi sozyv* (Moscow, 1966). Information on the lower officials was drawn primarily from lists of oblast deputies elected in 20 oblasti in February-March 1967. (The year of birth was included with the man's name and position.) The 20 oblasti do not include the giants of Moscow, Leningrad, and Sverdlovsk nor the small Siberian oblasti, but they constitute a representative cross section of the RSFSR oblasti.

[a]This table is limited to the RSFSR because the information about the other republics is too scattered to be trustworthy. However, the officials in the non-Russian areas appear to be somewhat younger. This is certainly true of the obkom first secretaries, the one category of officials on which complete information is available. The obkom first secretaries of the autonomous republics and oblasti of the RSFSR were born in 1915 on the average, those of the Ukrainain obkomy in 1916, those of the obkomy of other republics in 1919. The 5 obkom second secretaries of non-Russian oblasti on whom information is available were born in 1920 on the average, the 10 lower obkom secretaries in 1919, the 23 obkom department heads in 1924, the 29 gorkom first secretaries in 1924, the 40 raikom first secretaries in 1923.

[b]This column includes all the oblasti in the RSFSR, except for the autonomous republics and oblasti. The information is as of June 1966.

not, however, extend to the lower party apparatus. The officials at these levels reflect the ethnic diversity of the country. For example, of the 139 obkom first secretaries in the USSR in June 1966, 47 percent were Russians, 24 percent were Ukrainians, and the remaining 29 percent were divided among 24 nationalities. The ethnic differences among the obkom first secretaries were associated with significant differences in life experiences.

The potential cleavages of greatest interest are those associated with the differentiated structure of the apparatus itself. A number of officials work in the Central Committee secretariat in Moscow, but most are scattered across the country. Some work in rural raikomy, others in industri-

Table 3.2. Background of obkom first secretaries of different nationalities

|  | Agricultural or engineering education (%) | Experience as Komsomol officials[a] (%) | Experience as teachers (%) |
|---|---|---|---|
| Russians ($N = 66$) | 64 | 35 | 17 |
| In largest oblasti[b] | 82[c] | 18 | 18 |
| in large oblasti[b] | 67[c] | 40 | 13 |
| In medium and small oblasti[b] | 53[c] | 41 | 18 |
| Ukrainians ($N = 33$) | 64[c] | 21 | 15 |
| Other nationalities ($N = 40$) | 32[c] | 40 | 42 |

Sources: Bol. sov. entsik., 1966 yearbook, pp. 574-621, and Deputaty.

[a]This refers to Komsomol experience listed in biographical sources. Presumably most secretaries were active in the Komsomol while acquiring higher education.

[b]The "largest oblasti" are the 17 oblasti whose population permitted them 7 or more deputies in 1966. The "large oblasti" are the 15 with 5 or 6 deputies in 1966. The "medium and small oblasti" are the remaining 34.

[c]If we exclude the engineering and agricultural degrees received after the first secretary reached party or state posts at the oblast level, the percentages would be: All Russians: 55 percent; Russians in largest oblasti: 76 percent; Russians in large oblasti: 60 percent; Russians in medium and small oblasti: 41 percent; Ukrainians: 61 percent. Too little information is available about the date of graduation of the other first secretaries to permit any correction in the cited figure.

alized centers. Some lead party organizations in cotton growing areas in Uzbekistan, others head organizations in the Donbass coal region. Some work in the iron and steel centers in the Ukraine, while others work in the timbering-paper districts of Karelia.

Within any given party organization, the officials work within quite specialized subunits. There are three Central Committee departments dealing with foreign policy questions and thirteen handling various internal policy spheres: administrative organs (working on law and order questions), agriculture, chemical industry, construction, culture, defense industry, heavy industry, light industry and food industry, machinery industry, propaganda (working in part on the publishing industry), science and education, trade, financial, and planning organs, and transportation and communications.

The local party organs have also been organized along branch lines for the last two decades. Each republican central committee and obkom has had one secretary specializing [*vedaiushchii*] on industrial questions, one on agricultural questions, and one on cultural-education questions. (The last-named official has had the title "secretary handling ideological work," but leadership of agitation-propaganda work forms only a small part of his responsibility.) Under the supervision of the specialized secretaries have been a number of branch departments. A medium-sized obkom has had eight departments: administrative organs, agriculture, construction, industrial-transportation, light and food industry and trade, organizational-party work, propaganda-agitation, and science, colleges, and schools.

The differentiation in party structure has been accompanied by specialization in the career patterns of personnel In the Central Committee secretariat, for example, the head of the agriculture department in 1966 had long experience in agricultural administration (head of the Penza agriculture administration, RSFSR Deputy Minister of Agriculture, RSFSR Minister of Grain Products) and in party and soviet work in rural areas; the head of the heavy industry department was an engineer who has been a plant director for five years, and chairman of the Cheliabinsk regional economic council (*sovnarkhoz*) for two years; the head of the light industry and food industry department was a graduate of the Moscow Textile Institute and a former USSR Deputy Minister of the Textile Industry; the head of the transportation department was a graduate of the Leningrad Institute of Railroad Engineers with twenty-two years of administrative and scientific work in the railroad industry (including service as head of the Gorki railroad); the head of the chemical industry department was a graduate of the Moscow Institute of Chemical Machinery, who worked for a dozen years in the USSR Gosplan, rising to the post of deputy department head. The heads of the departments for the machinery, defense, and construction industries had only lower level administrative experience in their respective industries before entering party work, but their careers in the party seem to have been quite specialized ones; the head of the science and education department was a graduate of the Academy of Social Sciences, a doctor of historical science, and a man with eight years' experience as director of the Moldavian Party School and five years as deputy director for research at the Higher Party School.[9]

The specialization in career pattern within the Central Committee secretariat is not a post-Khrushchev innovation. Table 3.3 summarizes

Table 3.3. Educational background of Central Committee officials (in percentages)

| Central Committee Departments | University, social science, pedagogical | Engineering | Agriculture higher education | Agriculture special secondary education | Higher party school[a] | Other |
|---|---|---|---|---|---|---|
| Agriculture (N = 17) | – | – | 65[b] | 24 | 6 | 6 |
| Industry-construction (N = 18) | – | 89[c] | – | – | 6 | 6 |
| Party organs (N = 24) | 17 | 38 | 4 | – | 33 | 8 |
| Propaganda-culture (N = 30) | 67 | 7 | – | – | 10 | 17 |

Sources: The biographies were gathered from a decade of yearbooks of the Bol. sov. entsik., from the three volumes of Deputaty, and from a variety of Soviet newspapers (in the form of obituaries).

[a]The only officials included in this column are those for whom the Higher Party School was the only higher education listed in the biography. A number of officials hold two degrees: one received from an institute early in their career, one from the Higher Party School in mid-career.

[b]This figure includes two men who graduated from institutes for the mechanization of agriculture.

[c]This figure includes an architect with years of work in construction design and a graduate of the mechanics-mathematics division of Moscow University.

the educational background of 89 officials (heads of departments, deputy heads of departments, heads of sectors, and instructors) who have worked in the Central Committee secretariat at some time during the 1953-1966 period. These 89 include all the Central Committee officials of this period whose published biography indicated the Central Committee department in which the man was employed.

There are also striking differences in the work experience of the officials of different Central Committee departments. Thus, 70 percent of the known officials of the agriculture department had at least five years' experience in administrative posts in agriculture prior to their appointment in the Central Committee secretariat. Similarly, two-thirds of the officials of the industrial department had as least that many years in engineering-administrative positions in industry or construction, and over 55 percent had at least a decade of such experience. One-half of the officials in the propaganda-agitation, culture, and science-education departments had worked for at least five years in editorial work or in teaching, 40 percent for at least ten years. The officials of the party organs department, on the other hand, generally had longer experience in the Komsomol or party organs. Only one-third of these men had five years's experience in industry, agriculture, or teaching positions; only 8 percent had ten years of such experience.

Systematic information about the specialized officials of the local party organs is more difficult to collect than that about officials of the Central Committee secretariat. Nevertheless, the evidence suggests that a similar differentiation in career pattern has also taken place at this level. If we examine the men selected as republican secretaries for industry in 1966, for example, we find that they normally had an engineering diploma and often had held such posts as republican minister or plant manager. The secretaries for agriculture usually were agronomists with administrative experience in agriculture (in four cases as republican minister). The ideological secretaries usually had been educated in a university or a pedagogical institute, and their work experience normally had been in the Komsomol, education, newspaper, and cultural realms.[10]

Specialization in career pattern has even become quite frequent among the obkom first secretaries. At the time of the 1966 election to the Supreme Soviet, 19 of the first secretaries in the 25 most industrialized oblasti in the RSFSR and the Ukraine had engineering training, 2 had a technical secondary education, 2 graduated from a physics-mathematics division of the university, and 1 was an economist. On the other hand, in the 25 most important agricultural oblasti in the RSFSR there were only 4 engineers among the first secretaries (and one of them had graduated from an institute for the mechanization of agriculture), while 13 of the first secretaries were agronomists.[11]

The early work experience of the first secretaries in the most industrialized and the most important agricultural oblasti was as disparate as their education. Of the 25 secretaries in the agricultural oblasti, 10 had held posts in governmental administration of agriculture at the level of MTS (Machine Tractor Station) director or higher, and another 8 had once been first secretary of a rural raikom and/or head of the agriculture department of an obkom. By contrast, none of the first secretaries in the 25 most industrialized oblasti had held administrative jobs in agriculture at the level of MTS director or higher. Only 4 had been first secretary of a rural raikom, and in two of these cases the raion contained considerable industry.

These aggregate statistics reflect the frequent practice of selecting obkom first secretaries from men whose background especially prepares them to supervise the major branch of the economy in their oblast. Thus, in 1966 the obkom first secretaries in Kemerovo (the center of the Kuzbass) and in Donetsk (the center of the Donbass) were the former heads of a coal combine and a coal trust respectively. The first secretary of the Kharkov obkom was an engineer with twenty years of lower administrative work in machine-building plants (up to the level of shop head) before becoming party secretary of the Kharkov Transportation Machinery Works. On the other hand, in Belgorod, Smolensk, and Orenburg (oblasti whose population was over two-thirds rural in 1959), we find obkom first secretaries who were once MTS directors with years of subsequent party and soviet work primarily oriented toward agriculture; in North Kazakhstan, Kustanai, and Semipalatinsk oblasti in the Virgin Lands we find agronomists who had been minister or deputy minister in the republican ministries supervising agriculture.

There are, of course, limitations to the degree of specialization possible among the obkom first secretaries. As Khrushchev correctly noted when he proposed the bifurcation of the party apparatus in 1962, all oblasti are developing increasingly complex economies. Moreover, the basic job of the first secretary is to be the prefect in his region—to make judgments about relative priorities when the interests, the plans, and the directives of the local representatives of the various ministries come into conflict with each other.[12] Because of the nature of their role, "there is not a (single) question in the economic, cultural, and public life of the district in which the party organ would not be interested."[13] Consequently, even a first secretary who is a specialist on the main branch of the economy in his area will continually have to make decisions on questions on which he has little expertise.

One attempt to solve this problem has been to place in charge of each party organization a team of secretaries with a variety of specialties. For example, a new obkom first secretary was named in Rostov oblast in the latter half of 1966. He was an agronomist who had worked in agricultural research and teaching until the age of forty-two and then in agriculturally oriented party and soviet work for six years. Surely it was not an accident that he was buttressed by a second secretary who was an ideological specialist, by an industrial secretary who was an industrial specialist (a former director of a defense industry plant), and by a gorkom first secretary in Rostov with long experience in construction administration and the education of construction engineers.[14] Presumably such a combination of specialized knowledge implies the type of team decision making which Galbraith suggests is inevitable in very largescale organizations.[15]

Another solution to the wide range of demands on an obkom first secretary is to move specialists into party work at an early age (in some cases drawing them from Komsomol work) and to let them "specialize" on the skills of the general coordinator by being advanced through general leadership posts in progressively larger and more complex territorial units. Of course, many obkom first secretaries already have such a career pattern, and nearly all of the first secretaries with a more specialized background have some generalized supervisory experience before rising to their current position.

However, we should recognize that even career patterns with years of generalized party and soviet work may be far more specialized than seems on the surface. Consider, for example, the following two biographies: Konstantin Pysin was born in 1910 and graduated from the Perm Agriculture Institute in 1935.[16] After six years of work as a zootechnician and as a teacher at the agricultural institute, he moved into party work, first as instructor, then as head of a department, then as secretary of the Perm obkom. (Because of his background, it is likely that he was head of the agriculture department and then secretary for agriculture.) In 1947 he was named chairman of the Perm oblispolkom and in 1949 chairman of the Altai oblispolkom. From 1955 to 1961 he was first secretary of the Altai kraikom.

Aleksandr Tokarev was born in 1921, served in the army during the war, and then in 1949 graduated from the Kuibyshev Institute of Construction Engineers.[17] Upon graduation he served as Komsomol secretary and then deputy party secretary at an oil refinery construction site. In 1951 he became secretary of a gorkom and in 1952 the gorkom first secretary in the city in which the construction site was located. From 1955 to 1958 he was head of the construction department of the Kuibyshev obkom and from 1958 to 1959 a secretary of the obkom. In 1959 he was named chairman of the Kuibyshev oblispolkom, in 1963 first secretary of the Kuibyshev industrial obkom, and in 1964 first secretary of the Kuibyshev obkom.

In many ways these two biographies are those of typical apparatchiki. Yet they are the biographies of men with quite different experiences and expertise. Pysin has the career pattern essentially of an agricultural specialist, Tokarev one of an industrial-construction specialist. Both had ample preparation for the next post to which they were appointed—in Pysin's case First Deputy Minister, then Minister of Agriculture of the USSR, in Tokarev's case USSR Minister of Industrial Construction.

The type of generational, ethnic, educational, and occupational divisions which we have been examining need not, of course, be associated with policy differences among party officials. It is possible that some of the potential sources of division are not as politically important as commonly perceived interests and perspectives deriving from employment within the party apparatus. It is possible that men may perceive their interests in quite different ways than an outside observer would think likely or advantageous.

However, if we are to treat the party apparatus as a unified interest group in the political process, let us be fully aware of the assumptions we must accept. We must assume that the agriculture department and the defense industry department of the Central Committee (with their leaders of quite different backgrounds) have greater community of views and interests than do the agriculture department of the Central Committee and the Ministry of Agriculture. We must assume that the specialized local secretaries who have spent their lives in industrial, agricultural, and cultural-education work respectively, and who in the future will probably return to government work in their branch, function more as allies than as competitors in the policy sphere. We must assume that the former coal industry administrator who becomes obkom first secretary in the iron and coal oblast of Kemerovo has much the same set of perspectives on important political issues as the former agriculture administrator who becomes obkom first secretary in the flax oblast of Smolensk. We must assume that the construction engineer whose party and soviet work in urban areas apparently warranted his appointment as Minister of Industrial Construction has a set of interests and outlooks which are basically in common with the agronomist whose party and soviet work in rural regions earned him appointment as Minister of Agriculture.

Normally, when one thinks of the apparatchik, the first official that comes to mind is the regional first secretary—primarily the first secretary of the republican central committee and obkom (regional party committee) but also that of the gorkom (city committee) and the raikom (district committee). Like the French prefects, they are "the" representative of the center in each territorial unit, the men who must decide what the

center would want done in circumstances not foreseen in central directives.

The primary responsibility of the prefect is to enforce central priorities, but both the Soviet press and Western observers have noted the "localism" often displayed in their activity. From the point of view of the
group approach, however, this localism should be viewed not simply as a
shortcoming in the work of the party officials, but as a major symptom of
the group configuration of Soviet politics on certain issues, particularly
those of an appropriations nature.[18]

Any person reading Soviet press reports about the local party organs
will quickly notice that the party officials are not only supervising local
governmental officials, but are also appealing for funds, supplies, and
other types of support from party and state officials at higher territorial
levels. Consider, for example, the speeches of the obkom first secretaries
at the Twenty-third Party Congress in 1966. The first secretary of the
Gorky obkom asked the Council of Ministers to support the specialization
of the Gorky Auto Works and the development of a network of cooperat-
ing supplier-plants.[19] (In an earlier article in the republican newspaper,
Sovetskaya Rossia, he had advocated that these plants be established
within Gorky oblast.)[20] The first secretary of the Perm obkom spoke out
for the realization of the "centuries-old dream" of diverting part of the
water of the Pechera and Vishera Rivers into the Kama and the Volga.[21]
The first secretary of the Krasnoyarsk kraikom complained about the limited participation of the central research and design institutes in work associated with Siberian development, and he demanded improvement.[22]
The first secretary of the Primorsk kraikom called for a rapid expansion
both of the krai's coal-electricity energy base and of its acreage devoted to
rice cultivation.[23]

The public presentation of such claims and suggestions is not a new
development in the Soviet Union, nor is it limited to the party congresses.
Although public advocacy by party officials seems to be more frequent
in the 1960s than it was in the last decade of Stalin's life, even in the past
the local organs frequently expressed "to the ministries their ideas about
the best way of using local reserves and possibilities."[24] Indeed, in this respect the speeches of the party secretaries at the Nineteenth Party Congress in 1952 are almost indistinguishable from those made by their
counterparts fourteen years later.[25]

In advancing proposals to higher officials, the local party officials are
usually acting not alone but in conjunction with local governmental, economic, and/or scientific institutions. Indeed, instead of initiating proposals themselves, they often can be found supporting the ideas and interests of these other institutions. In one typical example the director of

the Dneprodzerzhinsk Metallurgy Works (one of the largest in the country) had been appealing to higher officials for funds to reconstruct the plant. "Why, new air heaters alone . . . would permit an increase in production of pig iron from each furnace by 27,000 tons a year and would achieve an annual economy of 400,000 rubles." The first secretary of the local gorkom wrote, "Of course, in such a situation the party gorkom had to harness itself in one team with the industrial administrators: to apply pressure, to push (*tolkat*), to solicit funds."[26]

This type of alliance, this "harnessing in one team" in the seeking of investment funds, is a completely normal feature of the Soviet administrative scene. It is true that the development of new facilities complicates the lives of local officials, who might dream of avoiding capital investment in a search for the peaceful life. However, they can never forget what Joseph Berliner called "the ratchet principle"—namely, the central practice of increasing the planned targets by a certain percentage every year.[27] The administrators know that next year's plan will be higher than this year's and that without new investment this plan will be extremely difficult to fulfill. Consequently, whatever difficulties will be created by the introduction of new equipment or the construction of new units or subunits, administrators must fight for them if they are to survive.[28] The local party secretaries, judged in large part on the basis of the economic performance of their region, have a similar interest in helping local administrators receive the funds and supplies they need. In addition, they undoubtedly observe many regional shortcomings which could be corrected, many local needs which could be satisfied, if only higher authorities could be persuaded to authorize the proper project.

For these reasons it is not surprising that in 1957 when the Minister of the Machinery Industry wrote about the communications which he had received from the provincial party and economic organizations, he warned of their local bias: "Analysis shows that they are chiefly demanding money for supplementary capital construction or are asking us to assign them material and equipment. . . . It is difficult to recall even one case of a refusal of capital construction because of a better utilization of the capacity of the enterprises." The minister did not feel it necessary to distinguish between communications from party officials and those from industrial administrators.[29]

Of course, the community of interest between a local party organ and any particular enterprise or institution in the region cannot be complete. The party officials' responsibility for resolving day-to-day conflicts among the local enterprises and institutions means that they must repeatedly take actions which impinge upon the interests of one or another of the state institutions. However, when funds are being sought from outside, the conflicts of interest between the regional first secretaries and the state officials are held to a minimum, for normally the local party officials need not choose among the various requests for funds advanced by local administrators.

At the center there undoubtedly has been fierce competition for funds among officials of the different branches of the economy, but this competition usually does not extend into the provinces. Once the central organs decide on the allocation of funds among the various ministries, each ministry has the funds for its branch at its disposal. Even in realms supervised by the local soviets, the oblast and the city are not allocated funds which their officials can then subdivide among the claimants. For example, the city soviet is not allocated money for culture and education and then permitted (or forced) to choose between building a new high school and a new theater. Nor is it allocated money for city services and then permitted to choose between a new hospital and a new department store. Rather, it is the oblast health department (or health officials at a higher level) which has the resources for new hospitals, the oblast education department which has the resources for new schools, and so forth. The officials of the city soviet can (and must) seek both the new hospital and the new high school, and the city party officials have no difficulty in supporting both proposals.

When the regional first secretaries deal with enterprises subordinated directly to republican or all-union ministries (for example, industrial enterprises), they find it even easier to support the claims of nearly all local administrators. They can support the expansion both of the chemical plant *and* of the steel plant, both of the defense industry plant *and* the textile plant. Only when the area contains a number of enterprises turning out precisely the same product (perhaps, for example, in coal mining) is there likely to be any necessity for the party officials to act as a filter for the proposals rather than as a transmitter or supporter of them.

Indeed, the local party officials frequently may not even have to choose between types of appropriations for a given plant. Except on marginal matters, the plant director does not have the authority independently to determine the structure of investment within the plant. In particular, he is not faced with the necessity (or the possibility) of deciding to use a lump-sum ministerial appropriation for a new apartment house or new equipment. Ministerial funds for factory housing and new equipment come from different sources—in essence from different deputy ministers—and the plant manager can fight for both simultaneously. Therefore, the local party officials can also ally themselves with the managers on both appeals.

At the same time that the nature of the Soviet appropriations process reduces the conflicts between the first secretary and the other officials in his city or region, it magnifies the conflicts among the first secretaries of different cities and regions. The crucial fact about the advocacy role of the local party organs is that they are all engaged in it. With each organ suggesting projects or demanding more supplies and funds, the result (as in all bureaucratic situations) is that there cannot be enough funds to finance all proposals. Inevitably, the seeking of funds becomes a competitive process, and the regional first secretaries collectively find it quite impossible to serve as a unified force in this type of appropriations politics.

When one examines the role of the provincial officials in the appropriations process, the analogy which repeatedly comes to mind is the seeking of defense contracts in the United States. Just as the traditional American categories of "labor," "management," "Democrat," and "Republican" lose almost all real meaning in this process as the alliances center upon certain key companies and the communities in which they are located, so the categories of "party" and "state" have little relevance for understanding the Soviet appropriations process, at least once the basic rate of investment is decided. The major conflicts here involve a series of shifting groups comprising both party and state officials. In the struggle for a new hospital, a new steel plant, a new dam, there will be one group of state and party officials in one city or region struggling for a particular project and another group in another city or region struggling for another project or projects.

The cleavages among the regional first secretaries on micro-appropriations questions are relatively easy to document. Nonetheless, to say that these men do not function as a unified group in the appropriations process is not necessarily to deny that they constitute a meaningful group in regard to other political issues. The question is: are there circumstances in which the regional first secretaries do, in fact, share a community of interest and act as a unified interest group?

Few questions about the Soviet political system have produced more extensive and dogmatic discussion and less empirical investigation and careful thought than this one. In our assessment of the apparatchiki, we have failed in the past to make a distinction between their approach and attitude on questions involving the fundamentals of the political system and their position on the typical political conflict which does not challenge the system as they perceive it. When in doubt about the approach and behavior of the party officials on a particular question of internal policy, we have repeatedly assumed the rigidity and dogmatism which we find in Communists in other settings.

Before speaking with confidence about the policy positions of the regional first secretaries, their approach to major questions, and the way they perceive their own interests, we need a series of thorough studies of developments in various policy realms over a ten-year-period—studies set within the framework of a sound comparative knowledge of the phenomenon of bureaucratic politics and based upon a combination of content analysis, career pattern study, and interview techniques. At this stage it is a mistake to pretend to greater knowledge about the policy positions of the regional first secretaries than we actually have. Consequently, it seems more useful to point to conceptions about the party secretaries which are open to question and to suggest possibilities about their role which deserve detailed consideration in future studies.

Perhaps the basic political issue in the Soviet Union has been the priority to be given heavy industry, light industry, and agriculture; and on this question it seems fairly clear that there has been a good deal of cleavage among the regional first secretaries. The outlook of these officials on macro-appropriations questions often seems affected by the nature of their region and their own personal background. At the party congresses, for example, the first secretaries usually propose various investment projects for their region, and the type of project chosen for inclusion in their short speeches varies considerably from one secretary to another. It is by no means certain that the type of specific suggestions given priority in a secretary's speech corresponds to his position on overall investment priorities, but there are suggestive differences among first secretaries of different backgrounds.

At the Twenty-third Party Congress, for example, the speeches of the republican and obkom first secretaries who were engineers were quite unlike those given by the first secretaries who were not engineers. In the speeches of the five first secretaries who were agronomists, 303 lines (as reported in the Stenographic Report)[30] were devoted to policy suggestions and investment demands related to agriculture, the rural sector, and agriculture-oriented industry (the agriculture machinery and food-processing industries), while 127 lines were devoted to suggestions with respect to industrial development (excluding the agriculture-oriented industries). Indeed, if we exclude the first secretary of the Ulianovsk obkom, who devoted most of his speech to the reconstruction of Ulianovsk in preparation for the hundreth anniversary of Lenin's birth, the ration would be 303 to 87. In the speeches of the eleven first secretaries who were engineers, we find only 69 lines devoted to agriculture-related suggestions (including the expansion of the industries connected with agriculture) as compared with 513 lines to suggestions about the industrial sector. The seventeen secretaries with neither engineering nor agronomy degrees were more balanced in their treatment—339 lines to industry compared with 294 lines to agriculture. Among this latter group, however, the three who were leaders in one of the 25 most industrialized oblasti devoted 92 lines to industry and 17 to agriculture.

While the precise numbers of lines have limited significance, it is highly probable that the differences in the speeches reflect real cleavages among the first secretaries. The crucial question is, do these men have an institutional interest on macro-appropriations questions which transcends the pressures toward disunity among them? Or, at a minimum, is a particular set of appropriations priorities accepted by a clear enough majority to say that on balance the first secretaries constitute a meaningful interest group in this respect? If so, in which direction do their interests and attitudes point?

Unfortunately, several contrasting a priori arguments can be advanced on this question. On the one hand, the party's commitment to modernization and industrial development has surely attracted to it those men who are positively oriented to the urban sector, industrial growth, and the future. It might further be argued that the legitimacy of one-party rule ultimately rests upon a policy of rapid economic growth. For these reasons (as well as a possible dogmatic commitment to old ideological positions) the first secretaries might be said to share a set of attitudes which make them one of the major forces supporting the high-tempo development of heavy industry.

On the other hand, it might well be argued that the immediate interests of the first secretaries lead most of them to oppose the priority of heavy industry. For years the greatest danger for the obkom first secretaries has arisen from the agricultural sector, for the low priority assigned to agriculture has made plan fulfillment much more difficult in this realm than in industry. The many obkom secretaries who were driven to false reporting and who were removed prior to the Twenty-second Congress can scarcely have been comforted by the thought that the emphasis upon heavy industry makes the position of the party apparatus as a whole more secure. A second major threat to a first secretary has been that of a large demonstration by the local population. The 1959 demonstration in Temir-Tau, for example, resulted in the obkom first secretary being reduced to the level of shift head in a plant,[31] while the 1962 Novocherkassk demonstration led to the obkom leader being transferred to lower level diplomatic work until after Khrushchev's removal.[32] A reduction in the emphasis placed upon heavy industry might reduce both of these dangers for the first secretaries, at least in the short run.

The second set of arguments seems more convincing, at least if we limit the argument to recent years. Although the first secretaries certainly are not united on the heavy industry issue, I suspect that the most powerful concentration of political support for agricultural, rural expenditures in the Soviet Union comes from the rural raikom secretaries, from among the republican and obkom first secretaries of the less industrialized areas, and from the specialized secretaries for agricultural and possibly ideological-cultural questions. Moreover, the frequent demand by urban party officials for an increase in consumer goods production by heavy industry plants (and their frequent complaints that the heavy industry ministries are cutting back on such production) indicate at least some ambivalence on the heavy industry question even on their part.

Although many of the major issues in Soviet politics center on appropriations questions, there are, of course, other issues whose budgetary implications are at best indirect. Among these are the degree of economic reform in industry and agriculture and the degree of freedom to be permitted the intellectual. Included in the general question of the freedom for the intellectual are two further subsets of questions: the prerequisites of "law and order" and the structure of the decision making process. It is on these questions more than on any others that the apparatchik has the reputation in the West of being a conservative, a supporter of the status quo, even a "neo-Stalinist." In the words of Brzezinski and Huntington: "The engineering background of the Soviet apparatchik is supplemented by intense and continuing political training and many years of direct occupational experience in politics. Political experience and engineering background combine to give Soviet leaders a highly focused, direct, down-to-earth, problem-solving approach, without concern for legal niceties and with little tendency toward compromise solutions."[33] These images of the apparatchik probably have a good deal of truth in them, at least with respect to many party officials. However, they must not be accepted uncritically.

In the first place, it would be a major mistake to think of all regional first secretaries as men infused with an "ideological style," as men with a "rigid and closed set of rules of conduct spelled out by the ideology," as men "with little tendency toward compromise solutions."[34] The assignment of the role of the prefect to the local party organs has virtually required the first secretaries—even those of the Stalin period—to acquire a balancing, incremental perspective on many issues and to develop bargaining techniques. The first secretaries have had to compromise, to resolve conflicts among specialists in circumstances in which both sides in the dispute are "right" in terms of party policy and goals; they have had to learn the arts of persuasion and of mobilization of support in seeking funds from higher territorial levels and even in obtaining certain kinds of behavior from powerful local subordinates; they have had to learn how to permit and even require violation of the law and the plan in some circumstances while maintaining high "moral tone" in the administrative apparatus. In short, as Brzezinski and Huntington recognize at one point, the first secretary must be "an expert in dealing simultaneously with a variety of issues and pressures, balancing one against another, attempting to resolve problems at the least cost to the greatest number of interests."[35]

Of course, to say that the party officials often are "rational, analytical, and empirical in their political action," that they often display "open, bargaining attitudes" and a "pragmatic, instrumental style,"[36] is not to deny that they may have quite rigid, ideologically conditioned views on *some* subjects. The combination of an instrumental, pragmatic approach on some questions and a dogmatic, rigid approach on others is quite normal—in fact inevitable—in participants in all political systems. The problem is, on what questions are the first secretaries dogmatically agreed on the nature of the answers?

It is beyond the scope of this chapter—and beyond the knowledge of its author—to analyze the various policy positions of the first secretaries. One would certainly expect the overwhelming majority to take for granted the wisdom of governmental ownership and planning of industry and agriculture; the desirability of a political order which avoids the factional squabbling and "irresponsible" criticism of a multiparty system; the desirability (if perhaps not the absolute necessity) of writers and artists providing moral inspiration to the citizens and particularly to the youth; the need of "society" to protect itself against those malcontents who spread "malicious lies" about it; the need of the Soviet Union to protect itself against "American imperialism"; and the desirability of supporting those foreigners fighting against private ownership social systems. On these types of questions the apparatus is presumably a unified interest group supporting major elements of the status quo.

This does not necessarily mean that all party officials dogmatically support all aspects of the existing policies in these spheres, or even that they are the most vigorous supporters of these policies. On all of the issues enumerated in the last paragraph, the position of the leading state and economic administrators is probably little different from that of the party secretaries, and on each issue (except perhaps that of foreign policy) there are other subgroups within the elite who are likely to support the status quo more intensely than the first secretaries.

For example, the apparent rejection by the first secretaries of radical and rapid movement toward market socialism likely does not result from worry about the ideological respectability of profits, incentives, and so forth. Rather, it likely stems from their membership in two larger groups which also include the great majority of the important industrial administrators: first, the engineering-managerial personnel who have dominated Soviet industrial administration and much of the political system in recent decades—men whose training has not accustomed them to the idea of an "invisible hand" and whose position might be severely shaken in an economic system in which different skills (like those of the economist) become more vital; second, the middle-aged, middle-class men who have achieved high status and economic comfort, but who may have an intense fear (perhaps reinforced by the Yugoslav experience) that market mechanisms produce inflation.

Within these major groups, the regional first secretaries may actually be among those most receptive to the initial steps in economic reform. The potential impact of the local organs upon economic decisions made within the region is much greater than on decisions made at higher territorial levels, and the devolution of authority (and particularly investment funds) to the plant level would significantly broaden the scope of action of party functionaries. For this reason it is not surprising that one of the most prevalent themes in articles by party officials on the economic reform has been criticism of the ministerial and financial personnel (those with most to lose in the reform) who restrict even those rights which the managers have already been granted.

In other major policy realms as well, the regional first secretaries are unlikely to be dogmatic in their support of the status quo as the other major groups benefiting directly from it. On literary and artistic questions, the party officials—even those in ideological work—are probably far less intense in their opposition to experimentation in style than many of the leading officials of the writers' and artists' unions. A Komsomol official with whom I once talked expressed the exasperated belief that an all-out struggle against abstract art is not worth the bother—a feeling that I suspect is widely shared. Similarly, the opposition of functionaries to most types of sociological and economic research is likely to be less than that of the academic political economists. On questions of law and order, one would expect the party officials to be essentially "conservative" in their approach and not to show tolerance toward "agitators." Yet even on this question many officials may be more receptive than other groups to the proposition that stability depends upon the correction of social evils and that the latter in turn requires a reasonably free flow of "responsible" criticism.

Of course, on many of the issues raised in the last paragraph there may be as little unity among the first secretaries as there is on appropriations questions. There may be conservative and liberal wings of the apparatus, with each position on an issue being strongly rooted among officials of particular backgrounds or areas. The first secretaries with the background of an industrial administrator (particularly those from heavy or defense industry) may tend to be conservative or even reactionary with respect to literary dissidence, market socialism, and a reduced priority for heavy industry; the younger first secretaries with a Komsomol background are, I suspect, often relatively liberal on these questions. Even if these suppositions are accurate, however, it is unlikely that knowledge of an official's conservative or liberal stand on one issue will reveal his position on all issues. It seems clear, for example, that the leaders of the Leningrad party organization have been quite reactionary in their relationships with literary dissidents, but most vigorous in their support for the development of concrete sociological investigation.[37]

Usually there is one question on which politicians can be expected to be quite conservative—the need to support the political structures in which they have learned to operate and which confer power and status upon them. Certainly, party officials are unlikely to lead the fight for a multi-party system and were undoubtedly prominent among those who were disturbed by the frequent reorganizations of the Khrushchev period, particularly by the bifurcation of the party apparatus.[38] Even on the question of the role and nature of the party apparatus, however, the regional first secretaries may not be completely united and rigid supporters of the organizational status quo. It is possible that many might come—or already have come—to favor basic changes in the mechanisms by which the General Secretary has exercised control over the apparatus. Considering that they were the major source of support for both Stalin and Khruschev in their rise to power, the first secretaries reaped fewer benefits than they might have expected. Even in the post-Stalin period, they found the authority of their sovnarkhoz quickly whittled away, and were themselves subjected to a large-scale purge in 1960-61; the apparatus itself was torn asunder in 1962. They even suffered the ignominy of being unable to hire good typists and stenographers because pay rates for these positions were set lower than those in other institutions.[39]

If a coalition of leaders attempting to limit the power of the General Secretary struck upon the device of restricting his ability to remove key officials in the lower apparatus, this proposal might win considerable support among the local officials. The regional first secretaries might be made responsible to the local organization, or, once selected from above, they might be given immunity from removal by the General Secretary. In practice, this seems to have taken place in the immediate post-Khrushchev period, for almost all republican and obkom first secretaries (at least those who were full members of the Central Committee) either retained their posts through 1968 or were given another job which normally would warrant Central Committee membership. If such a practice were instituted on a longterm basis, indeed, if there were any permanent limitation on the ability of the General Secretary to remove disloyal (or inefficient) party officials, it would constitute a radical transformation in the political system. Although the present tendency toward "respect for cadres" may be relatively short-lived, even the possibility that the regional first secretaries might support such an important change in the political system should remind us of the need to exercise care in generalizing about them.

Although Western scholars focus upon the regional first secretaries as the epitome of the apparatchik, the typical official, in numerical terms, is the employee of a specialized department of a party organ. With the exception of a few senior secretaries, all of the employees of the key Central Committee secretariat fit within this category. The Central Commitee officials are probably of primary interest to a student of the Soviet political system, but because of the greater availability of information on the specialized officials of the local organs, we shall examine them first.

The practice of naming specialists to the apparatus has usually been attributed to a desire of the leadership to provide the first secretaries with the expert staff assistance which is necessary to control the specialists in the state and economic apparatus. This interpretation is unquestionably correct, but we should be careful about deducing the nature of these Soviet policitians from the original functions assigned to them. Like the first secretaries, they have also been assigned—or at least have assumed—the responsibility of supporting, of pushing, and of fighting for investment projects relating to the branch of the economy they supervise. This responsibility is vital in determining their role in the policy-making process.

The first secretaries of local organs are active in advancing and supporting local development projects, but much of the working support for these projects is undoubtedly provided by the specialized secretary and department most directly involved. Since one of the normal techniques for developing support for a project is to speak out for it in a public speech or article, the extent of the participation of the specialized officials in the appropriations process may be readily discerned. In a speech at a republican party congress, a republican secretary for agriculture may "propose that the opening of the pastures on the Zaunguz plateau, in the southeastern and southwestern Kara-Kums, and in the Kara-Kum Canal zone be considered, [for, he asserted] this will open the gate to large-scale livestock raising in Tashauz oblast."[40] A deputy head of the industrial-transportation department of the Kazakhstan central committee may write an article in *Ekonomicheskaya gazeta,* complaining that the expansion of oil production in the new Mangyshlak field is being delayed by the failure of central authorities to make sufficient preparation for the transportation of the oil in 1968 and 1969, and he may end the article with the plea that action be taken.[41] An ideological secretary of the Bashkiria obkom may report that the drive for universal secondary education is gaining success, but that in the process it is creating a serious shortage of ninth-grade teachers in the area. Consequently, he may call for the establishment of a pedagogical institute in Ufa to solve this problem.[42]

The specialized party officials do not limit their support to specific local projects; they also publicly propose the appropriation of funds to benefit their branch on a nationwide basis. Thus the head of the industrial-transportation department of the Krasnodar kraikom together with the head of the Krasnodar Oil Prospecting Trust asserted that recent successes in experimental drilling of deep oil wells in their region justified (indeed, made imperative) the mass production of the equipment necessary for this work.[43] In another article, the agricultural secretary of the Pskov obkom recognized that "Yes, we now receive more funds [for land reclamation] than before," but continued: "Often [the funds] do not have an impact because they are not invested in an integrated fashion. Let's say, the situation has become better with fertilizers, but there are few machines for applying them and only a small number of poorly equipped agro-chemical laboratories to consult with the kolkhozy and sovkhozy on how to apply the mineral fertilizers."[44] The Pskov secretary bluntly insisted, "If we want to intensify agricultural production in the Non-Black-Earth region on a modern level, then it is necessary first of all to create a durable production-technical base for land-reclamation and to improve the supplies situation."[45]

It is important to note that the secretaries for ideological questions also participate in this aspect of the appropriations process, and it is vital to understand the nature of their participation. As indicated earlier, the responsibilities of these secretaries are not limited to the supervision of propaganda and agitation and to the exercise of ideological control over the creative intelligentsia. They also have many down-to-earth responsibilities in the cultural-education realm. For example, the ideological functionaries may at times appeal publicly for an increase in quantity and quality of film strips for the party's political education program. But their participation in the appropriations process is more vigorous on other questions.

A large portion of the time of the ideological officials must be devoted to the school system—and in considerable part to its financing and supplying. We have already mentioned the ideological secretary of the Bashkiria obkom who fought for a new pedagogical institute. Even more frequently, the problem is to ensure that the various agencies responsible for elementary and secondary school funding and construction perform this task faithfully. Thus, the ideological secretary of the Krasnodar kraikom wrote an article in the newspaper of the Russian Republic criticizing the Ministry of Agriculture for creating a smaller, worse equipped school network in the sovkhoz settlements than the kolkhozy were creating in the kolkhoz settlements.[46] He also pointed to the need to solve the "painful problem" of shortages of school furniture and laboratory equipment. The ideological secretary of the Penza obkom went further. He acknowledged that the present practice of financing school construction through the enterprises and kolkhozy resulted in sufficient funds for this purpose, but complained that the absence of centralized supplying of construction materials and equipment created great problems. "Construction materials and equipment have to be beat out with all truths and nontruths."[47]

Judging from their articles in the press, the ideological secretaries fully realize that shaping the citizens' attitudes requires more than exposing them to Marxism-Leninism and shielding them from hostile ideologies. In an article about the education of persons in their late teens, the ideological secretary of the Bashkiria obkom seemed quite sensitive to the importance of jobs for high school graduates and of meaningful training on their first jobs. While indicating that the obkom had been quite interested in ensuring that the local economic administrators hired and trained recent graduates, he stated that several policy changes were demanded at the national level. He proposed that the planning organs and ministries begin locating more plants in small and medium-sized cities to ease the difficulties of placement there. Moreover, he called upon the USSR State Committee for Labor and Wages to introduce a system of material incentives to reward foremen who assumed the responsibility of training high school graduates on their new jobs.[48]

Similarly, in an article dealing with the problems of developing a positive worldview among young people, the ideological secretary of the Uzbekistan central committee asserted that a lack of concern for young people on the part of some administrators seriously hampered this work. He demanded greater managerial sensitivity concerning the need for adequate sports facilities and decent dormitories.[49] Two months prior to calling for better schools in the sovkhozy, the ideological secretary of the Krasnodar kraikom declared that production esthetics and city beautification were vital programs in shaping the cultural outlook of Soviet citizens. He insisted that they receive greater attention (and presumably funds).[50]

In appealing for funds, the specialized officials of a particular local party organ sometimes operate as a unified interest group. Since the funds for each branch are controlled by the respective ministries, the specialized officials can function together as a team, each attempting to obtain projects for the region by tapping a different set of central funds. There are, however, limits to the extent of the community of interests among the specialized officials of a particular organ.

In the first place, of course, some of their appeals go beyond a claim for a larger share of the branch's funds. It is one thing to call for the establishment of a local pedagogical institute; it is something else to call for a large-scale, integrated land-reclamation program. In the real world, it may be quite impossible to institute at the same time a large-scale expansion in the production of school furniture, in the development of new oil fields, in the land-reclamation program, and in the city beautification program. Consequently, when the specialized officials make appeals that require macro-appropriations, their interests come into sharp conflict with each other.

In the second place, even on micro-appropriations questions there can be a great difference in the intensity of the support which the bureau and the first secretary give to a project. It is one thing for the ideological secretary to write of the need for a pedagogical institute and even to gain the endorsement of the bureau and the first secretary for the project. It is quite a different matter if the first secretary places the institute at the top of his list of priority projects for the region and is willing to "bang the desk" when he visits the Central Committee secretariat and the Council of Ministers in Moscow. In attempting to win this type of support from the first secretary, the interests of the specialized officials may come into conflict in a fundamental way.

Finally, the last stages of the appropriations process—the appropriations of real men and materials for the construction of the project—produce further conflicts of interest among the specialized officials. To obtain appropriations in the sense of money authorizations is far easier than to ensure the "mastering" (*osvoeniye*) of the funds. For example, a sovkhoz which I visited in 1967 had had no difficulty in obtaining the funds for a palace of culture, but the project had remained uncompleted for several years. The raion authorities would not include it in the list of the priority projects to be built by the overburdened local construction trust. The problem is typical and becomes particularly great in those cases in which the allocation of supplies is not organized in a centralized fashion. Decisions about the priority to be given construction projects cause the most severe competition among the specialized officials. In the Kazakhstan Party Congress of 1961 this competition came to the surface in a strong complaint by the republican secretary for industry: "For two years the plans for capital investment in housing, culture, education, public health, and communal construction have been overfulfilled. The plan for capital investment in agriculture has been overfulfilled by almost a billion rubles. However, we have far from mastered the funds allocated for the development of heavy industry and the construction industry."[51]

On these aspects of the appropriations process group conflict is far different from that suggested by those analyses which emphasize the conflict between the party and the state, the apparatchik and the manager, the ideologues and the intelligentsia. On these questions, the key groupings are usually formed along functional lines, as the party secretaries ally themselves with, and defend the interests of, state officials over whom at other times they exercise control. The obkom secretary for agriculture, the deputy chairman of the executive committee of the oblast soviet for agriculture, the head of the oblast agriculture administration (the direct subordinate of the ministry), and the head of the agriculture department of the party obkom are likely to be natural allies in a struggle with, for example, the obkom secretary for ideological questions, the deputy chairman of the executive committee of the oblast soviet for cultural-education questions, the head of the oblast education department, and the head of the science, higher education, and schools department of the obkom. For this reason, it was not surprising to hear a young and by no means doctrinaire director of an art museum exclaim in a 1967 conversation, "Where would we be without the party obkom?" In a conflict with the bank over funding, he had found the obkom (presumably first and foremost the ideological officials) the only effective source of local support.

Of course, on many issues the essential conflicts take place within the confines of one branch of the economy rather than between branches. Should priority be given to the development of heavy industry or light industry, to the development of the Virgin Lands or to the reclamation of the western lands? How much authority should be delegated from the ministry to the plant manager or the university rector? To what extent should experimentation be permitted within the theaters and the art galleries? At what stage should defense attorneys participate in criminal investigations? On these questions do the specialized officials have a different party perspective than their counterparts in the governmental and economic hierarchies?

To some extent these questions are answered by the very structure of the apparatus. Because a local party organ has only one secretary for industry, it is obvious that the policy positions of this offical will not always coincide with those both of the heavy industry and the light industry administrators of the area. Similarly, since the administrative organs department oversees the activities of the police, the procuracy, the courts, and presumably the defense attorneys, its officials would find it impossible to reflect mechanically the views of all the men they supervise, regardless of their own wishes.

Although there is ample room for a distinct party position on many issues, it is not at all clear what that position is—or, indeed, whether one actually exists. Certainly there is little evidence that the specialized party officials, even the ideological ones, are always the spokesmen for the dogmatic, ideological position on a given issue. The specialized functionaries do not have the same range of coordinating responsibilities as the first secretaries, but they, too, must make a continuing series of hard choices among widely varying claims within their branch. They, too, must develop some of the politician's skills and behavior in their participation in the appropriation process. As the ideological officials fight "with all truths and nontruths" for materials and equipment for school construction and attempt to persuade local plant managers to improve sports facilities and to employ school dropouts, they are far more likely to develop into pragmatic politicians than mere ideologues preoccupied with the intricacies of Marxist philosophy.

In practice, the relation of the specialized officials and the state administrators varies considerably from one issue to another. In the cultural-education area, for example, the ideological officials may well be more dubious about the showing of foreign films than are the theater managers who are more immediately worried about fulfilling their attendance plan. Yet most ideological officials are probably more willing to tolerate artistic innovation than many conservative writers, and more eager to encourage sociological research than many political economists.

To the extent that the specialized officials have an identifiable group position on intrabranch questions, it is likely that these positions are associated with the party organ's responsibility for regional coordination and political stability. The major difference between ideological officials and the educational administrators is likely to involve the education of potential dropouts rather than the ideological content of the curriculum. Most Soviet educators seem dedicated to a program designed for the college-bound; the ideological officials often seem more concerned with the dangers of idle teenagers wandering the streets. The industrial party officials are probably more sensitive than the industrial administrators about the need to hire soon-to-be-drafted teenagers, to improve working conditions at the factory, and to produce more small-scale consumers' goods out of scrap material.

A critical question is whether these hypotheses are valid so far as the specialized officials of the Central Committee secretariat are concerned. Do these officials take a "presidial perspective" on policy questions, or do their attitudes often correspond to those of the respective specialized officials of the local party organs and the administrators they supervise?[52]

Unfortunately, as all scholars concerned with the Soviet Union have found reason to lament, it is precisely when we turn to a discussion of the Central Committee apparatus that the problem of information becomes the most acute. Soviet newspapers seldom provide much information about the inner workings of the party organ to which they are directly subordinate, and the central press adheres to this rule even more closely than the local press. If we take an interest group approach, however, we begin with great skepticism about the likelihood of a common set of values within such an internally differentiated institution as the Central Committee secretariat—or, at least, a common set of values with respect to the typical "within-system" political conflicts of Soviet society. The limited information available indicates that this skepticism is justified.

Perhaps the surest indication of cleavage within the Central Committee secretariat is the nature of the job which its officials have been assigned. In particular, the responsibility for "verification of the fulfillment of party and state decisions" has important implications for the role of the secretariat in the policy process. Each party member is obligated by the party to "speak out against any actions which harm the party and the state and to inform the party organs, right up to the Central Committee, about them,"[53] and the party organs are obligated to investigate these complaints and to correct the situation reported. The Central Committee officials also are given the responsibility of seeking information on their own. For example, in 1962 the party secretary of the Minsk Automatic Lines Works reported, "Long in advance of the plenary session [of the Central Committee on leadership of industry] a representative of the Central Committee came to our plant. He asked what questions concerning the leadership of the economy and particularly industry agitated us, and he said that the Central Committee would like to know our opinion on these questions—the opinion of the party *aktiv* and the leaders and employees of the plant."[54]

In performing their information-collecting functions, the specialized party officials repeatedly learn of the need for more funds and supplies. When, for example, the officials of the agriculture department check on the fulfillment of the Central Committee decree on irrigation and land reclamation, they obviously are told privately what the Pskov secretary said in public: "Often [the funds] do not have an impact because they are not invested in an integrated fashion." They are told, "If we want to intensify agricultural production in the Non-Black-Earth region on a modern level, then we first of all must create a durable production-technical base for land-reclamation and must improve the supplies situation.'' As the top party leaders ask the specialized officials how the performance of their branch could be improved, the latter frequently must pass along the investment suggestions and demands of ministerial and lower party officials, and the information and suggestions emanating from each Central Committee department must to a considerable degree reflect the differences of opinion among these officials.

Party spokesmen continually emphasize that verification of performance entails the responsibility not only to report shortcomings, but also to see that they are removed. Western scholars have emphasized that this responsibility requires the specialized party officials to prod their ministry or ministries to use existing resources more effectively, but it would be a mistake to focus exclusively upon the tensions built into the relationship of the ministries and the Central Committee secretariat. The very nature of their duties identifies the specialized party officials with the major goals assigned the ministries they supervise. It is inevitable, for example, that the head of the oil industry sector of the Central Committee's heavy industry department will adhere to the position he enunciated in *Ekonomicheskaya gazeta* in 1968: ''It is very important to speed the introduction of new capacity in the oil industry. This means we must increase the known reserves, widen the scale of oil-well drilling, and perfect the exploitation of the deposits.''[55]

Since significant increase in productivity in modern industry requires investment, it is also inevitable that party officials dedicated to the development of their branch must fight for the necessary funds. And so, the same head of the oil industry sector raises his voice publicly for the ''integrated automation and telemechanization of the production processes.''[56] Similarly, the head of the agriculture department of the Central Committee can be found stating that the agricultural machinery plants must develop a wider assortment of machines to deal with the peculiarities of different zones of the country, while two Central Committee officials specializing in light industry demand an increase in the quantity and an improvement in the quality of machines producing shoes.[57]

In practice, it is highly probable that on fundamental appropriations questions each department usually works together with the relevant ministries as the combined representative of their branch. In the conflict which flared over the level of agricultural investment in the late 1950s, for example, Khrushchev has testified that the party and governmental officials specializing in agriculture functioned as allies:

At the end of 1959, at the December plenum of the Central Committee of the CPSU, our party worked out new important measures in the agricultural realm . . . I should tell you, when we prepared for this plenum, our agricultural organs— the departments of the Central Committee for the union republics and the RSFSR and the ministries of agriculture—worked out fairly broad proposals for the development of all branches of agriculture in the Soviet Union. We rejected these proposals. The Central Committee considers that the basic boundaries of the development of agriculture are well stated in the seven-year plan.[58]

It seems certain that the ''metal-eaters'' on the other side of the issue likewise included within their ranks both party officials (for example, the iron and steel sector of the heavy industry department) and governmental officials (for example, the Ministry of Ferrous Metallurgy). Such behavior seems almost certainly to be the norm rather than the exception.

On intrabranch questions there is less inherent reason to assume a community of interests and viewpoints between the officials of the Central Committee department and the ministerial officials they supervise. As Fainsod has pointed out, the basic rationale for the creation of a duplicate set of ''ministries'' in the Central Committee secretariat is to provide the party leadership with diversity in information and policy suggestions:

> By pitting the competitive hierarchies of administration, party, and secret police against each other at lower levels of the governmental structure, [the leadership] frees itself from exclusive dependence on any single channel of fact gathering and encourages rivalries among the various agencies to correct distortion and prevent concealment. In this fashion it mobilizes the cumulative resources which competition sometimes generates.[59]

If the overlapping of the party and state institutions is to serve this function, then one would expect the party leadership to take steps to ensure some diversity in viewpoint between them. It would be logical to appoint a Central Committee secretary for agriculture whose general policy views on agriculture are known to differ somewhat from those of the Minister of Agriculture.

Yet despite the competition built into the secretariat-ministry relationship on intrabranch questions, there are a number of forces that tend to draw together the party and governmental officials dealing with a particular branch of the economy. There is frequent and intimate contact between such men, and common attitudes have ample opportunity to develop. The investigations carried out by the party officials bring them into close contact with ministerial personnel, but the interaction often takes more prolonged and often more cooperative forms. In the past—and probably at the present—officials of the Central Committee staff attended meetings of the collegia of the ministries and presumably participated in their discussions. Moreover, officials of the Central Committee secretariat and the state institutions usually seem to work together in the drafting of major decisions. Normally ad hoc bodies ("commissions") are formed, composed of representatives of the interested Central Committee department or departments, ministries, and state committees, as well as experts from the academic and scientific community. A commission may produce a draft decision which the top policy makers find unacceptable, as apparently was the case in the 1959 agricultural investment policy mentioned by Khrushchev; at other times it is probably more conscious of "political realities." Sometimes, particularly in a decision of the Secretariat alone, officials from the outside may be invited for long discussions on the draft. In the case of a 1957 decision on the historical journal, *Voprosy istorii,* for example, eight- to nine-hour discussions were held on two successive days, and the editors of the journal, the president and vice-president of the Academy of Sciences, and other representatives from the Academy of Sciences participated along with officials of the relevant Central Committee departments.[60]

In either case, however, the repeated give-and-take which this type of legislative process requires between party and state officials specializing on a given branch of the economy could be expected to push them toward a common definition of key problems and possible solutions for them. In the course of prolonged interaction with their state officials, the specialized functionaries may come to have a vision of the political world more similar to that of their counterparts in the government than to that of their nominal colleagues in other departments of the Central Committee. In fact, since the specialized party officials are usually drawn from those with administrative experience in their own field, these men may well have had a similar outlook before their appointment.

Of course, there are no institutions or groups of specialists without differences of opinion, and such differences surely exist between the officials of a Central Committee department and those whose work they oversee. Many policy differences must be essentially idiosyncratic in nature, but some undoubtedly reflect basic institutional differences. A department of the Central Committee, like that of a local party organ, has a broader set of responsibilities than any one ministry or state committee, and this inevitably prevents the development of a complete community of interests and views between a department and all the institutions it supervises. It should be noted, however, that the greater number of departments in the Central Committee secretariat reduces the number of state institutions within the jurisdiction of any one Central Committee department and, consequently, reduces the amount of conflict with the state apparatus. The head of the industrial-transportation department of a local party organ will inexorably come into conflict with some of the industrial administrators he supervises; however, it is at least within the realm of possibility that the head of the chemical industry department of the Central Committee and the Minister of the Chemical Industry might be in nearly complete agreement. Because of the greater specialization within the Central Committee secretariat, one would suspect that many of the department heads and particularly the sector heads often have a narrower perspective on a number of issues than do many specialized local party officials.

The crucial question, once again, is whether the officials of the Central Committee departments, more than those of the governmental agencies, are men with "an ideological form of political calculation and analysis" who act in accordance with a "rigid and closed . . . set of rules of conduct spelled out by the ideology."[61] As before, this is a difficult question to answer. The officials of the Central Committee departments seem to be guided by a willing or unwilling passion for anonymity, and their policy positions on intrabranch questions are seldom discernible.

The one piece of evidence that we have would by itself provide little reason to conclude that the officials of the Central Committee departments are as a whole more rigid than their counterparts in the ministries or state committees. When we look at year of birth and of party admission for the Central Committee department heads, the ministers, and the chairman of state committees who worked on internal policy questions in 1966,[62] we find that the department heads were on the average five years younger (1914 vs. 1909) and joined the party four years later (1939 vs. 1935). In some cases the contrast was striking. The head of the transportation and communications department of the Central Committee (a man who was born in 1917 and joined the party in 1943) oversaw ministers of railroads, communication, and merchant marine whose year of birth averaged 1902 and whose year of party admission averaged 1922.[63] The head of the light industry and food industry department of the Central Committee (born 1916) joined the party in 1941—a year after the Minister of the Food Industry (born 1899) and the Minister of the Fish Industry (born 1905) had already become Peoples' Commissar for the branch of industry they still head.[64] The head of the agriculture department of the Central Committee was nine years younger than the Minister of Agriculture and seventeen years younger than the Chairman of the State Committee for Deliveries; the head of the construction department was eleven years younger than the average age of the construction administrators who sat on the Council of Ministers.[65] Eight of the eleven ministers and chairmen of state committees cited in these examples had reached the level of minister by 1955, five of them by 1948. None of the four Central Committee department heads had held their post for as many as five years. (Indeed, at the time of the Twenty-third Congress in the spring of 1966, over three-quarters of the department heads dealing with internal policy had tenure of under two years.)

Age alone is, of course, not a conclusive indication of attitude. But in the absence of other evidence, there seems to be no a priori reason to believe that the ministers just discussed have been the pragmatic, innovative advocates of reform within their branch, while the younger department heads mentioned have been the hidebound opponents of change. Similarly, was Furtseva (Minister of Culture) who joined the party in 1930 at the age of twenty likely to be less ideological in her approach than Shauro-(head of the culture department of the Central Committee) who joined the party in 1940 at the age of twenty-eight?Was Stepakov (head of the propaganda department of the Central Committee) who first entered party work in 1944 after seven years of administrative work in industry and transportation necessarily more ideological than Mikhailov (Chairman of the State Committee of the Press) who was first secretary of the All-Union Komsomol from 1938 to 1952? The honest answer to all these questions is—we really do not know. But again we can say that the scholar who hypothesizes a Central Committee secretariat united in an ideological approach and opposing a more pragmatic, rational state administration should be aware of the assumptions he is making. In practice we have too often compared the attitudes of the Central Committee official with those of the intellectual—and the dissident intellectual at that —or perhaps we have been too much impressed by the mere designation "party." If we compare the ideological approach of Central Committee officials with that of top governmental administrators, we may be forced to make a more complex analysis than is customary.

If we seek issues on which the Central Committee secretariat is likely to be a group with unified interests in opposition to those of another group within the elite, we find few such issues readily discernible. Like the specialized officials of the local party organs, the officials of the Central Committee departments are probably more immediately aware of the implications of policy for political stability than are many of the state officials, and this awareness may well have an impact on their attitudes similar to that hypothesized for local party officials.

Moreover, the high rate of turnover among the department heads within a year of Khrushchev's removal (and a similarly high rate in 1953-55) suggests that there may be a close personal relationship between the General Secretary and the department heads and that the latter may be more sensitive than the governmental officials to the implications of policy for the stability of the position of the party leader. The department heads may be united in trying to defend the General Secretary's political position, and they may tend to close ranks when he is involved in a critical political conflict over a particular issue. Even in such a case, however, the department heads whose branches are threatened by the General Secretary's attitude surely emphasize to him the potential consequences of his position, and continue to attempt to produce one of those policy changes for which General Secretaries have been famous. When—as usually must be the case—the General Secretary tries to give himself flexibility by occupying a more centrist position, even the most loyal specialized party officials will be free to speak vigorously for their branch in intrabranch conflicts.

Paradoxically, the "within-system" issue on which the Central Committee officials may be most united is one which involves conflict with other parts of the party apparatus rather than with the ministerial officials. The Central Committee officials are located in the center; they work intimately with central state officials; they find it easier to influence policy in one nearby ministry than in fifteen scattered republics. While the specialized officials may eventually decide that they could have a greater impact on events through the use of centrally controlled economic levers, there is little reason to expect them to be dedicated to the principle of decentralization of policymaking authority. Particularly, given the overwhelming Russian domination of the Central Committee secretariat, they are probably quite unsympathetic to the idea of moving in the direction of genuine federalism. On the other hand, the lower party officials, whatever their devotion to the principle of a centralized party and state, are surely pressing for more decentralization on specific questions. This is an important cleavage and is likely to become even more so with the passage of time.

The emphasis throughout this chapter has been placed upon the divisions within the party apparatus and upon the complexity of the role of its officials in the decision making process. To the extent that this assessment is valid, it lends support to many of the key propositions of the interest group approach presented in the opening pages.

Beyond furnishing evidence that the phenomena emphasized by Bentley are present even in totalitarian regimes, does this study have any implications for comparative interest group theory? Does an examination of the party apparatus in the Soviet Union provide insights into the similarities and differences in the political processes of the Soviet Union and Western democracies?

On the surface at least, one sees striking differences between the interest group or groups described here and those usually described in Western interest group studies. In the West, attention is concentrated on associational interest groups (like the AMA or the AFL-CIO), which are autonomous vis-à-vis the government and able to provide "the average citizen with a large number of channels of access to the political elite."[66] But the persons discussed in this essay all occupy elite positions within the political machine itself. All have been appointed by the leaders on whom they make demands, and they may be removed by these leaders. Moreover, while associational groups may use a variety of techniques (including strikes, demonstrations, and so forth) to dramatize and elicit support for their demands, the party officials in the Soviet Union—particularly the Central Committee officials—are severely limited in what they can say publicly, and especially in how they can say it.

It has been argued that evidence of "subsystem autonomy" in a Western democracy and the lack of it in a totalitarian regime is a crucial distinction in defining the nature of the political systems:

> A totalitarian system in a nominal sense has all the structures and subsystems of roles that exist in a democratic system, but rather than being autonomous, the interaction of these political substructures is hierarchically controlled. In conversion or process terms, the flow of inputs from the society is suppressed or strictly regulated. Consequently, we cannot speak of interest groups, media of communication, and political parties as constituting an autonomous political infrastructure. They are to be viewed more as mobilization structures contributing to the regulative, extractive, and symbolic capabilities than as substructures creating the basis for a responsive capability. . . .
>
> This implies that *regardless* of the personal desires and ideological commitments of the political leaders, it will be very difficult for such systems to develop a broad responsive capability. We can predict that systems of this class will continue to show a limited range of responsiveness as long as subsystem autonomy remains low and differentiation high.[67]

This line of argument, however, gives rise to serious questions, particularly if one accepts Bentley's interest approach. He argued that a government must be responsive to some interest or interests, but that in the nature of things it cannot be completely responsive to all interests. The crucial question, therefore, is: to whose interests is policy responsive?

It would certainly simplify the comparative study of political systems if we could assume that the elite members of the institutional groups which comprise "the gigantic bureaucracy-party organizational complex" in a country such as the Soviet Union represent essentially their own interests, and not those of the farmers, workers, and clerks whom they supervise. It would also be convenient if we could assume that through the presence of "numerous and autonomous associational groups, with access to political agencies through a variety of legitimate channels" "the institutional interests can be checked and combined with other interests."[68]

It is tempting to make such a priori assumptions—but highly dangerous. In the first place, it is by no means certain that institutional interest groups always represent the interests of the top administrators of the institution alone. In any country, as Almond and Powell point out, "elite representation may . . . serve as a channel for interest groups which have no other means of articulation. In the 1830's and 1840's in Great Britain certain aristocratic and middle-class members of Parliament took it upon themselves to articulate the interests of the working class. Their work on Committees of Inquiry and the like did much to promote the passage of factory and mines legislation."[69] When governmental and party officials specializing in agriculture appeal for additional machinery and fertilizer, when they call for a more effective incentive system to stimulate production, they represent some of the vital interests of the peasant. The subordination of nearly all rank and file Soviet citizens to some ministry or state committee provides all citizens with institutional leaders who have ample incentives to learn their grievances. These leaders know, to quote Almond and Powell, that "peasants on collective farms and workers in factories [can] bargain with their rates of output."[70]

In the second place, it is by no means certain that Western associational interest groups—particularly the large ones usually emphasized by scholars—should be viewed as "channels of access to the political elite [through which] . . . the citizen can easily voice his demands."[71] Mancur Olson has correctly asserted that membership in large associational groups in the United States usually results from compulsion or from tangible benefits other than interest representation.[72] His analysis would lead one to expect few membership challenges to the group leadership—even if the interest representation is considered inadequate. Or, at least, one would expect major challenges only when there is a level of dissatisfaction which would be readily discernible in any political system.

Olson's argument tends to be supported by the empirical work of a leading American specialist on the subject, the late V. O. Key, Jr. At the end of a lifetime of study, Key concluded that "to a considerable degree the work of the spokesmen of private groups, both large and small, proceeds without extensive involvement of either the membership or a wider public."[73] He depicted interest group leaders less as the representatives of autonomous groups than as members of a common political elite—a "leadership echelon." At times he found it possible to speak of this echelon in the singular, attaching great importance to "the motives that actuate the leadership echelon, the values that it holds, . . . the rules of the political game to which it adheres, . . . the expectations which it entertains about its own status in society, and perhaps . . . some of the objective circumstances, both material and institutional, in which it functions."[74] Key even hypothesized that "the pluralistic interaction among leadership echelons may occur, and may be tolerable, precisely because leadership clusters can command only a relatively small following among the masses."[75]

Charles Lindblom has interpreted the activity of associational interest groups in a similar manner, contending that "interest-group leaders will be listened to with respect not because they wield power but because they are perceived to be representative of interests entitled (by the accepted norms of rules governing the few activists) to be heard and accorded consideration." He continues: "The big engine of interest-group participation in the play of power . . . is persuasion . . . Interest-groups are highly-skilled practitioners of partisan analysis; it is perhaps their main source of influence or power . . . Their educational or persuasive work is typically more restricted . . . to showing the proximate policy maker how a policy desired by the interest-group squares with the policy-maker's philosophy, values, or principles."[76] Lindblom did not hesitate to point up the obvious implication of this interpretation: "If . . . their powers are largely those of partisan analysis, then, great as they are, they are nevertheless constrained by the fundamental values of . . . proximate policy-makers to whom they appeal."[77]

On an observational level, the Western interest groups described by Key and Lindblom and the Soviet groups described in this essay have many more similarities than suggested in Almond and Powell's book. In both countries members of the political elite claim to speak for broader groups within society. In both countries these avowed elite representatives of interests advance their case largely through persuasion. Even the fact that the elite representatives of interests in the Soviet Union are administratively responsible to the top political leaders may make them little less autonomous than are the appointed leaders of military establishments throughout the world.

Thus, the questions to which we must return are: for whom *do* the specialized elites in a country speak? To what extent do they serve as channels through which all significant interests in society can be equitably represented in the political process? And, of course, ultimately we face the question that Bentley raised with respect to a despotic ruler (and also a democracy): which interests "are most directly represented through him, . . . which almost seem not to be represented through him at all, or to be represented to a different degree or in a different manner.''?[78] These are the questions we must answer before we can say anything meaningful about the responsiveness of different political systems.

Unfortunately, a study of an interest group such as the party apparatus or even of the multitude of groups of which different party officials are members does little to answer these questions. The interest group approach really suggests that we study not only the interest groups themselves, but also the relationship among them. If we are to compare how interests are represented in different political systems, we may have to take seriously Lasswell's definition of politics and begin to explore the question—who, in fact, gets what in different political systems? It is this type of exploration that will be necessary before we can make a definite judgment about the role of the party apparatchiki as an interest group in Soviet society.

# 4

# Political Participation in the Soviet Union

In many ways one of the crucial questions for an understanding of the Soviet Union is the nature of the role of political participation in the political system. To what extent can people speak out? To what extent are they drawn into committees and councils which have an impact on their place of work and residence? To what extent do they participate in what we would call local or national policymaking? And, of course, what impact does such participation have upon decisions which are taken?

In recent years a number of scholars have treated the fall of Khrushchev as a watershed in the history of citizen participation in the Soviet Union. Khrushchev's introduction of the concept of the "all-people's state," his advocacy of the gradual transfer of functions from state to public organizations, his insistence that millions of citizens be drawn into part-time work in the soviets, the other governmental agencies and the public organizations (some of them newly created)—all of these, it is said, reflected his "populism." "The first secretary formed an alliance with the people against bureaucracy . . . [He] encouraged a measure of popular participation in the execution if not the formulation of public policy."[1]

According to this line of analysis, Brezhnev and Kosygin embody the successful counter-revolution of the bureaucrats—of the "clerks," in Zbigniew Brzezinski's phrase. In this view, the present leaders (and those they represent) are imbued with the career official's sense of rationality, and they distrust the dilettantism, irregularity, unpredictability, and amateur interference in decision making that they believe participation to involve:

> For Khrushchev the impulsive adventurer, fervent ideologue, "democratic popularizer," and restless pragmatist—the means of sociopolitical organization and advance emphasized public-spiritedness and participation in societal and administrative affairs. By contrast, for the more cautious, faceless, and systematic Brezhnev and Kosygin . . . the solution lies in bureaucratic instrumentalities perfected according to the principles of scientific Communism and the law of economic development.[2]

And, in fact, it is argued, "since Khrushchev's fall the new leadership has reexamined and curtailed the excessive practice of drawing rank-and-file party members and the general public into the work of party and state organs."[3]

Although there is a widespread impression of a post-Khrushchev counter-revolution against popular participation in decision making, little systematic research has actually been conducted on the subject, and a few voices have been raised to challenge this view.[4] This is a question that deserves far more careful study than it has hitherto received, and this chapter attempts to make the initial, exploratory groundwork for such a study. The empirical core will be a detailed examination of the evidence, both ideological and statistical, that seems pertinent for an analysis of the trends in political participation in the Khrushchev and Brezhnev periods. However, the most important questions about Soviet political participation are qualitative rather than quantitative in nature, and they involve comparisions among political systems more than comparisons over time within one political system. The exploration of these questions is not a simple matter of examining official Soviet statements and statistics; rather, it requires the most careful thought about the methodology of comparing subtle phenomena across political systems. A short discussion can scarcely treat this matter in a comprehensive manner, but will at least try to indicate some of the considerations that are important for such an analysis.

In some respects the removal of Khrushchev in 1964 did bring change in Soviet policies with respect to public participation. On the ideological level, a number of leading Soviet scholars (sometimes reversing earlier positions) began to speak not of the "withering away of the state", but of the need for "the preservation of the leading role of the state."[5] Moreover, although the virtues of the state have been extrolled, post-Khrushchev leaders have seldom used the phrase "the all-people's state." One scholar analysing the Soviet system in these terms in 1973 had to go back to 1964 to find a Brezhnev quotation employing the term.[6]

These theoretical reformulations have been accompanied by organizational change as well. The Union of Sports Unions and Organizations —the most dramatic example of the transfer of governmental functions to public organizations—was transformed once more into a State Committee for Sports and Physical Culture. A voluntary Volgograd trade union obkom of the machine-building industry, which had been hailed in 1962 as part of a new trend in trade union work, was discovered to have three full-time staff members on a 1973 visit. The change had occurred about five years earlier, its chairman stated.[7] The number of totally voluntary departments of the soviets in the Russian Republic declined from 6,212 on 1 January 1964 to 5,037 in 1969.[8]

Although the fall of Khrushchev unquestionably had an impact on policies with respect to citizen participation, we must be very careful in specifying the nature of this impact. In the ideological realm, for example, it would be wrong to suggest that Khrushchev's ideological innovations have been totally reversed. Scholars frequently continue to speak of the "all-people's state," and one recently insisted that "as a basic principle, all authors unquestionably recognize the existence of two basic stages of the development of the Soviet state: the stage of the state of the dictatorship of the proletariat and the stage of the all-people's state."[9] This author used the term "people's power" [*narodovlastie*] to describe the Soviet system, and he defined "power" [*vlast*] as the ability to compel another to carry out one's will—an ability that may be exercised through legal authority or persuasion but which is always backed up by force.[10]

The most responsible Soviet spokesmen usually avoid phrases like "people's power" or "all-people's state," but they consistently treat the present period as a quite distinct one: the period of 'developed socialism' [*razvityi sotsializm*]. This special period is the product of the 'scientific-technical revolution,' and it is explicitly stated that this revolution 'influences the forms and methods of the organization of social-political life, as well as the active enlistment of the toilers in participation in governmental affairs and in social-political activities.' In particular, the rising educational level associated with this revolution is seen as creating a citizenry that 'clearly [can] carry out the functions of governmental leadership in a qualified, competent manner.'[11] Finally, it is contended the growth in the ability of the public to participate in political affairs has been accompanied by the party's determination to encourage it:

> The KPSS consistently carries out measures to perfect democratic institutions in all spheres of public and state life. Each Soviet man has the guaranteed opportunity to take part in the discussion and decision of important problems of national, republican, oblast, city, or raion scale. Besides that, in their work collectives Soviet people daily decide a multitude of questions connected with the administration of their enterprises, institutions, and organizations.[12]

Words, of course, can be very cheap. It is hard to forget that the Great Purge occurred immediately after (and to some extent simultaneously with) the introduction of the present Soviet Constitution and a voluminous discussion of the democratic processes and protection of individual rights supposedly guaranteed by it. However, if the argument is about the nature of the words, the nature of the ideology, then a change of phraseology should not lead us to claim a retreat from ideological commitment to popular participation—especially when the changes involve a Westernization of phraseology, as the discussion moves from one of "withering away" to one of the impact of education in "developed socialism." After all, Khrushchev's "all-people's state" and "transition to communism" scarcely promised a quick disappearance of the state (let alone the party), and it is significant that the man who first used the phrase "developed socialism" in print (Fedor Burlatsky) is the same scholar who was most closely associated in print with the phrase "all-people's state."[13]

The statistics of the post-Khrushchev period also indicate a continuation of the rise in citizen participation that began in the mid-1950s (see table 4.1). To be sure, the rate of increase in most types of participation has been slower in the last decade than it was in the previous one, but it has been strikingly higher than the increase in the adult population. Indeed, it has been particularly high, given the fact that the group entering young adulthood in recent years has been the abnormally small cohort born during World War II.[14] Thus, the much publicized decline in the number of new admissions into the party is, as table 4.2 suggests, the result not of a decrease in the percentage of real eligibles admitted into the party, but a decrease in the pool of eligibles from which party members are usually drawn.[15]

Moreover, while the Brezhnev era has not been noted for creating new organizations designed to draw the citizens into public life (like the *druzhiny*), some actions were taken to facilitate the access of citizens to the decision making process. For example, in 1969 Kolkhoz Councils were created at the center and at the raion, oblast, and republic levels. These councils were headed by the top agricultural administrator at each level, and, at the all-Union level at least, the council's membership was overwhelmingly administrative or professional in occupation. Its 125 members in 1969 included 25 regional, republican, or central administrators, 56 kolkhoz chairmen, 18 middle-level kolkhoz administrators, 11 kolkhoz professionals, 6 link-leaders and senior shepherds, and only 8 rank-and-file kolkhozniki.[16] Nevertheless, to the extent that they have been effective, the Councils do give over 65,000 persons a greater opportunity to provide advice to the top agricultural officials at each level.[17]

Similarly, the granting of the right of control (*pravo kontrolia*) to the party organizations of educational and scientific institutions—while often interpreted as a strengthening of party control—has probably resulted primarily in the admission of less elite elements into the decision

Table 4.1. Political participation in the USSR, 1954-73

| Group | 1954-55 | Increase 1954-63 (%) | 1963-64 | Increase 1963-72 (%) | 1972-73 |
|---|---|---|---|---|---|
| Adult population[a] | 120,751,000 | 16 | 140,000,000 | 12 | 156,507,828 |
| Party members and candidates[b] | 6,864,864 | 51 | 10,387,196 | 43 | 14,821,031 |
| Deputies to local soviets[c] | 1,536,310 | 27 | 1,959,565 | 12 | 2,193,086 |
| Trade union members[d] | 40,240,000 | 60 | 68,175,600 | 44 | 98,000,000 |
| Komsomol members[e] | 18,825,324 | 17 | 22,000,000 | 41 | 31,000,000 |
| Controllers[f] | 0 | – | 4,300,000 | 109 | 9,000,000 |
| Activists in independent organizations[g] | ? | – | 20,000,000 | 25 | 25,000,000 |
| Druzhinniki[h] | 0 | – | 5,500,000 | 27 | 7,000,000 |

[a]The effective adult population is measured by the number of persons registered to vote in the elections. In years when comparable election and census data are available, the adult population as measured by electoral registration is 2-3 percent lower than that measured by the census.

Figures for 1954, *Pravda*, March 18, 1954, p. 1; for 1963, ibid., March 7, 1963, p. 1 and March 21, 1963, p. 1; for 1973, ibid., June 23, 1973, p. 1.

[b]Figures for 1954 and 1963, T. H. Rigby, *Communist Party Membership in the U.S.S.R. 1917-1967* (Princeton, N.J., 1968), p. 53; for January 1, 1973—*Partiinaia zhizn'*, 1973, no. 14, p. 10.

[c]Figures for 1955 and 1963, N. A. Petrovichev et al. *Partiinoe stroitel'stvo* (Moscow, 1972), p. 403; for 1973, *Pravda*, June 23, 1973, p. 3.

(continued)

dFigures for 1954 and 1963, Petrovichev, *Partiinoe stroitel'stvo*, p. 411; for 1972, *Partiinaia zhizn'*, 1972, no. 21, p. 11.

eFigures for 1954, *Komsomol'skaya pravda*, March 20, 1954, translated in *The Current Digest of the Soviet Press*, vol. VI, no. 13 (March 12, 1954), p. 9; for 1964, V. M. Chkhikvadze, ed., *Sotsializm i narodovlastie* (Moscow, 1965), p. 86; for 1973, *Ezhegodnik Bol'shoi Sovetskoi Entsiklopedii 1973* (Moscow, 1973), p. 18. The proportion of young people of the appropriate age group who are in the Komsomol rose from 34 percent in 1959 to 43 percent in 1965 to over 50 percent in 1970, according to *Slavnyi put' leninskogo komsomola* (Moscow, 1974), vol. II, pp. 469, 580.

fFigures for 1964, *Kommunist*, 1964, no. 13, p. 123; for 1973, *Sovetskaia Rossiia*, March 15, 1973, p. 1.

gFigure for 1964, Chkhikvadze, *Sotsializm*, p. 84; for 1970, *Partiinaia zhizn'*, 1970, no. 13, p. 9.

hFigures for 1963, V. E. Poletaev, ed., *Rabochii klass SSSR* (Moscow, 1969), p. 425; for 1971, F. S. Razarenov, comp., *Narodnomu druzhinniku* (Moscow, 1973), p. 115.

**Table 4.2.** Party saturation by age group, 1965, 1967, 1973 (percentages)

| Age Group | 1965 | 1967 | 1973 |
|---|---|---|---|
| 18-25 | 3.1 | 2.2 | 2.5 |
| 26-40 | 11.0 | 11.5 | 11.2 |
| 41-50 | 10.7 | 11.8 | 13.0 |
| 51 + | 5.5 | 6.5 | 8.0 |
| Total | 7.9 | 8.3 | 8.9 |

*Sources:* The age distribution of party members is found in *Partiinaia zhizn'*, 1965, no. 10, p. 13; 1967, no. 19, pp. 9, 16; 1973, no. 14, p. 19. The age distribution of the population in 1965 and 1967 is extrapolated from 1959 and 1970 census data: *Itogi vsesoiuznoi perepisi naseleniia 1970 goda* (Moscow, 1972), vol. II, pp. 12-13. The age distribution of the population in 1973 comes from *Narodnoe khoziaistvo SSSR v 1972 g.* (Moscow, 1973), p. 34. In the case of 1965, the age categories were actually 18-25, 26-39, 40-49, and 50.

making processes of these bodies. In the higher educational institutions, for example, the rector had been advised by a scholarly council composed of the institute's or university's administrators and leading professors. To a large extent, this council has been a committee of party members (192 of the 233 members of the scholarly councils in Tomsk were party members in 1973[18]), but the party organization as a whole is much less elite in nature, containing, on the average, 42 percent of the institution's faculty.[19] Even the party bureau (the party committee in large institutes) includes not only full professors and administrators, but also students, graduate students, and junior faculty. Moreover, the party committee, unlike the scholarly council, need not wait for the rector to initiate an issue, and, in case of disagreement with the rector, it can take the dispute to the district party committee. If the party committee has become a more important center of discussion and decision, it may well be that younger viewpoints are now better heard and represented. (A professor discussing this question in private conversation cited a curriculum decision in which this had, in fact, occurred.)

Probably most important of all has been the emphasis placed by the post-Khrushchev leadership upon the need for science, specialized knowledge, and information feedback.[20] While this policy may have served to undercut the rationale for some uninformed public interference in the political-administrative process,[21] it has surely also accelerated the use of outside scholars and specialists as consultants (as paid consultants as well as members of the various voluntary commissions and councils). The scientific emphasis has also contributed in a major way to the development of policy-oriented research and to its legitimacy as a source of information for policy makers.

The creation of the Council of Kolkhozy, the granting of the *pravo kontrolya* to the party organizations of scientific-educational institutions, and the increased emphasis upon scientific information may have been primarily of benefit to potential participants in "middle-class" (really upper-stratum) occupations, but the statistical evidence suggests that the trend towards greater worker-peasant participation which began in the Khrushchev period continued after his removal (see table 4.3).

Some of the evidence relating to worker-peasant political participation is particularly suspect because of quirks in the Soviet definitions of "worker" and "peasant."[22] However, the pattern is also present in cases in which this definitional problem is minimal (as in the percentage of workers selected as deputies to the city soviet) or nonexistent (as in the private count of workers and peasants who became deputies to the Supreme Soviet). It is also found in a number of other cases not included in table 4.3. For example, the number of workers and peasants (defined in Western terms) identified among the full members of the republican party central committees increased from 5.2 percent in 1961 to 7.6 percent in 1971.[23]

Some could argue that all of the evidence presented about political participation in the Soviet Union is completely suspect to the point of demonstrating nothing about the trends in participation. It is well established that in the Stalin period official statistics on the subject were grossly inflated. For example, a Soviet sociologist, Iu. E. Volkov, asserts that 25,000 persons were listed as the *aktiv* of the standing committees of the local soviets in Sverdlovsk oblast in 1954, but that "in practice, as an investigation we conducted in that year with Iu. G. Sudnitsyn showed, these 'activists' were in a majority of cases listed only on paper . . . With a few exceptions, the standing committees did not work in practice."[24] One could contend that the expansion in participation during the last decade is simply an increase in the number of "paper activists" and that hard-to-measure changes in political atmosphere have been far more significant in defining and reducing the significance of citizen participation in the Soviet Union.

It is, of course, within the realm of possibility that such a contention is accurate, for the published Soviet statistics clearly are inflated. Lower officials have little incentive to purge nonactive "activists" from their

**Table 4.3.** Worker-peasant participation in the USSR, 1954-73 (in percentage of total group involvement)

|  | 1954-55 | 1963-64 | 1972-73 |
|---|---|---|---|
| Party members (workers and kolkhozniki)[a] | 49.1 | 53.8 | 55.4 |
| Party members (workers alone)[b] | 32.0 | 37.3 | 40.7 |
| Deputies to local soviets (workers)[c] | 10.6 | 26.9 | 39.3 |
| Deputies to city soviets (workers)[d] | 27.7 | 47.2 | 59.5 |
| Deputies to Supreme Soviet (workers and peasants, narrowly defined)[e] | 11 | 20 | 36 |
| Deputies to Supreme Soviet (workers and peasants, reasonably defined)[e] | 14 | 32 | 42 |

[a]Figures for 1956 and 1964, Rigby, *Communist Party Membership*, pp. 325, 306; for 1973, *Partiinaia zhizn'*, 1973, no. 14, p. 15.

[b]Figures for 1956 and 1964, Rigby, p. 325; for 1973, *Partiinaia zhizn'*, 1973, no. 14, p. 15.

[c]Figures for 1955 and 1963, Poletaev, *Rabochii klass SSSR*, p. 405; for 1973, *Pravda*, June 23, 1973, p. 3.

[d]Figures for 1955 and 1963, Poletaev, p. 405; for 1973, *Pravda*, June 23, 1973, p. 3.

[e]These percentages were based upon my own count from the press at the time of the 1954, 1962, and 1974 elections to the Supreme Soviet. The narrow definition excludes anyone with any supervisory responsibility. However, Western censuses do not include foremen and sub-foremen among white-collar employees, and surely the link leaders and *starshie* categories in agriculture and the brigadier and *starshie* categories in industry are peasants and workers by any reasonable comparative definition. They are included in the last entry in the table. However, even the "reasonably defined" workers and peasants exclude industrial foremen and agricultural brigadiers and heads of livestock farms on the ground that these positions are increasingly reserved for the technically trained.

lists, and the number of meaningful participants is far lower than officially claimed. The number of influential participants is still lower. Whether Soviet authorities discuss the earliest forms of participation ("Pioneer self-administration" in the schools), the later types of participation in public work such as house committees or the druzhiny, or the presumably more important types of participation such as membership in the party or selection as a deputy to the local soviet, they always report the existence not only of activists who are "up to their ears" (*po makushku*) in work, but also of the "eternal passives"—those "who stand at the side."[25] The situation can reach the extreme of council members in young people's dormitories being "at times" appointed by the adult supervisor of the dormitory (the *vospitatel'*) or being elected without their knowledge or consent. "It is not astonishing that after such 'election's [only] one or two activists remain in the council after six months."[26]

Yet if the question is simply one of trends, it can be forcefully argued that the burden of proof is upon those who doubt the direction of the change. Soviet participation statistics, including those of the Khrushchev era, have always overstated the degree of participation, but they need not be regarded as totally fraudulent. The mere possibility that a statistical rise in participation may be accompanied by a decline in its meaningfulness does not require us to assert that this is a certainty or even a probability. Western observers have been so obsessed by the fear of being taken in by Soviet propaganda that they have too often based their judgments about the Soviet Union on the worst conceivable possibility, not on the most probable.

In particular, those arguing that there has been a decline in the meaningfulness of political participation in the Soviet Union despite the statistical evidence, must contend with two basic facts. First, the educational level of the Soviet population is increasing—and fairly rapidly at that. The proportion of the population with at least some high-school education has risen from 26 percent in 1959 to 48 percent in 1970—and to 59 percent for the urban population and to nearly 90 percent in the age group under thirty. The percentage with a complete secondary education or better has increased from 14 percent in 1959 to 24 percent in 1970—and to 33 percent in the urban areas. If we insist that the scale and meaningfulness of citizen participation has declined in the face of this type of rise in educational level, we are postulating a rather striking development in the light of what we have learned about the relationship of participation and education in the West and in the Soviet Union,[27] and this in the face of a reported rise in the quantity of participation. It is a possibility, but not one for which we have any real evidence.

Second, there is one type of political participation that is visible to us in the West: the articles and books that appear in print. Here we need not rely on statistics alone (although those on the number of letters to editors show the same continued growth in participation observed in other areas[28]), but we can read the debates for ourselves and judge their nature. If we do this, we find that nearly all the debates are richer and freer than they were under Khrushchev. The documentation which can be used to support arguments is fuller, the freedom to aggregate complaints and proposals is greater. Proposals or criticisms of the status quo sometimes must be phrased with care, and the most radical ones may be restricted to specialized journals or books (the change in the contents of books has been especially striking), but there are few ideas that cannot be expressed in print in one form or the other. The increase in freedom of within-system expression has been less than many intellectuals anticipated—or hoped for—in 1965, but we are comparing the experience of the Brezhnev period with the experience of the early 1960s—not with the hopes of 1965.

The direction of change in the amount of political participation is not the only question to raise. The nature of that participation and the degree of its impact in comparative terms is of more crucial importance. Explicitly or implicitly, our ultimate interest must be a comparison of the Soviet political system with other systems—particularly those in which we live. How similar or dissimilar are they? What are the causes and consequences of the various similarities and differences?

One very important group of scholars has answered these questions very forthrightly. They have not only recognized the existence of participation, but have placed it at the center of comparative analysis. "The Soviet regime is not merely an authoritarian government, consisting, as it were, of a small elite group above the masses of a static, traditional society in the nature of some Middle Eastern countries. Rather, it is a dynamic totalitarian government which sets as its ideal the total and active involvement of all citizens in the affairs of a rapidly changing and ever more complex society.[29] Indeed, the leading theorists of totalitarianism have insisted that "if there were no controlled intermediate organizations in all spheres of society, people would be free to regroup along lines independent of the regime. That is why it is of the utmost importance to totalitarian regimes to keep the population active in these controlled groups."[30]

In this view, however, " 'popular participation' in the Soviet Union is vastly different from that in democratic countries, and indeed in many respects a total inversion."[31] In the words of Brzezinski and Huntington, "the Soviet regime increasingly uses political participation to control its people [and] the controls produced by political participation flow in one direction only."[32] (Both quotations have deliberately been taken from works that refer to the Khrushchev era. The Brezhnev regime is often now compared to a Khrushchev regime that is unrecognizable in the Western scholarly literature of that time.)

But what is the basis for such judgments? Some types of political participation are, of course, observably different from their couterparts in the West. (That involved in electoral and pre-electoral activity is an obvious example.) Yet this is not true of many types of participation. Letters to the editor or the publication of articles in journals, personal appeals to governmental or political officials, membership in many types of committees (various types of student committees, house or street committees, parents' committees in the school, various committees at the place of work), participation in various citywide councils or commissions—so far as can be observed by an outsider, these activities seem little different on the surface from their counterparts in the West.

The examples refer to local decision making, but the same point could be made about top policymaking. We see policy discussions in the Soviet press. We must assume that this discussion is read by an attentive public and that individuals do arrive at opinions about the validity of various positions. How do we know that the most basic Soviet policy decisions (whether to pursue a policy of détente or not, to emphasize law and order or to permit wider dissent, to emphasize industrial growth or other competing values, to conduct a war on poverty in the countryside or expand the highway network and automobile production) are not responses to shifts in the moods and opinions in this attentive public? That is, how do we know that citizen participation in public policy discussions is not decisive in shaping major Soviet policies?

In the past this type of methodological question has not been given much attention in the West. Our basic view—our basic paradigm—of the Soviet system has been that of a directed society, and this view has little room in it for the flow of power or control upwards. As a consequence, we have instinctively looked for evidence that political participation has a limited impact on decisions taken in the Soviet Union. And, in fact, we have found much such evidence in the Soviet press itself (for example, the discussion about participation in dormitory councils). We have instinctively wondered whether participation might not serve other functions than those of influencing decision making. And, in fact, we have found many such functions. Popular participation in the Soviet Union has, indeed, often strengthened the identification of the citizen with the regime and its policy, it has created a pool of unpaid labor for tasks considered important for the regime, it has served as a prod to the performance of lower-level bureaucrats, it has supplied the policy maker with feedback information, it has provided a socially acceptable safety-valve for popular discontent, and so forth.

None of these traditional judgments about political participation in the Soviet Union is wrong. Yet we have often stopped our analysis at this point and have not really reflected on the fact that similar judgments could be made about political participation in the West. If we are trying to compare citizen participation in the Soviet Union with actual participation in other countries, then it is not enough to demonstrate the existence of limitations both on the scale of that participation and on its impact. That is a universal. Nor is it enough to say that political participation serves many functions of benefit to the elite and to the system as a whole. That too is a universal.[33] The questions we need to ask are: how do the limitations on political participation in the Soviet Union compare with those in the West? Does participation in the Soviet Union have an impact on decision outcomes at the same time that it serves the other functions which have been postulated?

For the purpose of comparison, consider, for example, the situation in the United States. The level of political participation as reported in repeated public opinion surveys is quite low. Only one quarter of the respondents to one national survey claim to have discussed public affairs with other people as much as once a week and the same percentage said that they never participate in this activity.[34] Only 32 percent of the population report being active in at least one organization involved in community problems, such organizations being defined broadly enough to include trade unions, PTAs, scouting organizations, fraternity groups, and so forth.[35] The proportion of respondents who claim *ever* to have contacted local officials about some problem is in the 20-30 percent range, and only 15-20 percent make such a claim with respect to the national or state level.[36] No more than 2 percent assert than they have ever "written a letter to the editor of a newspaper or magazine giving political opinions."[37] Reported participation in marches and demonstrations is also extremely low, and in a 1970 national survey only a bare majority of the respondents even conditionally approved of people in general "taking part in protest meetings or marches that are permitted by the local authorities."[38]

The extent to which this public participation has an impact upon decision making in the United States is a controversial subject. Many on the left assert that it has almost no impact at all. Leading pluralists like Robert Dahl have a more complex analysis of this phenomenon. They believe that elections give the masses an indirect influence, but they too suggest that only a relatively small percentage of the population has any direct impact.[39] Even on such decisions as the location of a school and the seeking of redevelopment funds from the federal government, Dahl found that the influentials were a handful of people who took a particular interest in the policy question at issue.

According to Dahl, much participation in New Haven followed the pattern of the PTA in the school. In this organization, Dahl concluded, most members have little influence. Many may be quite inactive, having joined because of pressure from their children to fulfill the classroom membership quota. Others may simply attend one or two meetings a year in order to watch some short program and to meet their children's teachers. Indeed, this pattern was so widespread that Dahl was led to summarize the overall function of the PTA in the following terms:

> Ostensibly . . . a Parent-Teachers' Association is a democratic organization of parents and teachers associated with a particular school, brought into being and sustained by their joint interests. In practice, a PTA is usually an instrument of the school administrator. Indeed, an ambitious principal will ordinarily regard an active PTA as an indispensable means to his success. If no PTA exists, he will create one; if one exists, he will try to maintain it at a high level of activity. [40]

Yet Dahl did find a few PTA members who were active. They made suggestions to the principal about the school; they took part in the process by which money, materials, and teachers are allocated among different schools. These active members may, in fact, influence decisions in ways important to themselves:

> As long as the principal keeps the active PTA members moderately satisfied, he will appear to have the "backing of the parents" for his programs and policies . . . A shrewd principal often uses the PTA to find out what problems are in parents' minds; he then brings about some adjustments in the school's program or perhaps allays the concern of parents simply by discussing the problems with them . . . Some female Machiavellians even look upon PTA activity as a way of assuring favorable treatment for their own children. And they may be right, for . . . the principal is likely to conclude that it is safer to ignore the difficulties of a child whose parents are not interested enough to participate in the PTA than the problems of a child whose mother is a PTA activist. The PTA is also a legitimate channel through which potential leaders may enter into the school system, test themselves, gain experience, and pass into the ranks of the leaders. [41]

One may, of course, make the value judgment that this type of impact is meaningless and may simply interpret participation in terms of cooption. And some persons make precisely this judgment. Yet American political events of the last decade have demonstrated just how high a value people can place on minor decisions made by minor administrators. Should a specific professor be hired or given tenure? Should undergraduates be admitted to the stacks of a new library? Where should a new college gymnasium be located? All these minor questions have provoked riots or strikes at various American and Canadian universities. As Verba and Nie assert in discussing the American situation, "the narrower decisions deserve closer study in terms of who can influence them, and how benefits are allocated through them. For the individual involved, such interactions with the government are important indeed."[42]

Whatever judgment is made about such questions, the crucial precondition for an understanding of the Soviet political system must be a determination to maintain comparability in our analysis. Above all, we must realize that, to begin to speak of similarities with the New Haven that Dahl describes, we need not say that everyone participates nor that every participant is active and influential. We need not find an equal proportion of workers and white-collar employees, only some representation from all classes. We need not demand that the citizen participation be able to change the fundamentals of the political, economic, or social system abruptly. If Soviet mechanisms for public participation do no more than provide the opportunity for a very small percentage of the population to inform themselves about some specialized realm of decision making and to have some impact on those decisions, they still may be quite significant from a comparative point of view.

We must also recognize that the participation rates in the Soviet Union are quite high in comparison with those in the West. (For example, approximately 27 percent of all Soviet citizens over thirty years of age with at least 10 years of schooling are members of the Communist party—approximately 44 percent of all males with these characteristics.) We must recognize that in the Soviet Union, where all "local and state politics" essentially center on decisions made by governmental and party administrators, many of the activities which we have dismissed as "the prodding of administrators" are quite similar to activities which we define as political in the West.

Of course, the actual impact of Soviet political participation— whether a direct impact of citizen participants on detailed decisions or an indirect impact of public discussion on major policies—remains an open question. When we begin to ask about this matter in interviews, however, we are told about the professor at the Leningrad Financial Institute whom the city government asks to sit on various budgetary councils and commissions and whose advice is often accepted by them, about the criminologist at Moscow University who is a deputy of the raion soviet and a member of its law enforcement standing committee and claims she spends as much time on these activities as on her scholarly work, about the locomotive engineer on the presidium of the trade union council of the October Railway Line in Leningrad who successfully fought for a change in the scheduling of engineers' runs to permit them more predictability in their days off, about a party committee in a higher educational

institute which regularly takes decisions about the appointment of department heads and other questions by formal votes that frequently are
not unanimous.

Possibly there were exaggerations in the examples offered in interviews; possibly the frequency and significance of the impact on decisions
in the Soviet Union is less than in the West. We do not really know. We
(and this "we" includes all social scientists, not just specialists on the
Soviet Union) have given very little thought to the methodological
question of how to determine whether the citizens in one country have
more influence than those in another. In the case of the Soviet Union, we
have simply been governed by our ideological assumptions about the
consequences of competitive elections. Indeed, we have been led by our
directed society paradigm not even to see phenomena such as citizen input which do not correspond to the paradigm or to interpret these phenomena differently from the way we would in the West.

It is far from satisfying to end with the words "We do not know,'
but perhaps at some time even they can be of value. In particular, they
can be of value if they produce at least a bit of agnosticism about the paradigm that has directed our work for so many years—if they persuade us
to subject it to test rather than merely take it for granted, if they lead us
to realize how many of our assumptions about the Soviet Union actually
are no more than assumptions, to let our research questions be shaped by
paradigms that encourage us to look for societal inputs. We may find that
research on these questions is not as difficult as we have assumed and that
it may become easier as time passes. True, even with such research, we
may still not feel certain about the impact of participation upon policy
outcomes in the Soviet Union but if that experience then leads us to explore how much we really know about that impact in the West, we may
be in a position to make a major contribution to social science theory.

# 5

# Party Saturation
# in the Soviet Union

From a comparative standpoint, perhaps the most distinctive feature of the Communist party is the nature of its membership policy. Lenin insisted that prospective members had not only to accept the basic philosophy of the party, but also to work actively to achieve its goals. The demand that party members be revolutionaries became anachronistic after 1917, but it evolved into the requirement that they devote their entire life to the construction of socialism and eventually communism. The result of this membership policy has, of course, been the admission of only a relatively small minority of the total population into the party. Soviet authorities term the party a "vanguard" of the Soviet people, a collection of the "best representatives" of the Soviet people; Westerners often called it "an elite, not a mass organization."[1]

Yet it is risky to label the Communist party of the Soviet Union an elite organization, for this word conjures up quite different images for different people.[2] In one well-known study T. B. Bottomore defines "elite" broadly—"functional, mainly occupational groups which have status (for whatever reason) in a society"—and he suggests that this definition is widely employed.[3] Explicitly or implicitly, however, other scholars use the concept much more narrowly. Thus "elite studies" in the Soviet-East European field frequently focus upon Central Committee membership, while the chapter on the Soviet Union in a book entitled *World Revolutionary Elites* is limited to an examination of the Politburo.[4]

What type of elite should we have in mind when we think of the Communist party of the Soviet Union? Is it the rather narrow elite implied in such phrases as "a secular priesthood" or even "the leading personnel of any organization or group, the commanders and their essential staffs . . . with a general sprinkling of industrial workers and a very small peasant component?"[5] Or is it a broad elite—perhaps even "the attentive public," to use a familiar phrase from American political science?

The most obvious way to determine the relative exclusiveness of the party elite in the Soviet Union is to calculate the degree of party saturation in Soviet society—the percentage of party members among Soviet citizens or special groups of Soviet citizens.[6] One could simply divide the number of party members (14,821,031 on January 1, 1973, including 450,506 candidates) by the number of Soviet citizens. If this is done, the party saturation in the population as a whole turns out to be 5.8 percent on that date, 6.0 percent if the candidates are included as well.[7] The percentages produced by this method are rather low, and it is not surprising that they have been cited most often in works emphasizing the closed nature of party membership.[8]

In at least one respect, however, it seems misleading to use the total Soviet population as the denominator in a calculation of party saturation. One-third of the population is under eighteen (the age at which admission to the party is permitted), and many scholars have decided to exclude this group from their analysis of party statistics. In their view, the meaningful saturation level is the percentage of Party membership (including candidates) among the *adult* population, and the figure comes to 8.9 percent in 1973, not 6.0 percent.[9] This figure suggests a somewhat broader Party membership, and it was the one used at the Twenty-Fourth Party Congress in 1971.[10]

Despite official Soviet endorsement of this second method I would, nevertheless, argue that it too fails to give an accurate impression of the degree of party saturation in contemporary Soviet society.

In the first place, while the age of eighteen is the theoretical minimum for party admission, in practice few Soviet citizens enter the party at such an early age. We have no complete Soviet data on this question for the pre-Brezhnev era, but the average age of party admission was 31 in 1965 and 27 in 1975.[11] An examination of the biographies of the 1958-1970 deputies to the Supreme Soviet suggests this pattern is found throughout the postwar period. If anything, the deputies should be atypically "political" in their attitudes and behavior, but the deputies who joined the party after 1946 did so at the average age of 29.4 years. Only 8 percent of all the deputies joined before the age of 23, 18 percent before the age of 25. The data further suggest—although the deputies may well be unrepresentative on this point—that the age of party admission has risen somewhat in the 1960s. The 293 deputies who joined the Party in 1960 or later did so at the average age of 31.7 years.[12]

The limited information available on party age distribution clearly supports the conclusions drawn from the data on Supreme Soviet deputies, at least to the extent of indicating that the mid- and late twenties is the earliest age at which substantial numbers of Soviet citizens enter the Party. While 20 percent of the adult population were between the ages of 18 and 25 in 1973, only 5.7 percent of the party members were in this under-26 age group.[13] The 1973 party saturation in this group can easily be determined by dividing the number of adults of this age into the number of party members in the group, and, as indicated in table 5.1, it proves to have been only 2.5 percent.

If we subtract the total population and the party members in the 18-25 age group from the statistics for the adult population as a whole, we can place the party saturation in the age group of 26 and over at 10.5 percent, in contrast to 8.9 percent for the adult population as a whole. The level of party saturation was also low among those persons between the ages of 26 and 30 and among those over 60. If these groups are also subtracted from the total, 1973 party saturation rises to 12.6 percent among adults aged 31 to 60, as can be calculated from table 5.1.

A second reason for not limiting our analysis to party saturation within the adult population as a whole is the great imbalance in the number of men and women in the party. As has often been noted, women are grossly underrepresented in the party, comprising 3,412,029 (or 23.0 percent) of the 14,821,031 members and candidates in 1973.[14] However, the converse of this statistic has usually been ignored—the gross overrepresentation of men in the party, and, therefore, the higher saturation rates among men than among the population as a whole. If the number of males in the adult population (that is, those eighteen and over) is divided into the number of males in the party, the result is a saturation figure of 15.6 percent in 1973, quite a difference from the 8.9 percent in the overall adult population.

Table 5.1. Party saturation, by age group, 1973.

| Age group | Total population | Party members | Party saturation (%) |
|---|---|---|---|
| 18-25 | 32,939,000 | 834,166 | 2.5 |
| 26-30 | 13,869,000 | 1,101,794 | 7.9 |
| 31-40 | 36,736,000 | 4,588,939 | 12.5 |
| 41-50 | 33,406,000 | 4,329,005 | 13.0 |
| 51-60 | 19,725,000 | 2,425,048 | 12.3 |
| 61 + | 29,613,000 | 1,542,079 | 5.2 |
| Total | 166,288,000 | 14,821,031 | 8.9 |

Sources: The number of party members by age is found in *Partiinaia zhizn'* no. 14 (July 1973), p. 19. The population data are extrapolated from *Narodnoe khoziaistvo v 1972 g.* (Moscow: Statistika, 1973), p. 34.

Obviously, the patterns of party membership by age and sex, when taken together, produce even higher figures for the percentage of men between the ages of 31 and 60 who are party members. Unfortunately, information is not published on the age distribution of party membership for each sex, and we are compelled to rely upon some assumption in making estimates on this subject. The most obvious and easiest assumption is that the age distribution among men and women party members is the same, but there are some difficulties with this supposition. In the first place, 35 percent of all women are over the age of 50 compared with 23 percent of the men,[15] and this might lead one to suspect a disproportionate number of older women party members. In the second place, young women with children may find the responsibilities of party membership particularly burdensome, and they may join at a later age than men, when they have more time. In the third place, however, the percentage of women admitted into the party has been increasing in recent years: 18.0 percent of the new candidates in 1956-1961, 21.7 percent in 1962-1965, 25.7 percent in 1966-1970, and 29.0 percent in 1971-1972.[16] If party admission occurs at the same average age for men and women, there should be larger percentages of women in younger age brackets. In the fourth place, the sex ratios among educated citizens are quite different at different ages. In the 20-29 age group in 1970, there were 22 percent more women than men who had a complete secondary education or better, but in the over-50 group there were 6 percent more men, despite the far greater number of women in general of this age.[17] Given the association of party membership and education, this too might lead one to hypothesize a disproportionate number of younger women party members.

There is no way to determine which of these distortions are most important, but fortunately, they work at cross purposes and may tend to cancel each other out. Even more important, as table 5.2 and 5.3 indicate, the use of different assumptions in calculating the rates of party saturation among men and women does not changes the results in a major way, in particular among those in the 31-60 age group. Whichever method is used, it turns out that 21-22 percent of the men between the ages of 31 and 60 were party members in 1973. If we make a few more assumptions, then we can estimate that this figure rises to the vicinity of 25 percent for men in this age group in urban areas.[18] (Of course, as table 5.3 indicates, the proportion of women who are party members is correspondingly low.)

As has been repeatedly reported, party membership in the Soviet Union varies not only with age and sex, but also with socioeconomic variables such as education and occupation. Thus, in 1973, 32 percent of those with a complete higher education were party members, compared

**Table 5.2.** Party saturation among men, by age group, 1973.

| Age group | Total population | Party members and party saturation | | | | | |
|---|---|---|---|---|---|---|---|
| | | Methodology A | | Methodology B | | Methodology C | |
| 18 – 25 | 16,727,000 | 640,000 | 3.8% | 682,000 | 4.1% | 592,000 | 3.5% |
| 26 – 30 | 6,884,000 | 849,000 | 12.3 | 893,000 | 13.0 | 792,000 | 11.5 |
| 31 – 40 | 17,985,000 | 3,531,000 | 19.6 | 3,692,000 | 20.5 | 3,438,000 | 19.1 |
| 41 – 50 | 14,909,000 | 3,333,000 | 22.4 | 3,358,000 | 22.5 | 3,380,000 | 22.7 |
| 51 – 60 | 7,821,000 | 1,869,000 | 23.9 | 1,792,000 | 22.9 | 1,940,000 | 24.8 |
| 61 + | 8,754,000 | 1,187,000 | 13.6 | 992,000 | 11.3 | 1,267,000 | 14.5 |
| Total | 73,080,000 | 11,409,000 | 100 | 11,409,000 | 100 | 11,409,000 | 100 |

Methodology A assumes an identical age distribution for men and women party members. Methodology B attempts to correct this distribution for the difference in the age distribution of men and women as a whole. Methodology C assumes that the age distribution varies with the percentage of women admitted into the party when each age group was around 30. It assumes 29 percent women in the 18-25 group, 28 percent in the 26-30 group, 25 percent in the 31-40 group, 22 percent in the 41-50 group, 20 percent in the 51-60 group, and 18 percent in the over-61 group.

**Table 5.3.** Party saturation among women, by age group, 1973.

| Age group | Total population | Party members and party saturation | | | | | |
|---|---|---|---|---|---|---|---|
| | | Methodology A | | Methodology B | | Methodology C | |
| 18 – 25 | 16,212,000 | 194,000 | 1.2% | 152,000 | .9% | 242,000 | 1.5% |
| 26 – 30 | 6,985,000 | 253,000 | 3.6 | 209,000 | 3.0 | 310,000 | 4.4 |
| 31 – 40 | 18,751,000 | 1,058,000 | 5.6 | 889,000 | 4.7 | 1,150,000 | 6.1 |
| 41 – 50 | 18,497,000 | 996,000 | 5.4 | 974,000 | 5.3 | 950,000 | 5.1 |
| 51 – 60 | 11,904,000 | 556,000 | 4.7 | 636,000 | 5.3 | 485,000 | 4.1 |
| 61 + | 20,859,000 | 355,000 | 1.7 | 552,000 | 2.6 | 275,000 | 1.3 |
| Total | 93,208,000 | 3,412,000 | 100 | 3,412,000 | 100 | 3,412,000 | 100 |

with 11.7 percent of those with incomplete higher education, 12.1 percent of those with complete secondary education, 6.7 percent of those
with incomplete secondary education, and 2.6 percent of those without
any high school education[19] (These percentages are based on figures
which include all persons over the age of nine.)

While these statistics correctly indicate the correlation of party
membership and education, they are misleading, for they are not adjusted for age and include persons in school, even elementary school
pupils over the age of nine. They exaggerate some of the differences in
the saturation rates among persons of different educational backgrounds,
for all of the college graduates are old enough to be admitted into the
party, while all the other educational groups include younger persons.
For example, the explanation for the relatively low party saturation
among those with incomplete higher education is that this group includes
large numbers of people still in college—people who generally are below
the age at which most admission into the party takes place.

Data on the age distribution of those with different levels of education are not available for 1973, but they were published in the 1970 census. The overall saturation levels were a bit lower in 1970 (10.6 percent
among those over 30, compared with 10.8 percent in 1973), but the difference are small enough that the 1970 statistics should be quite adequate
for our purposes. What they clearly demonstrate, as table 5.4 shows, is

Table 5.4. Party saturation among persons over thirty, by level of education,
1970

| Level of education | Total population | Party members | Party saturation (%) |
|---|---|---|---|
| Complete higher | 6,377,000 | 2,265,000 | 35.5 |
| Incomplete higher | 945,000 | 285,000 | 30.2 |
| Complete secondary | 17,097,000 | 4,033,000 | 23.6 |
| Incomplete secondary | 22,915,000 | 3,037,000 | 13.3 |
| Complete and incomplete elementary | 67,495,000 | 2,556,000 | 3.8 |
| Total | 114,829,000 | 12,176,000 | 10.6 |

*Sources:* Data for party members were extrapolated from *Partiinaia zhizn'*
no. 14 (July 1973), p. 16; total population, *Itogi vsesoiuznoi perepisi naseleniia
1970 goda* (Moscow, Statistika, 1972), III, 6-7.

that party membership really begins to take on a mass character among those persons over 30 years of age who have at least a high school education. Of this group 27 percent are party members, and this figure includes women as well as men.

When we attempt to distinguish between levels of party saturation among men and women of different educational levels, we are on less certain grounds in our extrapolations. In addition to making assumptions about the similarity or dissimilarity of the general age distribution among men and women party members, we must also speculate about the pattern of educational distribution among party members of different sexes. Again, as tables 5.5 and 5.6 demonstrate, we face the problem that the various educational groups within the population as a whole are not divided proportionately among men and women. There are nearly 20 percent more men with higher education, but nearly one and three-quarters times as many women as men with elementary education. In particular, in 1970 there were 24,350,000 women over the age of 55 who never attended high school, compared with 10,495,000 men;[20] and this interaction of the uncertainties in age and education distributions of party members is a worrisome fact.

Nevertheless, any attempt to explore the consequences of our assumptions reveals that, as in the case of age distribution, it would take very extraordinary irregularities to affect the saturation rates by more than a few percentage points. Thus, Methodology B of tables 5.5 and 5.6 pro-

Table 5.5. Party saturation among men over thirty, by level of education, 1970.

| Level of education | Total population | Party members and party saturation | | | |
|---|---|---|---|---|---|
| | | Methodology A | | Methodology B | |
| Complete higher | 3,464,000 | 1,744,000 | 50.3% | 1,870,000 | 54.5% |
| Incomplete higher | 525,000 | 219,000 | 41.7 | 237,000 | 45.1 |
| Complete secondary | 7,869,000 | 3,105,000 | 39.5 | 3,116,000 | 39.6 |
| Incomplete secondary | 10,746,000 | 2,338,000 | 21.8 | 2,364,000 | 22.0 |
| Complete and incomplete elementary | 24,506,000 | 1,968,000 | 8.0 | 1,787,000 | 7.3 |
| Total | 47,110,000 | 9,374,000 | 19.9 | 9,374,000 | 19.9 |

In methodology A, it is simply assumed that 77 percent of the Communists in each education group are men. In methodology B, an attempt is made to adjust for the differences in the distribution of men and women in each group.

Table 5.6. Party saturation among women over thirty, by level of education, 1970

| Level of education | Total population | Party members and party saturation | | | |
|---|---|---|---|---|---|
| | | Methodology A | | Methodology B | |
| Complete higher | 2,913,000 | 521,000 | 17.8% | 395,000 | 13.6% |
| Incomplete higher | 420,000 | 66,000 | 15.7 | 48,000 | 11.4 |
| Complete secondary | 9,228,000 | 928,000 | 10.1 | 917,000 | 9.9 |
| Incomplete secondary | 12,169,000 | 699,000 | 5.7 | 673,000 | 5.5 |
| Complete and incomplete elementary | 42,989,000 | 588,000 | 1.4 | 769,000 | 1.8 |
| Total | 67,719,000 | 2,802,000 | 4.1 | 2,802,000 | 4.1 |

duces an estimated party saturation of 10.8 percent among women over 30 with at least a secondary degree, compared with 44 percent of the men with these characteristics. If we made the extreme assumption that the number of women Communists over 30 with a secondary degree were to be 50 percent greater (that is, 2,040,000 such women instead of 1,360,000, 73 percent of all women Communists instead of 49 percent), the saturation rate among this group would rise only to 16.2 percent and that among comparable men would decline only to 38.3 percent. Even if there were not a single woman party member without a secondary degree (which obviously is untrue), then 32 percent of all men over 30 with a secondary degree or better would still be party members.

In short, when we talk we talk about party membership among men in the Soviet Union, we are talking about a political activity that is extremely widespread in comparison with the typical levels of political activity in the West—particularly among men who have at least ten years of schooling (the amount required for a secondary school degree) and who have reached the age of "settling down."[21]

It could be argued, of course, that this discussion places far too much emphasis upon party membership among men and that very high rates of membership among educated males over 30 says little about the dispersion of potential influence—except that it is not dispersed to women. However, at a minimum, the relatively late age of party admission and the male-female imbalance within the membership do have the consequence of ensuring a far wider representation of mature family units within the party than is indicated by overall party statistics. If there is frequent communication within the family, if husbands pass on privileged information received through the party channel of communication, if they use their access to communicate the grievances of their respective wives and children as well as their own, then the large proportion of men enrolled in the party implies that the benefits of party membership are much more broadly diffused among family units than we have realized.

Moreover, even the participation rates among women over 30 with at least secondary education—low as they are in comparison with those of Soviet men—are fairly comparable with rates found in the West, at least if membership were to entail considerable activity. To think of such a Communist party as a "priesthood" makes no sense at all, and even to call it "an elite" requires us to recognize that it is, indeed, "an elite of a rather peculiar kind."[22]

The analysis of party saturation has thus far been essentially limited to one particular date. Yet major longitudinal questions obviously are close to the surface, for the percentage of Soviet citizens with higher and secondary education is rising rapidly. If the levels of party saturation among the respective educational groups remain the same, then the size of the party must also increase rapidly. Conversely, if party membership does not grow sufficiently, then the saturation levels among the better-educated citizens inevitably will decline.

The possibility of a change in the levels of party saturation is raised even more strongly by a reduction in the rate of growth of party membership over the last decade.[23] In July 1965 the Central Committee passed a decision "About Serious Deficiencies in the Work of the Kharkov Oblast Party Organization in Party Admission and the Training of Young Communists," which called upon lower party organs to take greater care in admitting new members—implicitly to raise their standards.[24] Following this decision, the number of persons admitted into the party did decrease. In the period 1962-1965, 760,000 persons a year became candidate members of the party, but this figure dropped to 600,000 a year in the period 1966-1970 and to 493,000 in 1971 and 469,000 in 1972.[25]

Yet these figures can be—and often have been—misleading to the outside observer. In the first place, even with the reduced rates of admission, the number of party members increased 26 percent from 1965 to 1973, compared with only 11.2 percent for the adult population (as measured by the number of persons registered to vote in the elections).[26] The second and even more important fact is that party members are not admitted from the population as a whole, but for the most part from a relatively narrow band of the population: those between their mid-twenties and mid-thirties. Because of the very low birth rates during World War II, there has been an abnormally small age cohort affecting the various institutions through which it passes, and over the last decade it has been reaching the age of party admission. Quite aside from questions of party policy, the number of admissions into the party would have dropped sharply unless the saturation rates among young adults had increased rapidly.

The nature of the World War II baby problem can easily be gleaned from an examination of the statistics on age distribution in the 1970 census. In that year there were nearly 25 million persons in the 5-9 and 10-14 age groupings and 22 million between the ages of 15 and 19. However, there were only 17.1 million persons between the ages of 20 and 24 and 13.8 million in the 25-29 group. The 30-34 age group, on the other hand, contained 21 million people.[27] The meaning of this "trough" in the population for the level of party saturation is clearly indicated in table 5.7: the number of persons admitted into the party could decline sharply, but the saturation rates among the age groups during which admission usually occurs could remain fundamentally unchanged.

It should be noted that the significance of the demographic factor for the pattern of party admission is not limited to the last decade. For example, at least a part of the explanation for the major increase in party membership in the 1950s and early 1960s must be the differences in World War II losses among different age groups. There were 57 million persons between the age of 20 and 34 in 1959, an average of 3.8 million

Table 5.7. Party saturation, by age group, 1965, 1967, 1973.

| Age group | 1965[a] | 1967 | 1973 |
|-----------|---------|------|------|
| 18 – 25   | 3.1%    | 2.2% | 2.5% |
| 26 – 40   | 11.0    | 11.5 | 11.2 |
| 41 – 50   | 10.7    | 11.8 | 13.0 |
| 51 +      | 5.5     | 6.5  | 8.0  |
| Total     | 7.9     | 8.3  | 8.9  |

Sources: Partiinaia zhizn', no. 10 (May 1965), p. 13; no. 19 (October 1967), pp. 9, 16; no. 14 (July 1973), p. 19. The 1965 and 1967 age distributions were extrapolated from the 1959 and 1970 census data. The age distribution for 1973 came from Narodnoe khoziaistvo v 1972 g., p. 34.

[a]The age categories in the data were actually 18-25, 26-39, 40-49, and 50 + .

for each year, while there were but 2.2 million persons for each year, in the 35-44 age group (the one that had been knocking on the doors of the party in the previous decade).[28]

Similarly, the 1970 census figures make it perfectly clear that the Soviet leadership will soon face a basic decision with respect to the nature of party membership. By 1950 the effects of World War II had ended, and for 15 years thereafter nearly 5 million babies a year were born and survived. In the mid-1970s this group is just beginning to reach the age of large-scale party admission. If the intake of new members were to continue to drop (or even to rise very slowly), the saturation rates would be affected significantly.

The question of the stability of party saturation among men and among education groups is much more difficult to discuss. We have seen that the percentage of women admitted to the party has been increasing in recent years, but the exact meaning of this change is unclear. The saturation levels for all those over 40 has been rising during the last decade, and conceivably some of the increase in the percentage of women members is reflected in this fact, for, of course, these are the age levels at which women begin to outnumber men. The percentage of women among political and administrative officials has risen from 27 to 34 between 1959 and 1970, that among enterprise officials from 14 to 17,[29] and conceivably many of these women are being admitted into the party in middle age when their children have become older and they have more time for outside activities. However, this is merely speculation—and not very confident speculation at that—and the plotting of the actual trend in saturation rates among men (which at the most still involves a change of not over a percentage point or two in the younger age brackets) is too sensitive to the methodological differences embodied in tables 5.2 and 5.3 to be done with any assurance at all. In any case, if the trend toward the admission of more women were to continue—and it certainly did in the 1973-1975 period[30]—obviously the maintenance of the existing saturation rates among men would require a larger intake of new members than would otherwise be necessary.

Trends in party saturation among educational groups are even more difficult to discuss, for information about the age distribution of persons with various levels of education is available only at the time of the census. This statistic is vital because of the continuing sharp rise in the educational level of those in their twenties. If we forget about age distribution and simply divide the number of Communists with a given education level by the total number of persons with that education, we find (as table 5.8 demonstrates) that party saturation among college graduates has remained essentially stable in the post-Khrushchev period, despite the increase in

Table 5.8. Party saturation among college graduates of all ages, 1959-1973.

| Year | Communists with higher education | Persons with higher education | Party saturation (%) |
|------|----------------------------------|-------------------------------|----------------------|
| 1959 | 1,047,864 | 3,800,000 | 27.6 |
| 1965 | 1,763,262 | 5,600,000 | 31.5 |
| 1967 | 2,097,055 | 6,400,000 | 32.8 |
| 1971 | 2,819,642 | 8,800,000 | 32.0 |
| 1973 | 3,209,605 | 10,000,000 | 32.1 |

Sources: *Partiinaia zhizn'*, no. 5 (May 1965), p. 11; no. 19 (October 1967), p. 4; no. 14 (August 1973), p. 16; *Narodnoe khoziaistvo v 1964 g.*, p. 33; *1967 g.*, p. 34; *1970 g.*, p. 23; *1972 g.*, p. 38.

the proportion of young people in this group. (The variations in table 5.8 are statistically insignificant, for they could simply be the result of rounding in the data.)

By contrast, the saturation rate among those who have only graduated from secondary school or who have incomplete higher education has been declining fairly steadily. (See table 5.9.) However, it is not altogether clear what this decline means, for the category includes many young persons who would not normally become party members. Thus, of the 39,500,000 persons with complete secondary education in 1970, 14 percent were under the age of 20, and another 37 percent were between the ages of 20 and 29. Partly because of party emphasis on universal secondary education, partly because of the differences in the birth rates during and after World War II, the number of young people with secondary education has increased enormously in the post-Khrushchev period. (The number of those in the "complete secondary education" category rose 2,687,000 a year in the period 1965 to 1973, compared with 800,000 a year from 1959 to 1965.)[31]

The real question about the levels of party saturation among those over 30 with secondary education is, as it often has been in previous analyses, the policy of party admission to be followed in the near and intermediate future. The bulge of post-World War II babies, whose leading edge is 27-28 years of age in 1975 is also (perhaps with a few years' delay) the bulge of secondary school graduates approaching the age of party admission. However, if we make the rather modest assumption that 65 percent of those between the ages of 10 and 19 in 1970 will eventually complete at least the ten years of schooling required for a secondary de-

**Table 5.9.** Party saturation among persons of all ages with incomplete higher and complete secondary education, 1959-1973.

| Year | Communists with incomplete higher and complete secondary education | Persons with incomplete higher and complete secondary education | Party saturation (%) |
|------|------|------|------|
| 1959 | 2,334,958 | 19,500,000 | 12.0 |
| 1965 | 2,843,260 | 25,000,000 | 15.4 |
| 1967 | 4,319,104 | 29,200,000 | 14.8 |
| 1971 | 5,270,953 | 41,800,000 | 12.6 |
| 1973 | 5,672,926 | 46,900,000 | 12.1 |

gree (and 53 percent of those in the 20-29 age cohort in 1970 had already done so), then the maintenance of the existing saturation rates for educational levels would eventually require two and a half times as many party members from the cohort as from the 20-29 age cohort in 1959 even though the younger group is only some 21 percent larger in size. (See table 5.10.) If one attempted the dubious projections necessary to distinguish between those with higher education and those with secondary education, the number of party admissions required for stable saturation would be even higher.

It would be interesting to try to predict the policy of party admission to be followed in the future. The number of admissions has already begun to rise, for the average annual intake of new candidates in the 1973-1975 period was 543,000, compared with 469,000 new candidates in 1972.[32] Moreover, in late 1976 the Central Committee issued a new decision which, although somewhat ambivalent in character, almost surely calls for an increase in the rate of party admission.[33]

The crucial variable is, however, the degree of increase. When this question was raised with several highly placed Soviet social scientists who should be in a position to know, they gave every indication of never having thought of the implications of the changes in birth rates for levels of party saturation—and, indeed, of not having thought much at all about saturation levels by age and education group, particularly among men. One scholar insisted that he would certainly have heard about a debate on this question within the upper echelons if it were occurring and that he has heard nothing.

Whatever the future policy may be, we in the West must be very careful in our analysis of what is happening. In particular, we must be

**Table 5.10.** Hypothetical number of Communists among three ten-year age cohorts, 1959-1970.

| Level of education | Persons with indicated education | Hypothesized Party saturation (%) | Hypothesized Communists |
|---|---|---|---|
| *20-29 age cohort, 1959* | | | |
| Secondary or higher | 8,711,000 | 27.0 | 2,350,000 |
| Incomplete secondary | 12,380,000 | 13.3 | 1,650,000 |
| Elementary or less | 17,433,000 | 3.8 | 660,000 |
| Total | 38,524,000 | | 4,660,000 |
| *20-29 age cohort, 1970* | | | |
| Secondary or higher | 16,251,000 | 27.0 | 4,390,000 |
| Incomplete secondary | 11,058,000 | 13.3 | 1,470,000 |
| Elementary or less | 3,567,000 | 3.8 | 140,000 |
| Total | 30,876,000 | | 6,000,000 |
| *10-19 age cohort, 1970* | | | |
| Secondary or higher | 30,225,000[a] | 27.0 | 8,240,000 |
| Incomplete secondary | 14,000,000[a] | 13.3 | 1,860,000 |
| Elementary or less | 2,000,000[a] | 3.8 | 750,000 |
| Total | 46,225,000 | | 10,850,000 |

*Sources:* The hypothesized party saturation rates are taken from table 5.4, the population data from *Itogi vsesoiuznoi perepisi naseleniia, 1970 goda,* III, 6-7, and *Itogi vsesoiuznoi perepisi naseleniia 1959 goda, SSSR* (Moscow: Statistika, 1962), pp. 74-75.

[a]Estimates are based on the assumption that 65 percent of the cohort will eventually receive a secondary degree or better and that the number without any high school education will continue to decline. Some small mortality is also assumed.

keenly aware of the implications of the fluctuations in the size of age cohorts produced by World War II. It would be very easy to interpret an increase in party admissions as a movement towards a more open party when, in fact, a small increase in admissions might denote lower saturation rates among groups that have had fairly free access to the party in the past.

To the extent that membership in the Communist party has meaning, the mass character of the "elite" party is a key fact about the USSR that has not been sufficiently absorbed into our understanding of that country. Some might contend, of course, that the degree of party saturation, whether among men or women, has little importance and that the entire statistical exercise in which we have engaged is essentially irrelevant. And, certainly, it is true that every Soviet citizen could be enrolled in the party tomorrow and that such a development might have little more meaning than the universal participation of Soviet adults in elections to the Supreme Soviet.

Yet so far as can be judged membership in the party usually is quite a different matter than voting in elections to the soviets. It involves the obligation to take on "party assignments" (frequently participation and leadership in activities of nonparty institutions and committees), and it provides the member with the opportunity to receive certain information that is not published in the press. When a number of people begin to participate in this type of political and social activity and become knowledgeable about it, everything that we have learned about the political process suggests that responsible officials will sometimes be responsive to some of the input, if nothing else for reasons of morale.

Although many party members remain relatively inactive,[34] the proportion of adult men in the party is very high in comparison with the proportion of politically active adults in the West, and the number of Soviet citizens who participate in nonparty institutions is even higher. Large numbers of party members could be relatively inactive or without influence, and there still would be ample room for the type of limited direct citizen impact on decisions found in the West by such scholars as Robert Dahl. Even if political participation were limited to active party members—and clearly it is not—we need to revise any notion that the Soviet population is peculiarly apolitical in comparative terms.

# 6

## The Impact of Participation: Women and the Women's Issue in Soviet Policy Debates

It is a truism to say that individuals participating on committees and councils must at times affect the nature of the decisions being taken. Although they don't have final authority, citizen participants surely must find that their suggestions or objections are sometimes reflected in the final decisions, and even the overall mood of the committee meeting may sometimes affect the basic direction of the decision. Political scientists often choose to study the influence of individuals or groups on specific decisions, for this type of inquiry is usually characterized by the relative ease of obtaining information. But such studies seldom have any theoretical interest unless existing theory suggests that certain types of influence do not exist and one can demonstrate the contrary. The question that is of major theoretical interest is the impact—or the lack of it—of broader scale participation upon broader decisions and the relationship of different institutional arrangements such as competitive elections to that impact.

It is difficult enough to study the impact of participation in any country, and, of course, the problem of access to data makes it much more difficult in the Soviet case. Intuitively, it would seem that variations in the rates of participation of broad groups with defined goals would be associated with variations in the final policy outcomes. If so, a test of the impact of participation might be the presence or absence of such variation in outcome in the face of variation in participation.

The problem in using an outcome-related methodology in the study of the Soviet Union was to find a broad group with identifiable views, with measurable variations in participation rates from time to time or place to place, and with comparable variations in relevant policy outcomes. An examination of newspaper reports of sessions of the oblast soviets held in the RSFSR from 1967 to 1975 revealed that there was a major variation from oblast to oblast in the participation rate of at least one major group in this forum: women. Thus from 1967 to 1971 they

were only 9 percent of the speakers in soviet sessions in the Tuva
Autonomous Republic and a low 12 percent in Briansk and Voronezh
oblasts, compared at the other extreme with 33 percent of the speakers in
Novgorod oblast and the Chechen-Ingush Autonomous Republic and 37
percent in Kaliningrad oblast. Given this variation, it seems worthwhile
to look at the participation of women in Soviet political life more fully, to
see what issues Soviet women raise in policy debates, and to try to ascertain whether the variations in participation rates in the oblast soviets are
associated in any meaningful way with variations in outcome on some
issue or issues of relevance to women.

    Women's political participation is a many-faceted phenomenon, for
there are various policy discussions in the Soviet Union and they take
place in many settings. At one extreme are the sensitive and secret
debates within the Party Politburo, at the other are the published letters
and articles in soviet newspapers and journals. In between are the myriad
of committee and council discussions such as those which revolve around
local school policy in the district soviet, the teacher's council at the
school, or even the school's parent committee. It would be a mistake to
restrict ourselves to any one type or level of discussion, for the generalizations appropriate to one are seldom universally valid.

    As Western scholarship has emphasized, very few women participate
in the policy debates that take place at the highest level: around the table
at the Politburo, the Secretariat, the Council of Ministers, the collegia of
the ministries, the party bureaus at the republican and oblast level. With
the exception of Ekaterina Furtseva, no woman has ever been named to
the Politburo, and since the early 1920s female representation on the
Central Committee has been no more than 4.2 percent of the membership (3.3 percent in the Central Committee elected at the Twenty-Fifth
Party Congress in 1976—2.8 percent of the voting members and 4.4 percent of the candidate members).[1]

    Similarly, Ekaterina Furtseva and Mariia D. Kovrigina (the Minister
of Health in the mid-1950s) have been the only women ministers in the
postwar period, and Furtseva has been the only female Central Committee secretary. They have been the only women with the right to take part
in the debates in the Council of Ministers and the Secretariat. Presently
there is no woman among the heads of the Central Committee departments (otdels), and there has not been one in the whole postwar period.
Also there seems to be but two women among the approximately 200
deputy department heads and section (sektor) heads of the Central Committee.[2] In April 1975, the number of women among the 550 to 560
deputy ministers and deputy chairmen of state committees on the USSR

Council of Ministers was limited to 7.[3] Consequently, there also must be little female participation in the party-governmental committee meetings attended by officials just below the top level.

The participation rate for women in the top republican and regional collegial bodies is not much higher than in the center. In 1976, 3.8 percent of the members of the republican party bureaus were women,[4] close to the 3.2 percent found by Joel Moses in his study of obkom bureau-level officials in the RSFSR and the Ukraine.[5] In 1975 the proportion of women in the inner core of the executive committees of the oblast soviets in the RSFSR—the chairmen, deputy chairmen, and secretaries of the executive committees—was a great deal higher at 7.8 percent. (Among the other members of the executive committees, which usually include from 7 to 11 persons, the percentage of women rises to 15 percent.) In large cities in the RSFSR, women constituted 21 percent of the members of the executive committee other than chairman, deputy chairmen and secretary.[6]

Yet these figures should not lead us to think that women do not participate in Soviet decision making or in political policy discussions. In the first place, it should be noted that female participation in the large policy bodies with formal authority is much higher than in the inner bureaus, and it is higher at lower territorial levels than in the center. Thus, in early 1976, 31 percent of the USSR Supreme Soviet deputies were women, 35 percent of the deputies at the union republic level, 39 percent of those at the autonomous republic level, 46 percent of those at the oblast level, and 48 percent of those in the cities, raions, and villages.[7] Even within the party the percentage of women among committee members seems to rise sharply in party organs below the central level. In 1975-76, women comprised 23 percent of the members and candidate members of republican and regional party central committees and auditing committees, 29 percent of those members at the city and district level, 25 percent of the members of the party committees and party bureaus of the primary organization, and 31.5 percent of the secretaries of the primary party organizations.[8]

The proportion of women among the speakers at sessions of the large formally supreme bodies is fairly low at the higher levels of the party organizations, but more substantial within the soviets. Only 2 percent of the speakers at the sessions of the all-Union Party Central Committee from 1965 to 1974 were women, 8 percent of those at fifteen sessions of republican central committees in mid-1975, and 10 percent of those in 24 plenary sessions of regional party committees in early 1975.[9] The proportion of female deputies taking part in the work of the Supreme Soviet has not been much higher: 10.5 percent of the speakers at the 1966-73 sessions of the Supreme Soviet, 13 percent of the speakers in committee sessions held from 1968 to 1975.[10] However, in eight republican supreme soviet sessions in mid-1975 women's participation stood at 20 percent and in the soviet sessions of the RSFSR oblasts, krais, and autonomous republics from 1967 to 1975 at 24 percent.[11] (The rate of female participation in the Supreme Soviet debates show no change in pattern over time, but in the regions it rose from 20 percent in 1967-69 to 22 percent in 1969-71, 24 percent in 1971-73, and 30 percent in 1973-75.) In 76 sessions of city soviets in the RSFSR oblast capitals in 1975, women comprised 31 percent of the speakers.[12]

Women's participation in the trade unions is also comparatively high. Almost one-half of the chairmen of trade union organizations at the enterprise level are women,[13] as are 46.1 percent of the members of the republican, krai, and oblast councils and auditing commissions and 34.5 percent of the members of the All-Union Central Council of Trade Unions (VTsSPS).[14] Fifteen percent of the speakers at the 1973-75 plenary sessions of the VTsSPS were women, as were 35 percent of the speakers at 14 oblast trade union conferences early in the year.[15] In addition, the Presidium of the VTsSPS has a commission for work among women, and it in turn has counterparts in the enterprises and farms.[16]

This type of participation could, of course, be dismissed as ritualistic or ceremonial in nature, but such an interpretation would overlook the nature of the audience at the sessions in question. In addition to the nonelite deputies and delegates, the party, soviet, and even trade union meetings invariably are also attended by the top decision makers and administrators in the area, and, whatever the likelihood that an argument made by a speaker will affect the law or resolution adopted at the time, this argument unquestionably does reach those who make subsequent decisions. Even judging by truncated and censored press reports, it also is unquestionably true that speeches in the oblast soviets and other conferences, just like published articles, do not merely reflect a set party line, but generally contain concrete suggestions on matters within the competence of local officials. There is no reason to doubt the autonomy of most of the suggestions being made; there is every reason to assume that they represent a serious attempt to influence party and governmental decisions.

A second fact to remember about female participation is that it varies with the type of policy area (see tables 6.1 and 6.2), and it can become substantial in some areas—notably that of health, education, and welfare. (For several reasons it seems to me far more appropriate to use the "heath-education-welfare" label rather than that of "indoctrination" in describing the center of women's political involvement.[17]) Thus,

Table 6.1. Women speakers by policy subject in soviet sessions of RSFSR
oblasts, krais, and autonomous republics, 1967-75

| Subject of the soviet session | Total number of speakers[a] | Percentage of women |
|---|---|---|
| Health | 507 | 37.7 |
| Socialist obligations taken in honor of holidays | 958 | 35.6 |
| Culture | 291 | 33.3 |
| Education and youth questions | 1261 | 28.9 |
| Trade, services, housing, utilities | 1714 | 26.7 |
| Next year's plan and budget | 5039 | 24.9 |
| Report of the Executive committee | 1646 | 24.4 |
| Industry and consumer goods production | 810 | 23.8 |
| Conservation | 291 | 21.5 |
| Agriculture | 2083 | 19.6 |
| Miscellaneous | 536 | 18.5 |
| Law enforcement and the courts | 453 | 18.1 |
| Construction | 1542 | 13.7 |

Source: Oblast newspaper clippings on the soviet sessions in 60 of the 71 oblasts, krais, and autonomous republics of the RSFSR.

[a]The column "total number of speakers" refers to the total number whose sex was determined. Basically, variations in this column from topic to topic reflect variations in the number of sessions devoted to each topic.

while only 10.5 percent of all speakers in Supreme Soviet sessions from 1966 to 1973 were women, the proportion of women participants in the discussions on health, education, and family matters rose to 31 percent, and the proportion of women speakers in such committee sessions to 24 percent. In the regional soviets the proportion of female speakers in sessions devoted to health, education, or culture was 32 percent compared with 23 percent in sessions devoted to other subjects.

Indeed, the health-education-welfare-culture area is one in which a significant number of women can participate even in debates within the inner committees on which top officials sit. Table 6.2 indicates the proportion of women in top policy positions in this area in the union republics in 1975, and the same pattern is found within the RSFSR regions. Women constitute 11 percent of the ideological secretaries of the RSFSR

**Table 6.2.** Women among top republican officials by area of specialty, summer 1975

| Type of institution | Number of officials | Percentage of women |
|---|---|---|
| Control instruments[a] | 99 | 0.0 |
| Heavy industry, construction, transportation[b] | 156 | 0.6 |
| Agriculture[c] | 89 | 1.1 |
| Light industry, trade, consumer services[d] | 146 | 8.9 |
| Health, education, culture[e] | 115 | 13.0 |
| Social security[f] | 15 | 60.0 |
| The mass media (or "indoctrination")[g] | 86 | 0.0 |

*Sources:* The various Russian-language republican newspapers in the summer of 1975, particularly the issues of June 19th which contained lists of newly elected deputies to the republican Supreme Soviet and then the issues devoted to the subsequent session of the Supreme Soviet.

[a]The officials included here are the organizational secretary of the Party Central Committee, the head of the organizational-party work and administrative organs departments of the Central Committee, the Chairman of the KGB, the Minister of Internal Affairs, the Prokuror, and the Chairman of the People's Control Committee. There are no women among the Ministers of Finance and the Chairmen of Gosplan, who might also be included in this category.

[b]The officials included here are the deputy chairmen of the Council of Ministers supervising these branches, the heads of the industrial-transportation departments of the Party Central Committee, the various construction ministers, the Chairman of Gosstroi, the Minister of Automobile Transportation, the Minister of the Timber and Woodworking Industry, and occasional additional heavy industry ministers named in different republics.

[c]The officials included here are the agricultural secretary of the Party Central Committee, the deputy chairmen of the Council of Ministers supervising agriculture, the head of the agricultural department of the Central Committee, the Minister of Agriculture, the Minister of Reclamation and Water Resources, the Minister of Procurements, and (in one case) the Minister of State Farms.

[d]The officials included here are the deputy chairmen of the Council of Ministers supervising these branches, the head of the light industry-food industry

department of the Party Central Committee, the head of the trade-services or of the trade-planning-financial organs department of the Central Committee (whichever existed in the republic), the Minister of Consumer Services, the Minister of Communal Economy, the Minister of the Food Industry, the Minister of Light Industry, the Minister of Local Industry, the Minister of the Meat and Dairy Industry, the Minister of Trade, and several light industry ministers specific to individual republics.

ᵉThe officials included here are the deputy chairman of the Council of Ministers supervising these branches, the heads of the science-education and culture departments of the Party Central Committee, the Minister of Culture, the Minister of Education, the Minister of Health, the Minister of Higher and Specialized Secondary Education, and the Chairman of the State Committee for Vocational-Technical Education. If the last two types of official (which include no women) are excluded, the percentage of women in the category rises to 16.9.

ᶠThe official included in this category is the Minister of Social Security. If this offical is included with the health-education-culture officials in a general health-education-welfare category, the percentage of women in it would be 18.4 percent —23.1 percent if the higher education and vocational education heads are excluded.

ᵍThe officials included in this category are the head of the propaganda-agitation department of the Party Central Committee, the Chairman of the State Committee for Television and Radio, the Chairman of the State Committee for Publishing, the Chairman of the State Committee for Movies, and the editors of the leading Russian-language and native-language newspaper respectively.

Left out of the table were a few positions unoccupied in the summer of 1975, and a few occupants who were not identified by sex.

---

regional Party committees (the secretary in charge of health-education-welfare questions, as well as propaganda and agitation) identified in the 1966-75 period (N = 113); 11 percent of the heads of the regional education departments in that republic (N = 107); 16 percent of the heads of the regional health departments (N = 116); 31 percent of the heads of the regional social security departments (N = 108); 16 percent of the regional culture departments (N = 99); 20 percent of the deputy chairmen of the executive committees of the regional soviets who are in charge of education-health-culture questions (N = 117); and 34 percent of the heads of the science-education departments of the regional party committees (N = 32). The percent of women was even high among the chairmen of the relevant standing committees of the regional soviets: 32

percent of the chairmen of the education committees and 50 percent of the health and social security committees.[18]

At the city level, the proportion of women among education-health officials in the large cities of the RSFSR is considerably higher than at the regional level. For example, 36 percent of heads of city education departments (N = 36), 23 percent of the city health departments (N = 34) and approximately 50 percent of the deputy chairmen of the executive committees in 1975 were women (N = 34), and this figures stood at 42 percent for 52 "ideological secretaries" of the city party committees in the 1967-75 period. On this type of question, women clearly are in a position to make their voices heard.

A third fact to keep in mind about female participation is that participation in policy debates is scarcely limited to those who sit in legislative bodies or hold high administrative posts. If the rates of participation of American women in policy discussions were judged by the percentage of women in Congress or in the cabinets of the federal or state governments, the conclusions would be little more accurate than if such a judgment were made with respect to the Soviet Union. As Norton Dodge has rightly emphasized,[19] women are extemely well represented among Soviet professionals normally involved in policy advocacy and analysis as part of their vocation (thus in 1970 they constituted 43 percent of the college teachers, 40 percent of the scientists, 45 percent of the journalists and writers, and 82 percent of the economists and planners), and they comprised 32 percent of the "leaders of organs of state administration, Party, Komsomol, trade union, and other public organizations, and their structural subdivisions."[20] Even in the Central Committee apparatus, it seems that more than 18 percent of those responsible staff officials below the level of section head are women—at least among those staff officials who stay in the apparatus until the age of fifty.[21]

Women also, of course, have the opportunity to join voluntary public organizations and participate in their discussions, but the scale of this participation is difficult to determine because of lack of data. Nevertheless, girls and young women are often as politically active in school or young adulthood as their male counterparts—probably much more so in school.[22] Even in the Komsomol they comprised 52.4 percent of the membership in 1974 and 57.1 percent of the secretaries of the Komsomol primary party organization.[23] However, the overall level of female participation declines precipitously with marriage and especially with the birth of a child. Only 23 percent of the party members are women, a figure which means that some 5 percent of all women between the ages of 31 and 60 are party members, compared with some 22 percent of all men of that age group. Although statistics about female involvement in other public organizations are seldom published, Soviet scholars privately report a tendency towards sex segregation in the patterns of participation. Some public organizations are said to be overwhelmingly male in composition (like the auxiliary police or *druzhinniki*), while others (like library and club councils and the parents' committees in schools) are said to be predominantly female in their active membership.[24]

Finally, women also communicate directly with the political authorities or the newspapers, either to register a complaint or to make a policy suggestion. (Twenty percent of the articles and letters with suggestions for change or criticisms published in *Pravda* and *Izvestiia* in early 1975 were written by women; 44 percent of those in *Sovetskaia kultura*—an organ of the Party Central Committee that deals with culture both in the literary-artistic and anthropological senses of the word.

Despite various shortcomings in the published statistics, it is not difficult to gain a rough sense of the degree of women's participation in Soviet policy debates. However, for any analysis of the impact of their participation it is crucial to determine its contents. Are there issues that are of special interest to women that might serve as an indicator of the effect of variations in womens participation?

In principle, it should be easy to compare the contents of women's and men's contributions to Soviet policy debates, at least if one assumes that the published debate is representative of the positions that would also be taken in committee sessions. One could look at women's articles in different forums—perhaps distinguishing among the policy positions taken by women of differing backgrounds—and compare these articles with those written by men of various backgrounds. Such a study would be very illuminating—all the more so because no one has ever attempted to analyze the scope of Soviet published debates and the patterns within them in any comprehensive way, even aside from the question of distinctions between male and female participation. Unfortunately such a study would be very time-consuming if done correctly, and it really requires lengthy treatment.

Here it is impossible to do more than to advance several impressionistic conclusions based on cursory reading and conversations with Soviet citizens—but supplemented by a careful examination of a few months of *Pravda, Izvestiia,* and *Sovetskaia kultura* in late 1974 and early 1975. Nevertheless, even this limited type of immersion in Soviet sources leaves clear impressions about certain types of themes or subjects that are raised in articles and letters written by women.

The first strong impression created by an examination of women's views in the Soviet Union is the absence of any widespread sense of grievance of the type found among Western feminists. This is not a controversial conclusion, for it had been expressed by all Westerners who have looked at the question and it is shared by Soviet scholars with whom one discusses it. One scholar at the Institute of State and Law in Moscow summarized the prevailing attitude succinctly when told that I was writing an article on the "women's question" (*zhenskii vopros*) in the Soviet Union. "It will be a short article," he predicted.

To be sure, the Soviet press does reveal a sense that the behavior and roles of men and women are different in many respects. Statements appear to the effect that girls are more conscientious than boys in school and therefore receive higher grades;[25] that many men believe that "women's work lowers a man" and therefore there is usually real inequality in the division of labor between husband and wife in household duties;[26] that, as a consequence, marriage usually produces a major decline in the level of political activity of young female party members.[27] These assertions are occasionally supplemented by complaints of unfair treatment at work. Thus, one woman foreman reported that her fuel apparatus plant has a "woman's shop" in which women perform basically the same job as men in the other shops but are given the smaller parts to make because their hands are smaller and more agile. Since smaller parts are less expensive and wages are based on piece-work, the women's wages are, in practice, lower than those of men doing the same work.[28]

What seems to be absent from the published Soviet discussion of the position of women is the view that all differences in treatment are wrong or that women are subject to systematic discrimination by the government and employers (and in the Soviet Union they are essentially the same). There are newspaper articles and pieces of fiction that suggest that a woman's lot can be very difficult in the Soviet Union if she must combine a job with housework and the raising of more than one child and has a typical Soviet husband with traditional attitudes toward housework. (These problems are perhaps best expressed in a short novella in *Novyi mir*, Nataliia Baranskaia's *Nedelia kak nedelia*.[29] While policy implications are sometimes drawn in such articles (that labor-saving appliances should be produced in greater quantity, that more efficient procedures should be introduced in the stores, that part-time jobs should be created for women), the problem normally is seen only as one of changing husbands' attitudes.[30] A female newspaper correspondent expressed this attitude clearly when asked why there were many more articles on sex roles and on inequality in the distribution of household duties printed in *Sovetskaia kultura* than in *Pravda* and *Izvestiia*. The answer, she stated, was that these are, after all, "cultural questions" (in the anthropological sense of the word), not political ones.

The degree to which a universalized sense of grievance has failed to develop is best illustrated in a frequently appearing type of article complaining about the low level of pay and the poor working conditions in some occupation or line of work. The article typically refers to the difficulties of attracting and keeping qualified personnel in the occupation, and demands an improvement in wages and working conditions in order to correct the situation. In December 1974 alone, *Pravda* and *Sovetskaia kultura* carried such articles about livestock workers, bookkeepers, sales clerks, waitresses, seamstresses, and graduates of library schools.[31] In practice, low-paying jobs usually contain large percentages of women, and, consequently, these complaints really represent appeals for an improvement in the situation of a group of women. Yet not a single article mentioned that part of the problem might be a tendency—unconscious or otherwise—for women's jobs to be underpaid. The articles written by women were no different in this respect than those written by men.

It could be argued, of course, that Soviet censorship prevents the expression of a sense of discrimination that, in actuality, is deeply felt. Such a possibility is a real one, for while there inevitably must be at least a few ardent feminists in the Soviet Union, no frontal attack on the way women are treated is ever published. However, before concluding that the censorship is creating a totally distorted view of the opinions of Soviet women, two facts should be taken into consideration.

First, there are other policy areas—like that involving the countryside—where a real sense of discrimination does ooze through and around the censor's filter into the Soviet press. The women's question is not so sensitive that one would expect a deep sense of grievance about it to be stifled more effectively than one with respect to the countryside. Yet no such sense emerges from the press, except on the issue of husbands' sharing household chores.

In the second place, when leading women intellectuals in the Soviet Union talk with a Westerner, they often make statements which would not be anticipated if they had been exposed to Western feminist arguments in private and knew the connotations that might be drawn from their words. For example, despite the large number of female heads of household in the Soviet Union as elsewhere, one major woman scholar quite casually explained low wages for doctors by asserting that doctors are predominantly women, that their salaries usually are the second salaries in the family, and that the question of higher wages is of secondary importance (*na vtoroi plan*) for them. Another spoke of the super-feminist of the "women's department type" (*zhenotdelskogo tipa*) as a phenomenon of the past, and fortunately so. Several spoke of lower rates of political participation of women as the result of a natural and not particularly worrisome division of labor: both men and women have regular jobs, and the man combines his with political activities (really duties) and the woman hers with household responsibilities.

Few Soviet women with whom I have spoken would have any quarrel with the female vice-president of the Academy of Pedagogical Sciences and a member of the Presidium of the Committee of Soviet Women who asserted in a published interview that "woman by her biological essence is a mother—a teacher-trainer (*vospitatel'nitsa*)" and that she has "an inborn ability to deal with small children, an instinctive pedagogical approach." This scholar stated that girls rightfully cannot enter 135 of 1110 professions taught in technicums because of the need to consider the girl's "motherly mission," and she defended the preference given to boys in admission to pedagogical institutes (apparently almost any boy who applies is admitted) on the grounds that men teachers are needed in the upper grades so that boys can receive "uncompromising male conversation" (*beskompromissnye muzhskie razgovory*).[32]

What then do women write about that seems to differ from the letters and articles written by men? One of the most frequent types of women's communication is the defense of professional or occupational interests—an appeal either for better working conditions for themselves or for policy change and better funding for the function they perform, the clientele they serve. Men's articles and letters are quite similar in this respect, but the considerable sex segregation within the economy means that men and women often are defending the interests and perspectives of different occupations and professions. Appeals for expenditures in the health-education-culture realm are more likely to be written by women (and to benefit women employed in these realms) than are appeals for support of heavy industry.

A second type of frequent communication by women to the newspapers flows from their child-raising and shopping responsibilities. Again and again one reads a complaint about the quality of some particular consumers goods item, an appeal for more daycare centers, a demand for a change in the local bus schedules or routes to facilitate the dropping off or picking up of children, a complaint about some grievance of her child (for example, the quality of the New Year's tree in the classroom), a plea that musical education be made available to the average child. Many men also write about the quality of specific goods sold in the stores, but the public defense of the interests of the family's children seems predominantly to be an activity of women.

A third center of interest for women writers, as their greater participation in *Sovietskaia kultura* than in *Pravda* and *Izvestiia* suggests, is the realm of culture, broadly defined. Women letter-writers often express interest in literature or the movies. A suggestion that better care be give a poet's grave is apt to emanate from a woman, and a debate on the "star system" in Soviet entertainment is likely to be a woman's debate in large part.[33] Women also seem disproportionately to be the source of demands for *"kulturnost"* in behavior (the offenders usually are said to be men) or in entertainment (the offenders seem to be those who cater to teenagers' tastes).

Of course, it should be emphasized once more that many of these conclusions are tentative. Not only do we lack reliable data from public opinion surveys of women's attitudes, but even judgments about the content of women's published contributions to the debate are not supported by a sound statistical analysis of a large number of Soviet articles. Nevertheless, the judgments derive from a considerable reading of the press, and they are not likely to be totally incorrect. Clearly there is reliable evidence on the distribution of women among various professions, and there is widespread testimony that women bear a disproportionate share of the responsibility for housework, shopping, and child-raising. It would scarcely be surprising that their participation in policy debates flows primarily from the activities to which they devote much of their time. We still badly need a comprehensive survey of the patterns of debate and of de facto freedom to publish in the Soviet Union, and an attempt to compare men's and women's contributions to the debate would be an excellent format for such a study.

When we turn to the question of the impact of this participation by women upon policy outcomes, we must face up to perhaps the most difficult problem in political science: the measurement of power. Political science has been very unsuccessful in determining the degree to which a given group has influence or power in the policy arena—the degree to which any participation has an impact—and almost no effort has been made to study the question seriously in the Soviet context.

Obviously we are in no position to observe the impact of women's participation in the Soviet Union—if, indeed, that would be the proper methodology in any case—but there are a few pieces of indirect outcome data that are at least tantalizing in their implication that participation does have an impact. Of course, the first major fact about the women's participation is that its level is considerably lower overall than that of men. A second fact is that women do not raise in print the argument that they are systematically discriminated against in the economy and that wages in women's jobs are systematically lower. If it were hypothesized that participation has an impact in this realm, then one would expect that men's wages would rise faster than women's and that there would be little tendency (despite a very large-scale program in the Brezhnev era to promote greater equality in income distribution)[34] for wages in low paid women's jobs to rise quickly. Unfortunately, we have no information on women's wages, and even the general wage data available on a year-to-year basis relates to very broad branches. However, as table 6.3 indicates, even this information suggests strongly that despite the wage equalization program the wages in branches employing a high proportion of women rose more slowly than in those with more men. The effect is particularly strong if the three branches with a small number of employees—art, credit and state insurance, and communications—are excluded. Correlation is not the same as cause-and-effect, but, at least, the pattern is of the predicted type.

Yet another major fact about women's participation is that it varies considerably from region to region, at least in the regional soviets. What this variation reflects is uncertain, but clearly it is not a random phenomenon. If the variation were random, there should be no correlation between the percentage of women speaking in 1967-71 sessions of an oblast session and the percentage speaking in the 1971-75 sessions, but, in fact, there is a .53 correlation, indicating substantial continuity over time.[35] Women's participation in oblast soviets tends to be slightly greater in more urbanized areas, but this factor explains little of the variation. Most of the variation must be related to such factors as the traditions or political culture of the area, the values of the local elite, the preferences of top regional officials, the degree to which women seek to speak, and so forth.

Regional variation is also pronounced on almost any social welfare indicator that can be imagined. Despite the expectations to which our image of a highly centralized system would lead—and contrary to my own expectations of a few years ago—such indicators as the number of hospital beds per capita, the number of square meters of housing per capita, the proportion of preschool children in daycare centers, and the retail-trade turnover (and, surely, therefore, wages) per capita all differ widely from region to region, both in terms of the concrete number at a particular time and the speed with which the service is being developed. Presumably something must explain these variations, and, at least to the extent that they do not reflect demographic variations built into central appropriation formulas, that explanation surely is related to the power and influence of the different groups involved in the various localities.

In trying to determine whether the regional variation in women's participation is associated with variations in policy outcomes, one is drawn to the availability of preschool daycare as the indicator most closely related to women's concerns on which good regional data is available over

Table 6.3. Wage growth and percentage of women by branch of the economy, 1965-73

| Branch of the economy | Percentage of women in branch | Total number of employees (in thousands) | Ruble wage 1965 | Ruble wage 1973 | Percentage growth in ruble wage 1965-73 |
|---|---|---|---|---|---|
| Transportation | 24 | 8705 | 106.0 | 156.7 | 47.8 |
| Construction | 29 | 10091 | 111.9 | 163.6 | 46.2 |
| Sovkhozy and other state agricultural enterprises[a] | 45 | 9211 | 74.6 | 117.5 | 57.5 |
| Art | 45 | 434 | 78.2 | 99.0 | 26.6 |
| Science | 49 | 3735 | 116.8 | 147.3 | 26.1 |
| Industry | 49 | 32875 | 104.2 | 147.2 | 43.2 |
| Housing, communal economy, and consumer services | 53 | 3527 | 72.0 | 102.0 | 41.7 |
| State and political apparatus | 63 | 2087 | 105.9 | 126.2 | 19.2 |
| Communications | 68 | 1465 | 74.2 | 107.5 | 44.9 |
| Education and culture | 73 | 8708 | 93.6 | 120.5 | 28.7 |
| Trade and public eating | 76 | 8392 | 75.2 | 101.8 | 35.4 |
| Credit and state insurance | 80 | 465 | 86.3 | 123.1 | 42.6 |
| Health, physical culture, social security | 85 | 5522 | 79.0 | 99.0 | 25.3 |
| National average | 52 | 97466 | 96.5 | 134.9 | 39.8 |

Source: Narodnoe khoziaistvo SSSR v 1973 g. (Moscow, Statistika, 1974), pp. 583 and 586-587.

[a] The Soviet data on the basis of which this table is constructed excludes collective farmers.

time. It is a policy concern that is actually expressed by Soviet women in the press, and it would also be predicted to be a major policy concern if the views of Soviet women were actually closer to those of Western feminists than this essay has suggested. Moreover, it has been a policy area of considerable activity during the Khrushchev and Brezhnev periods, with a major increase in the proportion of preschool children enrolled in these institutions during these years. In 1959 approximately 12 percent of children up to age six in the RSFSR were in nursery school or kindergarden, but this figure rose to approximately 39 percent in 1970.

On the daycare indicator, as on others, there was great diversity from region to region in 1970. The proportion of children enrolled in such institutions ranged from 10 percent in the Dagestan Autonomous Republic at one extreme to 70 percent in Magadan oblast and the Komi Autonomous Republic at the other. Unfortunately, information is not available to me on the regional levels of women's participation for the whole span of years in which the 1959-70 rates of growth in daycare centers were really determined, but it does turn out that those regions with highest female participation rates in the regional soviets from 1967 to 1971 also had the most complete daycare facilities in 1970. (Correlation = .19) As table 6.4 indicates, those regions with a high rate of female participation were particularly unlikely to have a poor record in providing daycare facilities, while those with a low rate were particularly unlikely to have an excellent record.

A good deal of the statistical association between women's participation in regional soviets and the level of daycare being provided in 1970 seems related to differences in levels of urbanization from region to region. However, if regression analysis is used to calculate the relationship between the level of urbanization and proportion of children in daycare institutions across regions and one then compares each region's actual record with that which the regression equation would have predicted for its level of urbanization, women's participation again seems related to deviations from the norm, particularly in those cases in which the participation was especially low. In the 20 oblasts and autonomous republics in which women constituted less than 19 percent of the speakers, only 6 had a higher percentage of children in daycare centers than would be predicted for their level of urbanization, while 14 had a lower percentage than predicted. (27 of the other oblasts and autonomous republics had a better than expected record, 18 a worse than expected one.)

A more meaningful indicator of the possible impact of participation would be the relationship of the percentage of women speakers to the record established by the region after the participation had taken place. Unfortunately, data has not been available on the number of children up

Table 6.4. Relation of children in daycare centers to women speakers in soviet sessions in RSFSR oblasts and autonomous republics, 1970 (percentages)

| Women speakers in soviet sessions 1967-71 | Children in daycare centers[a] | | |
|---|---|---|---|
| | 41 plus | 25-41 | Under 25 |
| 22 | 52 | 41 | 7 |
| | (N = 14) | (N = 11) | (N = 2) |
| 19-22 | 39 | 28 | 33 |
| | (N = 7) | (N = 5) | (N = 6) |
| Under 19 | 20 | 65 | 25 |
| | (N = 2) | (N = 13) | (N = 5) |

Sources: The information on percentage of women speakers was based on the author's count of speakers reported in newspaper clippings of the oblast soviet sessions. That on the number of children aged 0-6 in the RSFSR regions was extrapolated from *Itogi vsesoiuznoi perepisi naseleniia 1970 goda* (Moscow, Statistika, 1973), II, pp. 76-162. The date on the number of children in daycare institutions comes from *Narodnoe khoziaistvo RSFSR v 1958 g.* (Moscow, Gosstatizdat, 1959), pp. 495-498 and *Narodnoe khoziaistvo RSFSR v 1969 g.* (Moscow, Statistika, 1970), pp. 384-387.

[a]The term "day-care centers" includes nursery schools (*iasli*) and kindergardens (*detskie sady*).

to age six at the oblast level other than in census years, but the annual statistical handbooks of the RSFSR do reveal the number of children in pre-school institutions in each region. From this source it is at least possible to determine the percentage increase in the number of such children from the beginning of 1970 to the beginning of 1974 and to compare the results with the data on 1967-1971 women's participation.

In practice, it naturally turns out that the regions with the highest proportion of children enrolled in preschool institutions in 1970 were the regions with the smallest percentage increase in the number of children enrolled from 1970 to 1974. (The correlation between 1970 enrollment and 1970-74 percentage increase is -.41.) If the system was already excellent, it had little room or reason for especially rapid improvement. Given the already noted relationship between the 1970 level of daycare provided and that of 1967-71 women's participation in the regional soviets, it follows that many of the regions with a high percentage of women speakers inevitably had a slow growth in their daycare systems between 1970 and 1974. Conversely, those regions with a poor daycare system in 1970 (and, concurrently, low levels of women's participation in the soviets on the average) not unnaturally showed an above-average percentage increase simply because of the small size of the original base. The consequence of these two factors is a negative correlation ( – .15) between the 1970-74 growth in number of children in daycare institutions and the 1967-71 levels of participation.

Yet there were regions which provided a middle-range level of daycare in 1970, and in these cases the picture is quite different than the overall correlation suggests.[36] In the 25 oblasts and autonomous republics that had from 25 percent to 40 percent of the children in daycare institutions in 1970, there was a fairly strong relationship between women's participation in the soviets and the 1970-74 percentage rate of growth in the number of children enrolled in daycare institutions. Of those 12 regions in which at least 22 percent of the speakers were women, 10 experienced a 15 percent or higher increase in the number of children enrolled, while 2 had a lower growth rate; of those 18 regions with less than 22 percent female speakers, 5 had at least a 15 percent increase in number of children enrolled, while 13 had a lesser increase.

One can, of course, make what one wants of the data. The strength of the statistical relationships is not extremely high—as no one would expect it to be. Certainly it would be desirable to have a longer run of data on women's participation to judge whether the relationship is a consistent one. Certainly it could be argued that it is the presence of daycare centers that permits participation, rather than participation that leads to greater attention to women's concerns. (However, women elected to the regional soviets scarcely are likely to have trouble finding places in daycare centers for their own children.) Certainly it is quite possible that participation in the oblast soviet is less important in its own right and simply reflects general participation rates in the oblast, including other institutions and settings in which the real impact is made.

Nevertheless, we *do* remain with the fact that there is tremendous variation in the percentage of women speaking in soviet sessions from one region to another. From the perspective of the directed society models, this is a surprising finding in itself. We *do* remain with the fact that this variation was correlated with the relative performance of the region in providing daycare facilities. At a minimum, this correlation suggests the need to continue to explore the relationship of local participation to differences in outcomes, and it further suggests the need to give more thought to participation in institutions that we have dismissed as purely ceremonial in character—and more thought to the role of the institutions themselves. If relationships prove to exist on other questions as well, and I suspect they will, then obviously there would be no reason to believe that it is only women's participation that has impact. And, of course, as has been seen, the differentials in the level of male and female participation has not been associated with a lower level of wages for the sex that participates the most.

# 7

# Centralization and Decentralization in the Soviet Administrative System

One of the most difficult variables to determine is the real degree of centralization or decentralization in any governmental or administrative system, for formal rules and decrees often bear little relationship to actual administrative behavior in this respect. The problem of analysis is particularly difficult in the Soviet Union, where local governmental units officially have been subordinated both to the local authorities and to a ministerial line-of-command. In such a situation very important variations could occur in the relative influence of the "vertical" and "horizontal" supervisors without any formal legal change taking place. The subject is as vital to study as it is difficult, involving questions of administrative practice and the meaningfulness of Soviet democracy in the localities.

A scholar studying the extent of centralization or decentralization in a foreign country—especially one with an economic, political, and social system unlike his own—faces particular difficulties. He does not have the citizen's understanding of informal "rules" of behavior, and he may find it hard to obtain many interviews with administrative officials. For this reason he often must try to utilize nontraditional methodologies, hoping thereby to ascertain indirectly what is not easy to learn directly.

This chapter will attempt to use one such nontraditional methodology in judging the trend in the degree of centralization in one aspect of the Soviet administrative system: budgeting and planning in public health. It is based on the assumption that in a system in which plans and budgets are confirmed at higher levels, the patterns of policy outcomes that emerge over time may illuminate the real degree of centralization in the system. The more the regional variation deviates from announced central norms, the more the center presumably is willing to permit greater regional autonomy in decision making. Or perhaps in a system with subordination of local administrative units both to a ministry and to local authorities, greater regional variation may show that the local authorities (or the local public) have greater influence over the local administrative unit relative to that of the ministerial line of command.

A complete picture of the degree of regional variation would require an examination of many policy outcomes, but this task needs far more time and information. Since this essay is more an illustration of a methodology than a definitive statement about the Soviet administrative system, it will focus on a single indicator—the number of hospital beds per 10,000 population—but the indicator chosen is the crucial one on which other health planning and budgeting is based in the Soviet Union, as in many other countries. Moreover, it is an indicator on which there are central norms against which one can judge actual regional performance. The impression of centralization or decentralization that is conveyed by this narrower study can be confirmed or refuted by an examination of different types of regional data in other policy areas.

The precise formulas for the calculation of hospital bed norms in the Soviet Union do not seem to have been published, but clearly they provide for some variation in the number of hospital beds per 10,000 population to correspond to demographic variations in the regions. The most important of these is obviously the relative size of the region's urban and rural population, for in recent years the norm for rural areas has been placed at 90-110 beds per 10,000 population and that for urban areas at 110-130 beds.[1] These norms are not absolutely obligatory, and health authorities are instructed, where possible, to utilize local resources in improving health services even beyond the norms. Nevertheless, the norms are meaningful in the planning and budgetary process, and the stronger the intention of central authorities to maintain uniform national standards, the more closely one would expect the actual regional figures to approximate the norms.

If it is assumed that the center has planned for the number of hospital beds per 10,000 population in the different oblasts on the basis of the percentage of urban population in a region, then one can take the *actual* figures for hospital beds per 10,000 population and for percentage of urban population in each oblast and utilize regression analysis to calculate the actual statistical relationship between the two variables at any specific time for which the statistical handbooks provide data.[2] When this is done, the formula that most closely expresses the statistical relationship in the data for the krais, oblasts, and autonomous republics of the RSFSR on January 1, 1974 is: beds in an oblast equals 87 plus .54 times the percentage of urban population in the oblast. Thus, according to this formula, an oblast with 100 percent rural population should have had 87 beds per 10,000 population in 1974, while one with 100 percent urban population should have had 141 beds. An oblast with 60 percent urban population should have had 119 beds—87 plus (.54 times 60).[3]

What is important for an understanding of the degree of centralization in the administrative system is not the regression formula itself, but the amount of variance it explains—the degree to which the actual number of beds in the respective oblasts corresponds to the number which the formula predicts for them on the basis of the percentage of their urban population. In a totally centralized system with very rigid norms, each oblast presumably would have almost precisely the number of beds appropiate for its percentage of urban population, and this fact would be expressed in an explained variance figure approaching 1.0. In a more decentralized system in which the horizontal supervision is stronger, there presumably would be much more variation from the norm, as different local priorities, financial resources, capabilities of local leaders, and other factors associated with the phrase "local democracy" affected the outcome. In the most extreme such cases the explained variance would drop towards 0.0.

To understand trends in the degree of centralization over time, one should employ such an analysis for each of a number of years and examine the changes that occur. The results of this analysis are found in table 7.1. From the beginning it should be recognized that regression analysis can be sensitive to extreme cases, and summary figures such as presented in table 7.1 should be interpreted with great care. However, the actual scatterplots of the data (for example, see figures 1 and 2) indicate no major irregularities (especially once Magadan oblast is removed), and hence the normal interpretations of the statistics are likely to be accurate.

Table 7.1 contains four columns, and three of the four have a distinctive meaning. The figures in the column labeled "Constant" indicate the number of beds per 10,000 population that would be found in the average hypothetical oblast with a zero percent urban population. While a striking change in the overall equation might distort the meaning of these statistics, the steady rise in the constant basically testifies to the persistent party policy of promoting a continuous increase in the number of hospital beds in the country as a whole.

The figures in the column labeled "B slopes" indicate the number of beds per 10,000 population that should be added to the constant for each percentage point of urban population in a given oblast. In general, the greater this figure, the greater the difference between the number of beds in urbanized and rural oblasts. The differences between many of these slopes are, in practice, quite small, but since the mid-1960s and particularly since 1970, there does seem to have been a significant decline in their size. This decrease presumably means an increase in the relative level of appropriations for hospital beds in rural areas as compared with

Table 7.1. Regression formulas and explained variances with respect to the relationship between beds/10,000 population and percentage of urban population in oblasts[a] and autonomous republics of the RSFSR, 1957-74

| Year | Constant | B slope | Correlation | Explained variance |
|---|---|---|---|---|
| 1/1/1957 | 42 | 0.63 | 0.68 | 0.47 |
| 1/1/1958 | 43 | .65 | .70 | .49 |
| 1/1/1959 | 44 | .66 | .68 | .46 |
| 1/1/1960 | 46 | .68 | .68 | .47 |
| 1/1/1961 | 48 | .70 | .68 | .47 |
| 1/1/1962 | 50 | .71 | .69 | .47 |
| 1/1/1963 | 54 | .70 | .66 | .44 |
| 1/1/1964 | 56 | .69 | .66 | .43 |
| 1/1/1965 | 60 | .67 | .65 | .43 |
| 1/1/1966 | 62 | .68 | .66 | .43 |
| 1/1/1967 | 66 | .65 | .64 | .42 |
| 1/1/1968 | 69 | .65 | .62 | .39 |
| 1/1/1969 | 70 | .66 | .60 | .37 |
| 1/1/1970 | 72 | .68 | .58 | .34 |
| 1/1/1971 | 76 | .67 | .55 | .30 |
| 1/1/1972 | 81 | .61 | .52 | .27 |
| 1/1/1973 | 84 | .57 | .46 | .21 |
| 1/1/1974 | 87 | .54 | .46 | .21 |

[a]Magadan oblast is excluded from the calculations.

urban areas—a trend toward greater equalization of conditions between the city and the country. It may well reflect the impact of the 1969 decision of the Central Committee and the Council of Ministers dealing with public health.

The interpretation of the columns entitled "Correlation" and "Explained Variance" (explained variance is the correlation squared) is a much more subjective matter. As figure 1 from 1958 indicates, an explained variance of .49 still involves considerable dispersion from a straight line, while figure 2 from 1974 demonstrates that an explained variance of .21 still has a discernible pattern. A scholar is free to emphasize that either of these explained variances is quite high or that either still leaves much to be explained.

Whatever the significance of the absolute figures in these columns,

Figure 1. Urban Population and Beds per 10,000 Population. RSFSR Regions, January 1, 1958.

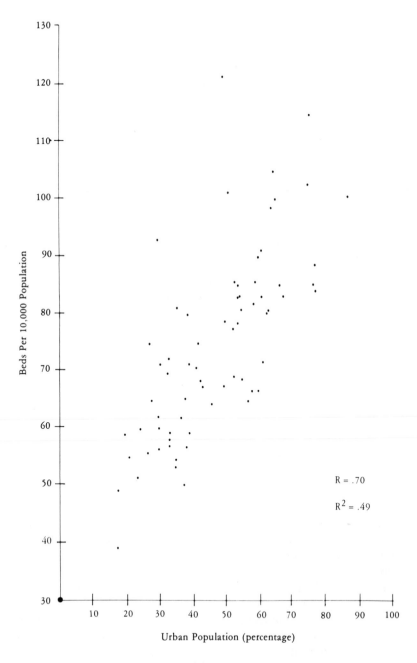

Figure 2. Urban Population and Beds per 10,000 Population. RSFSR Regions, January 1, 1974.

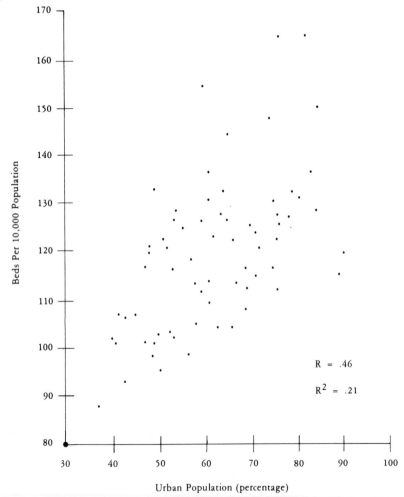

Urban Population (percentage)

the trend in the magnitude of explained variance over time seems to have an obvious meaning. Throughout the late 1950s and early 1960s the figures are quite stable, but in the second half of the 1960s they begin to drop—a process that accelerates in the early 1970s. It seems clear that while the process of plan and budget confirmation remained much the same during this entire period, the localities were, in later years, given a greater de facto opportunity to deviate from central norms in accordance with local priorities and capabilities. The data suggest that at least in this key aspect of public health planning there was a trend in the direction of decentralization in the late 1960s and early 1970s in the form of greater power for the local soviets and for those political forces and influences that shape their decisions.

Since there is variation in per capita hospital beds from region to region, even controlling for the proportion of urban population, other factors than the enforcement of central norms obviously are at work in health planning. The next step must be an attempt to explore what these factors might be.

If one examines the figures for any one year, the available indicator that is most overwhelmingly associated with the regional variations in beds per capita is retail trade turnover per capita in the oblast—an indicator that almost surely is closely linked with the oblast's per capita income and the financial resources available in it. For example, the correlation between per capita trade turnover and per capita beds was .80 in 1965, .76 in 1970, and .73 in 1974. Indeed, if per capita retail trade turnover and percentage of urban population are both used as independent variables in a multiple regression equation, the latter adds almost nothing to the explained variance, suggesting the availability of local resources is crucial.

However, from the point of view of an analysis of the dynamics of decision making—or even of the analysis of a recent year—it is highly misleading to emphasize the high correlation between retail trade per capita and beds per capita. Whatever produced the high correlation in 1965 (and, of course, in earlier years as well), the stock of beds that existed in 1965 remained in existence. If both trade turnover and number of beds in an oblast continue to grow incrementally each year (as they will tend to do if lower administrators are encouraged to begin the compilation of the plan by taking the previous year's figures and increasing them by a moderate percentage), the correlation will remain high even if the relationship is no longer important in determining the size of the increase in the number of beds. The fact that the correlation between beds per capita in 1965 and 1974 was .88 and that between retail trade turnover per capita in 1965 and 1973 was .96 testifies to the proposition that the growth was, in fact, incremental.

Thus, for an understanding of decision making in the late 1960s and early 1970s, the focus of analysis must be the size of the increase in beds per 10,000 population from 1965 to 1973. The regional variation in this increase was enormous, ranging from 2 beds per 10,000 population in Kaliningrad oblast to 45 beds in Kurgan oblast. For an analysis of this variation, the important fact is not the .73 correlation between per capita retail trade and per capita hospital beds in 1973, but the .18 correlation between the level of retail trade per capita in 1970 and the increase in the

number of beds per capita. The regions with the most resources as reflected in retail trade turnover had, on the average, smaller increases in
their number of hospital beds per capita.

The factor that is most strongly associated with increase in per capita
beds is the increase in the level of urbanization in the oblast. In the
period 1970 to 1974, when the trend towards decentralization seemed
most pronounced, there was a .53 correlation between these two variables. Yet even this correlation means that 28 percent of the variance has
been explained and 72 percent is still to be explained by other variables.

In regression analysis one standard technique for trying to ascertain
other factors that are at work is an examination of residuals. This involves
an examination on a case-by-case basis of the differences between the
actual figures for each oblast and the figures predicted by the regression
equation and an attempt to ascertain which factors are associated with
actual figures that are respectively higher or lower than the predicted
ones. Thus, in the case at hand, the formula that best relates the 1970-74
increase in the number of beds per capita per 10,000 population to the increase in the level of urban population is: 3.7 plus (1.39 times the
number of percentage points by which the percentage of urban population rose). For example, by this formula, Tambov oblast, whose urban
population rose from 39 percent to 45 percent in these years, would be
predicted to have an increase of 12 hospital beds per 10,000 population
(3.7 plus 1.39 times 6), as would Kirov oblast and Omsk oblast each rising from 55 to 61 percent, and Novgorod oblast which rose from 53 percent to 59 percent. In practice, the increase in beds per 10,000 population
for Tambov oblast was 18 beds, for Kirov oblast 14 beds, for Omsk oblast
8 beds, and for Novgorod oblast 16 beds. The residuals for the four
oblasts were $+6$, $+2$, $-4$, and $+4$ respectively.

As one examines various factors that might explain the deviation of
actual increases in beds per 10,000 population from predicted increases,
one important factor is the number of hospital beds existing in an oblast
in 1970. To be specific, the party did seem to be making an effort to
equalize the number of beds per oblast, presumably by directing extra
funds to those oblasts with the lowest number of beds. The average oblast
had 110 beds per 10,000 population in 1970, but 20 oblasts had fewer
than 100. These were predominantly rural oblasts, and most were undergoing rapid urbanization. (70 percent had an above average percentage
point increase in the percentage of urban population.) As a consequence,
the predicted increase in the number of beds for these 20 oblasts would
have been above average in any case, but, in practice, 15 of the 20 had an
actual increase that was even above the level predicted. Conversely, in the
10 oblasts with over 125 beds per 10,000 population in 1970, only 3 had a

greater increase in the number of beds than predicted, while 7 had a smaller increase.

Another factor that some Soviet newspaper and journal articles and a number of American Sovietologists might consider important is the rate of industrial development in the region. Funds for social services are often provided not only by the relevant ministry, but by the industrial ministries as well, and a heavy influx of industrial investment funds could be associated with an influx of social funds from industrial ministries at the same time.[4] There is, in fact, a small correlation between the rate of industrial development in an oblast and the size of the increase in its hospital beds per capita (.20 in 1965-73; .13 in 1970-73), but these correlations are much smaller than those with growth in percentage of urban population and this factor turns out not to be important in distinguishing between oblasts that did better or worse than predicted by growth in urban population.

On the surface it would therefore seem that much of the unexplained variance in growth of hospital beds must be explained in large part by local political factors: the values of the local population, the capabilities and values of relevant officials in the leadership stratum, the influence of different social groups, and so forth. Unfortunately, a foreigner faces enormous difficulties in measuring such political factors, for the necessary data often cannot be obtained. In two cases, however, there is local political information available to the author, and this information does suggest that the realm is worth exploring.

One type of available political information that might be relevant to variation in growth in the number of hospital beds is the amount of attention given it by local political authorities. The one such indicator that was available was the subject-matter of sessions of the regional soviets, and it does turn out that there was considerable variation in the subjects with which they dealt. Between July 1968 and December 1971, 27 of 49 oblast and krai soviets discussed health questions at one of their sessions, and 22 did not.[5] Of the 27 oblasts in which such a discussion took place, 16 had a bigger growth in the number of hospital beds from 1970 to 1974 than predicted, and 11 a smaller increase; of the 22 oblasts in which there was no such discussion, 8 had a better than predicted increase while 14 had a smaller one.

Another factor that was also associated with the oblast's performance in terms of increase in hospital beds per 10,000 population was the length in office of certain top officials in the oblast—specifically the chairman of the oblispolkom, the head of the oblast health department, and the first secretary of the party obkom. In the 23 oblasts and autonomous republics in which a new chairman of the oblispolkom (or chairman of the council

Table 7.2. Relationship of change in oblispolkom chairman, head of oblast health department, and obkom first secretary to increase in hospital beds per 10,000 population, 1970-74

| Number of changes among the three officials in an oblast, 1969-72 | A larger increase in number of beds than predicted[a] | A smaller increase in number of beds than predicted |
|---|---|---|
| 3 officials changed | 3 | 1 |
| 2 officials changed | 12 | 2 |
| 1 official changed | 8 | 9 |
| No officials changed | 12 | 19 |
| Insufficient information | 1 | 4 |

[a]The prediction, as indicated in the text, comes from a regression equation that relates increase in the number of hospital beds per capita to the percentage-point increase in the percentage of urban population in an oblast.

of ministers in the case of the autonomous republics) was selected in the 1969 to 1972 period, 14 had a larger increase in the number of beds than expected, 9 a smaller one; in the other oblasts, 21 had a larger increase, 24 a smaller.[6] In those 21 oblasts where a new head of the oblast health department was appointed, 15 had a larger increase than predicted, 6 a smaller; in other oblasts 20 had a larger increase, 24 a smaller one. In those 19 oblasts where a new obkom first secretary was elected, 15 had a better record than predicted, while 5 had a poorer one; in the other 52 oblasts, 22 had a better record and 30 a worse one. As table 7.2 indicates, the difference in oblast performance becomes especially striking when one looks at these changes in top officials in cumulative form. It would seem either that a new political or administrative figure is more vigorous in promoting growth in the first years of his or her tenure, or is perhaps more successful in obtaining funds from the republic level at this time.

In conclusion, therefore, it seems that there may be concrete indicators to help illuminate the local political factors that produce some of the variation from locality to locality in the Soviet Union. In any case the scale of variation from oblast to oblast makes it clear that models (notably the totalitarian model and its related successors) implying that all decisions are made in Moscow have serious defects. Of course, any thorough understanding of the Soviet administrative system would require a study of variations in many policy areas and at the city and raion level as well as the oblast and the autonomous republic. It would require an examination of other political factors such as variations in the opinions and priorities of the population and local leaders—an examination that is far beyond the capabilities of a foreign scholar. It is be be hoped that Soviet scholars will find this methodology useful for improving the understanding of the Soviet administrative system, and of the principles of scientific organization of administrative labor (NOUT) in a socialist society.

*Afternote:* This article was written for and submitted to *Sovetskoe gosudarstvo i pravo* in hope that the time might be ripe for this journal to follow the lead of other Soviet journals in less sensitive fields that publish articles by Americans, but the expectation proved mistaken. In some respects the focus that was chosen for this purpose was not precisely the same that it would have been if written originally for a Western audience, for the assumption and interests of the Soviet and Western audiences are different. It does not seem desirable or proper to rewrite the article with a change in focus, but an afternote may be useful in emphasizing several aspects of the article that seem crucial in terms of Western theory.

If written for Western specialists on the Soviet Union, who have often been exposed to the argument that the Brezhnev era has been one of recentralization in political-administrative authority, this essay unquestionably would have attacked that notion more directly. The statistical relationships with respect to political influences are not enormously strong and it may be misleading to conclude the essay with them. The data in table 7.1 are, I think, of quite a different quality, and I believe them to be very sound support for the basic conclusion about the decentralization of real authority in this one policy area. As I argued in the first chapter, I also believe that this decentralization of real power is a general one in the Brezhnev era, but of course the picture almost surely varies somewhat from question to question and from policy area to policy area.

A Western focus would also have emphasized more strongly the basic fact of great variation from region to region on almost any statistical index that is available.[7] The reader may feel some skepticism about the extent to which the impact of holding an oblast soviet session or the change of oblast officials has been conclusively demonstrated (just as similar skepticism may have arisen about the impact of women's participation). An open mind is always advisable until more data are available, yet one fact is indisputable. The regional variation is so great and so "random" in many respects that it absolutely *must* be produced by some local factor either in the present or the past. There is no other explanation that is reasonable. And to the extent that local factors are important, this not only undercuts many of the assumptions of the totalitarian and directed society models, but also reemphasizes the point that the much-maligned citizen participation in local administration is dealing with questions of real importance.

Finally, while the author of *The Soviet Prefects* is scarcely likely to argue that the local party organs are an insignificant factor in the regional decision making process, it is interesting that factors like the topic of the oblast soviet session, the percentage of women speaking in oblast soviet sessions, and a change in the head of the health department of the oblast soviet turn out to be related with variations in indicators such as beds per 10,000 population and growth in the number of children in daycare centers. When we speak of an "oblast," we are dealing with a unit comparable to an American state. Obviously neither the first secretary, the bureau, or even the ideological secretary of such a unit can decide every question in it, and it may well be that the party organs concentrate so heavily on economic matters that the soviet officials frequently have considerable leeway on other matters. It certainly is a question that deserves much more serious research.

# II

## Implications for
## Social Science Theory

# 8

# Inputs and Responsiveness in American Political Science

One of the most striking features of the Soviet political system has been the extent to which the citizenry have been encouraged to engage in "demand input" or "interest articulation," to use the influential concepts of David Easton and Gabriel Almond respectively. The Soviet Union has been a participatory society in almost all senses of the phrase, and the large-scale political efforts that Westerners usually have labeled "mobilization" have in large part been the mobilization of people into political participation of one type or another.

There have, of course, been limitations on the type of major policy demands that can be articulated in the Soviet Union and on the way of representing interests, but party insistence on widespread "criticism and self-criticism" has been, in practice, an insistence on the widespread input of demands as defined in political science. Even in the most repressive years of the late Stalin period, Alex Inkeles (scarcely a pro-Soviet scholar) could describe the situation in the following terms: "It has indeed been remarked that in the United States one criticizes the President but little else, whereas in the Soviet Union one never criticizes Stalin or his policy but does criticize virtually everything else. This generalization is certainly too broad, but it represents an element of reality . . . This criticism gives the people a channel of communication with the party, a means for expressing grievances and complaints and addressing appeals to the distant foci of power in Moscow and elsewhere."[1] In fact, as specialists on the Soviet Union have long recognized, one of the distinguishing features of Stalin's regime was a multiplicity of overlapping institutions providing channels of communication upwards.

Yet the major literature of comparative political science has been strikingly limited in recognizing and evaluating societal inputs in the Soviet Union. Some of the foremost scholars seem flatly to deny their existence, readily observable even under Stalin, and others have fallen into a pronounced inconsistency, as they acknowledge an increase in freedom of debate in one part of their analysis while suggesting its near-total absence in another. Most frequently, as they have compared the Soviet

Union and the West, they have unconsciously shifted their definitions of concepts like "demands," "interest articulation," or "policy initiation" in such a way as to emphasize the freedom of such activity in the West and the well-known party restrictions on it in the Soviet Union.

Whenever major theorists consistently make statements that they themselves would reject upon reflection, there is every reason to think that theory is affecting perception. Indeed, the more obvious the denial of reality that is involved, the more central the theoretical assumptions at work and the greater the need to reexamine the theory in an effort to learn what has gone wrong. Just as clearly the place at which theory and reality diverge so greatly is an excellent point at which to begin the re-examination. If we look at the difficulties in the treatment of demand inputs and interest articulation in the Soviet Union and at the theories (especially the theory of responsiveness) that seem associated with the difficulties, we can explore some of the types of revision of theory that seem suggested by the Soviet experience.

The problems of comparative analysis of inputs in the Soviet Union and the West have been manifold. Perhaps the most basic, as Alfred Meyer has emphasized,[2] is a tendency for scholars to shift the focus of analysis as they turn their attention to the Soviet Union, to raise different questions and study different phenomena, and to define concepts in different ways—without realizing that they have done so. As a consequence, when they discuss the Soviet Union and the West, they unknowingly often compare noncomparable phenomena and therefore inevitably find major differences in the political systems even beyond those that the data might suggest. Invariably, it might be added, the result is to place the Soviet Union in a more unfavorable light.

Consider, for example, the influential textbook on "the governing of men" by Austin Ranney. In the chapter on the nature and determinants of public opinion, the early section is illustrated almost exclusively with American examples and deals with the diversity within public opinion produced by such factors as selective perception, a variety of group memberships, and different socialization experiences. The concluding section on "Public Opinion in USSR" deals, however, entirely with Soviet *policy* toward opinion formation and therefore is limited to a discussion of criticism and self-criticism as traditionally defined, agitation-propaganda, and Lenin's conception of the masses.

Ranney's conclusions flow naturally from his approach. He emphasizes the pluralism in the structure of political inputs in countries such as the United States and the lack of such pluralism in the Soviet Union. In that country "the masses are not . . . permitted to attack the Communist regime in any way, or to attack the party's policies, or to criticize the top leaders of the party . . . Ordinary workers at a collective farm would certainly be hustled off to a slave-labor camp if they publicly argued that the whole idea of collective farms is bad.''[3] Ranney acknowledges that "the Communists have been far from completely successful in molding the opinion of the masses" and that "the party knows that some of the Russian masses hold opinions other than those it prescribes,"[4] but even after accepting V. O. Key's definition of public opinion as "those opinions held by private persons which governments find it prudent to heed," he still summarizes the situation in the Soviet Union in 1965 in the following manner: "The only issues that are genuinely 'controversial' . . . are those on which the government allows 'controversy' . . . Only on these issues can 'public opinion' in anything like the democratic sense be said to exist."[5]

Ranney's approach is not unique. As William Mitchell has pointed out, "Hardly a volume on [totalitarian societies] is without chapters on schools, propaganda, and indoctrination, while very few books on American *politics* treat the same institutions and phenomena."[6] Indeed, the major comparative theorists have been actively hostile to the assertions of the Left that political inputs from American society are significantly shaped, conditioned, or manipulated by the educational system or mass media, even to the point of suggesting that such assertions are nonverifiable and therefore illegitimate.[7] The contrary is true in work on the Soviet Union, and Carl Friedrich is quite typical in emphasizing that suppression of dissent results from the "internalization of ideology." After recognizing the considerable degree of consensus on fundamentals existing in Soviet society in 1965, he contended that "such consensus and the procedures it makes possible ought not to be confused with those of representative government . . . [The] thought control dehumanizes the subjects of the regime by depriving them of a chance for independent thought and judgment."[8]

Not only are different phenomena brought to the center of attention in comparative analysis of the Soviet Union and the West, but commonplace phenomena are often defined in different ways, thereby ensuring that, in practice, different phenomena will be discussed under the same label. A typical example has already been given: Ranney's defining "public opinion" in a way ("those opinions held by private persons which governments find it prudent to heed") clearly requiring that it be present even in Stalin's Soviet Union, but then asserting that public opinion (in quotation marks) can only exist in the Soviet Union on issues that the leadership permits to be controversial.

Such shifts in definition occur repeatedly. In David Easton's *A Sys-*

*tems Analysis of Political Life,* for example, two of the central concepts are "demands" and "gatekeepers." "Demands" is one of the two most important categories of inputs discussed by Easton (the other is "supports"), and it is defined in the broadest terms:

> A demand may be defined as an expression of opinion that an authoritative allocation with regard to a particular subject matter should or should not be made by those responsible for doing so . . . It matters little whether the demand so stated has been voiced to a friend over cocktails, to a fellow-worker between bites of a sandwhich on the end of an I-beam, to fellow sufferers before a meeting of the local ratepayers association or as a complaint, in a traditional society, to a neighboring hawker at a bazaar. Nor does it matter whether the demand has been uttered in public to rouse public support or in secret to get the ear of an effective official or powerful person . . . A call for a binding decision is no less a demand if it is highly general, vague, and complex. Broad pleas for better government, for a more vigorous defense policy, or for greater attention to the underprivileged, without specification of the exact steps to be taken, represent such highly generalized demands.[9]

Easton then introduces the concept of "gateway" to indicate the "structural points in the system . . . regulating the flow along the demand channels,"[10] and he emphasizes the great number of such gateways in a political system such as the American.

> The occupants of the [gateway] roles, whether they are individuals or groups are the gatekeepers . . . Gatekeepers are not only those who initiate a demand by first voicing it; the term also designates those whose actions, once a demand is moving through the channels of the system, at some point have the opportunity to determine its destiny . . . In democracies as we know them today, the formal capacity to convert wants to demands is broadly diffused throughout the system. Each person may tend to his own gate, is even encouraged to do so by injunctions to participate actively in politics . . . If not every man becomes his own converter . . . popular gatekeepers do constitute numerous, widespread structural points through which demands may enter a system.[11]

If we are to take this seriously, then any Soviet worker who tells a friend on the other end of an I-beam, "the government should improve the housing situation" is not only making an input into the political system, but is serving as a gatekeeper who is converting wants into demands. It is perfectly obvious that there is an enormous number of demands and gatekeepers in the Soviet system by these definitions—in fact, a much larger number than in Western political systems, for in a country in which housing is government-owned, even an appeal for a new apartment and for repairs by the landlord fits within these categories.[12]

But how are demands and gatekeepers in the Soviet Union analyzed in *A Systems Analysis of Political Life?*

> The operating rules of [modern totalitarian or dictatorial] regimes . . . require that any want seeking political expression must secure validation through the approval of the leadership or of cadre groups in an approved political party which is close enough to the leadership to be able to interpret its desires and intentions. By thus imposing limits on those who may act as gatekeepers in the conversion of wants to demands, access to the political process is limited and the leadership is able effectively to help regulate the entry of demands. In systems such as these based as they are on the limitation of want conversion, input overload would scarcely be likely to occur or even threaten.[13]

Later in the book Easton makes a similar point, seeming to deny the existence of nearly all demand input from outside ''a restricted elite:'' ''In those systems in which a restricted elite possesses a monopoly over the input of demands, as in various totalitarian regimes, and where whatever popular demands that may be permitted are carefully guided into channels controlled by the elite, volume of demands need not present a major problem. Even though the USSR is a major industrial nation, the Supreme Soviet typically needs to meet only a few weeks a year, so sheltered is it from any influx of demands.''[14]

What is happening in this analysis? How can Easton conceivably deny the existence of a large number of demands in the Soviet Union when it is absolutely obvious, as James Oliver has pointed out, that ''the [Soviet] regime that has undertaken, with great pride and deliberate purpose, more activities than any in modern history [clearly] is confronted with demands covering a wider range of subjects than any regime in history.''[15] How can he deny a problem of demand overload when reformist Soviet economists have repeatedly—and correctly—emphasized that the danger of overload for the top decision makers is very great indeed? The answer is simple. Easton is not taking his own definitions seriously. In the Soviet case—and sometimes in his discussion of the West—Easton is thinking of *effective* demands and of demands involving major policy change, and his image of gatekeepers really is that of the persons at the gates of the transmissions channels, not of those who convert wants into demands.

The same problem of shifting definition arises in Gabriel Almond's use of the phrase ''interest articulation.'' The formal definition, as in the previous case, is a very broad one: ''the process by which individuals and groups make demands upon the political decision makers.''[16] "Interest articulation'' is, to be sure, more limited than Easton's "input of demands,'' for Almond apparently restricts the concept to articulation directly or indirectly aimed at political decision makers and thereby presumably excludes both the demand made to the fellow-worker on the I-beam and the request for an apartment made to the low-level administrator in the housing office. However, an article on the economic reform or other policy question, any bureaucratic policy memorandum, or any letter written to the Central Committee or top governmental officials clearly is part of an interest-articulation process, and, just as clearly, this process has been a rich one in the post-Stalin era and far from non-existent in the last years of Stalin's life.

In one section of the basic statement on comparative politics written by Almond in conjunction with G. Bingham Powell, there is, indeed, some recognition that "demands in some form are made by the peasantry, by non-Russian ethnic groups, by professional and technical personnel, by groups within the bureaucracy, and by groups within the party.'' The totalitarian model is explicitly criticized for suggesting "that there is little or no responsive capacity in the Soviet Union.''[17]

Nevertheless, the basic treatment of Soviet interest articulation in Almond and Powell's *Comparative Politics* flows straight from the totalitarian model. The book contains numerous statements that, if taken seriously, deny the type of interest articulation involved in, for example, the economic debate.

> In systems such as those of Soviet Russia and Communist China . . . interest articulation takes the form of very low-level suggestions within specific bounds, or receives only latent expression . . . Even in the course of the recent relaxation, the elites have been very sensitive to any hint of criticism of the society, let alone the regime, by writers and intellectuals . . . The mass media do not function as internal interest-articulation channels except in the form of channels for individual complaints regarding lower level bureaucratic officials . . . We cannot speak of interest groups, media of communication, and political parties as constituting an autonomous political infrastructure. They are to be viewed more as mobilization structures contributing to the regulative, extractive, and symbolic capabilities rather than as substructures creating the basis for a responsive capacity.[18]

Almond, like Easton, usually really has effective interest articulation in mind, the kind of articulation that a government definitely has to take into account, and he too combines this shift in definition with an extremely traditional view of the structure of power in the Soviet Union.

In Zbigniew Brzezinski and Samuel Huntington's *Political Power*

*USA/USSR,* the picture is more mixed. The book represented a major breakthrough in Soviet studies and was the first in recent years to devote considerable attention to the policy process in the Soviet Union, or, at least, a policy process other than a personalistic conflict among Politburo members and cliques. Its authors recognize the existence of "orthodox dissent" in the Soviet Union and acknowledge that "undoubtedly ideas and proposals do drift up the Party and governmental hierarchies."[19] They see "bargaining and deciding" taking place within a "hierarchical context composed of three types of group": "amorphous social forces," "specific interest groups," and "policy groups."

In their view, the "policy groups" (which include "the military, the heavy-industry and light industry managers, the agricultural experts, and finally the state bureaucrats") "come the closest to participating in the policy-making process, as both claimants and advisors." While they are "careful not to cross the shadowy line between advocacy and pressure . . . they advocate to the political leadership certain courses of action; they have their own professional or specialized newspapers which, at times and subject to over-all Party control, can become important vehicles for expressing specific points of view."[20]

Yet elsewhere, and particularly in their explicitly comparative statements, Brzezinski and Huntington's analysis is little affected by this awareness. The processes of "socialization" in the United States are contrasted with those of "politicization" in the Soviet Union. Individual participation is described in terms that suggest it has no impact: "The Soviet regime increasingly uses political participation to control its people [and] the controls produced by political participation flow in one direction alone."[21] The newspapers that earlier had been described as important vehicles for expressing specific points of view come to be discussed in totally different terms. The book emphasizes the "diversity of opinion represented by the American [newspapers and journals]," as well as the efforts of the major American interests to influence public opinion, but it then continues, "No parallel or even analogy to this is remotely present in the Soviet Union; the Soviet citizen has access only to official sources of information, designed to elicit from him the desirable political reaction." Later it asserts that "while the Soviet government would like to stimulate more public criticism of performance, it is still unwilling to allow public criticism of policy."[22]

The treatment of "policy initiation" is even more striking. The subject is discussed in a section entitled "Initiation: Bubble Up and Trickle Down," a title that epitomizes the analysis. The authors accept Dean Acheson's summary description of the American policy making process— "The springs of policy bubble up; they do not trickle down"—but, despite their earlier statement about the drift of ideas and proposals up the party and governmental hierarchies, they now describe Soviet policy initiation solely in trickle-down terms: "The initiative in formulating most important policy measures probably rests with the Central Committee Secretaries and the departments of the central apparat."[23] In the course of the analysis both of "policy initiative" and of "criticism of policy," the word "policy" has shifted its meaning from that of "any governmental decision" to that of "major decisions by the top officials," while the definition of "initiation" has shifted from the "origin of ideas" to "the final drafting of a formal policy decision."

The statements that have been quoted have deliberately been taken from the works of the very best comparative theorists in the political science of their generation. At times one can sense the nature of the sophisticated position these men would take in private conversation if the inconsistencies were pointed out, and clearly they would be quick to repudiate or reformulate many of the more extreme statements that have been quoted. The fact remains, however, that as these scholars reviewed their manuscripts, their galleys, and their page proofs, they were not sufficiently struck by the inconsistency among their various statements (or between their statements and their own knowledge) to rephrase the statements.

The crucial question is: why has it been so difficult for the foremost political scientists of their generation to admit what is obvious to any reasonably attentive reader of the American press? Why is it so difficult to admit that the party has, in fact, permitted a great deal of criticism of Soviet society and party policy, that the Soviet mass media serve as important interest articulation channels, that policy ideas "bubble up" in the Soviet Union as well as in the United States, and so forth?

There are, no doubt, a number of answers to these questions. One possibility, of course, is that comparative political scientists have remained prisoners of the old "atomization of society" images and have been slow to appreciate the actual extent to which demand input has been permitted in the Soviet Union. A second possibility is that their perception of the Soviet Union has been excessively affected by the ideology of their own society and by the pressures created by the McCarthy era, causing them to differentiate Soviet socialism from welfare-state liberalism in the sharpest possible terms. A third possibility is that intellectuals unknowingly have a distinct class bias, that they unconsciously judge political systems almost exclusively by the way these systems treat intellectuals such as themselves, and that the Soviet restrictions on Western-oriented dissidents have unduly colored the interpretation of Soviet within-system politics.

All of these explanations contain considerable elements of truth. Yet an even larger part of the answer must be sought in another direction—in some of the basic assumptions of American political science about the sources of power in a political system and about the preconditions of a responsive political system. Scholars have often unconsciously assumed that inputs almost inexorably flow through to policy outcomes, and, perceiving Soviet outcomes that do not correspond to their notions of responsiveness, they often have failed to see the kind of inputs that would create difficulties for their assumptions. If a scholar admits that there are societal inputs into the "black box" of the Soviet political system, he often seems to fear that he is admitting that governmental decisions reflect these inputs—or, perhaps worse, that the party leaders are a kind of barometer rather than the directors of society. If he admits that "pressure groups" or "interest groups" exist in Soviet society rather than merely "aspiration groups" (a distinction made privately by one of the leading scholars of the mid-1960s), then he seems to feel that he must concede that the party leadership accedes to pressure.

Nowhere, of course, will one find major American political scientists flatly expressing the opinions attributed to them in the previous paragraph, and the point is difficult to document in definitive terms. No one scholar agrees completely with another, and a number of the leading ones have further clouded the issue by moving back and forth between an analysis of the actual American political system and an analysis of an ideal-type democracy (whatever term is used) in a way that sometimes leaves it unclear what the subject of a particular sentence is. Yet in a broader sense it appears that those scholars working within the dominant pluralist school have shared a number of fundamental, often unspoken assumptions about the principles by which political systems do and should operate. It is these basic assumptions rather than the scholars' opinions about the American political system that I am trying to capture.

Certainly, it can be said as an absolute minimum that since the turn of the century American political science has been deeply absorbed in the study of what are now called "inputs." The group approach, of which Bentley was only one of the early (and actually one of the minor) proponents,[24] was little more than an exhortation to focus upon those persons and institutions most prominently engaged in the articulation of demands, and the widespread interest in political parties likewise reflects a concern with institutions that perform (or can perform) the functions of initiating either discreet policy proposals or more comprehensive and integrated political programs.

The political authorities themselves have not, of course, been neglected in political science, but frequently they have been treated as instruments of mediation among the interests rather than as independent actors. As early as 1914 A. Lawrence Lowell spoke of the democratic politician as a "broker." His "most universal function," Lowell said, "is to bring men together in masses on some middle ground where they can combine to carry out a common policy . . . . The number of statesmen who strive to carry into effect a personal policy of their own on any large scale by leading and educating the community is very small."[25] A half century later Brzezinski and Huntington used almost identical language: "To the politician . . . agreement almost becomes an end in itself quite apart from the substance of what is agreed upon . . . The fact of agreement is a major accomplishment, something in which he can take pride."[26] The politician's work becomes summarized in different homey metaphors emphasizing the limited nature of his role: "patching up an old system,"[27] "the art of muddling through."[28]

With the political authorities being treated as brokers—and brokers committed to incrementalism at that,[29] the inputs themselves and the interests represented in them emerged as the truly significant factor in the political process. In the past this set of assumptions was most clearly expressed in the frequent use of the word "equilibrium" by nearly all major political scientists of the first half of the century to describe the configuration of group pressures that seemed to determine policy.[30] In the words of V. O. Key, "The structure of political power may be pictured as a more or less unstable equilibrium among competing interests . . . The political equilibrium among social groups is from time to time disturbed. One class or group becomes discontented with the existing state of things and the processes of politics go into operation to create a new equilibrium. The politician finds himself in the middle—and belabored from all sides—as he seeks to contrive a formula to maintain peace among conflicting interests."[31]

Indeed, sometimes in this image there seemed to be little need for political brokering among major conflicting interests. Policy making often was seen as a compartmentalized process with each group dominating policy questions of greatest concern to it and sometimes even merging with the governmental agencies responsible for these questions.[32] In its less extreme form a scholar might merely suggest the existence of "minorities rule" in which "the making of governmental decisions is not a majestic march of great majorities united upon certain matters of basic policy [but] is the steady appeasement of relatively small groups."[33]

Obviously no serious scholar ever assumed that the steady appeasement of small groups or the adjustment of the equilibrium among groups is an easy task, and Dahl's study of New Haven is typical in its open admiration for the role played by the city's mayor in its political process. Nevertheless, the overall logic of the basic assumption seemed fairly straightforward: to the extent that politicians are doing their job properly (and competitive elections are supposed to maximize the likelihood that this will be the case, at least in the long run), the wishes of the minorities and the veto groups should be the crucial determinant of most policy questions of primary interest to them individually, and the relative intensity of feeling and power among the groups should be decisive on questions involving several of them. That is, assuming a properly functioning political system, the analysis seems implicitly to assume a position that H. L. Childs enunciated explicitly in the 1930s: "Were it possible to plot pressure groups objectively as parallelograms of forces and compute the resultant, significant predictions might be made not only as to what party platforms are likely to be, which parties will win, but also as to significant trends in public policy."[34]

Although it is no longer fashionable to speak of an "equilibrium,"[35] the introduction of the systems approach into much of recent political science theory has served to strengthen the emphasis upon inputs as a causative factor. Not only have concepts such as "demands," "inputs," "input structures," "channels," "interest articulation," and "communications systems" become core elements in theory, but Easton's great emphasis upon channels of access and Almond's even greater emphasis upon the "autonomy" of input structures as key indicators in distinguishing among political systems clearly seem to imply that the access of inputs is far more critical than the nature of the decision makers they ultimately reach.

Indeed, even the equilibrium concept has been smuggled into systems-oriented theory in a number of ways. For example, the central role given to the "bargaining" culture and to mutual adjustment as defining elements in the "civic culture" seems to be pointing to characteristics of a population that are necessary for a smoothly functioning equilibrium.[36] However, the presence of an equilibrium model is implied even more strongly by the frequent use of the concepts of "feedback" and "responsiveness" in this type of approach.

Scholars who discuss feedback (the two most prominent are David Easton and Karl Deutsch) invariably assert that governments need not respond to the information feedback that they receive from society, but the term remains a very dangerous one. It comes from the field of cybernetics and refers to mechanisms such as thermostats that not only collect information about the environment (the temperature in the case of the thermostat), but also utilize this information to regulate the unit's actions. Obviously, a thermostat does not set the temperature it desires, but when the goals of the system are defined very broadly (like systems maintenance), as they often are in this approach, demands and feedback become virtually indistinguishable from an outside observer's point of view. Whatever Deutsch may mean in concrete political terms by statements such as the following, they leave a strong impression of an equilibrium mechanism at work: "By feedback is meant a communications network that produces action in response to an input of information, and *includes the results of its own action in the new information by which it modifies its subsequent behavior* [The italics are Deutsch's.] . . . If the feedback is well designed, the result will be a series of diminishing mistakes—a dwindling series of under- and over-corrections converging on the goals."[37]

Perhaps most important of all in imbedding the equilibrium concept in systems-influenced political science has been the widespread use of the terms "responsive" and "responsive capacity" to refer to political systems that are considered superior from the point of view of democratic values. The terms "responsive" or "responsiveness" seldom are defined with precision, but the most explicit definition has been provided by David Easton: "Responsiveness . . . will be interpreted to mean first, that the authorities are willing to take . . . information into account and give it consideration in their outputs and second, that they do so positively in the sense that they seek to use it to help avert discontent or to satisfy grievances over the initial outputs or some unfulfilled demand."[38] Gabriel Almond defines "responsive capacity" as "the openness of the political system to demands coming from various groups in the society, or from the international political system."[39] He never specifies the exact nature of a responsive political system, but it obviously is one with high responsive capacity. It is a system that is accommodating to the "inputs of demands from groups in society," that is concerned with "giving the people 'what they want.' " It is one in in which "the elites must manifestly and positively incorporate the interests of the major groups in society."[40]

There are many reasons why scholars have come to speak so often of "responsiveness" or "responsive political systems."[41] One of the most important, surely, has been the obvious and growing inadequacy of traditional classifications of government in the face of the variety of political regimes that have arisen in the twentieth century. Thus, for example, the word "democracy" traditionally was applied both to a particular set of institutions (those involving competitive elections) and to the political consequences those institutions were thought to produce: a willingness of political leaders to listen to the wishes of the public, a style of decision making that incorporates broad consultation, a protection of civil liberties, and so forth. However, as elections, even formally competitive elections, become associated in the Third World with regimes of the most diverse characteristics, the dual meaning of democracy often caused it to be misleading in its implications.

A similar problem was created by a proliferation of types of regime that seemed to fit best within the traditional categories of monarchy or dictatorship. Even leaving aside the monarchies of the British type, scholars certainly felt that Tito's Yugoslavia was more democratic (in the noninstitutional sense) than Stalin's Russia, whatever the very considerable similarities in formal structure. Certain of the dictatorships of the Third World seemed even less like the Soviet Union of the 1930s and the 1940s, and, in fact, they seemed more democratic than some Third World nations with electoral mechanisms. Yet the institutional meanings of democracy made that word seem inappropriate to use in analyzing them.

In practice, the concept of "responsive" arose as a category that could convey the noninstitutional meanings of democracy (or really constitutional democracy) and denote approval. In a number of respects the choice was an excellent one. The word does have the connotations that are desired, and it easily lends itself to marginal comparisons. One can say without semantic difficulty that the Yugoslavian political system is more responsive than the Soviet or that the British political system is more responsive than the Italian, and no institutional implications have been created.

But how does one actually tell whether one political system is more responsive than another? After all, every society contains a variety of wants, demands, suggestions, and pressures, and often they push in quite different, even opposite directions. No political system can be fully responsive to all the demands and pressures, and no political system can avoid having its decisions correspond to someone's wishes. As Almond and Powell recognize, "in a sense every political system is responsive to something. The political system must be responding to some set of internal or external pressures or demands."[42]

How are we to judge whether the pressures to which a government responds warrant it being termed responsive? How, for example, are we to compare the American political system in the period 1931 to 1937 with the German political system of the same period? In both countries a deep dissatisfaction with the consequences of the economic depression led to a change of political leadership in 1933. By 1937 the new German leadership had instituted policies that achieved full employment and economic prosperity, while the unemployment rate in the United States stood at well over 10 percent. Should the German system be considered the more responsive one in this period?

What are we to say if a political system is quite responsive to a large segment of the population but is almost totally nonresponsive to a significant minority? If—speaking hypothetically—the Nazi system had met every criterion of responsiveness in relationship to the non-Jewish population, and had, in accordance with majority desire, placed Jews in concentration camps, could it have been called responsive? Given its almost total lack of responsiveness to the black population for decades, can the American political system be considered responsive during that period? Indeed, leaving aside the question of general labeling, what action *should* a responsive government have taken if the majority in a southern American town wanted complete segregation and inferior schools for the black minority, while active members of the black community were demonstrating for an end to such programs?

To what extent do our criteria for ascertaining responsiveness involve an insistence that the government be a passive referee playing "the inert part of a cash register, ringing up the additions and withdrawals of strength, a mindless balance pointing and marking the weight and distribution of power among the contending groups?"[43] After all, the very word "responsive" is passive in nature—a fact that is thrown into even clearer relief when it is compared with its once popular generic counterpart, "responsible." A responsible government seems to be one that takes actions and then assumes responsibility for them at the next election; a responsive government has none of these connotations.

To be sure, the leading political scientists writing about responsiveness, just like those advancing an equilibrium analysis earlier, certainly did not want to suggest that a responsive political system was incompatible with executive leadership. Most of these scholars were New Deal liberals, and they were writing at a time when such liberals were seeking a strong president rather than speaking of the need to curb one. They continually asserted that a responsive political system need not and should not be of the cash register type.

But if the British government can still basically be a responsive one even if it abolishes the death penalty in the face of a public opinion poll showing 80 percent popular support for capital punishment, and if some of the modernizing governments in the Third World can be considered responsive, how do we distinguish responsive executive leadership from the modernization pushed by Stalin in the 1930s? If we answer by insisting that responsive leadership be subject to the regular test of a popular election, then are we not faced again with our original problem—the need for a term that does not automatically link the institutions of a democracy with a democratic or responsive political system?

Some of the questions that have been raised are rhetorical in nature, and some have answers that are obvious. However, some of the obvious answers are not really compatible, and they still raise the question—how *do* we judge that one political system is, in fact, more or less responsive than a second system?

In practice, it seems that our judgments have been based primarily on the degree to which civil rights (as defined in the West) are guaranteed in a particular country. A responsive political system is one in which the government does not restrict the citizens' right to speak out, guarantees them due process and the right to a fair trial, and leaves them secure from sudden and drastic interference in their property, status, and role. That is, any governmentally-sponsored change affecting the individual in these respects will be taken in an accommodating manner and then only incrementally. A responsive political system is a constitutional system in a broad sense of that term.

That scholars should instinctively judge responsiveness on the basis of such constitutional indicators is not surprising. The scholars being discussed did place the American political system generally within the responsive category, and they did perceive these characteristics to be present within it. Moreover, the characteristics have the enormous advantage, first, of being readily observable, and, second, of not forcing the scholar to face up to the type of dilemmas discussed, for they can be shared fairly universally by the citizenry.

Yet constitutional indicators are at best indirect indicators of responsiveness in any generic sense of that concept. They can be used as that type of indicator only if certain assumptions are made. One basically *must* assume that the freedom to speak out, the freedom to make inputs, will be accompanied by governmental policies that incorporate these inputs in some roughly proportionate manner. One *must* assume that the incremental changes will be in the direction that the moving equilibrium of inputs suggests, at least to the extent that minorities rule does not permit all inputs to be incorporated in policy. And, to repeat, there are many indications that such assumptions have been unconsciously made, not the least of which is the enormous difficulty that comparative political science has had in acknowledging the existence of inputs in the Soviet Union.

Nevertheless, a fact remains a fact. There are inputs in the Soviet political system. There are many channels of access through which those inputs flow to the decision makers. And these facts are true of the Stalin period as well as of the succeeding years. If our unconscious theoretical assumptions lead us to resist these obvious facts, then we need to reexamine those assumptions closely.

The first conclusion to be drawn from the argument of this chapter is, of course, the self-evident and seemingly trivial one that we should start taking seriously the proposition that inputs do not flow directly through to outputs and that a free flow of inputs does not necessarily mean that all inputs are proportionately represented in policy. This conclusion is scarcely revolutionary, for every major political science theorist has made it. Nevertheless, surely it is not without meaning that so many scholars claim that *other* scholars fall into the parallelogram of forces or the equilibrium trap. Surely it is not accidental that such a universally disavowed theory has inspired such frequent attack nor that it has needed to be disavowed so often. Recognizing the truth of an idea can be quite different from taking it seriously.

If we seriously renounce any tendency to treat inputs as causal agents, we may discover rather quickly why this renunciation has been so difficult in practice. The implications of this action are much more far-reaching than would seem on the surface.

In the first place, the great advantage of any explicit or implicit theory that emphasizes the importance of inputs is that it focuses our attention upon phenomena that are relatively easy to observe and study, particularly in comparison with the workings of the "black box" of the decision making process and of the decision makers' minds. If it is not enough to rely upon inputs and the freedom to make them, then we are driven to use quite different methodologies in dealing with some of the basic questions of political science. The work of the political scientists is enormously complicated in the process, and the results of the other methodologies may, at times, be very disquieting.

In the second place, unless some verifiable indicators of responsiveness can be developed that are not based on input data, an abandonment of causal assumptions about inputs also means an abandonment of the concept of responsiveness as an empirical category in political science. And such an abandonment, besides leaving us with our original problems in classification of governments, may further force us to face up to the real dilemmas of political life in a way that we have unconsciously sought to avoid.

As one reflects upon the earlier pluralist discussion of equilibrium or the more recent discussion of responsiveness, one is struck by the number of classic dilemmas of political theory that it either solves or ignores depending upon one's point of view. The world of the American pluralist is not a Hobbesian one of brutish struggle nor a Marxian one of irreconcilable class conflict. It is not haunted by fears of governmental threats to individual liberty or majority tyranny over the minority. In Dahl's words, "if majority rule is mostly a myth, then majority tyranny is mostly a myth too. For if the majority cannot rule, surely it cannot be tyrannical."[44] This world may contain a population that is not very well informed, interested, or rational, but that is not a cause for undue concern because interests are represented by a series of agents who have the necessary information and understanding of the situation.

In many ways the responsive political system is similar to that represented in a sober anarchist or Marxist postrevolutionary ideal. Society, while reasonably integrated both in its values and its need for interdependence, is still quite compartmentalized in the sense that one group's freedom of action within the narrow realm of primary interest to itself seldom interferes with other groups' freedom of action in their 'realm. Every group can function more or less autonomously. "Conflicts over issues related to divisions of the total economic pie, influence over various institutions, symbolic status and opportunity, continue,"[45] but no group need lose seriously in these conflicts, at least in the short run. The conflicts can be resolved through mutual adjustment, compromise, accommodation, bargaining, and so forth. There is no need for societal stability to be maintained by force, except in the case of individual deviants. Power is not seen in zero-sum terms, being exercised by one group over another. Rather it is merely the means through which society achieves its collective aims.[46] In the words of Karl Marx, "the state withers away."

All have agreed that the Marxist image of the political system of the Communist stage is an attractive one, but non-Marxists have raised the most serious doubts about the real world possibility of its enactment, even aside from its assumptions about the control of individual deviance. We should really ask ourselves if our ideal types of responsive systems, of equilibrium systems, of reconciliation systems are ultimately much more realistic. Even if we don't fall into the trap of confusing ideal type with reality (a danger that many fail to avoid), we should ask ourselves if we aren't trying to hide from the fact that there are always winners and losers in political-social systems and that strong governmental action against the status quo may be as responsive to disadvantaged groups as conciliatory and incremental governmental action is to those with more to lose.

When our criteria for judging responsiveness rest so heavily on the types of freedom of demand input found in the West, we should question whether we really are not trying to avoid any serious normative evaluation of Western systems with those based on different principles. Or, to phrase it as C. B. Macpherson would, are we convinced that we are not trying to avoid the question whether "liberal" (or "constitutional") regimes and "democratic" regimes are inevitably and in all circumstances always identical?[47] Are we certain that—to paraphrase the late Charles Wilson of General Motors—we are not simply assuming that what is good for the intellectuals like ourselves is good for the country? One would certainly hope that this assumption is accurate, but if we are to be true to our self-conception as intellectuals it should not be a question closed by definition.

# 9

# Communications and Persuasion in the Analysis of Inputs

The long-term assumptions in American political science about the importance of inputs in the political process are the product of many factors, but one obvious reason for giving them importance is that there actually must *be* some relationship between inputs and governmental decisions. The Soviet experience teaches us more than that the input of demands is universal. It also indicates that governments think it useful to place restrictions on certain types of expression of views. Stalin obviously did not feel that he had to function as a passive barometer who registered the societal pressures impinging on him, but just as obviously he also seemed to believe that a free public flow of ideas would somehow limit his own freedom of action.

Neither Stalin nor his successors nor innumerable governmental officials in a variety of countries can be considered infallible in their judgments, but the presumption must be strong that they have accurately perceived something about the impact of the input process upon decision making. What is their insight? The Soviet leaders apparently have not been much concerned about "channel overload" or about access of demands to themselves. What have they been trying to accomplish with their elaborate and costly system of censorship and their large network of secret police agents? An answer to this question may bring us to a better understanding of what in the input process is crucial in its impact upon the distribution of power.

It is universally agreed that public demand articulation in the Soviet Union has been strikingly different in scope and character in the post-Stalin period from what it had been earlier. It is also agreed that something has happened to the distribution of power and influence in the same period. In practice, the leader now operates under more effective restraints than Stalin did, and there seems to be more pluralism in the distribution of influence among the elite. Whatever the connection between these two developments, an examination of the changes in the input process that occurred after 1953 seems the best way to pinpoint those aspects of the process that may be peculiarly sensitive in their power implications.

Perhaps the quickest way to understand the differences in the input process that occurred after Stalin's death is to examine the contents of two more or less randomly-chosen months of *Pravda* and *Izvestiia*—December 1951 and December 1971.[1] The issues of these months, which seem quite typical for the respective periods, remind us first, of course, that there are major similarities between the Soviet press of 1951 and 1971. Censorship was in force in both years, and it was not a formality. In 1966 one party official expressed party policy very directly: "In our country each person who considers himself an artist has the right to create freely and to write what he desires without the slightest restriction. But in similar measure the party and our governmental organs enjoy the right of free choice on what to publish."[2] *Pravda* and *Izvestiia* in 1971 reflected these policies as much as in 1951. Many articles were published to reassure the Soviet citizen of the benevolence of the Soviet system and of party policy, and there was no frontal attack either on the system or the leading party organs. Certain types of information never appeared, including any criticism of any Politburo member or even any real indication of the variation in policy views among the party leaders.

Another similarity between the press of 1951 and 1971 is much less appreciated in the West: at both times the newspapers contained a number of demands (in Easton's sense of the term) for change in specific policies followed by the party. Although Western scholars have sometimes suggested that only lower-level bureaucrats could be criticized in the Soviet press of the Stalin years and then only for improper implementation of policy, this view is simply incorrect.

The 1951 issues did, in fact, include a number of suggestions for minor changes in ministerial policies (for example, an improvement in the way ski production was organized, the need for a new movie studio in Belorussia, a change in the system of school inspectors to make the number in each district proportionate to the number of schools in it),[3] but there were other articles with more far-reaching policy implications. Even in this one month the two central Soviet newspapers carried a number of articles that, in sum, constituted a cautious, collective attack on many of the defects in economic administration and planning that were to lie at the center of the reforms taken later in the decade. Thus an article on the Kazakhstan Party Congress reported that the Chairman of the Kazakh Council of Ministers spoke about "the urgent problems in creating a reliable feed base for agriculture," and an article written by the Leningrad obkom secretary specializing in agriculture appealed for more mechanization of work in orchards. An obkom first secretary asserted that the MTS section agronomists should, so far as possible, be individually assigned to serve a kolkhoz and be actually attached to it. The head of a store complained that the crockery factories, with the agreement of the Ministry of Trade, shipped all dishes in one predetermined assortment that included many more tea cups than the consumers wanted, and he asked that the shipments vary in response to consumer demand. Both the head of construction of the Great Turkmen Canal and the director of the giant Leningrad plant Elektrosila demanded that the scientific institutes render more consistent and concrete help in solving specific problems of the construction trusts and industrial enterprises, but an academician praised the existing level of cooperation of scientific institutes and industrial plants and stated that the scientists should concentrate on "big" theoretical and economic problems. His suggestion for improving contact between science and industry was to increase the numbers of conferences at which scientists could report their results to industrial administrators.[4]

There were, however, several significant differences between the 1951 and the 1971 issues. In the first place, the newspapers had been expanded somewhat in size,[5] and some of the additional space had been allocated to demand articulation. In December 1951 the two newspapers carried a total of 46 articles and letters (29 of them explicitly labeled as letters) which contained some demand for change other than one made by a *Pravda* or *Izvestiia* correspondent or by an official calling for an improvement in the work of some person or institution he supervised. In December 1971 *Pravda* and *Izvestiia* carried 101 critical articles and letters fitting within these categories, 54 of them letters.[6] In addition, excerpts from 24 other critical letters were printed in survey articles or in articles written by a newspaper correspondent. The number of letters alone rose from .52 an issue in 1951 to 1.5 an issue in 1971 (including those excerpted in the surveys).[7]

A second difference between the issues of 1951 and those of 1971 is in the kind of people whose demand articulation was published. In both years the authors of critical articles and letters came overwhelmingly from white collar workers (93 percent of the total in 1951 and 89 percent in 1971), but a significant change occurred in the authorship of the long articles in the sample. In 1951 there were but 13 such articles, and 9 were written by highly elite figures—the first secretary of the Komsomol, a republican party first secretary, a chairman of a republican council of ministers, three party obkom secretaries, the head of construction of the Great Turkmen Canal, the director of a giant Leningrad plant, and a member of the Academy of Sciences. In 1971 there were 43 of these long articles, and only 14 of their authors occupied positions comparable to those held by the 9 elite writers of 1951.

Perhaps the most interesting fact about the writers of long articles articulating demands is the rise in the proportion of academic and scientific personnel among them. In 1971, 15 of these articles (35 percent of the total) were authored by a person of this background, compared with only 1 in 1951. Indeed, in the long articles devoted almost exclusively to proposals for policy change (other articles were essentially reports of actual experience with a very brief and often minor demand attached), the academic and scientific personnel constituted 46 percent of the authors. Whereas the one 1951 article written by a scientist raised what Brzezinski and Huntington call a "defensive" interest[8] (in this case, the maintenance of the autonomy of the scientist from the industrial managers), the articles in 1971 centered on general policy questions—usually questions on which the educator or scientist had specialized knowledge.

The third difference between critical articles published in *Pravda* and *Izvestiia* in 1951 and 1971 is in the content and manner of presentation. In the earlier issues the articles involved the input of a demand in pure and simple terms. An author usually presented a single demand and made little attempt to treat a problem as a whole or to suggest the need for interrelated policy measures. Moreover, the demands were seldom accompanied by the type of factual information that would make the demand most compelling. A person could say in print that there was an urgent need to strengthen the feed base for livestock, but he could not support his policy proposal by pointing out that, despite a significant increase in population, the number of livestock was still well below the 1928 level or that the production of grain was below that of 1940. Such facts were state secrets, not to be published.

The situation in 1971 had changed very considerably. Take, for example, a *Pravda* article authored by a professor at the Timiriazev Agricultural Academy.[9] It began with a brief mention of the large investments being made in agriculture and the significant growth in the production of agricultural machinery, but turned very quickly to its major subject—the problems not solved by current agricultural policy. The professor reported that the average kolkhoz had 138 rubles worth of agricultural machinery and equipment for every 100 rubles worth of tractors, but the experience of progressive farms demonstrates that the ratio should be at least 2:1 and perhaps 3:1. He placed the blame squarely on past policy, and, while acknowledging that the recently adopted five-year plan was moving in the right direction (tractors were to increase by 25 percent as against a 65 percent rise for agricultural machinery), he asserted that "the optimal relationship will still not be achieved" even with the new planned rates of production. His conclusion was expressed very directly. "Consequently, it is extremely indispensable that the plan for the production of agricultural machinery be significantly overfulfilled both through a fuller use of internal reserves and a seeking of additional financial and material resources.''

The professor further argued that even if the plan were changed, the difficulties would not be completely solved. One problem was that the new machines being produced, although higher in price by some 20-25 percent, were not correspondingly more productive in terms of the work they do. ''When new models are worked out and introduced, proper attention is not given to comparative economic evaluation . . . It is necessary to raise the responsibility and material interest of the designers in creating economically profitable machines.'' A second problem, the professor contended, was too few trained personnel on the farm. He reported that ''research conducted by scholars'' shows that the number of machine operators should be increased by one-and-a-half times, and he further maintained that the level of their preparation should be raised. In addition, he suggested that the ratio of engineers and technicians to machine operators (now 41 per 1000) be brought closer to the ratio of engineers and technicians to workers found in industry (147 per 1000). He listed a number of steps (most of them expensive) that he believed necessary to improve the personnel situation.

Another 1971 article—one written by a correspondent of *Izvestiia* —had many of the same characteristics. The correspondent discussed the general relationship of the public services sector to their clientele, citing a number of cases in which the rights of customers are regularly ignored. Porters are supposed to make up the beds in train compartments, but they don't; the bureau for the exchange of apartments charges seven rubles for doing absolutely nothing except registering the exchange; collective farms receive materials from the Agricultural Supply Agency only if they furnish the workers for repair or construction work and allow the Supply Agency to include the work in its plan; a customer goes into a store near closing time and is refused service because, as he is frankly told, the store has already fulfilled its sales plan and overfulfillment might lead to a higher plan in the future.

The correspondent did not suggest a specific program to solve these problems, but he did not hesitate either to point to general principles that he believed to be illustrated by the problems or to draw general conclusions from them.

> Monopoly in the providing of a service creates the conditions for ''the application of pressure on the client.'' The client and his partner are unequal, and the client suffers most often . . . A conflict of interests, separate special plan indicators which drag the partners in different directions

—this is the most frequent reason that the economic "orchestra" turns
into a Krylov quartet. The economic reform is removing this discordance
and is uniting the partners. But at the XXIVth Party Congress it was emphasized (and not without reason) that this process is a long one and that
far from all of the problems have been solved . . . It is necessary to think
how all the levers of economic reform can be brought into full conformity
with the demands of the time. Then the client will be the dearest and most
desired guest in any of the service spheres. [10]

What is so different about these two articles and those that had been
published in the Stalin era? In the first place, of course, a much greater
level of information and degree of documentation was permitted in 1971
than in 1951. Radical demands—or at least demands with fairly radical
implications—often could be published under Stalin, but he seemed
wary of allowing the type of persuasive argumentation that might make a
demand compelling.

In the second place, the demands of 1971 were much more detailed
and comprehensive. The proposal that agricultural production be increased and the proposal that there be a change in the proportion of
agricultural machinery and tractors produced are both—to use Easton's
definition of a demand—"an expression of opinion that an authoritative
allocation with regard to a particular subject matter should or should not
be made by those responsible for doing so." While one might think that
Stalin would be less concerned about the technical proposal than the
general one, the reverse was the case. He often seemed less sensitive about
the enunciation of a goal than about the publication of seemingly non-
sensitive technical information and of concrete and detailed legitimate
policy suggestions on how to achieve an important goal. He was quite
willing to tolerate a public appeal for a restructuring of the incentive
system for industrial managers (indeed, Liberman himself made such an
appeal in *Trud* in 1949), but he would not permit an open debate on the
details of such a restructuring.

In the third place, the articles of 1971 often could attribute shortcomings to more general causes. In 1951 the arguments that were presented to support a demand were directed mostly at the alleged sins of a
single institution or official, and even an article that was actually a proposal for major change in agricultural policy would be phrased as a criticism of the Ministry of Agriculture. "Objective reasons" were often explicitly and scornfully rejected as an explanation for some deficiency. In
1971, on the other hand, press articles took for granted that objective factors (including the basic organizational structure and incentive systems)
were important in determining economic-social relationships, and, in

fact, the articles tended to concentrate precisely on the objective factors that dictate this or that policy change. It is symptomatic that the article on agricultural reform discussed above did not even mention the Ministry of Agriculture, but was simply directed at general policy.

In practice, the expression of ideas became much freer in the Soviet Union after the death of Stalin, but censorship has, of course, continued to exist, and the laws prohibiting "anti-Soviet propaganda and agitation" and "slanderous fabrications which defame the Soviet state and social system" have, if anything, been strengthened. Some statements still result in prosecution, and many more types are excluded from published media of communication. If an examination of the differences between 1951 and 1971 articles may give us some idea about the relative sensitivity of various types of communication, then an examination of the types of restrictions maintained by Stalin's successors may help to indicate the nature of the next level of sensitivity.

If the average American citizen or even the average scholar were asked the purpose of the censorship and the laws restraining freedom of expression in the Soviet Union, the instinctive answer would be: to prevent the Soviet people from being exposed to dangerous ideas, to criticism of the political leadership and the fundamentals of the Soviet system. Despite the elements of truth in this answer (particularly so far as criticism of the leadership is concerned), it is still astonishingly misleading in many respects.

In the first place, "the fundamentals of the culture" or "the principles of middle-class respectability" seem a far more sensitive topic to the leadership than the fundamentals of the political, economic, or social system. An article defending the gay life or charging discrimination against homosexuals would be totally prohibited, as would one suggesting advantages in a drug subculture or damning the work ethic. Articles advocating more sexual freedom or pornography could not be expressed in forthright terms. Indeed, some of the tightest censorship is directed at work that normally would not be included in demand input or interest articulation at all, let alone be considered politically subversive: pornographic books and magazines, comic books, romance magazines or novels, "I Love Lucy" types of television programs, or soap operas. Given the fact that such material is at the heart of working class culture in the United States and that the American Left labels it the real "opium of the people" at the present time, it is striking that a leadership interested in a quiescent population has been so hostile to it.

Discussion of the need for fundamental political, economic, or social change, on the other hand, is far more possible in the Soviet Union. Of course, no one can publish a direct and frontal attack upon the system in the sense in which American radicals use that word in their criticism of the United States. No one can publish an article asserting that capitalism is better than socialism or even that Yugoslavian or Hungarian socialism is better than Soviet socialism, nor can they argue that the Soviet Union is not a democracy, a true federal state, or essentially a just society. It is also impossible to criticize the Politburo members in print either collectively or as individuals.

Yet in the name of perfecting socialism, democracy, the federal system, or social justice in the Soviet Union, Soviet citizens can make the most basic (if carefully worded) criticisms of what Westerners certainly would consider the fundamentals of the system. They can propose policy change that, from our perspective, would transform these fundamentals in a basic way. They can propose economic changes that would move the Soviet Union well towards market socialism, political changes that would (according to our theories at least) increase the impact of public opinion upon governmental decisions, and social change that would substantially improve the lot of the disadvantaged. The tone and language that must be used does not alter the fact that the contents and implications of the advocacy are quite radical.

Moreover, the exposure of the Soviet citizen to dangerous political ideas goes far beyond those contained in advocacy articles written by Soviet citizens. Even the republican and regional newspapers (generally the most tightly censored of the printed media) print such opinions as that the Soviet political system is totalitarian in nature, that the Soviet economy is in a state of "crisis" and is characterized by "technical backwardness,"[11] that Soviet federalism is a sham hiding Great-Russian domination, that Professor Seton Watson believes Soviet policy in the socialist camp is similar to the policy of the imperialists,[12] that religion is persecuted in the Soviet Union and that Marxism-Leninism is a "theology,"[13] and so forth.

Competing ideologies are likewise given enormous coverage in the Sovet press, and the attentive Soviet reader surely has a far clearer understanding of the convergence doctrine, and specifically of the views of Zbigniew Brzezinski and Daniel Bell, than the average American social scientist, let alone the average American citizen. Daniel Bell is quoted incessantly in the republican press as stating, for example, that "the scientific-technical revolution . . . inevitably leads to the end of ideology . . . It always and everywhere produces commonality in technology and methods of industrial leadership, the development of similar ways of life among all peoples, and common social problems."[14] "The well-known English sociologist" Bottomore (to use the label provided for the reader in Kirgiziia) is said to believe that "almost all Western society has turned into a high middle class."[15] The Italian church is reported to feel that Christianity can help Marxism by providing criticism from the "ethical point of view."[16] By their nature, short newspaper articles cannot develop such points at much length, but there are innumerable journal articles and books published in the Soviet Union that do so in great detail.

To be sure, the various criticisms and ideological deviations were not praised or defended in the articles where they appeared. Instead, the articles being quoted were discussing "bourgeois falsification" and were subjecting the ideas to severe attack. But the fact remains that this type of wildly unorthodox idea does reach a mass audience and does so with the reported endorsement of a Western scholar. In fact, given the frequency with which these various "falsifications" are reported, the Soviet citizen gains the clear impression that they must be widely advanced in the West, and specifically by leading Western scholars.

Both policy toward criticism of the political-economic-social system and the widespread coverage given "bourgeois falsification" presumably bespeak a belief of the party leadership that the way in which ideas are presented is far more crucial in posing a political danger than are the ideas themselves. Western ideas do not seem so threatening if Westerners cannot properly defend them and if Soviet authors cannot give them domestic legitimization. Proposal of fundamental change need not be intolerable if it does not acknowledge that it is challenging the fundamentals and if it is not accompanied by sweeping condemnations and especially condemnations in comparison with other countries.

This assumption about the importance of the manner of presentation and the determination flowing from it to regulate the manner of presentation is not limited to criticisms or demands of a fundamental nature. Even in the case of the most legitimate and least dangerous ideas—those that can be quite freely and vigorously supported and documented in the press—there exist the strictest restrictions on the type of dramatization of support that is permitted. In the United States it is taken for granted that persons making a protest or advocating a new line of action will form a committee or an organization, that they will picket governmental buildings, that they will hand out leaflets, that they will gather signatures for petitions. Such persons also may wear buttons on their lapels, place bumper stickers on their cars, or insert advertisements in the newspapers. If they want to maximize news coverage, they will try some highly dramatic gesture—dairymen pouring milk onto the fields or feminists burning their bras—and even if the dramatic action is formally illegal, as in the case of some sit-ins or the blocking of a street, it often will be very lightly punished, if at all.

In the Soviet Union, however, such dramatization of protest is completely illegal, regardless of the legitimacy of the demand involved. The only exception seems to be a privately organized petition or delegation to the local authorities on some grievance such as maintenance of an apartment house, but even on such an issue no one can picket an offending administrative agency, handout a mimeographed complaint, or collect signatures for the petition on the street. A street demonstration, let alone a sit-in, is likely to be included among those "group actions which violate public order in a coarse manner" that are prohibited by Article 190-3 of the RSFSR Criminal Code. Soviet law also prohibits the formation of groups whose sole purpose is the advancement of the economic or political interests of their members,[17] and hence, with the rarest exceptions, there can be no organizations promoting a particular piece of legislation or protesting some development or some administrative action (even by low-level bureaucrats).

The Party leadership has, of course, been willing for spokesmen of different viewpoints to build support for many types of ideas through argumentation in articles and books. It has permitted—and, in fact, required—the formation of innumerable organizations, committees, and councils on some territorial, occupational, institutional, or even "hobby" basis, and has allowed these public organizations to defend many types of interests of their members. But this is where it draws the line.

The reasons for the near-total prohibition of issue interest groups and of public dramatization of support for a complaint or a policy proposal are not totally clear. One explanation may be an extreme sensitivity toward any open challenge to authority that may derive from some kind of psychological insecurity as much as from a rational calculation of the dangers created by it. Certainly large numbers of Americans seem very upset by open challenges to authority and react quite negatively to them, and perhaps the Soviet response should be understood partially in similar terms.

A second possible explanation may be that the leadership fears that open demonstration will be taken as a barometer of intensity of support for an idea or a proposal. They may feel that they cannot claim to speak for the public if they go against such demonstration and that, consequently, their hand would be forced—a position they would reject on even the least sensitive issues. The same consideration might raise questions about the publication of letters and articles in the printed media, but at least in this situation the popular sense of intensity and breath of public opinion can be controlled in various ways.

A third possible explanation for the prohibitions against public dramatization of interest articulation may be a determination of the leadership to keep the size and nature of the audience for a demand or a criticism under tight control. Certainly this consideration does seem to be an important one in the regime's policy toward the spread of unconventional ideas. In practice, the mass medium with the widest audience (television) is the one that carries the least critical information and the fewest demands for major policy change, while the specialized and scholarly books and journals having a narrow readership are the scene of the most sensitive debates. *Pravda* and *Izvestiia,* which reach a more general "attentive public" audience, are more cautious than the specialized journals, while the local press (the most widely read of the newspapers) is even more cautious. In like fashion, as illustrated in table 9.1, there also tends to be a strong relationship between the number of copies printed of a book or journal and the conventionality of the ideas published in it.[18]

**Table 9.1.** The size of edition of Soviet books discussing the American political system, 1965-69

| Image of American political system | 5000 copies and under (%) | 5001- 10,000 copies (%) | Over 10,000 copies (%) | Total % |
|---|---|---|---|---|
| Traditional image (N = 16) | 13 | 25 | 62 | 100 |
| Intermediate image (N = 19) | 42 | 32 | 26 | 100 |
| Unconventional image (N = 12) | 67 | 33 | — | 100 |

*Sources:* The books and the image of the American political system they embody are drawn from the footnotes of Franklyn Griffiths, *Images, Politics, Arms Control: Aspects and Implications of Postwar Soviet Policy Toward the United States* (Ph.D. diss., Columbia University, 1972), chap. 2. All books of the years 1965-69 mentioned in the dissertation have been included in this analysis, except for two books published by remote republican presses and four books which could not be located. The size of edition (*tirazh*) was found in the back of each book. "Traditional image" is equivalent to Griffiths' "Image I" and "Image II;" "Intermediate image" is Griffiths' "Image III," and "Unconventional" is his "Image IV."

By limiting certain debates to more specialized publications, the regime does not actually prevent anyone from reading them.[19] But since the average citizen or even scholar in any country rarely looks at such sources if they are outside his or her field of specialization, this way of limiting debate can make it as invisible to the vast majority of the educated public as if there were an actual censorship aimed at them alone. Few politically significant debates in the Soviet Union (the notable examples are in the foreign policy and defense realms) are restricted totally to the specialized media, but by retaining and exercising control over the location and size of publication, the regime obviously believes that it can narrow the dissemination of certain criticisms and policy suggestion while satisfying its desire for specialist input that is informed by substantial communication among experts.

From this perspective, it may well be that the controls over the open dramatization of completely legitimate demands stem from the fact that such dramatization is indiscriminate in whom it reaches. Any passer-by can observe a picket line or be handed a leaflet. If such activity became permissible in the case of legitimate complaints, the problem of drawing the line between legitimate and illegitimate issues would immediately arise, and the regime may feel that its ability to regulate the flow of debate and protest to different audiences in any subtle and smooth manner would be seriously compromised.

Despite the great differences in the communications policies followed in the Stalin and post-Stalin periods, there are still certain similarities in the principles that govern them. First, both leaderships have been more preoccupied with regulating horizontal communication among the citizenry than with communications between the citizens and the political authorities. Second, they both showed considerable concern with the nature of the audience to which particular types of communication are directed. Both have been much less concerned about exchanges among specialists than communication to a broad audience, but one of the most useful ways of visualizing the changes in communication policy is in terms of a greater breadth in audience to which and within which a freer flow of policy-relevant information was permitted. Third, both leaderships apparently believed that the horizontal communication of demands is less worrisome than disseminating information and documentation that would legitimate demands. A demand or criticism that cannot be persuasively and authoritatively defended does not seem nearly as threatening.

As one thinks about the priority of concerns of the Soviet leadership, it is striking how rarely these concerns are placed at the center of analysis in comparative political science. Thus, Easton makes almost no effort to distinguish between different types of demand and gives little attention to horizontal communication. Similarly Almond places such phenomena as scholarly development of policy solutions—and apparently even the struggle for such solutions—within his definition of interest aggregation rather than that of interest articulation, but then discusses interest aggregation almost exclusively in terms of political parties. His chapter on communication deals primarily with vertical communication.

In short, one consequence of the concentration on inputs, particularly on demands, has been to turn attention away from the horizontal processes by which demands and especially policies are formulated and by which support for them is generated. And, if the Soviet leaders are right in the nature of their fears, this is a misdirection of attention. An earlier generation of political scientists often defined democracy more as a process in which involved citizens talked about issues and came to a consensus or at least a decision about them than as one of the input of clashing and discreet interests or demands. (The work of Ernest Barker is typical of this earlier school.) Whatever the naivete of this position, especially in its implication of mass involvement in this process, it may have represented an insight about the sources of political power that needs to be reincorporated more fully into political science theorizing.

In particular, the question of audience access is one that deserves the most careful consideration, for it may be as relevant for understanding countries like the United States as it is for the Soviet Union. That American dissidents almost invariably can find some outlet for their ideas says much about the United States as a liberal society, but, particularly in a country where elections are the ultimate arbiter in the choice of leader, the degree to which dissident ideas (with persuasive argumentation behind them) can reach a mass audience may be the crucial factor in determining whether these ideas have much chance for success. If the subject of analysis is the power of the top 10-15 percent of the population, of the New Class, in different political systems, then perhaps the willingness of the Soviet regime to have its citizens exposed to the unsupported ideas of the "bourgeois falsifiers" may say something of general interest about the likely impact of certain types of ideas. Given the very low level of political policy information of the mass of the population on most issues in all countries, the processes by which ideas penetrate to politically relevant elements of the population and especially the processes by which ideas and policies are changed, are enormously more complex than any facile statements about the autonomy of the media of communications would indicate.

# 10

# The Soviet Experience and the Measurement of Power

Over the last two decades, specialists on the Soviet Union have been grappling with the problem of reconceptualizing the Soviet political system. All have come to recognize the existence of groups and group activities in the Soviet Union, and some have no hesitation in using the term "interest group." All have come to recognize some element of pluralism among the Soviet elite, and some are willing even to move away from Gabriel Almond's emphasis upon the lack of "autonomy" among the elites. Whatever label or image is employed, everyone now sees a relationship between the leadership and the top elite that is far different from that depicted in the totalitarian model. In the past the bureaucracy, the New Class (even those at the level of Central Committee members) were included among the acted-upon, but now even those who retain a directed-society view of the Soviet Union have almost all slipped into talking about a society directed or dominated by an elite rather than the political leader or Politburo.

But what about the relationship between the masses (the bottom 85-90 percent of the population) and the elite—either a broadly defined elite such as the top 10-15 percent of the population or a more narrowly defined political elite? Little attention has been given to this question—except perhaps by those who suggest (wrongly, I think) that the fall of Khrushchev brought the end of a period of populism, an end to a period emphasizing "public-spiritness and participation in societal and administrative affairs." This matter deserves very serious study, and this chapter is essentially devoted to a preliminary exploration of the issues involved in it.

However, since the starting point for a discussion of the power relationship between the elite and the masses must be the basic methodological question of how to ascertain this relationship, an examination of the situation in the Soviet Union may also serve a broader purpose. The long debate in political science about the measurement of power has been closely linked with a debate on the structure of power in the American local community and, by implication, in the American political system as a whole. As a result, each side in the debate on methodology has been unconsciously afraid that the acceptance of the other side's methodological insights would imply acceptance of the other's empirical and normative judgments about the American system.

For this reason, a change in the setting of the methodological debate may be quite helpful—and particularly a change in which many of the normative implications are reversed. The example of the Soviet political system may be especially useful for this purpose, for the major scholars who deny the existence of elite rule in the American system (and who evaluate the system favorably) generally have visualized the Soviet system in elite terms (and have evaluated it unfavorably). If the methodological issues are discussed in this context as well as in the American, it may be easier to analyze them on their own merits and to promote the cause of methodological advance.

It is easy to say that a crucial and relatively unexplored aspect of the structure of power in the Soviet Union is the power relationship between the masses and other elements of society. The principal question is—how do we tell what this relationship actually is. While this matter has been vigorously debated, no agreement has been reached. The problem is essentially twofold. In the first place, the most widely-used Western definitions of power or influence have tended to follow the lines enunciated by Robert Dahl—namely that "A has power over B to the extent that he can get B to do something that B would not otherwise do."[1] Unfortunately, in practice, one can seldom be certain what B would have done otherwise. In addition, C, D, E, F, and G are usually also trying to influence B's behavior. Even if we know that B would have preferred to do something else, how do we know that it was A who had the power? It is a cliche of political biography that even the major political actors themselves often are not fully conscious of the factors influencing their decisions and actions.

In the second place, power is clearly situational and relational in nature. In the words of V. O. Key, power is not "a substance that could be poured into a keg, stored, and drawn upon as the need arises."[2] It varies with the issue at stake and the circumstances existing at the moment. The unquestioned power of the Soviet Union to crush Rumania in a war is not easily translated into an ability of the Soviet Union to compel Rumania to accept the Soviet position on all questions. The same point obviously could be made with respect to the United States and North Vietnam or Saudi Arabia, or to any other political actors in any political arena. To quote from Key once more, "Such notions of power as . . . something a person does or does not have convey a truncated or partial conception of the reality of power."[3]

If this conception of power is correct, how do we compare the distribution of power in two communities or two countries? In particular, how do we gauge the relative power or influence of broad groups within society—if we are interested, for example, in demonstrating that competitive elections do or do not increase the power of the masses in the United States in comparison with those in the Soviet Union? Since the power relationships among the political leadership, the elite, and the masses vary from situation to situation and from issue to issue in any country, how do we judge whether on balance the political leadership or the elite in one country is more powerful than in another? If we try to compare the distribution of power, are we not forced to treat power in aggregated terms, even though we know it is illegitimate to do so?

Surprisingly, the political science literature on the measurement of power, despite its great volume, sheds very little light on this crucial comparative problem. As phrases such as "who governs?" suggest, the focus of much of the literature has been upon the study of the direct exercise of power. The most important direct participants in the vast majority of instances have been elite in character, at least to the extent that those in the middle class or the upper-stratum are considered in the elite. Hence the central issue has often been the nature of elite participation, specifically the degree of pluralism within it.

Although various participants in the debate have attempted to speak about indirect influence, they have—as their respective opponents have charged—done so on the basis of very little empirical evidence.[4] Unfortunately for our purposes, any influence of the broad mass of the population upon policy, strong or weak, is overwhelmingly indirect in nature. It is registered almost exclusively in the form of decision makers' anticipation of the population's reaction to the results of policy, whether this be votes in an election, riots or the lack of them, high productivity or low, and so forth.[5] As a consequence, any methodology which focuses on the exercise of direct power is bound to be deficient from our point of view.

In addition, the literature on the measurement of power has been conducted more as a debate than as a cumulative development of position. Thus, the most systematic and valuable recent attempt to formalize the study of power—that made some fifteen years ago by Robert Dahl and several of his students (notably Nelson Polsby)—was explicitly a response to assertions about elite rule in the United States made by Floyd Hunter, C. Wright Mills, and several other sociologists. The opposing position then came to be developed largely as a response to Dahl. Both the original contributions of Dahl and his protagonists, as well as the ensuing discussion, tended to focus more on the weakness of each other's position than to move toward a consideration of the best way to analyze the distribution of power in comparative terms.

Consequently, as we try to utilize this methodological literature in understanding the distribution of power in the Soviet Union, we must never lose sight of the fact that most of the authors had limited aims. Robert Dahl, for example, did not attempt to measure the distribution of power directly in his analysis, particularly the distribution of indirect power or influence. In fact he was perfectly willing to concede that "the distribution of influence in most sectors of policy [in the United States] is far indeed from perfect equality." He sought no more than to prove the nonexistence of a ruling elite: "To condemn our political system for inequality is one thing; to condemn it for being dominated by a ruling elite is another."[6]

For his limited purpose, Dahl tried to sidestep the difficulties of aggregating power by setting up his protagonists' position as a null hypothesis and seeing whether it could be disconfirmed. He tried to define the conditions that would be necessary to declare that a society was elite-dominated. A ruling elite, he argued, should be defined as "a group of people who to some degree exercise power or influence over other actors in the system . . . a controlling group . . . a minority of individuals whose preferences regularly prevail in cases of difference of preference on key political issues." Dahl contended that the existence of a ruling elite could be demonstrated only if one found, first, that "the hypothetical ruling elite is a well-defined group," second, that "the hypothetical ruling elite prefers one alternative and other actors in the system prefer other alternatives," and third, that "in all or very nearly all of these cases the alternative preferred by the ruling elite is actually adopted." Unless these conditions are met, Dahl felt, "the hypothesis (that the system is dominated by the specified ruling elite) is clearly false."[7]

Nelson Polsby was even more explicit in his use of a null hypothesis test. He surveyed the books of those who spoke of elite rule in American communities and drew out "five assertions . . . about power" which he believed common to the "stratification thesis" developed in them:

1. *The upper class rules in local community life* . . . The group with the highest social-economic standing has the most power.
2. *Political and civic leaders are subordinate to the upper class* . . . They are held to take orders from or do the bidding of the upper class.
3. *A single 'power elite' rules in the community* . . . By a single power elite . . . [is meant] a small group, not selected by some democratic means, which [is] united in its policy aims and consistently [gets] its way in more than one significant policy area.
4. *The upper-class power elite rules in its own interests.*
5. *Social conflict takes place between the upper and lower classes* . . . Social conflict is primarily a matter of interclass warfare.[8]

When the evidence of the American community was applied against these null-hypothesis tests, Dahl and Polsby found no ruling group which could pass them. Dahl concluded that New Haven is a city "dominated by many different sets of leaders, each having access to a different combination of political resources . . . [a city with], in short, a pluralist system."[9] In another place, he expressed his belief that "New Haven is similar to many communities and strikingly similar in many ways to the United States as a whole."[10] Polsby likewise argued that the books of those who formulated the "stratification thesis" did not demonstrate the validity of the thesis and that their approach had led to "the systematic misreporting of facts and to the formulation of vague, ambiguous, unrealistic, and unprovable assertions."[11] Sometimes Dahl and Polsby incautiously moved to more general statements about the distribution of power (like Dahl's statement that "there is even a sense in which nobody runs the community")[12] but, strictly speaking, their aim was simply to disprove the notion that a narrow business, or social super-elite dominates decision making.

Critics of Dahl's approach have contended that the study of the outcomes of political issues is not the best way to reveal power relationships, that power may be exercised covertly through the shaping of values, the determination of the agenda, or the creation of a sense of hopelessness among one's opponents. In addition, many have questioned whether a city "dominated by many different sets of leaders" has, "in short, a pluralist system." Yet while the critics have insisted on the importance of "non-decisions," their efforts to formulate methodologies for studying them have been poorly developed, and they made no effort to try to compare the degree of power exercised in different systems.[13]

What then do we do if we want to analyze the power of the broad population in the Soviet Union in comparative terms? Almost any technique will demonstrate that there is inequality of power in the Soviet Union. The average rank-and-file citizen clearly does not have the same impact on decisions as more active participants in those decisions: party officials, governmental administrators, scholarly specialists, interested in upper-stratum citizens participating on commissions or councils. But, of course, even Dahl acknowledged that the distribution of power in the United States "is far indeed from perfect equality." How do we judge whether the degree of inequality is different in the two countries?

Since a great many American scholars have analyzed the Soviet Union in ruling elite terms, it might at least be useful to use the Dahl-Polsby null hypothesis technique in the Soviet context. To be sure, specialists on

the Soviet Union have disagreed on the nature of the Soviet elite; some
have contended that the elite—at least at times—has been as small as one
man, while others have spoken of the Politburo, the party apparatus, or
even a group as broad as the New Class.[14] Yet many have seen the relationship between the elite, however defined, and the masses in essentially "they - we" terms. Perhaps the Dahl-Polsby null hypothesis test
will at least demonstrate that the Soviet Union is (or was) elite-dominated
in contrast to the United States.

In practice, however, if we attempt to examine the Soviet experience—even the experience of the Stalin period—in light of the Dahl
and Polsby null hypotheses, the result is no different than in the American case. Even for Stalin's Soviet Union, the hypothesis of a ruling elite is
disconfirmed.

Polsby's null hypothesis test—his "stratification thesis"—is drawn
from the works of others and relates directly to their view of the American scene, and, therefore, it is not a proper test for ruling elite domination in another country. Nevertheless, the test does embody a number of
the critical themes in the debate, and it may be instructive to note that
the Soviet political system of the Stalin era does fail several of its requirements. It seems quite wrong, for instance, to state that the Soviet political
leaders were subordinate to the upper class. They either dominated that
class or, better, were part of it, depending upon how the upper class is
defined. Moreover, any Soviet elite that is broader than one man clearly
has been divided. Even in the late Stalin period there were readily apparent conflicts between Malenkov, on the one hand, and Zhdanov and
then Khrushchev, on the other, as well as between Stalin and many of
the other Politburo members. The departmental conflicts among top
ministerial officials were even more obvious. Finally, political conflicts
within the Soviet system generally took place less between the ruling elite
and the masses than among members of different sectors of the elite.[15]

Whatever the validity of using Polsby's stratification thesis as our
null hypothesis, there should be no question about the appropriateness
of Dahl's key test. Yet, if we ask whether the alternative preferred by the
ruling elite was adopted in all or nearly all of the cases of conflict between
the masses and the elite in the Stalin period, again the answer is no. Consider the question of agricultural organization. In the 1920s Stalin and
his lieutenants preferred state farms over collective farms. They felt compelled to adopt the latter. Stalin then wanted rapid collectivization, but
he had to retreat with his "Dizziness from Success" speech and to accept
incremental collectivization over a five-year period. Indeed, he eventually
had to forego complete collectivization and permit the continued existence of private plots and privately owned cows and fowl. In 1937 (a good
year for the socialized sector) the private plot produced 52 percent of the

country's potatoes and vegetables, 71 percent of its meat, 57 percent of its fruit, 43 percent of its wool, and 71 percent of its milk.[16] Except for the production of grain and technical crops such as cotton, collectivization remained only partial throughout the Stalin years.

Collectivization was not the only realm in which leadership preferences did not prevail during the Stalin period. In the rapid industrialization drive, Stalin thought it necessary to sacrifice some of the most sacred ideological preferences and to yield to the desires of administrative personnel and skilled labor for an end to the egalitarian wage and status programs of the 1920s.[17] (The change in this period was so great that Nicholas S. Timasheff entitled a 400-page book on the subject, *The Great Retreat.*[18]) Even when Stalin's preferences were enacted into law, the enforcement of that law often yielded to popular pressure. For example, the ban on the subordination of women to men in Moslem areas of the Soviet Union was motivated by a set of reinforcing economic, ideological, and political factors, but in practice only sporadic attempts were made to enforce it in the rural areas.

If it is impossible to say that "in all or very all of [the cases in the Stalin era] the alternative preferred by the ruling elite [was] actually adopted," then it is even easier to use to test to discredit a ruling elite thesis so far as the 1950s and the 1960s are concerned.[19] At a minimum, the determination of the post-Stalin leadership to enforce its preferences was much weaker than that of its predecessor, and, in practice, its policy was much more ambivalent. If a policy area such as education is studied, the cleavages are readily apparent and deviation from Khrushchev's enunciated preferences are not difficult to document.[20] An examination of the structure of power in the Soviet city by a similar procedure also disconfirms any notion of a ruling elite there.[21]

There would seem to be two ways to look at the results that have emerged from our use of the Dahl null hypothesis test in the Soviet context. One possible conclusion is that even under Stalin power and influence were more dispersed than the totalitarian model suggested, and that substantial elements of pluralism have always existed within the Soviet Union. This conclusion is at least partially warranted. A second possible conclusion is that a test for ruling elite domination that cannot be passed by Stalin's Soviet Union is not altogether a reasonable one. It might be argued that the test is useful in pointing to the dispersion of power and influence that exists in any large-scale political system, but it does not help us to distinguish the degrees of inequality of power found in the real world. And, in fact, it seems to me that this conclusion is also warranted.

Basically, the fact that Dahl and his associates were responding to a very simplistically stated elite theory made the task of discrediting it too easy, and they were not led to explore the problems of analyzing a more sophisticated theory. Thus, for example, there is no reason to think only of the possibility of a narrow business ruling elite. Dahl and Polsby both defined an elite simply as "a minority of individuals whose preferences regularly prevail in cases of differences in preference on key political issues."[22] (A small group chosen through democratic processes is excluded.) By this definition, the entire white minority in South Africa could be seen (and, I would think, quite rightly so) as a ruling elite vis-a-vis the black majority. Similarly, it should be at least thinkable to speak of an elite comprising the top 1-2 percent of society in socioeconomic standing or even the top 10-15 percent. Such an elite would still be very small in relation to society as a whole, but quite large in number. Two percent of New Haven's adult population would be some 2,000 people, while 10 percent would be 10,000. In the United States as a whole, the figure would range between 2,500,000 and 12,500,000 persons.

Similarly, there is no inherent reason to insist upon a united elite. If we were to discover that the Politburo members, and only the Politburo members, had the overwhelmingly decisive role in all major Soviet decisions, would the additional discovery that the Politburo had two factions disqualify it as a ruling elite? Does the fact that the whites in South Africa govern themselves through democratic institutions, and are frequently divided on policy issues, change the fact that collectively they constitute a minority ruling elite in the country? Certainly these questions could be answered affirmatively, and one could insist on a narrow definition of the term "ruling elite." However, if this narrow definition is then used in a null hypothesis test, rejection of the hypothesis in no way allows us to conclude that power and influence are widely dispersed (except, perhaps, within the elite), that "nobody rules."

Indeed, pluralists have always assumed that each person has a multiplicity of interests—or group memberships, to make the same point in different language. They normally take for granted that a group which is united on one issue will be split on others. Thus, the fact that one Air Force general may advocate emphasis upon missiles while another supports bombers does not preclude the possibility that they are members of an Air Force "group," fairly united on a number of issues involving the Air Force as a whole. Similarly, competition among the Air Force, the Army, and the Navy for funds does not necessarily imply to the pluralist that these groups do not unite in the battle for defense needs in the budget as a whole.

Why then should conflicts within the "power elite" be cited as evidence against C. Wright Mills' contention that this group dominates policy making on certain fundamental questions? An empirical study might cast doubt on the existence of such a group or on its dominance in the policy process, but divisions within the group scarcely make it impossible in principle that the industrial and military elites basically are (or perhaps were) united in promoting a particular foreign policy line toward the Soviet Union and revolutionary regimes in the Third World.

One could at least imagine an elite theory that would require very few assumptions about unity within the elite. First, such a theory would have to assume that, whatever the conflicts in the policy process, those influential within it are members of a narrow circle of the community. (Again, however, let us remember that 10 percent of the American adult population is a narrow group that includes over 12,000,000 persons.) There might be—indeed, surely would be—vigorous debates within "the club," but nonmembers would usually not be invited to participate in a significant way nor would their wishes be considered very seriously. Second, the theory would have to assume that, to the extent that members of the elite share interests with members of the nonelite (and this is inevitable), the degree of support for various proposals among the nonelites would not be a very significant factor in determining the outcome. (It is unrealistic, however, to assume that the masses are totally without influence in any situation.) Third, it would probably have to assume that the relatively narrow elite would have at least some interests in common that are not widely shared by the rest of the population, but these interests might be little more than the protection of existing inequalities in income distribution and property ownership.

How such an elite theory would be verified or disconfirmed is not the subject of discussion at this point, but it is crucial to recognize that Dahl's basic test for ruling elite domination would always disconfirm the existence of this or almost any elite. To demand that "in all or very nearly all of [the cases of conflict of preference] the alternative preferred by the ruling elite is actually adopted" is to forget the essential point of Dahl's own insight about power: that power varies with the situation and that only God is omnipotent. No individual person, and certainly no ruling group in a complex society, is ever able to achieve or acquire anything he or it wants. In part, the problem is that wants tend to expand if they are satisfied. The more fundamental problem, however, is that a person or group is not limited to one preference and that there may be trade-offs among them.

Thus, the conventional explanation for Stalin's "Great Retreat" from the ideological preference for wage and status egalitarianism is that he had an ever greater preference for rapid industrialization, a preference based in large part upon an intense desire to strengthen the Soviet defense capacity. Stalin found out, so it is argued, that incentive wage systems and status distinctions are necessary for the maximization of industrial growth, and he reconciled himself to such "imperatives of industrialization" in order to reach this goal.[23]

If this argument is true—and I see no reason to challenge it—what should we say about Stalin's ability to achieve his preferences in this realm? On the one hand, the real and potential resistance of the industrial elite and skilled labor force to central decrees did compel Stalin to yield on key preferences. On the other hand, as Jeremy Azrael has documented, Stalin was able to push a tempo of industrial growth that was more rapid than even the industrial elite desired.[24]

The analysis of the preferences of any political leadership is further complicated by the fact that one of its preferences surely is for the population to accord it some support and legitimacy. To some extent, it inevitably will adjust its decisions and behavior to maintain this support. Indeed, Arthur Bentley insisted that "except in the case of a subjected population immediately under the heel of the conquerer under conditions of most primitive oppression, the ruling class is to a certain extent the chosen (that is, the accepted) ruler of the ruled class, not merely its master, but also its representative; and the despot at the top of the system is representative both of his own class, and to a smaller, but none the less real, extent of the ruled class as well."[25] Bentley may have overstated the point, but there is an element of truth in his position.

The situation with respect to "the alternative preferred" by the population is just as complex as it is with respect to that of the political leaders or the elite. Let us imagine, hypothetically, that an institution, a community, or a nation actually has a ruling group, but a ruling group which, of course, is not omnipotent. Under these conditions, nonelite citizens who desire to promote their preferences through political action could choose between one or two strategies. One possible strategy would be to seek the overthrow of the ruling group and the establishment either of a new ruling group or a new kind of political system. The other would be to assume that the ruling group, like any ruling group, will surely yield on some questions and then try to affect the decisions on those questions. Employing the second strategy, the non-elite citizens would define politics as "the art of the possible" and would continually make demands or suggestions on issues that do not seem critical to the ruling elite at the moment.

If, however, there actually were a society dominated by a ruling group, if the nonelite members of the population chose the nonrevolutionary strategy, could the existence of the ruling group be identified by Dahl's test? Assuming that the nonelite citizens behave intelligently, the answer is a flat no. The proper strategy for the citizenry would be to move the political battleline to the point where the ruling elite might well adjust its policies. If they have judged the power situation correctly, they will, in fact, have a fair chance of winning. And, as a consequence, Dahl's test will always demonstrate that no ruling elite exists.

The problem can be illustrated by examples from a number of different areas. For example, in race relations in the American South a half century ago, there surely were blacks who pressed for incremental changes within the segregated system—perhaps an additional teacher for their school or even the construction of a new building, a new drinking fountain in the city hall, better care for the "Colored Only" restrooms. And surely they sometimes won on these issues.[26] The change in their power today is measured not so much by a high percentage of victories in current conflicts, as by the fact that the conflicts now concern the presence of black teachers and principals in schools with large percentages of white students.

Likewise in the realm of international affairs, the power relationship between Rumania and the Soviet Union is not adequately summarized by noting that Rumania wins on most of the open issues between the two countries—for example, an integrated Comecon, the timing of Rumanian recognition of West Germany, and the amount of support given by Rumania to the Soviet Union on the China question. A crucially relevant fact is that control of Bessarabia (Moldavia), Rumanian withdrawal from the Warsaw Pact, or Rumanian entry into the Common Market have not become political issues between the two countries.

The locus of power in universities is yet another question to which it is not enough to answer that each side sometimes wins in student-faculty conflicts. If the battle rages over faculty-student parity on tenure committees, the relative influence of the two groups is not what it was in the past when the issue was whether women could visit the men's dorms for twenty hours a week instead of fifteen. And the relative influence of faculty and students would be still different if students felt strong enough to push for decision making by committees, the members of which are chosen in joint student-faculty elections in which each student and each member of the staff have one vote.

In short, if persons or groups can never have everything they want, the critical indicator of relative power is not simply victory or defeat on issues which arise. Rather it is the nature of the issue on which the struggle takes place. Let us say, speaking very unrealistically, that A and B each have 100 preferences that come into conflict. What is crucial in defining their power or influence vis-à-vis each other is the ranking of the preference on which they do battle. If A has achieved 90 of his preferences and

the contest concerns his 91st, his power relationship to B is radically different from what it would be if he had achieved only 10 and the conflict
centers on his 11th. To use an analogy from the game of football, on
whose end of the field is the line of scrimmage located? Who has "field
position?" The analogy would be even more accurate if football games
were scored on the basis of the amount of time spent in the opponent's
end of the field.

Other authors have made many of these points in different form.
Andrew McFarland, for example, has emphasized the need to take the
importance of a decision into account, and, following the lead of James
Fesler, has cited the case of Soviet industrial administration as one of
"spurious pluralism" in which power is decentralized on routine rather
than important issues.[27] The Bachrach-Baratz criticism of Dahl essentially
is of a similar nature. However, to say that the importance of issues is a
critical element in the measurement of power, to say that field position
best corresponds to our intuitive notion of the meaning of power, is not
to say how one judges an issue's importance or a person's field position,
especially in comparative situations. Authors such as McFarland have
done a better job in emphasizing the difficulties in judging the importance of an issue than in telling us how to take advantage of their insight.[28]

There was, after all, a very sound reason for the methodological
approach used by Dahl and Polsby and specifically for their use of a null
hypothesis test. Power *is* situational and relational; it is *not* really an ag-
gregative entity. But if we cannot fruitfully use a null hypothesis test, we
face the problem of measuring power in aggregate terms if we still want
to compare the distribution of power in different political systems—if we
want to say, for example, that the existence of competitive elections
means that the power position of the bottom 80-90 percent of the population in the West is stronger than that of their counterparts in the Soviet
Union. We know that it is fundamentally wrong to treat power in this
way, we know that we are attempting to square the circle, but we also
know that the attempt is necessary if we want to answer the questions
long considered basic in political science.

What is the way out of this methodological box? In particular, since
we know that power is distributed unequally but widely in all political systems (and hence have proved nothing in comparative terms if we
demonstrate either inequality or dispersion of power in any country), how
do we compare the levels of inequality that do exist? We assume that
competitive elections increase the influence of the masses upon public
policy, but how do we demonstrate that this is so?[29] Or, on the contrary,

how does the classical Marxist demonstrate that the masses have less political power in systems with private ownership of the means of production? Or, to leave the realm of East-West comparisons, how do we judge whether parliamentary systems have a different impact on the distribution of power than presidential systems or whether decentralization of functions to the state, city, or community level has an impact on the power of the poor vis-a-vis other social groups?

Part of the answer surely lies in the abandonment of any attempt to speak of a ruling elite in a way which implies all-or-nothing possession of power. The use of the Dahl-Polsby test in the Stalin case strongly suggests that there is not—that there cannot be—a society in which all power is concentrated in a few hands and in which the broad population has none. All citizens must have a modicum of direct or indirect influence in certain situations (if nothing else, as rulers anticipate their reactions), and the gradations in influence and power between different strata of society must be incremental in nature. Inequalities in the distribution of power surely must be visualized along lines analogous to the Lorenz curves of income distribution.[30] Therefore, the question for comparative political scientists should not be "Does a ruling elite exist in Country A or Country B?" Instead, it should be "How does the relative power of the top 1 percent of the population (or the top 5 percent or the top 10 percent) vary from political system to political system?" Above all, "What factors are associated with these variations?"

Another part of the answer must be a keen awareness of the unpleasant fact that we all are in deep trouble as we try to answer some of the most important questions about political systems in general and about the Soviet Union specifically. However, it may be that awareness of our problem may be of some help in our efforts to solve it. If we recognize that any methodology being used must inevitably be flawed, we may perhaps be in a better position to use a number of imperfect techniques in attempting to tease out partial clues with respect to the questions that interest us. After all, while a circle cannot be squared in literal terms, it is possible to draw a square with essentially the same area as a given circle.

In appealing for eclecticism in our attempts to compare the power distribution in different political systems, one need not say much about the possible advantage of examining open political conflicts or of seeking information about the preference of different groups.[31] The cases for these methodologies have often been advanced. Less, however, has been said about the possibility of inferring power relationships from an examination of societal outcomes, and this methodology deserves much more serious attention than it has received. We have looked at governmental decisions (outputs) and even at their impact, but it may be that an examination of relationships and distributions of values in society—whether produced by governmental action or not prevented by it—will be indispensable to shed more light on nondecisions, on the importance of decision, on field position.

The use of societal outcomes as an indicator of differences in the relative power of the actors involved clearly does have major flaws as a methodology, for differences in outcomes may easily result from other factors. Actually, Polsby has suggested that four such factors are possible: irrationalities in decision making, influences intruding from outside the arena in which the actors are struggling, outcomes occurring without anyone making a conscious decision, and the conscious desire of the powerful to satisfy the desires of the nonpowerful.[32] In fact, one might add that differences in outcomes in different settings can reflect differences in the values of any of the actors, the apparently nonpowerful as well as the apparently powerful.

Yet such criticisms would be more compelling if other methodologies existed with fewer shortcomings, and it may be that they should be treated as cautionary warnings rather than decisive arguments. If we examine areas in which mass values and elite interests may be assumed to be more or less comparable, the difficulties are somewhat reduced. For example, in one of his more recent books, *Polyarchy*, Dahl tried to determine whether land distribution is more egalitarian in countries with democratic institutions, hoping to ascertain thereby whether democratic institutions seem to affect the power of the masses. The Communist countries were excluded from the calculation, but in the rest of the world democratic insititutions do seem to be associated with more equal distribution of land ownership.[33] This technique, assuming that one tries to control for other variables such as level of industrial development, seems well worth emulating.

Income distribution is another indicator that intuitively seems to be useful for inferring power relationships among broad strata of the population. Income is helpful in achieving most other values, and one would think that the middle and lower levels of society would use whatever power is at their disposal to maximize their share of national income. Certainly this hypothesis about democracy has been advanced by political philosophers since the time of Plato and Aristotle. It seems to run contrary to intuitive reason to say that the masses in Country A have a great deal of power while those in Country B have little, if the masses in Country A receive no more and perhaps less of a share of national income than those in Country B.[34]

There are innumerable other comparative outcomes that may shed light on power relationships in ways not attained by other methodologies.

Surely, for example, the power of American doctors is best illustrated not by the series of gradual defeats they have suffered on governmental health programs, but by the fact that much more comprehensive programs are found in other countries of the industrial world, and are enormously popular.[35] Similarly the power of those with high socioeconomic status in the New Haven area is better understood if one moves beyond that area and compares the situation there with that in, say, Toronto, Canada. In the Canadian case, the well-to-do suburbs were compelled to accept amalgamation with the city and the greater equality in taxes and services that accompanied it; in New Haven, the city inhabitants have so little confidence about their field position that the question is not raised in the state legislature. With the development of a strong interest in policy studies in the discipline, there is certain to be far more information available on outcomes in the future, and it should be easier to find evidence of relevance for a comparative understanding of the distribution of power.

Although the major lesson of this methodological exploration for specialists on the Soviet Union is that we face great difficulties in judging the relative power of the Soviet masses, there are other important implications for our understanding of the Soviet Union. By far the most important has little to do with the reasonableness or unreasonableness of the Dahl test as a means of verifying ruling elite hypotheses. The key fact is that we have regularly advanced such hypotheses about the Soviet Union, but never have linked our analysis with what has probably been one of the most prominent methodological disputes in political science in recent years. We have not tried to utilize the basic methodology our colleagues have used in studying similar questions in the West, and we have not heeded their many warnings about possible difficulties in assertions about ruling elite domination.

The results have been disastrous for our comparisons of the Soviet Union and the West. If in our comparative statements about the structure of power, our conclusions about the West rest on an approach like that employed by Dahl and Polsby, which measures power by examining the outcomes in conflicts over issues, while those about the Soviet Union are based on a C. Wright Mills-like approach which emphasizes the potential power of the elite if it wants to impose its will, then obviously the results are not going to be comparable. Yet this is precisely what has occurred.

In trying to understand the Soviet political system, we continually focus on the question: Does the political leadership or the elite have the final authority to force through any policy that it desires? Does not the existence of Party *nomenklatura* mean that the political leadership has final control over the careers of the leaders of the institutional interest groups and that, therefore, these ultimately are not autonomous? And, of course, we rightly answer, "Yes, at least to the extent that those at the top are willing to accept costs that their actions may entail."

On the other hand, we condemn those who suggest that the power of a Western elite is to be measured by what it can do if it is united and determined. Indeed, so far as government is concerned, we simply take for granted that it is the body that can make "authoritative allocations of values" and can enforce them with coercion, and our analysis is concerned with the nature of the groups, persons, and values that shape the authoritative allocations. In doing this, we insist that we must look at real world behavior. We know that a British Parliament may have unlimited legal power but, in practice, may be severely limited by a number of political norms and unwritten constraints. We know that even in a presidential system, the political leadership as a whole, including the Supreme Court, can incarcerate native-born Japanese-Americans in camps if it is united and believes that such action is necessary. We never assume that just because the military is in the *nomenklatura* of Western civilian authorities, it has no autonomy as an interest group.

Similarly, although the pluralist approach is highly suspicious of allegations that an elite dominates through the shaping of values, our analysis of the Soviet Union regularly deals with indoctrination and "the internalization of ideology" and the restraints on mass freedom and power that are involved in them. We regularly attribute values and interests to Soviet citizens in precisely the terms Polsby criticized so severely in his discussion of "false consciousness."[36]

This type of comparative analysis of the Soviet Union and the West is, unfortunately, not an isolated phenomenon. Our comparisons all too often have rested on different definitions of our concepts, on the application of different methodologies, and on the asking of different questions. Even if the Soviet and Western political systems were identical, this practice would inevitably result in our images of them being different. Unless we become much more aware of the need for consistency in definitions and standards, we open ourselves to the charge that Western social science sometimes is not all that different from the way it is described in the Soviet press.

A second implication of the methodological issues we discussed is the need to give much serious thought to our assumptions about the distribution of power between the elite and the masses in the Soviet Union. Certainly we should exercise extreme caution in speaking of ruling elite (for example New Class) domination in the Soviet Union. Perhaps there is some reasonable way to define the concept of a ruling elite so that we can demonstrate whether one does or does not actually exist in a country, but it is not readily apparent. The New Left political scientists who charge that the United States is elite-dominated have been no more successful in doing this than have their methodological opponents, and the suspicion must be very strong that we are dealing with a normative rather than an empirical category.

Indeed, if we take societal outcomes seriously as an indicator of power, even the question of the relative power of the masses and the broad elite in the United States and the Soviet Union becomes a live one. Obviously, power is distributed unequally in the Soviet Union, being correlated with socioeconomic status and educational level.[37] But the fundamental question is again the comparative one. Does the existence of competitive elections, the right to form autonomous organizations, and the right to engage in confrontation politics (including the right to strike in the economic sphere) mean that the masses in the West have more power vis-a-vis the elite than in the Soviet Union?

The masses in the West may well have more power than do the Soviet masses, but there are certain indicators that do not seem to reflect it. One is the case of income distribution. There is some argument in the West about the distribution of income in Communist countries (and for good reason, given the data problems), but it is obvious that income distribution in the East is basically as egalitarian as in the West. If property income, especially potential income from property, is taken into account, it is probably more egalitarian.

Similarly, an examination of urban politics in countries such as the United States and Canada reveals that one of the major values of the upper strata of society has been the establishment of exclusive neighborhoods where taxes are lower, schools and services are better, and, above all, the neighbors are of similar socio-economic status. Yet, with the exception of an extremely narrow elite, the Soviet New Class has not been able to achieve such exclusiveness in its neighborhoods.

These examples do not demonstrate that our conceptions about the relative power of elite and the masses in the East and West must be reversed. Even if the outcome method of measuring power is accepted, the continued existence of collectivization in the Soviet Union is an outcome as well as the great increases in the peasants' share of national income in the last two decades. Nevertheless, the examples—and there are many more—suggest the need for a bit of caution and even skepticism about generalizations which in the past have often been facilely reached largely on the basis of faith. We should at least feel some wariness in calling the Soviet Union a peculiarly elite-dominated society, given its income distribution and its pattern of urban housing, and the growing egalitarianism in income distribution should make us think twice before stating that the power of the masses has declined since 1964 in the Soviet Union.

Outcome analysis also suggests caution in some of our analysis of Eastern Europe. When we note that both Tito and Dubchek have been associated with policies of greater income inequality, we should at least consider the possibility that "States' Rights" may have the same conservative social consequences in the Communist world as they have had in the United States, and that Dubchek may have received strong political support from the elite of the Czech skilled labor force at Skoda and from many in the middle class at least as much because of his wage policy as his policy of political reform.

It may be that the major differences in the distribution of power in the Soviet Union and the West are to be found not in the relationship between the top 10-15 percent and the bottom 85-90 percent of the population, but in the distribution of power within the top 10-15 percent. The old pluralist conception of "veto groups" in the American political system has been subject to severe criticism, but it may not be far wrong for groups whose members are near the top of the socioeconomic hierarchy, as are all persons with professional or managerial occupations. Civil rights for dissenters tend also, in practice, to mean more autonomy for iconoclasts within these strata. These concepts have had much less relevance for understanding the Soviet Union, particularly in the past.[38]

Basically, however, our real knowledge about the distribution of power either in the Soviet Union or the West is still rudimentary at best, and it will not become better until we face up to the methodological issues. It may be that a comparative examination of societal outcomes—of who gets what—in the East and the West will require us to use the word "power" in contexts which violate our intuitive sense of what that word means. We may be driven to the conclusion that the concept of power is so ambiguous and unmeasurable as to be worthless and that, like the concepts of phlogiston and the ether in the natural sciences, it should be abandoned if the social sciences are to advance.[39] Rather than trying to analyze the relationship between institutions and power perhaps it is more useful to study the relationship of such institutions as competitive elections to variables such as income distribution, the ability of upper-strata professional groups to defend their professional autonomy, the treatment of dissidents, and so forth. Ultimately it is not power that interests us, but the concrete meaning of power relationships for the way in which people live.

Whatever conclusions we may reach, an examination of outcomes clearly will provide clues to questions which are of crucial interest to political scientists and specialists on the Soviet Union—at least if these outcomes are continually evaluated from their theoretical significance. At a minimum, such an examination will lead us to a more sophisticated understanding of how policy is formulated and will point us toward issue conflicts whose significance has not been appreciated. At a maximum, it may lead to renewed thought about (and perhaps a better understanding of) some of the most fundamental questions in the history of political and social philosophy. What are the factors that lead to power for the broad masses of the population? What are the consequences of the type of competitive elections, issue interest-groups, and confrontation politics that exist in the West?

# 11

## The Comparative Approach and the Study of the Soviet Union

Over the last several decades political scientists have increasingly extolled the virtues of the comparative approach as the path to a better understanding of the political process. It is a belief I fully share. Nevertheless, one of my recurrent themes is that, so far as our understanding of the Soviet Union is concerned, the use of the comparative approach has not always had the beneficial results claimed for it. Indeed, the most oversimplified statements about the Soviet Union, ones that would be most readily cited as exhibiting an ideological or Cold War bias, are usually found in comparative books and articles—including those written by the foremost comparative theorists—rather than in books on the Soviet Union itself.

There has been some tendency to treat the difficulties in the comparative analysis of the Soviet Union simply as the temporary product of the Cold War or of some other area-specific factor, but it seems to me that much more basic methodological problems are also involved. If we speak facilely of "Cold War literature," we will fail to face up to difficulties that far transcend the Soviet-American comparison and fail to adopt the types of research strategies that are necessary to break Soviet studies out of the ghetto in which it is located.

Why has the comparative approach contributed so little to our understanding of the Soviet Union? One reason, of course, is the impact of scholars' values upon the questions they ask and the conclusions they draw. It is, of course, a cliché to say that scholarship cannot be value-free, but the methodological literature does not sufficiently emphasize that the value problem is especially great in comparative work that deals with the fundamentals of competing political-social systems, one of them our own.

Obviously the study of the Soviet Union has touched an extraordinary number of the values and interests of Western scholars. These scholars have had the normal class bias of those in the top 5 to 10 percent in socioeconomic status as well as the bias of the intellectual in favor of intellectual freedom. Those with foreign policy interests have often been led to study and emphasize the regressive aspects of the system in order to counteract Soviet propaganda which has presented an extremely distorted image of the degree of democracy and intellectual freedom in the Soviet Union. Those with a liberal domestic outlook often have felt a strong need to counteract the Far Right tendencies (especially in the McCarthy era) to equate the welfare state and Communism, and in the process many may have unconsciously been tempted to play down Soviet phenomena like governmental welfare state programs that were close to the liberal goals. Finally, a great many Soviet specialists have come from a Russian or East European background—some from families that fled the Communists, others from families which left during the pogroms at the turn of the century—and this background may have made them acutely aware of certain types of discrimination or oppression and may have led them to make these phenomena a central test of the overall nature of the system.

One might think that scholars using a comparative approach would be less affected by these problems—that a rigorous use of comparative definitions and standards would permit a more objective analysis than a methodology without such standards of comparison. Yet nothing is easier than permitting definitions and standards to shift in a way that makes the results congenial to the value system.

Indeed, it is in comparative studies—at least when dealing with important questions—that it is psychologically most difficult to reduce the impact of values. After all, it is not an enormous challenge to one's values to recognize that the Soviet system has certain strong points or virtues. The longevity of the system requires some explanation and a totally negative picture might not only lack credibility, but also convey the sense of imminent Soviet collapse and therefore the lack of a long-term challenge. Similarly, it is reasonably easy in emotional terms to say that conditions in the Soviet Union have been improving, for such a view can be coupled with the notion that the change is not as rapid as it should be or that the consequence of the change is to make the Soviet system more like our own.

However, from the psychological point of view it is extremely difficult to make a comparative statement suggesting that the Soviet Union is better than the United States—or even as good as the United States by some important, value-laden criterion. It is one thing to say that there has been some dispersion of power in the Soviet system; it would be quite another to assert that the masses in the Soviet Union have much the same amount of power as those in the United States. In fact, in many cases it is difficult even to use words like ''pluralism,'' ''political participation,'' or "interest group" in describing the Soviet system because of their strong and positive normative overtones. In the Soviet Union, the censorship permits a great deal of criticism of Soviet reality, but is exceedingly strict in dealing with comparative statements that might be less than favorable to the Soviet system. This type of sensitivity is clearly a universal one.

The value problem is such a serious one in comparative work that one is almost tempted to counsel more narrowly focused research in order to minimize it. Yet the problem will not disappear, for almost any meaningful generalization about a political system (that, for example, the Soviet system is elite-dominated) is implicitly comparative in nature, and a failure to make the comparison explicit does not mean that it isn't there.

Although scholarship can never be value-free, continued emphasis of that fact may be of some use. Scholars have a tendency to recognize their commitment to democracy and liberal values in the introductions of their books and then to assume that such a recognition guarantees objectivity. Clearly such a formal acknowledgment of values is not enough. What is needed is more of the spirit behind the conception of a null hypothesis: that a scholar should be responsible for trying to prove the hypothesis that he opposes, and try to disprove his own hypothesis. When we know that our values are, in part, deeply involved on some question, we should perhaps feel a special responsibility to look for evidence that is opposite to that which we would like to find. No doubt this is a utopian notion, but if our commitment is to the liberal values with respect to the search for truth, we might at least posit it as an unattainable goal towards which we aspire and strive.

The great shortcomings in the comparision of the Soviet and Western political systems are not, however, simply the product of the values of the scholars involved. A second contributing factor has been the scholarly methodology dominant in the great flowering of comparative studies since the mid-1950s.

A central feature of the expansion of comparative political science in the last two decades was the first serious focusing of attention on the less industrialized countries of Asia, Africa, and Latin America and, as a consequence, on the politics of development. As the need for developmental categories and theories became clear, the scholars whose work seemed most relevant and proved most influential were the great sociologists, Max Weber and Talcott Parsons. Weber's analyses of modernization and traditional, charismatic, and rational-legal authority—particularly as interpreted by Parsons and amplified by his "pattern variables"—became the backbone of the rapidly multiplying work on the politics of "traditional," "transitional," and "modern" society.

On balance, political science has benefited immensely from the insights of developmental sociology, but in several respects the impact of Weber and Parsons on the discipline has been unfortunate. Specifically, many political scientists have adopted not only the basic analysis of Weber and Parsons, but also its framework: the ideal type as used by Weber and the emphasis upon comprehensive systems analysis found in Parsons. These methodologies, as they have often been used in political science, have had a number of negative consequences that are especially potent in the comparison of the Soviet Union and the West.

A great deal could be said about systems analysis—some of it laudatory. Certainly this volume has been heavily influenced by the tendency of systems analysis to focus upon functions and processes rather than upon legal structures. However, the aspect of systems theory that has had a most baneful effect upon the Soviet-Western comparison has been the insistence upon the need to define the boundaries between the political system and other social systems. To quote Almond and Powell:

> What do we mean by "system"? A system implies the interdependence of parts, and a boundary of some kind between it and its environment . . . A system starts somewhere and stops somewhere. . . . In dealing with social systems, of which political systems are a class, the problem of boundary is not . . . easy. Social systems are made up not of individuals, but of roles . . . The same individuals who perform roles in the political system perform roles in other social systems such as the economy, the religious community, the family, and voluntary associations. As individuals expose themselves to political communication, form interest groups, vote, or pay taxes, they shift from nonpolitical to political roles.
>
> The problem of boundaries takes on special significance because systems theory usually divides interaction processes into three phases—input, conversion, output . . . The inputs and outputs, which involve the political system with other social systems, are transactions between the system and its environment; the conversion processes are internal to the political system. When we talk about the sources of inputs, their number, content, and intensity, and how they enter the political system, and of the number and content of outputs and how they leave the political system and affect other social systems, we shall in effect be talking about the boundaries of the political system.[1]

The meaning of this analysis is not totally clear, but it seems to make some intuitive sense in the case of countries such as the United States. One can see private individuals and institutions making demands on the government or rendering support to it; one sees interaction among political actors through which demands are converted into policy. In the case of countries like the Soviet Union, on the other hand, the concept of political boundary is much more difficult to visualize. In practical terms all citizens are governmental employees, and virtually all members of the elite would be labeled politicians or governmental administrators in the normal American usage of the words. How then do we define the boundary between the political system and the other systems? Where, for example, do the minister and other officials of the Ministry of Health fit into the analysis? Are they leading members of the medical community (they are, in fact, doctors) or are they key participants in the conversion process? In their political roles are they more the sources of inputs or are they primarily responsible for the authoritative determination of the outputs in their field?

It might seem that these questions are naively worded and that they pose no major problems for systems analysis. Almond and Powell are not talking about some boundary between politicians and private citizens, between political institutions and nonpolitical institutions. To use older terminology, they are not talking about a boundary between state institutions and society. They are talking about roles, and they recognize that individuals and institutions play a variety of roles. The obvious answer to the questions of the last paragraph is that the officials of the Ministry of Health, like governmental officials in any country, perform all the roles mentioned, depending upon the particular context.

In practice, however, it is extremely difficult to restrict analysis consistently to the level of abstract roles. Moreover, it is not altogether clear what problems are solved or illuminated if this is done. In practice, social systems tend to become associated with more concrete institutions, the political system with political institutions, and certain political institutions with certain political funtions:

> The *governmental structures,* particularly the bureaucracy, makes it possible for the political leaders to communicate directions for rule implementation to various political officeholders in an efficient and unambiguous fashion . . . The courts and various governmental agencies are the major agencies through which redress of grievances or *registration of demands* [my italics] is undertaken . . . The governmental structures also supply large amounts of general information to the public.
>
> The *"input"* structures, such as interest groups and parties constitute yet another significant information channel. By their very nature they are engaged in transmitting popular and special-interest demands to the political leadership.[2]

As the role analysis becomes reified, the concept of boundary begins to create major difficulties in trying to understand the Soviet Union and to compare it with non-Communist societies. Ministerial and party officials inexorably come to be placed on the political system side of the boundary, and hence there are few influential figures left on the other side of the boundary to articulate societal interests. With the society's major interest groups being institutional ones, it seemingly becomes impossible to acknowledge that they might have any autonomy. The whole advantage of looking at functions and processes instead of formal institutions becomes completely lost, and a system with Western institutions (even Western capitalist systems) becomes, by definition, the only one with true "responsive capacity."

A second problem that the Weberian and Parsonian categories of analysis have introduced into comparative political studies has been associated with Max Weber's "ideal type." The ideal type is not, of course, a description of an ideal system in the sense of a perfect system, but the distillation of the essential features of a particular type of institution, society, of phenomenon. In the words of Horace M. Miner, it is "a mental construct. It is a concept derived from observable reality but not conforming to it in detail. Some aspects of that reality are selected and accentuated in defining the type, because of the apparent interdependence and theoretical importance. However, ideal types are not classifications. No actual society will comform completely to such a type. When used as a basis of comparison with life situations, however, the type suggests possible hypotheses and lines of investigations. Thus ideal types are tools to be used in the analysis of empirical reality."[3]

In the study of political systems, the use of ideal types forces the scholar to create neatly defined, logically consistent categories, and it tempts him to emphasize differences rather than similarities among the ideal types, particularly if their number is small. Of course, this need not be disadvantageous if the ideal type is used for the purpose for which it was originally intended: that is, to provide a backdrop against which "the real situation or action is compared and surveyed for the explication of certain of its significant components."[4] In this case, the deviations of reality from the ideal type may, as Miner indicated, suggest many fruitful lines of inquiry.

But it is one thing to take *one* ideal type and to compare the real situation in an institution, country, or even set of countries with it; it is much more dangerous to use several ideal types and to compare them as a first step in understanding the differences and similarities among *several* different institutions, countries, or set of countries. In the first case the deviations of reality from the ideal type are highlighted and the ideal type serves to raise questions or hypotheses for scholarly inquiry or reflection. In the second case, however, the deviations that do not fit the ideal type (for example, the policy debates in the Soviet press or the extreme disparity between upper-class and lower-class voting in American local

elections) are often dismissed or ignored as the comparative analysis focuses on the essential features of political systems or types of political
system. And not by coincidence the features thought of as essential tend
to be those of the ideal type which the particular political system is
thought to approach.

In short, the result of comparing ideal types may be a confusion or a
blending together of ideal type and reality. This danger may be particularly great—and the results particularly unfortunate—when the ideal
types to which one's own country is said to approximate are termed
"modern," "democratic," "responsive," and so forth, and those to
which the enemies are said to approximate are called "totalitarian,"
"ideological," and so forth.

In fact, those making the Soviet-American comparison have often
fallen into the trap of confusing reality and ideal type, as in this typical
passage from Almond and Powell's *Comparative Politics:* "Some political
systems are primarily regulative and extractive in character. Totalitarian
systems suppress demands coming from the international environment.
At the same time, they regulate and coerce behavior in their societies, and
seek to draw maximum resources from their population . . . In democracies outputs or regulation, extraction, and distribution are more affected
by imputs of demands from groups in society."[5] Are Almond and Powell
talking about ideal-type totalitarian and democratic political systems, or
Soviet and American society in 1966? Unfortunately, they are talking
about both, and in the process the analysis becomes extremely slippery
and ambiguous.

It may be unfair to attribute such problems in comparison to Weber's ideal type, for Weber himself advocated a different use for his tool.
Perhaps the problem is the compulsion of comparativists to classify and
categorize political systems—as Richard Fagen phrased it, "each political
scientist has been his own taxonomist."[6] Any such effort at classification
of political systems leads to simplification, and thus to the creation of
something like an ideal type; it also leads to a comparison of these simpli-
fied ideal types. It is very difficult for such comparision to contribute to a
more sophisticated understanding of individual countries, particularly
when the values of the scholarly community must inevitably affect the
criteria of classification selected.

If the development of the right system of classification of political
systems is not the most useful focus for comparative political studies,
what then should be our central concern? Ideally, we should attempt to
develop generalizations about the relationship of different variables that
cut across political systems. What is needed, in the words of Erik Hoff-

mann, is "more problem-centered research in Communist studies," in which the specialist seeks "to construct [or] to test empirical theory."[7]

But how is this type of research to be conducted? Hoffmann summarizes the standard methodological advice in the following terms:

> The Communist area specialist may have much to *contribute* to, and much to *gain* from, social science theory. Particularly important are theories and hypotheses of a "puzzle-solving" or an anomaly-reducing nature. Also of considerable importance are hypotheses that are both logically and topically-related—hypotheses that have been deduced from insightful and rigorous causal models or formulated axioms and theorems. Greater confirmation, disconfirmation, or refinement of the latter propositions helps to confirm, disconfirm, or refine the other propositions to which they are logically related and the larger theories of which they are a part . . . The social scientist needs reasonably clear, discrete, and theoretically significant concepts *prior* to measurement, data collection, quantification, theory testing, or comparative analysis . . . In the absence of a research design and conceptual orientation tailored to this purpose in the initial stages of data collection, any attempt to change focus significantly in mid-stream is bound to be less than satisfactory.[8]

This methodology has been distilled from that supposedly used in the natural sciences. However, even if it does accurately observe the situation in the natural sciences,[9] there are key differences between the natural sciences and the social sciences which social science methodologists do not sufficiently appreciate.

In the first place, the data base of the social sciences is quite unlike that in the natural sciences. Although the nucleus of the atom or the structure of the cell are enormously difficult to study, the scholarly models or theories dealing with them can be tested against a uniform reality. Whatever the country of a scholar, whatever the century of his research, the phenomenon being studied, the data against which the model or theory is tested, will remain the same. (Of course, new technology will change the observability of the phenomenon enormously.) In political science, on the other hand, the data are far less stable. Even if human behavior does not change as that behavior is studied and reported, even if human behavior does have the regularity of the physical world (and these are enormous "ifs"), this behavior appears in quite different forms from place to place and from time to time. For example, we never see "administrative behavior" or "roles" in the real world, only the functioning of organizations of different responsibilities, sizes, and social-political milieus.

The problem of data variability has tended to be obscured by the fact that much of political science theory is essentially based on the American experience and that the scholars—whether they realize it or not—come to the study of the United States with a great deal of knowledge that has been accumulated in a lifetime of study, personal experience, and exposure to the media. However, when the experience of foreign countries is used in testing theory, we usually do not have this advantage. We often must learn the basic facts about those countries before we can even know which body of data is relevant for testing which theory.

In the case of my own study of the local party organs in the Soviet Union,[10] for example, what body of theory would have been the most appropriate to test? Eventually the book was entitled *The Soviet Prefects,* and it discussed the local party organs within the framework of the theory of field administration and regional coordination, arguing that the party organs fulfilled functions vital for the operation of the administrative structure. The book would undoubtedly have made a more useful contribution to the theory of field administration if it had originally been organized around a test of specific hypotheses—or, at least, an exploration of general conclusions—in that theory.

Yet one fact cannot be ignored: if my study of the local party organs had been conducted in accordance with the principles of a narrow problem-solving approach, it certainly would not have tested any proposition at all involving regional coordination. Regretfully, I did not conceive of the local party organs as a coordinating agent when I began the study.[11] It took a year or so before I even realized that the relationship of the secretary of the primary party organization to the plant manager was fundamentally different from the relationship of the regional party secretaries to that manager. Given that level of conceptual confusion (and similar confusion about many other aspects of the work of the party officials), undertaking any explicit test of administrative theory would have been worse than useless.

The learning process involved in my study of the local party organs is far from unique. It has been this need to understand and describe the basic facts of a situation—to understand the nature of the relevant test for a particular theory—that had led social scientists to deviate from the experience of the natural sciences and to follow the time-consuming strategy of researching and writing books instead of concentrating almost exclusively on articles. It has been this need that has often required a change in theoretical focus midway through a study. And this need explains the sterility and banality of so many articles in comparative politics that do attempt to test theoretical hypotheses explicitly.

A second fundamental difference between the natural sciences and the social sciences is the absence of concentrated scholarly focus in the second discipline—the lack of an agreement upon the way to look at the subject matter. In contrast, the disciplines or subdisciplines of the natural sciences (particularly the ones whose success has preoccupied philosophers and methodologists) tend to have some very specific question or questions on which the vast majority in the field have implicitly or explicitly agreed to work—questions which arise from a particular framework of analysis or model. As Thomas Kuhn has emphasized, this agreement upon a paradigm (to use his term) has been the indispensable precondition for the great progress made in the natural sciences.[12]

As the result of their agreement upon a paradigm, the disciplines of the natural sciences develop a real ongoing tradition, and those within the discipline often have a clear conception of the specific problems that are on the agenda today, as well as of the lines of work that are likely to be most productive in the future. The confidence exuded by James Watson, when he summarized the state of research in his field, illustrates this phenomenon very well:

> During the past two decades the vast majority of our bio-chemically inclined biologists focussed their efforts on the bacterial cell. They did not want to risk almost certain failure by attacking the much more complicated cells of human beings before they thoroughly understood the fundamental chemical rules that make possible the existence of the bacterial cell . . .
>
> Because of the innumerable remaining major intellectual challenges still facing biology, it attracts, for the first time, many of the best students who wish to do science. On the whole, most opt for work with the higher cells of vertebrates, not because they know this is where the money lies, but because animal cells now seem intriguingly tractable, in much the same way that bacteria looked to me twenty-five years ago when I first began to work in a university laboratory.
>
> For fields of science have their own momentum or nonmomentum, depending on whether the current experimental techniques are capable of moving them forward. Often it is all too obvious that a given key question cannot be answered with the current instrumentation and that, barring some unexpected insight, it is best left for another generation of scholars to take up. This may well be the case today in the fields of human perception and memory where the frightful anatomical complexity of the vertebrate brain poses a virtually impenetrable jungle for even the most talented experimentalists.
>
> In contrast, there exists a firm basis for the belief that the essential biochemistry of human cells can be worked out within the next decade or two. Even though today we still are completely in the dark about how vertebrate chromosomes function and have no good ideas about the detailed architecture of the outside surfaces of normal cells, much less those of cancer cells, there already exist the experimental techniques and machines which, when correctly applied should quickly lead to important new concepts.[13]

What political scientist could have the slightest confidence in making any such statement about his own discipline? From the perspective of a Soviet scholar, Western social scientists undoubtedly do share a number of assumptions in common—maybe even a paradigm. But there is little agreement on the basic questions towards which problem solving should be directed. What, for example, do students of "organizational theory" really want to know? Is it how best to structure an organization? If so, what values do we use in defining "best?" Efficiency? Innovation? Achievement of the goals of the leadership? A decrease in alienation on the part of the employees? Quality of service to clientele? Or is it our purpose to describe how organizations actually function rather than how they might function better? If so, are we interested in their internal nature or in their relationship to society or to an elite, in the way they reach decisions, or in the values and interests they serve? Indeed, what is an organization? Is it some concrete formal institution as perceived by the man in the street or an abstract set of roles, expectations, regularities in behavior, or just what? There is no agreement, and this is a subfield with a fairly lengthy tradition.

Consequently, though a political scientist may be able to follow Watson's lead and state that a certain line of research or the testing of a certain hypothesis will be the most appropriate and timely way to advance some aspects of organizational theory, he does not have Watson's assurance that other scholars will join him in undertaking the numerous small studies that are necessary to build up and refine a theory. Indeed, he has no assurance that his results or even the theory on which he is working will be of much interest when the study is completed, for whole theoretical approaches prove to be passing fads. Group theory is an excellent example from the past, and all signs suggest that elite theory is facing such a fate in the near future.

Given the lack of an agreed-upon paradigm and the complexity of our data base, what methodology is likely to be most profitable to social scientists, especially graduate students and young scholars beginning their careers? Or, to focus the discussion more directly on the subject at hand, what research strategy and methodology should be recommended to scholars in the Soviet field—and, I suspect, to those in the general field of comparative politics as well?

The best starting point for any research strategy, particularly so far as doctoral candidates are concerned, is the choice of a topic which permits the scholar to gain a real "feel" for some reasonably complex situation or phenomenon. Only in this way is a scholar of comparative politics likely to pick up some of the basic information about a foreign culture that the student of American politics takes for granted. Only in this way is he or she likely to avoid gross errors in determining which phenomena are really anomalous in terms of theory and which are anomalous because they have been misperceived and misclassified.

Such a strategy has great potential value for the reader as well as for the scholar, especially the reader who is not interested in the author's theoretical framework. A book that is rich in detail and gives some "feel" for a situation may be of some use to almost any reader, for it may provide sufficient data to test other theoretical generalizations in an informal and partial manner. Articles and books which limit themselves to an explicit test of hypotheses, on the other hand, often lack this quality, particularly if they are based on coding and scaling techniques whose validity cannot be verified by the reader. The reader who does not trust the numbers in these studies will find the studies worthless, for they contain little else. In practice, the key factor in determining the acceptability of such tests of theory may be their congeniality to the reader's previous views.

A second feature of a productive research strategy surely must be a recognition of the value of comparative work, broadly defined. This is the only work that can indicate which characteristics of a country and its political-social system are distinctive and which are held in common with other countries. It alone can suggest whether a phenomenon needs to be explained by the distinctive history and culture of that country or by factors that transcend national boundaries.[14] It is only through such work that the most interesting questions for study are likely to be raised.

In many cases a scholar may not actually need to conduct a formal comparative study in order to obtain many of the advantages of the comparative approach. Broad and comparative reading on the subject under study may itself develop a new perspective on it and on the various forces at work.[15] For example, the fact that Soviet housing policy leads to integrated neighborhoods in terms of socioeconomic status may be given little attention by the Societ area specialist, for this question never becomes an explicit issue in the Soviet Union. Yet this fact takes on great theoretical interest when it is observed that a great many political issues in the United States revolve around the desire of citizens to exclude persons of lower status from the neighborhood school. Is human nature really different in the Soviet Union and the United States? Or does the inability of the Soviet "New Class" to gain the exclusivity of neighborhood generally won by their American counterparts indicate something important about power relationships in the Soviet Union and in the United States? At a minimum, one is led to explore the possibility that certain overt issues in Soviet urban politics (for example, the construction of cooperative housing or the shifting of housing from the control of industry to that of the soviets) may have class issues covertly imbedded in them.

A third feature of a productive research strategy should be a deter-

mination to contribute to theory in some sense. The only meaningful reason for a society to expend resources on research is the hope that it will
help to explain phenomena of interest and relevance to members of that
society. Since research on subjects such as the local party organs in the
Soviet Union seems of little inherent interest to American society, the
scholar surely has a responsibility to indicate how his study illuminates
questions of broader interest. This is just another way of saying that research has little intrinsic interest unless it has some theoretical relevance.

However, and this is vital to understand, the lack of an agreed-upon
focus or paradigm within political science creates a real problem in determining just what is theoretically relevant. Precisely because political
scientists work on different questions and within different traditions, a
scholar has a real choice as to which audience he will address, and he must
recognize that a contribution to the theory of one audience may contribute little to the theory of another. Indeed, scholars within one tradition
may be unfamiliar with generalizations and insights developed by colleagues in other fields who are working on overlapping problems, and,
consequently, an argument derived from the literature of one tradition
may be theoretically interesting to scholars working within another.

For example, if a scholar working on the Soviet administrative system in the 1960s read widely in Western administrative theory, he quickly
learned that the monist and Weberian bureaucratic models had been seriously discredited. But this was not the case in Soviet studies. As specialists on the Soviet Union began accepting Alfred Meyer's argument that
the bureaucratic model should be used in conceptualizing the Soviet system, they (like Meyer himself) essentially employed the monist bureaucratic model, whether they spoke of an "administrered society," an
"organizational society," or others.[16]

Nor had the monist model been fully discredited in the literature on
development administration. Scholars in this field, like those studying
the developing nations in general, have utilized concepts which, directly
or indirectly, have been drawn from the work of Max Weber rather than
from recent Western administrative theory. Recognizing that the bureaucracies of the Third World do not correspond closely to Weber's bureaucratic ideal-type, the scholars have usually attributed the deviations from
the ideal type to factors such as the persistence of traditional norms and
values rather than to imperfections in the ideal type as a representation of
an effective administrative structure.

Given these circumstances, a line of argument which might seem
stale to a scholar steeped in Western administrative theory could have
quite a different appearance to audiences working on the theories of Soviet evolution or of development administration—and conceivably it

could make a significant contribution to theoretical development in these fields. Similarly, a point taken for granted by Soviet specialists may be theoretically fresh to Western adminstrative theorists. In any specific case, one may approve of an author's choice of audience and hence of his theoretical focus, but methodologists should never forget that the lack of an agreed-upon paradigm requires any author to make some choice. They must understand that, whatever the nature of this choice, it inevitably reduces the relevance of a book or article for other audiences.

Those calling for a more theoretical approach in Soviet studies are basically saying that Soviet specialists have too often chosen the theoretical focus of greatest interest to other Soviet specialists and that this choice has had very unfortunate consequences. This criticism is quite accurate. Scholars generally do not read material that is not explicitly addressed to their own set of interests,[17] and the output of the massive research effort on the Soviet Union has not affected scholarly generalizations about the political process to the extent it should have. The area specialists could make a major contribution to the development of the discipline by redirecting the focus of their work, and they surely would find it in their self-interest to do so.

As we begin to address ourselves more to nonspecialist audiences, however, there is little reason for us to become entangled in formal methodological issues. Specialists on methodology engage in fierce battles on the meaning of such terms as theory, model, and ideal type, and they cannot agree among themselves on the nature of theory or model building. Some of the leading contemporary methodologists are scornful of the way many political scientists attempt to confirm hypotheses through the use of significance tests, and they suggest that this technique involves a basic misunderstanding and misapplication of the scientific method.[18] In these circumstances, why should we Soviet specialists wed ourselves blindly to any one side of this debate and take a pretentious attitude towards a scientific methodology that many methodologists disavow?

Our central task need not be a hopelessly esoteric one. We should simply find out what general questions interest non-Soviet specialists who are working on problems analogous to our own and then try to bring Soviet evidence to bear on these questions. This task is not always an easy one, for non-Soviet specialists themselves, including those who label themselves ''behaviorists,'' are often as atheoretical as specialists on the Soviet Union are accused of being. (Many are really American area studies specialists.) Nevertheless, the multiplicity of paradigms means a multiplicity of questions from which to choose, many of them basic ones requiring little knowledge of specialized terminology.

In examining these research questions we should remember that the best methodology is nothing more than the application of logical, commonsense rules on the marshaling of evidence with respect to controversial questions. When we are in a position to confirm or reject an interesting and clearly defined hypothesis in a definitive way, then certainly we should be purist in our choice and use of statistical techniques. But when we are not in such a position, when the problem is lack of clarity in the manner we view a phenomenon or conceptualize our hypothesis (and this is usually the case), it is foolish to feel constrained by statistical requirements that assume conditions we cannot satisfy in any case.

Why, for example, should we be bound by the textbook requirement that our hypotheses or even our basic research design be precisely defined before data collection is begun? Obviously a scholar should give as much thought as possible to a study at its inception, and this is all the more important if the data must be collected at one particular time, as when a questionnaire is administered. However, in studies that are really innovative, the scholar comes to see the research problem in a very different light after being submerged in the data, and it would be extremely foolish to define research in such a way as to preclude this possibility. Especially in the case of a dissertation, it might well be argued that a study which retains its original organization and conceptual framework from its inception to its completion is likely to be a failure, for the student has not really learned enough in the course of the work to cause a reconceptualization.

In Soviet studies particularly the best research strategy usually will be a "maxi-mini" one. Scholars should be aware of a large number of hypotheses that might be illuminated by their work—some sweeping in their import, some more modest—and they should be continually open to new hypotheses in the comparative literature they read while conducting their research. In this way the focus of the study can be adjusted, depending upon the availability of data and the interest of the findings. If information of relevance to the more ambitious theoretical concerns becomes available, then the scholar is in a position to take advantage of it; if such information proves more difficult to obtain, he or she will not be so tempted to test hypotheses which the available data neither confirm nor reject, for there is likely to be sufficient information on other hypotheses or questions to permit a solidly based contribution to the literature. If it seems advisable, the scholar should not be afraid to abandon the original focus altogether.

Our discussion may have led to the assumption that a great many questions have theoretical relevance for the students of political science, but, in practice, some questions obviously are more profitable to study than others; some approaches more fruitful to pursue. In the past, specialists on the Soviet Union have tended to concentrate on what David Easton would call "support questions": How has the Soviet regime or system maintained itself in power? Will it be able to do so in the future? It is conceivable that this approach could have led—and may still lead—to major theoretical advance in political science, particularly given the widespread concern of American political scientists with the sources of democratic stability. However, meaningful linkages have never developed between the literature on Soviet stability and that on the sources of stability in general. Specialists on the Soviet Union have almost never explored the possible impact of variables such as overlapping group memberships on Soviet stability,[19] while comparative theorists have become so ensnared in the language about boundaries between social, economic, and political systems that they find it extremely difficult to compare Western systems with those in which all spheres of the economy are nationalized.

Whatever the potential payoff from a comparative examination of support questions,[20] the entire demand-output side of Soviet politics has received little systematic attention, and research in this realm should prove highly rewarding at this time. The most advantageous focus would normally be one that centers on a specific policy area. Such a focus provides the scholar with an excellent opportunity to gain a good feel of the Soviet political system, for the various political actors—both institutions and individuals—can be observed as they interact on real problems rather than in the abstract. Moreover, interviewing of Soviet officials about institutions, processes, and influences becomes much simpler and more productive when the scholar can ask concrete and specific questions on matters that officials can discuss in a meaningful and nonideological way.

A policy approach can also greatly facilitate comparative study. When political scientists studied distribution questions, they tended to concentrate on the political process—the "when" and "how" of politics, to use Lasswell's terms—and to neglect the relationship of process to "who gets what." As a result, it has been very difficult to judge the extent to which differences in process, even such gross differences as the existence of competitive elections, have any meaningful impact on outcomes. An examination of specific policy areas helps to overcome this problem, while narrowing the focus to manageable proportions and permitting comparison on questions that generally are easy to handle in conceptual terms.

The illumination of the relationship of process to "who gets what" is likely to be particularly valuable if we do not limit our comparisons to "outputs" in Easton's sense of the term (actual decisions taken by the political authorities), but also give great attention to the outcomes in the policy area, broadly defined. That is, if we compare the actual distribution of value satisfaction, the actual pattern of "who gets what" in a policy area in the Soviet Union and elsewhere, if we do not worry at the beginning whether these outcomes are produced by governmental or nongovernmental action, then we often will be better sensitized to the type of impact produced by variations in political systems or in governmental decisions.

From this perspective, our research should begin with an exploration not of educational policy per se, but, for example, of the comparative percentage of various age groups enrolled in various educational institutions and the degree of social mobility associated with different patterns; an exploration not of tax and wage policy, but of the pattern of income distribution; not of policy with respect to urban-rural differences, but of the actual distribution of services between rural and urban sectors; not of policy toward women, but of the distribution of women in the labor force, the availability of day-care facilities, the relative structure of men's and women's time budgets, and so forth. Once the comparative outcomes are known, we can then begin to explore the factors and processes that produce the similarities and differences in outcomes. Of course, the task is not an easy one, but even the difficult examples are much more tractable than might be supposed.

A final possible advantage of a policy area approach is that it appears to be the next major candidate in the perennial search for paradigm agreement in the discipline. Clearly this analysis would have to move beyond its present preoccupation with budgetary data and would need to incorporate an analysis of impacts and outcomes in order to become a general guiding principle for research, but if it can do so it is an attractive candidate. The approach focuses upon a question—the relationship of political factors in "who gets what"—that everyone would recognize as central in the discipline and one that is broad enough to permit the incorporation of much previous work with a slight change of perspective. Often nothing more would be required than the treating as independent variables (that which does or does not explain differences which have been observed) factors which have been studied as dependent variables (the thing to be explained). Moreover, because of the range of policy areas and questions that are relevant, the approach would provide an ample choice of topics for scholars, many requiring the most advanced statistical methods, but others amenable to more qualitative research techniques.

It is quite probable, of course, that political science will remain without an agreed-upon paradigm, but at the least comparative analysis of policy and of impacts is likely to be at the center of major theoretical interest in political science during the next decade. Many practitioners of the comparative policy approach have concluded that politics does not matter and that political decisions overwhelmingly reflect underlying economic and social factors. This conclusion certainly has little claim to validity until it is tested against the experience of the Communist world, and for this reason there is much that we can contribute to the debate. Since, at a minimum, this approach would further our understanding of questions traditionally of interest to Soviet studies and widen our exposure to the comparative literature on these questions, we have little to lose and much to gain by exploring it vigorously.

# Notes

## Introduction

1. Joseph LaPalombara, "Monoliths or Plural Systems: Through Conceptual Lenses Darkly," *Studies in Comparative Communism,* 8 (Autumn 1975), 305-306, 322-328.

2. Alfred G. Meyer, "The Comparative Study of Communist Political Systems," *Slavic Review,* 26 (March 1967), 11.

3. Allen Kassof, "The Administered Society: Totalitarianism without Terror," *World Politics,* 16 (July 1964), 558-575.

4. T. H. Rigby, "Traditional, Market, and Organizational Societies," *World Politics,* 16 (July 1964), 539-540.

5. Zbigniew Brzezinski and Samuel P. Huntington, *Political Power USA/USSR* (New York, Viking Press, 1964), p. 71.

6. Ibid., p. 75.

7. Jerry F. Hough, *The Soviet Prefects* (Cambridge, Mass., Harvard University Press, 1969).

8. *Partiinaia zhizn',* no. 4 (February 1958), p. 5.

9. Quoted in Hough, *The Soviet Prefects,* pp. 199-205, 240-241.

10. William Taubman, *Governing the Soviet City* (New York, Praeger, 1973).

11. For example, see the discussion in Jeremy R. Azrael, *Managerial Power and Soviet Politics* (Cambridge, Mass., Harvard University Press, 1966), pp. 65-77.

12. This point is strongly argued in T. H. Rigby, *Communist Party Membership, 1917-1967* (Princeton, Princeton University Press, 1968), p. 571.

13. Jerry F. Hough, "The Brezhnev Era: The Man and the Regime," *Problems of Communism,* 25 (March-April 1976), 11-13.

14. These points are made at some length in "The Cultural Revolution in Historical Perspective," in Sheila Fitzpatrick, ed., *The Cultural Revolution in Russia, 1928-1931* (Bloomington, Ind., Indiana Press, 1977). For the argument that these generalizations even apply to the cultural realm, see Sheila Fitzpatrick, "Culture and Politics under Stalin: A Reappraisal," *Slavic Review,* 35 (June 1976), 211-231.

15. Peter Wiles, *Distribution of Income: East and West* (Amsterdam, North-Holland Publishing Co., 1974), p. 25.

## 1. The Soviet System: Petrification or Pluralism?

1. Allen Kassof, "The Administered Society: Totalitarianism without Terror," *World Politics,* 16 (July 1964), 558-575; T. H. Rigby, "Traditional, Market, and Organizational Societies and the USSR," ibid., 539-557; Zbigniew Brzezinski and Samuel P. Huntington, *Political Power USA/USSR* (New York, Viking Press, 1964); Carl A. Linden, *Khrushchev and the Soviet Leadership*

(Baltimore, Johns Hopkins University Press, 1966); Sidney I. Ploss, *Conflict and Decision-Making in Soviet Russia* (Princeton, Princeton University Press, 1965); Alfred G. Meyer, "USSR Incorporated," in Donald W. Treadgold, ed., *The Development of the USSR* (Seattle, University of Washington Press, 1964), pp. 21-28.

2. John A. Armstrong, "Comparative Politics and Communist Systems: Concluding Remarks," *Slavic Review,* 26 (March 1967), 27. Armstrong's remarks were made in a symposium, and he was supporting a point made earlier by Robert S. Sharlet (ibid., p. 24). See also Paul Hollander, "Observations on Bureaucracy, Totalitarianism, and the Comparative Study of Communism," *Slavic Review,* 26 (June 1967), 302-307, and for a more recent version of the model, Roy D. Laird, *The Soviet Paradigm* (New York, The Free Press, 1970).

3. Jeremy R. Azrael, "The Party and Society," in Allen Kassof, ed., *Prospects for Soviet Society* (New York, Frederick A. Praeger, 1968), pp. 70-73. The order of the sentences has been changed somewhat. In fairness, it should be noted that Azrael's analysis of the mobilizational nature of Soviet society seems to have changed since that article was written. See his "Varieties of De-Stalinization," in Chalmers Johnson, ed., *Change in Communist Systems* (Stanford, Stanford University Press, 1970), pp. 135-151.

4. Carl J. Friedrich and Zbigniew K. Brzezinski, *Totalitarian Dictatorship and Autocracy* (Cambridge, Mass., Harvard University Press, 1956), p. 74.

5. As Karl Mannheim has argued in his classic book on the subject, "There is implicit in the word 'ideology' the insight that in certain situations the collective unconscious of certain groups obscures the real condition of society both to itself and to others and thereby stabilizes it." *Ideology and Utopia* (New York, Harcourt, Brace, & World, 1965), p. 90.

6. Zbigniew Brzezinski, *Between Two Ages* (New York, Viking Press, 1970), p. 165. As its wording suggests, the model comes in a discussion of alternative paths of future Soviet development, and Brzezinski actually predicts a combination of petrification and technological adaptation in the 1970s. The model does seem, however, to summarize Brzezinski's analysis of the first five years of the Brezhnev period, and it is cited here for that purpose alone.

7. Leonard Schapiro, "Keynote—Compromise," *Problems of Communism,* 20 (July-August 1971), 2. I do not mean to suggest that Brzezinski would accept this interpretation, but only that it would make the model neat.

8. The view that Soviet politics revolves around conflict between a conservative party apparatus and a progressive state apparatus is an old and widely held one whose persistence defies explanation—at least in my view. Even the most obvious evidence seems to contradict it. For example, the men who in 1952 would have been called the two leading party apparatchiki after Stalin were Malenkov and Khrushchev, but they would hardly be regarded as the leading conservative figures of the post-Stalin era. For an examination of the more esoteric evidence on this point, see the chapter "The Party Apparatchiki" in this book.

9. Milovan Djilas, *The New Class* (New York, Frederick, A. Praeger, 1957), pp. 39-40. Djilas' definition of the party is quite different from that adopted in the previous variant, and it conveys a clearer impression of the meaning of this model. He conceives of the party not as the actual institution but as "the compact party, full of initiative," which, he says, "diminishes," "is disappearing," or "grows weaker."

10. The present General Secretary Leonid Brezhnev, and the de facto second

secretary of the Central Committee (Kirilenko) are ferrous metallurgy and aviation industry engineers, respectively, with extensive party work in centers of the defense and heavy industries. The Central Committee secretary handling the military, the defense industry, and the police (Ustinov) in 1971 was People's Commissar of the Munition Industry and then Minister of the Defense Industry from 1941 to 1957 before becoming the top official coordinating the defense industries in the Khrushchev era. The Chairman and the two First Deputy Chairmen of the Council of Ministers in 1971 did not have a heavy-industry background, but the eight Deputy Chairmen were all heavy-industry engineers. Six had been Ministers for some branch of heavy industry or the defense industry, and a seventh had been a Deputy Minister of Ferrous Metallurgy before becoming a top planning official with responsibility for that branch. In the three largest republics, the political leaders were former enterprise managers in the defense industry (Solomentsev in the RSFSR and Shelest in the Ukraine) or in nonferrous metallurgy (Kunaev in Kazakhstan). Since the mid-1950s, the obkom first secretaries in over 80 percent of the 25 most industrialized oblasts have been engineers (usually with substantial managerial experience), and nearly all these men come from heavy rather than light industry. While the percentage of all heavy-industry obkom first secretaries is not large, they have been concentrated in the populous, urbanized oblasts with large numbers of party members. In 1966, 146 units (small republics, oblasts, and the city of Moscow) sent delegates to the 23rd Party Congress. Less than a quarter of these units had first secretaries with a heavy-industry background, but they named over 40 percent of the delegates.

11. In the words of Alex Inkeles, "In most areas of life the best way to predict the attitudes, values, and orientations of men in the Soviet Union is to draw on the general knowledge that we have about men holding comparable positions in Western industrial societies." *Social Change in Soviet Russia* (Cambridge, Mass., Harvard University Press, 1968), p. 427.

12. Robert V. Daniels, "Soviet Politics Since Khrushchev," in John W. Strong, ed., *The Soviet Union under Brezhnev and Kosygin* (New York, Van Nostrand-Reinhold Co., 1971) pp. 22-23.

13. Brzezinski and Huntington, *Political Power, USA/USSR,* p. 196.

14. H. Gordon Skilling, "Groups in Soviet Politics: Some Hypotheses," in H. Gordon Skilling and Franklyn Griffiths, eds. *Interest Groups in Soviet Politics* (Princeton, N.J., Princeton University Press, 1971) p. 42.

15. Franklyn Griffiths, "A Tendency Analysis of Soviet Policy-Making," ibid., pp. 369-377.

16. Philip Stewart, "Soviet Interest Groups and the Policy Process," *World Politics,* 22 (Ocotober 1969), 50.

17. H. Gordon Skilling, "Interest Groups and Communist Politics: An Introduction," in Skilling and Griffiths, *Interest Groups in Soviet Politics,* p. 17.

18. Gabriel A. Almond and G. Bingham Powell, Jr., *Comparative Politics* (Boston, Little, Brown and Co., 1966), p. 57.

19. A. Lawrence Lowell, *Public Opinion and Popular Government* (New York, Longmans, Green and Co., 1914), pp. 61-62.

20. Robert A. Dahl, *A Preface to Democratic Theory* (Chicago, University of Chicago Press, 1956), pp. 27-28, 133, and 146.

21. Robert A. Dahl and Charles E. Lindblom, *Politics, Economics, and Welfare* (New York, Harper & Row, 1953), pp. 82-88.

22. Inkeles, *Social Change in Soviet Russia,* p. 431.

23. Brzezinski, *Between Two Ages,* p. 167.

24. Three republic KGB chairmen were elected to full membership in the republic party bureaus, and three to candidate membership, at the republic party congresses in February and March 1971. The fourth candidate member was named to the Belorussian party bureau the following July.

25. Documentation of this point is too scattered and voluminous to be compressed into a note of reasonable length. However, one need only refer to almost any Western article or book dealing with a specific Soviet policy area. Two such articles are Aryeh L. Unger, "Polit-informator or Agitator: A Decision Blocked," *Problems of Communism,* 19 (September-October 1970), 30-43, and Zev Katz, "Sociology in the Soviet Union," ibid., 20 (May-June 1971), 22-40.

26. See, for example, Grey Hodnett, "What's in a Nation?" ibid., 17 (September-October 1967), 2-15; and Franklyn Griffiths, "Images, Politics, Arms Control: Aspects and Implications of Postwar Soviet Policy toward the United States," (Ph.D. diss, Columbia University, 1972), esp. chap. 2.

27. *The New York Times,* September 13, 1971, p. 35.

28. For brief biographical notes about the dissenters, see Abraham Brumberg, ed., *In Quest of Justice* (New York, Frederick A. Praeger, 1970), pp. 464-474. Elsewhere Brumberg questions Khrushchev's liberalism by listing a number of his policies: "The restoration of the death penalty for economic crimes, and the unsavory 'vigilance campaign' of 1962-1963 with its heavy admixture of anti-semitism; the assault on private property in agriculture; the recurrent attack on the liberal intelligentsia, so reminiscent of Zhdanov's repressions of the late 1940s; the creation of quasi-legal bodies to administer justice outside of the confines of legally consituted bodies, such as the antiparasite legislation and comrades' courts. Finally, the creation of yet another 'cult of the individual' . . . with a dash of nepotism thrown in for good measure." "The Fall of Khruschchev: Causes and Repercussions," in John W. Strong, ed. *The Soviet Union under Brezhnev and Kosygin* (Princeton, N.J., Van Nostrand-Reinhold, 1971), pp. 11-12.

29. Zbigniew Brzezinski, *The Permanent Purge* (Cambridge, Mass., Harvard University Press, 1956), pp. 168-170.

30. In contrast to the Politburo, however, the Central Committee Secretariat remains overwhelmingly Russian. All but one of the secretaries and the department heads are Russian.

31. *Pravda,* March 31, 1971, p. 10.

32. Twenty-four obkom first secretaries appointed in this period were promoted from lesser positions within the same oblast. Eleven had been oblispolkom chairman; six had been obkom second secretary; five had been gorkom first secretary (a new and perhaps significant source of recruitment); and two had held other positions. However, only 35 percent of the new obkom first secretaries in republics other than the RSFSR were promoted from within the oblast. (This calculation excludes all newly formed oblasts.) Except in one case, the new first secretaries did come from within the republic in which the oblast was located.

33. *Pravda Ukrainy,* April 20, 1970, p. 1.

34. I am indebted to Donald Carlisle, professor of political science at Boston College and associate of the Russian Research Center, for the information about Ikramov and Khodzhaev.

35. Mirzoian was first secretary of the Kazakhstan kraikom and then of the republic central committee from 1933 to 1938. His name too was not even men-

tioned in a page-long article on the history of Kazakhstan in the 1930s that appeared in *Kazakhstanskaia pravda,* October 10, 1967, p. 3. The Azerbaidzhan
newspaper in which his biography was published was *Bakinskii rabochii,* December 1, 1967, p. 3.

36. John Armstrong, "The Ethnic Scene in the Soviet Union: The View of the
Dictatorship," in Erich Goldhagen, ed., *Ethnic Minorities in the Soviet Union*
(New York, Frederick A. Praeger, 1968), pp. 3-49.

37. Phillip Stewart, in reviewing this book in the May-June 1971 issue of *Problems of Communism,* mistook my thesis to be that of an all-powerful Soviet regional party first secretary. The confusion may arise from the old problem of distinguishing clearly between legitimate authority and real influence. The conventional Western conception portrayed the local party organs as a vital force in
pushing plant managers to technical innovation but considered party intervention
to be a quasi-legitimate (and on many questions an illegitimate) violation of the
chain of command. My own contention is that the situation is the reverse—that
the party organs have clear-cut legal authority but not a great deal of influence
with respect to technical policy and several other intra-industry questions. The evidence which Stewart cites from the book to challenge the thesis that he attributes
to me is actually the evidence that I presented to bolster my major thesis.

38. The resubordination of the raion agriculture administrations to the soviets
occurred in the summer of 1970. See *Pravda,* July 3, 1970, p. 3. The decrees referred to were published in *Pravda,* March 14, 1971, pp. 1-2, and March 20,
1971, p. 1. In evaluating the decrees, two facts should be kept in mind: any improvement in the position of the soviets begins from a very low point; and even
after the decrees, there have been complaints by local officials that the city soviets
still do not have adequate authority over housing construction and municipal services expenditures to be able to integrate such development into any meaningful
city plan.

39. In addition to the republic ministries of education and culture, state committees have been created for publishing, movie making, and television and
radio. Vocational education has also been raised to the state committee level in
many republics, and nearby half of the republics have ministries for higher and
secondary specialized education.

40. Even if one were to accept the relative status of the party apparatus as a reliable indicator, the picture is a mixed one. Three of the four Politburo members
newly elected in 1971 were party officials, but the long-term decline in the percentage of Party officials among the voting members of the all-Union Central
Committee has continued: from 56 percent in 1956 to 46 percent in 1961, 42 percent in 1966, and 39 percent in 1971. In the republics, apparatus representation
has remained essentially stable. The proportion of party officials among the voting members of the republic party bureaus has only risen from 57.2 percent in
1966 to 57.5 percent in 1971, while the difference in the proportion of party officials among the voting members of the republic central committees is not statistically significant—34.1 percent in 1966 and 33.4 percent in 1971. (The figures
do not include party officials below the level of raikom secretary and are based on
identifications of 93 percent of the 1966 republic central committee members and
92 percent of the members of the 1971 committees. Very few party officials will
be found among the unidentified.)

41. The lists of Central Committee members elected at each party congress
and the biographies of many of the members can be found in Boris Levytsky, *The*

*Soviet Political Elite* (Stanford, Calif., Hoover Institute on War, Revolution, and Peace, 1970). The 1971 figure excludes the worker and peasant members of the Central Committee. Data on the characteristics of the members elected in 1971 can be found in Robert H. Donaldson, "The 1971 Soviet Central Committee: An Assessment of the New Elite," *World Politics,* 24 (April 1972), 382-409.

42. All the agricultural ministries (including, for the first time, Reclamation, Selkhoztekhnika, and Rural Construction) are now represented by full members on the all-Union Central Committee, while the number of agricultural ministers (or chairmen of state committees) on the republican central committees has risen from 43 to 51. On the contrary, not a single light or food industry minister was included among the 42 ministers and chairmen of state committees named to the all-Union Central Committee, despite an increase of 15 such state officials on this body since 1966. The number of ministers and state committee chairmen from light industry and the municipal services on the republic central committees has remained virtually unchanged (58 in 1971 compared with 57 in 1966).

43. The members of republic central committees who are most difficult to identify are those chosen from among workers and collective farmers. The republic statistics must therefore be considered merely approximate.

44. Peter H. Solomon, "A New Soviet Administrative Ethos—Examples from Crime Prevention," paper prepared for the meetings of the Northeastern Slavic Conference, Montreal, 1971.

45. Janet Chapman, *Wage Variation in Soviet Industry,* (Santa Monica, Calif., Rand Corporation, 1970), Memorandum RM-6076-PR, p. 126. For a new discussion of Soviet wage policy pointing in the same direction, see Leonard Joel Kirsch, *Soviet Wages* (Cambridge, Mass., Massachusetts Institute of Technology Press, 1972).

46. *Pravda,* March 21, 1971, pp. 4-5. See also David W. Bronson and Constance B. Krueger, "The Revolution in Soviet Farm Household Income, 1953-1967," in James R. Millar, ed., *The Soviet Rural Community* (Urbana, Ill., University of Illinois Press, 1971), pp. 214-258. For a table giving the wage increases for various categories of employees in this period, see Jerry F. Hough, "The Brezhnev Era: The Man and the Regime," *Problems of Communism,* 25 (March-April 1976), 13.

47. There are various criteria by which the list of the top 50 or top 500 American corporations could be chosen. I have used market value of stock, for this methodology produces a list with many of the great growth companies on it. It is worth noting that the 22 growth companies on the list (those with a price/earning ratio of over 25 at the time) had chief executives with the same average age as the executives of the other 28 companies. The lists of corporations and chief officers are found in *Forbes,* May 15, 1971, pp. 91-92 and 128-161.

48. Inkeles, *Social Change in Soviet Russia,* p. 431.

49. The relationship of the elite and the disadvantaged in different political systems is, in particular, a problem that deserves very careful empirical consideration. In the September-October 1971 issue of *Problems of Communism* ("The Status of Soviet Women"—review, p. 62;, Ellen Mickiewicz expressed the traditional Western view when she asserted that "without a channel through which to influence politics, it is questionable whether Soviet women can assert their right to genuine equality." The model of institutional pluralism—and a good deal of comparative Soviet-American data on social welfare issues (and surely also on the

position of women)—suggests that this is not a closed question. For further discussion of this question, see the concluding chapters in this book.

50. Brzezinski, *Between Two Ages,* p. 167.

51. Myron Rush, "Brezhnev and the Succession Issue," *Problems of Communism,* 20 (July-August 1971), 9-15.

52. Daniels, "Soviet Politics Since Khrushchev," p. 20.

53. This figure is based on the list of delegates published at the end of the Stenographic Report of the Twenty-Third Party Congress. The list includes the region from which each delegate comes, and it is a simple matter to add the number of delegates for each region. The unit of analysis is the region specified in the list itself.

54. The Stenographic Report of the Twenty-Fourth Congress did not list the region of the delegates, and hence it was assumed that the relative number of delegates from each oblast and republic was the same in 1971 as in 1966.

55. For some time it has been the practice to appoint persons of the local nationality to the post of party first secretary in the non-Slavic republics, with a Russian sent in from the outside as second secretary. Many scholars consider the Russian second secretary to be the key figure in the republic as the representative of the center, but his actual relationship to the lower-level obkom, gorkom and raikom first secretaries is at present very unclear. In my view, the native first secretary now seems a more dominant figure than the Russian second secretary, and it is quite possible that the lower-level secretaries tend to be beholden to him.

56. Daniels believes that, in fact, "a fundamental change has occurred in the circuit of power . . . real control does not pass to the top leader, but flows instead from the top collective bodies around through the party organization" ("Soviet Politics Since Khrushchev," pp. 22-25). Daniels rests his argument largely on the psychological impact of Khrushchev's removal, but it could be hypothesized that the Politburo has been able to limit the General Secretary's source of power in a more direct manner. One possibility is that the responsibility for selecting obkom and republic party secretaries has been divided among several or perhaps many Politburo members. For example, the fact that Suslov attended a session of the Leningrad obkom that selected a new first secretary could conceivably denote his ability to select a man loyal to himself for that position. Another possibility is that except in cases of major scandal or mismanagement, the regional elite have been given control over the post of local first secretary. As mentioned earlier, a much higher percentage of obkom first secretaries have been selected from within the oblasts in recent years.

57. Rush, "Brezhnev and the Succession Issue," p. 10.

58. Daniels, "Soviet Politics Since Khrushchev," pp. 22-25.

59. In *Escape from Freedom* (New York, Farrar and Rinehart, 1941) Erich Fromm suggested that the break up of feudalism in Western Europe created major psychological disorientation, that the authoritarianism and determinism of early Protestantism provided some relief for these psychological strains, and that the success of the Protestant Reformation is to be explained in significant part by this fact. If the period 1860-1917 is viewed as one of the breakup of feudalism in Russia, then Fromm's analysis would seem to suggest a similar psychological disorientation and propensity to authoritarianism in its wake—and there are, in fact, many striking parallels between early Calvinism and Bolshevism, particularly as it developed under Stalin.

60. Alfred G. Meyer, "The Comparative Study of Communist Political Systems," *Slavic Review,* 26 (March 1967), 11. Meyer argues (and with good reason) that such notions are too often suspended in our study of the Soviet Union, and that our analysis of that country is seriously flawed by the use of "concepts and models reserved for it alone or for it and a few other systems considered inimical."

## 2. The Bureaucratic Model and the Nature of the Soviet System

1. Leon Trotsky, *The Revolution Betrayed* (Garden City, N. Y., Doubleday, Doran, 1937).

2. James Burnham, *The Managerial Revolution* (New York, John Day, 1941). Sociologists of language might find it interesting to explore how Burnham's term "managerial revolution" changed from one predicting convergence in the direction of the Soviet system into one suggesting evolution in the Western direction.

3. Barrington Moore, Jr., *Terror and Progress USSR* (Cambridge, Mass., Harvard University Press, 1954).

4. Alfred G. Meyer, "USSR, Incorporated," *Slavic Review,* 20 (October 1961), 370.

5. Zbigniew Brzezinski, "Victory of the Clerks," *The New Republic* 151 (November 14, 1964), 15 and 18.

6. Victor A. Thompson, *Modern Organization* (New York, Alfred A. Knopf, 1961), pp. 4 and 3.

7. Alfred G. Meyer, *The Soviet Political System* (New York, Random House, 1965), pp. 468 and 474.

8. Allen Kassof, "The Administered Society: Totalitarianism without Terror," *World Politics,* 16 (July 1964), 558-575; T. H. Rigby, "Traditional, Market, and Organizational Societies and the USSR," *ibid.,* pp. 539-557.

9. Moore, *Terror and Progress,* pp. 187-190; Barrington Moore, Jr., *Political Power and Social Theory* (Cambridge, Mass., Harvard University Press, 1958), pp. 19-20. Reinhard Bendix reveals much the same image of bureaucracy in his assertion that the Communist countries are not bureaucratic but postbureaucratic, since they "lack a concept of law in the sense of a system of relatively stable, impersonal, and nonpolitical norms and procedures" and since their leadership has a "determination to centralize decision-making under the auspices of a single party." "Bureaucracy," in *International Encyclopedia of the Social Sciences* (New York, Macmillan and Free Press, 1968), II, 206-219.

10. Trotsky, *The Revolution Betrayed,* pp. 93-94.

11. Brzezinski, "Victory of the Clerks," pp. 15-18; Zbigniew K. Brzezinski, *Between Two Ages* (New York, Viking, 1970), p. 165.

12. For a discussion of this point (with a different categorization of bureaucratic models), see David Lane, *Politics and Society in the USSR* (New York, Random House, 1971), pp. 175-178.

13. Leonard Schapiro, "Keynote—Compromise," *Problems of Communism,* 20 (July-August 1971), 2.

14. George Fischer, *The Soviet System and Modern Society* (New York, Atherton, 1968), pp. 15-18.

15. Zbigniew Brzezinski and Samuel P. Huntington, *Political Power USA/USSR* (New York, Viking, 1964), p. 196.

16. Zbigniew Brzezinski, "The Soviet Political System: Transformation or Degeneration?" *Problems of Communism,* 15 (January-February 1966), p. 10.

17. Vernon V. Aspaturian, "The Soviet Union," in Roy C. Macridis and Robert E. Ward, eds., *Modern Political Systems: Europe* (Englewood Cliffs, N. J., Prentice-Hall, 1968), p. 550.

18. H. Gordon Skilling and Franklyn Griffiths, eds. *Interest Groups in Soviet Politics* (Princeton, N. J., Princeton University Press, 1971), p. 24.

19. If anything, the normal criticism made of the college education of Soviet administrators is that it is too specialized.

20. For documentation and discussion of the points in this paragraph—see Jerry F. Hough, *The Soviet Prefects* (Cambridge, Mass., Harvard University Press, 1969), chap. 7.

21. *Deputaty Verkhovnogo Soveta SSSR, Vos'moi sozyy* (Moscow, Izdatel'stvo Izvestiia sovetov deputatov trudiashchikhsia SSSR, 1970), p. 222.

22. Actually relatively few leading party officials have a biography that is as exclusively political as Korotkov's. Not only do many move between the party and state hierarchics in mid-career, but a large number originally begin working in the state administration. Thus, 51 percent of the 1970 regional (obkom and kraikom) first secretaries did not hold their first party job until after their twenty-eighth birthday, 59 percent of those in the RSFSR. This pattern was particularly pronounced in the most populous regions of the Russian Republic, holding true for 90 percent of those first secretaries in the ten most populous regions and 73 percent of those in the next fifteen most populous one. The biographies of the first secretaries are all found in *Deputaty Verkhovnogo Soveta.*

23. *Deputaty Verkhovnogo Soveta*, pp. 110, 281, 397, and 429.

24. Such an image seems to be implied in Aspaturian's reference to the state bureaucrats as "the only institutional group which has custody of important symbols and credentials of legality." Aspaturian, "The Soviet Union," p. 550.

25. The biographies are drawn from *Deputaty Verkhovnogo Soveta.* The intertwining of the party and soviet institutions at this level is further reflected in the fact that 39 percent of the regional party first secretaries in 1970 were transferred to this post directly from work in the soviets, 31 percent from the position of chairman of the executive committee of the regional soviet.

26. Kassof, "The Administered Society," p. 559.

27. Peter M. Blau and Marshall W. Meyer, *Bureaucracy in Modern Society* (New York, Random House, 1971), pp. 144-145.

28. David Granick, *Management of the Industrial Firm in the USSR* (New York, Columbia University Press, 1954), p. 121.

29. Melville Dalton, *Men Who Manage* (New York, John Wiley, 1959), p. 265.

30. Jerome H. Skolnick, *Justice Without Trial* (New York, John Wiley, 1966), chaps. 1 and 11.

31. Max Weber, *The Theory of Economic and Social Organization*, trans. by A. M. Henderson and T. Parsons (New York, Free Press, 1947), p. 335.

32. Fischer, *The Soviet System and Modern Society*, pp. 16-17.

33. Kassof, "The Administered Society," pp. 558 and 560.

34. Weber, *The Theory of Economic and Social Organization*, p. 338.

35. Ernest S. Griffith, *The American System of Government* (London, Methuen, 1966), p. 86.

36. Weber, *The Theory of Economic and Social Organization*, p. 337.

37. Thompson, *Modern Organization*, pp. 6 and 13.

38. Herbert Kaufman, "The Growth of the Federal Personnel System," in Wallace S. Sayre, ed., *The Federal Government Service* (Englewood Cliffs, N. J.; Prentice-Hall, Inc., 1965), p. 11.

39. Anthony Downs, *Inside Bureaucracy* (Boston, Little, Brown and Co., 1967), pp. 92-101.

40. Blau and Meyer, *Bureaucracy in Modern Society*, p. 37.

41. Aaron Wildavsky, *The Politics of the Budgetary Process* (Boston, Little, Brown and Co., 1964), p. 162.

42. Ibid., p. 162.

43. Daniel Patrick Moynihan, *The Politics of a Guaranteed Income* (New York, Random House, 1973).

44. Thompson, *Modern Organization,* p. 89; see also Michel Crozier, *The Bureaucratic Phenomenon* (Chicago, University of Chicago Press, 1964), pp. 165-168.

45. Quoted in Austin Ranney, *The Governing of Men* (New York, Henry Holt, 1958), pp. 438-439.

46. John Kenneth Galbraith, *The New Industrial State* (Boston, Houghton Mifflin, 1967), pp. 76-77.

47. Thompson, *Modern Organization,* p. 186.

48. Galbraith, *The New Industrial State,* pp. 72-82. The italics are in the original.

49. Ibid., pp. 75-76. The italics are added.

50. Richard M. Cyert and James G. March, *A Behavioral Theory of the Firm* (Englewood Hills, N. J., Prentice-Hall, Inc., 1963), pp. 27-28.

51. Wildavsky, *Politics of the Budgetary Process,* pp. 12 and 70.

52. Herbert A. Simon, *Administrative Behavior* (New York, Macmillan, 1957), p. xxiv.

53. Downs, *Inside Bureaucracy,* p. 248.

54. Merle Fainsod, "Bureaucracy and Modernization: The Russian and Soviet Case," in Joseph LaPalombara, ed., *Bureaucracy and Political Development* (Princeton, N. J., Princeton University Press, 1963), p. 238.

55. Thompson, *Modern Organization,* pp. 19 and 163.

56. Ibid., pp. 163-164.

57. William Delaney, "The Development and Decline of Patrimonial and Bureaucratic Administration," *Administrative Science Quarterly,* 7 (March 1963), 498.

58. Crozier, *The Bureaucratic Phenomenon,* p. 185.

59. Ibid., p. 185.

60. Blau and Meyer, *Bureaucracy in Modern Society,* pp. 143-145.

61. See, for example, Robert V. Presthus, *The Organizational Society* (New York, Alfred A. Knopf, 1967).

62. Delaney, "The Development and Decline of Patrimonial and Bureaucratic Administration," p. 498.

63. Brzezinski and Huntington, *Political Power USA/USSR,* pp. 203-204.

64. Downs, *Inside Bureaucracy,* p. 164.

65. Crozier, *The Bureaucratic Phenomenon,* pp. 228-231.

66. Granick, *Management of the Industrial Firm;* Joseph S. Berliner, *Factory and Manager in the USSR* (Cambridge, Mass., Harvard University Press, 1957).

67. Vera S. Dunham, "The Party Secretary in Postwar Soviet Literature," (Cambridge, Mass., Harvard University Project on the Soviet Social System, 1953).

68. Hough, *The Soviet Prefects.*

69. Jeremy R. Azrael, *Managerial Power and Soviet Politics* (Cambridge, Mass., Harvard University Press, 1966).

70. Barry M. Richman, *Soviet Management* (Englewood Cliffs, N. J., Prentice-Hall, 1965).

71. Granick, *Management of the Industrial Firm*, pp. 263 and 285.

72. Wildavsky, *The Politics of the Budgetary Process*. See also Hough, *The Soviet Prefects*, pp. 256-271.

73. John A. Armstrong, "Sources of Administrative Behavior: Some Soviet and Western European Comparisons," *The American Political Science Review*, 59 (September 1965), 643-655.

74. Joel J. Schwartz and William R. Keech, "Group Influence and the Policy Process in the Soviet Union," *American Political Science Review*, 62 (September 1968), pp. 840-851; Philip P. Stewart, "Soviet Interest Groups and the Policy Process: The Repeal of Production Education," *World Politics*, 22 (October 1969), 29-50.

75. Hough, *The Soviet Prefects*, pp. 312-313 and 285-286.

76. Armstrong, "Sources of Administrative Behavior," p. 653.

77. L. G. Churchward, "Bureaucracy—USA: USSR," *Coexistence*, 5 (1968), pp. 202-203.

78. Meyer, "USSR, Incorporated," p. 370.

79. For a fascinating discussion of the interrelationships between scholars and administrators in the crime prevention realm, and of the movement of personnel from one category to another, see Peter H. Solomon, Jr., *Soviet Criminologists and Criminal Policy: Specialists in Soviet Policy-Making* (New York, Columbia University Press, forthcoming).

80. Cyert and March, *A Behaviorial Theory of the Firm*, pp. 19-20.

81. V. G. Afanasev, *Nauchnoe upravlenie obshchestva* (Moscow, Politizdat, 1968).

82. Robert V. Daniels, "Soviet Politics Since Khrushchev," in John W. Strong, ed., *The Soviet Union Under Brezhnev and Kosygin* (Princeton, N. J., Van Nostrand-Reinhold, 1971), pp. 22-23.

83. Alex Inkeles, *Social Change in Soviet Russia* (Cambridge, Mass., Harvard University Press, 1968), pp. 422 and 431.

### 3. The Party Apparatchiki and Interest Group Theory

1. Zbigniew Brzezinski and Samuel P. Huntington, *Political Power USA/USSR* (New York, Viking Press, 1964), p. 163.

2. Arthur F. Bentley, *The Process of Government* (Chicago, University of Chicago Press, 1908), p. 220.

3. Ibid., p. 207. See pp. 465-468 for Bentley's criticism of Marx's "hard and fast" classes.

4. Ibid., pp. 204, 270, 300.

5. These phrases are all taken from Alfred G. Meyer, *The Soviet Political System* (New York, Random House, 1965), pp. 238-243.

6. Mervyn Mathews estimates an apparatus of 95,000 persons, while Robert McNeal puts the number at 200,000. Mervyn Mathews, "Top Incomes in the USSR," *Survey* 21 (Summer 1975), 24, and Robert H. McNeal, "Paying for the Party," ibid., 22 (Spring 1976), 64. Mathews's figure seems extremely reasonable to me, with the proviso that it includes full-time raion-level instructors—a group that Mathews seems to exclude. The 1970 census reports 184,305 leading personnel (including instructors) of *all* party, Komsomol, trade union, and other public organizations in the Soviet Union. *Itogi vsesoiuznoi perepisi naseleniia 1970 goda* (Moscow, Statistika, 1973), VI, p. 23.

7. The biographies of the obkom first secretaries can be found in *Deputaty*

*Verkhovnogo Soveta SSSR, Sed'moi sozyv* (Moscow, Izdatel'stvo "Izvestiia," 1966). For the date of college graduation, one must refer to the 1966 yearbook of the *Bol'shaia sovetskaia entsiklopediia*, pp. 574-621. Unfortunately, this source includes only those obkom secretaries elected to the Central Committee or the Auditing Commission of the Party. All obkom first secretaries in the RSFSR were named to these bodies, but the first secretaries in the other republics have been represented less frequently.

8. The biographies of all department heads were printed in *Bol'shaia sovetskaia entsiklopediia*, 1966 yearbook, but this source does not list the nationality of these men. This information is found in *Deputaty* (1966), but not all department heads are included in this volume.

9. The department heads in 1966 were: agriculture, F. D. Kulakov; heavy industry, M. S. Solomentsev; light industry and the food industry, P. K. Sizov; transportation and communication, K. S. Simonov; chemical industry, V. M. Bushuev; machinery industry, V. S. Frolov; defense industry, I. D. Serbin; construction, A. E. Biriukov; science and education, S. P. Trapeznikov. Their biographies can be found in *Bol'shaia sovetskaia entsiklopediia*, 1966 yearbook, pp. 578, 580, 597, 611, 613, 615, 617.

10. These secretaries were selected at the republican party congresses held in February and March 1966. More information about them can be found in Jerry F. Hough, *The Soviet Prefects* (Cambridge, Mass., Harvard University Press, 1969), p. 36.

11. Information on regional industrial output is spotty, and the list of the most industrialized oblasts was compiled in the following manner. Since Soviet industry is overconcentrated in the larger cities, I took the 200 largest cities in the 1959 census and grouped them by oblasts. I assumed that the 25 oblasts containing these 200 cities were the most industrialized. But since agriculture clearly overshadows industry in three of the regions near the bottom of the list (Altai krai, Bashkiria ASSR, and Omsk oblast, in each of which the rural population constituted over 60 percent of the total population), I replaced them with three oblasts which just failed to make the top 25, but still occupied an important role in the country's industrial life—Ivanovo, Zaporozhe, and the Russified Karaganda in Kazakhstan.

The 25 most important agricultural oblasts are those with the largest rural populations, excluding the autonomous republics and those oblasts already included among the most industrialized.

12. See Hough, *The Soviet Prefects,* for an elaboration of this theme.

13. E. I. Bugaev and B. M. Leibson, *Besedy ob ustave* (Moscow, Gospolitizdat, 1962), p. 141.

14. The biography of the new first secretary, I. A. Bondarenko, is found in *Deputaty* (1966), p. 65. The biographies of the other secretaries were found in the oblast newspaper.

15. John Kenneth Galbraith, *The New Industrial State* (Boston, Houghton Mifflin, 1967), chap. VI.

16. *Deputaty* (1966), p. 372.

17. Ibid., p. 444.

18. The next four pages of this essay summarize material found in Hough, *The Soviet Prefects,* chap. XII.

19. *XXIII s''ezd kommunisticheskoi partii sovetskogo soiuza,* [29 marta-8 aprelia 1966 goda], *Stenograficheskii otchet* (Moscow, Politizdat, 1966), I, 198-199.

20. *Sovetskaia rossiia*, March 15, 1966

21. *XXIII s"ezd*, I, 542.

22. Ibid., p. 560.

23. Ibid., pp. 250-252.

24. *Kommunist*, no. 1 (January 1958), 61.

25. Leo Gruliow, ed., *Current Soviet Policies* (New York, Frederick A. Prae-ger, 1953). See, for example, pp. 145, 173, 174, 179, and 198. Examples are cited in Hough, *The Soviet Prefects*, pp. 258-259.

26. *Pravda ukrainy*, October 28, 1965.

27. Joseph Berliner, *Factory and Manager in the USSR* (Cambridge, Mass., Harvard University Press, 1957), pp. 78-79.

28. Another factor which may be important is the practice of basing the salary scale of the manager and other officials upon the size of their enterprise. Expansion of a plant may result in it moving into the next category.

29. *Pravda*, April 3, 1957.

30. The agronomist first secretaries (and the volume and page on which their speech begins in *XXIII s"ezd*) are I. I. Bodiul (I, 417), A. V. Georgiev (II, 75), D. Rasulov (I, 272), A. A. Skochilov (I, 584), and N. F. Vasilev (II, 143). The engineering first secretaries are A. F. Eshtokin (I, 572), K. I. Galanshin (I, 538), K. F. Katushev (I, 195), D. A. Kunaev (I, 148), K. K. Nikolaev (I, 332), N. N. Rodionov (I, 598), P. E. Shelest (I, 130), M. S. Solomentsev (I, 518), and V. S. Tolstikov (I, 140). The three other secretaries heading oblasts from among the 25 most industrialized are F. S. Goriachev (I, 157), F. A. Tabeev (I, 505), and A. F. Vatchenko (I, 512).

31. This was P. N. Isaev. The demonstration occurred between the time of the election to the 1958 Supreme Soviet and the publication of the biographical directory of deputies. His biographical entry does not mention his various party positions. *Deputaty Verkhovnogo Soveta SSSR, Piatvi sozyv* (Moscow, Izdatel'stvo "Izvestiia", 1959), p. 168.

32. This was A. V. Basov, *Bol'shaia sovetskaia entsiklopediia*, 1966 yearbook, p. 577.

33. Brzezinski and Huntington, *Political Power USA/USSR*, p. 146.

34. The first two phrases about ideological style come from Gabriel A. Almond and G. Bingham Powell, Jr., *Comparative Politics: A Developmental Approach* (Boston, Little, Brown and Co., 1966), pp. 60-61. Their discussion does not deal with the regional party secretaries, but rather with a type of political culture. The Soviet Union is, however, said to have such a political culture. See p. 312. The ideological-instrumental dichotomy is also analyzed in Brzezinski and Huntington, *Political Power USA/USSR*, particularly pp. 71-76.

35. Ibid., p. 141.

36. Again the phrases come from Almond and Powell, *Comparative Politics* (pp. 24, 61, 87) and were not used to describe party officials, but to epitomize the attitudes found in a culture with "full secularization."

37. The leading place of Leningrad in Soviet sociology is mentioned in Frederick C. Barghoorn, *Politics in the USSR* (Boston, Little, Brown and Co., 1966), p. 254. The Leningrad first secretary was also the most vociferous speaker in support of sociological research at the Twenty-Third Congress, *XXIII s"ezd*, I, 147.

38. For example, the first secretary of the Estonian Central Committee asserted at the Twenty-Third Congress, "We have experimented and reorganized too much [on structural questions]," and he received applause on this point. *XXIII s"ezd*, I, 443.

39. *Partiinaia zhizn'*, no. 22 (November 1965), p. 35.

40. *Turkmenskaia iskra*, September 17, 1961.

41. *Ekonomicheskaia gazeta*, no. 43 (October 1967), p. 15.

42. *Sovetskaia Rossiia*, June 22, 1966.

43. *Ekonomicheskaia gazeta*, no. 46 (November 1967), p. 29.

44. *Sovetskaia Rossiia*, January 22, 1966.

45. Ibid.,

46. *Sovetskaia Rossiia*, February 12, 1966.

47. Ibid., August 9, 1967.

48. Ibid., June 22, 1966.

49. *Izvestiia*, November 17, 1965.

50. Ibid., December 21, 1965.

51. *Kazakhstanskaia pravda*, September 30, 1961.

52. Brzezinski and Huntington, *Political Power USA/USSR*, p. 199.

53. Party Rules, Statute 2, *Pravda*, November 3, 1961.

54. *Sovetskaia Belorussia*, November 21, 1962.

55. *Ekonomicheskaia gazeta*, no. 51 (December 1968), p. 8.

56. Ibid., p. 8.

57. *Partiinaia zhizn'*, no. 5 (March 1958), p. 14, and no. 19 (October 1958), pp. 45-48.

58. N. S. Khrushchev, *Stroitel'stvo kommunizma v SSSR i razvitie sel'skogo khoziaistva* (Moscow, Gospolitizdat, 1963), IV, 109.

59. Fainsod, *How Russia Is Ruled*, p. 341.

60. Ibid., p. 339.

61. Almond and Powell, *Comparative Politics*, pp. 61 and 312.

62. In the foreign policy realm two of the department heads were born and joined the party over a decade prior to the average department head specializing on internal policy questions. However, even the four foreign policy department heads (Iu. V. Andropov, A. S. Paniushkin, B. N. Ponomarev, and D. P. Shevliagin) on the average were born and joined the party a year earlier than the top four state officials handling foreign policy questions (A. A. Gromyko, V. V. Kuznetsov, N. S. Patolichev, and S. A. Skachkov). *Bol'shaia sovetskaia entsiklopediia*, 1966 yearbook, pp. 575, 584, 597, 605, 607, 611, and 619.

63. The head of the transportation and communications department of the Central Committee was K. S. Simonov; the Minister of Railroads, B. P. Beshchev; the Minister of Communications, N. D. Psurtsev; and the Minister of the Merchant Marine, V. G. Bakaev. Ibid., pp. 577, 578, 608, and 611.

64. The head of the light industry and food industry department of the Central Committee was P. K. Sizov; the Minister of the Food Industry was V. P. Zotov; and the Minister of the Fish Industry was A. A. Ishkov. Ibid., pp. 589, 590, and 611.

65. The head of the agriculture department was F. D. Kulakov; the Minister of Agriculture was V. V. Matskevich; and the Chairman of the State Committee for Deliveries was L. R. Korniets. Ibid., pp. 595, 597, and 601. The head of the construction department was A. E. Biriukov, and the four construction administrators were I. A. Grishmanov, F. B. Iakubovsky, E. F. Kozhevnikov, and I. T. Novikov. Ibid., pp. 578, 584, 593, 604, and 621.

66. Almond and Powell, *Comparative Politics*, p. 169. This phrase was applied to "input" structures "such as interest groups and parties."

67. Ibid., pp. 312 and 325.

68. Ibid., p. 91.
69. Ibid., p. 84.
70. Ibid., p. 278.
71. Ibid., p. 169.
72. Mancur Olson, *The Logic of Collective Action* (Cambridge, Mass., Harvard University Press, 1965), pp. 5-16 and 132-167.
73. V. O. Key, Jr., *Public Opinion and American Democracy* (New York, Alfred A. Knopf, 1967), p. 530.
74. Ibid., p. 537.
75. Ibid., p. 530, n. 9.
76. Charles E. Lindblom, *The Policy-Making Process* (Englewood Cliffs, N. J., Prentice-Hall, 1968), pp. 64-65.
77. Ibid., p. 68.
78. Bentley, *The Process of Government*, p. 270.

### 4. Political Participation in the Soviet Union

1. Frederick C. Barghoorn, *Politics in the USSR,* 2nd ed. (Boston, Little, Brown and Co., 1972), p. 31.
2. Paul Cocks, "The Rationalization of Party Control," in Chalmers Johnson, ed., *Change in Communist Systems* (Stanford, Stanford University Press, 1970), p. 165.
3. Ibid., p. 178.
4. See, for example, Harvey Fireside, Reply to correspondence, *Problems of Communism,* 21 (November-December 1972), 91; Jan S. Adams, "People's Control in the Soviet Union," *Western Political Quarterly,* 20 (December 1967), 919-929; Ellen Mickiewicz, "Policy Applications of Public Opinion Research in the Soviet Union," *Public Opinion Quarterly,* 36 (Winter 1972-73), 566; D. Richard Little, "Mass Political Participation in the U.S. and the U.S.S.R.; A Conceptual Analysis," *Comparative Political Studies* 8(January 1976), 437-460.
5. Roger Kanet, "The Rise and Fall of the 'All-People's State': Recent Changes in the Soviet Theory of the State," *Soviet Studies,* 20 (July 1968), 92.
6. N. P. Farberov, "Sotsialisticheskoe gosudarstvo i pravo," in F. S. Razarenov, comp., *Narodnomu druzhinniku* (Moscow, Znanie, 1973), p. 19.
7. The regional committee was visited on June 26, 1973. The present chairman had been the voluntary chairman while working as an engineer at the Volgograd Tractor Works, but then became a full-time trade union official.
8. Ts. A. Iampolskaia, *Obshchestvennye organizatsii i razvitie sovetskoi sotsialisticheskoi gosudarstvennosti* (Moscow, Nauka, 1965), p. 82; N. P. Bannykh, *Uchastie obshchestvennosti v deiatel'nosti ispolkomov mestnykh sovetov* (Moscow, Iuridicheskaia literatura, 1972), p. 53. This decline seems to have been arrested in later years, for the number of volunteer departments in the RSFSR was put at 5,230 in1972. *Sovetskaia Rossiia,* February 27, 1973, p. 2.
9. L. A. Grigorian, *Narodovlastie v SSSR* (Moscow, Iuridicheskaia Literatura, 1972), p. 115.
10. Ibid., pp. 8-9.
11. These quotations are drawn from E. M. Chekharin and D. A. Kerimov, "Sotsialisticheskaia demokratiia na sovremennom etape kommunisticheskogo stroitel'stva," in D. A. Kerimov, ed., *XXIV s''ezd ob ukreplenii sovetskogo gosudarstva i razvitii sotsialisticheskoi demokratii* (Moscow, Mysl', 1973), pp. 11-12. Chekharin was deputy head of the science and education department of

the Party Central Committee at the time the article was probably written, but he had become rector of the Higher Party School by the time it was published. The phrase "developed socialism" is also used throughout a book by the quite conservative head of the science and education department of the Central Committee, S. P. Trapeznikov, *Na krutykh povorotakh istorii* (Moscow, Mysl', 1971).

12. Chekharin and Kerimov, "Sotsialisticheskaia demokratiia na sovremennom etape," p. 12.

13. F. M. Burlatskii, "O stroitel'stve razvitogo sotsialisticheskogo obshchestva," *Pravda,* December 21, 1966. For a bibliography of his earlier works on the state, see F. M. Burlatskii, *Lenin, gosudarstvo, politika* (Moscow, Nauka, 1970), p. 508. His "Voprosy gosudarstva v proekte Programmy KPSS," *Kommunist,* no. 13, 1961, pp. 37-48, is particularly important, for in the Soviet Union such an article is often written by a scholar who has had a hand in drafting the document that the article is explaining authoritatively for the first time.

14. Thus, in 1970, there were 25,000,000 persons in the age cohort 10-14, 22,000,000 who were 15-19 in age, 17,100,000 who were 20-24, 13,800,000 who were 25-29 (these, of course, were born during World War II), and 21,100,000 who were 30-34. *Itogi vsesoiuznoi perepisi naseleniia 1970 goda* (Moscow, Statistika, 1972), II, 13.

15. Formally, persons may join the party at the age of 18, but since World War II few have been permitted to become party members until their middle or late twenties. (This fact is suggested in table 4.2 and is also confirmed by an examination of the biographies of the 742 Supreme Soviet deputies of the last 15 years who joined the party after 1946. If anything, these deputies should be atypically "political" in their attitudes and behavior, but they joined the party at the average age of 29.4 years. Their biographies can be found in the volumes of *Deputaty Verkhovnogo Soveta SSSR* published by Izvestiia Publishing House, Moscow, shortly after the 1958, 1962, 1966, and 1970 elections to the Supreme Soviet.) Since the late 1960s the babies of World War II and the immediate postwar period grew up to the age during which party admission is normal.

16. *Pravda,* November 29, 1969, pp. 1-2.

17. *Partiinaia zhizn',* no. 11, 1973, pp. 44-47. This article provides a good summary of the work of the councils.

18. Ibid., no. 6, 1973, p. 35.

19. Ibid., no. 7, 1973, p. 14.

20. See Peter H. Solomon, Jr., "Specialists in Soviet Policy-Making: Criminologists and Criminal Policy in the 1960's" (Ph. D. diss., Columbia University, 1973), and Donald V. Schwartz, "Recent Soviet Adaptations of Systems Theory to Administrative Theory," *Journal of Comparative Administration,* vol. V (August 1973), 233-264.

21. T. H. Rigby goes so far as to say that "in more and more areas of Soviet life, effective decision making is coming to mean professional decision making, and this is clearly incompatible with the detailed supervision and control by party officials or by the 'party masses.' " T. H. Rigby, *Communist Party Membership in the U.S.S.R., 1917-1967* (Princeton, N.J., Princeton University Press, 1968), p. 525.

22. The basic problem is that the chairmen, lower administrative personnel, and trained specialists are counted as "collective farmers" rather than "white-collar employees," while sovkhoz and MTS "peasants" are counted in the "worker" category. (Sovkhoz and MTS administrators and professionals have

been considered "white-collar employees.") As a consequence, the abolition of the MTS in 1958 arbitrarily threw a large number of people from the "worker" to "kolkhoznik" category, while the transformation of many kolkhozy into sovkhozy has had precisely the opposite impact.

A second problem is that statistics on class composition of party membership refer not to current occupation but to the occupation which the person held at the time of entrance into the party. For a discussion of regional evidence on the number of current workers in the party, see Merle Fainsod and Jerry F. Hough, *How Russia Is Ruled,* 3rd ed. (Cambridge, Mass., Harvard University Press, 1978), chap. 9.

A third problem is that at the time of the 1970 census a number of menial white-collar occupations were transferred to the worker category, the most notable of them being *prodavets* or sales clerk. (*Itogi vsesoiuznoi perepisi naseleniia 1970 goda,* vol. VI, 4.) A comparison of the original estimates of the number of workers in *Narodnoe khoziaistvo SSSR* statistical handbooks with the post-1970 reworked estimates indicates that as many as a million and a half people were involved. However, relatively few of this type of personnel have been deputies or even party members, but the post-1970 growth in worker component in the party is small enough to be accounted for entirely by this redefinition.

23. This calculation is based on only 10 of the republics, for my examination of the press of the other republics in 1961 was not thorough enough to permit identification of a sufficient number of their Central Committee members. The proportion of members identified was the same in each year: 93.6 percent.

24. Iu. E. Volkov, *Tak rozhdaetsia kommunisticheskoe samoupravlenie* (Moscow, Mysl', 1965), p. 118.

25. For pupil participation in the schools, see N. G. Ogurtsov and V. P. Aleksandrova, *Vospitanie obshchestvennoi aktivnosti uchashchikhsia* (Minsk, Narodnaia Asveta, 1972), pp. 81-82, 146. For party members, see, for example, *Pravda,* July 4, 1973, p. 2. For sociological work on deputies, see Volkov, *Tak rozhdaetsia kommunisticheskoe samoupravlenie,* pp. 130-136.

26. *Molodoi kommunist,* no. 4, 1973, p. 31.

27. For example, if party membership data are analyzed in conjunction with census data, the following percentages of those 25 years of age and older in each education group turn out to be party members: 8th grade or less, 4 percent; incomplete secondary education, 11 percent; complete secondary education, 18 percent; incomplete higher education, approximately 22 percent; complete higher education, 31 percent; holders of a higher degree, 46 percent. The party data are extrapolated from *Partiinaia zhizn',* no. 14, 1973, pp. 16, 19. The number of persons with a higher degree (candidate or doctor of science) is found in *Narodnoe obrazovanie, nauka, i kultura v SSSR: Statisticheskii sbornik* (Moscow, Statistika, 1971), p. 246. The other census data are taken from *Itogi vsesoiuznoi perepisi naseleniia 1970 goda,* III, 6-7.

28. For example, *Pravda* received 360,000 communications a year in the mid-1960s, 409,000 in 1972. Mark W. Hopkins, *Mass Media in the Soviet Union* (New York, Pegasus, 1970), pp. 303-304; *Pravda,* January 8, 1973, p. 1.

29. Howard Swearer, "Popular Participation: Myths and Realities," *Problems of Communism,* 9 (September-October 1960), p. 42.

30. William Kornhauser, *The Politics of Mass Society* (Glencoe, Ill., Free Press, 1959), p. 82.

31. Swearer, "Popular Participation," p. 42.

32. Zbigniew Brzezinski and Samuel P. Huntington, *Political Power USA/-USSR* (New York, Viking Press, 1964), p. 93.

33. This point is emphasized in Little, "Mass Political Participation in the U.S. and the U.S.S.R."

34. Gabriel A. Almond and Sidney Verba, *Five Nation Study Codebook, US Volume* (Ann Arbor, Survey Research Center, University of Michigan, 1968), p. 18.

35. Sidney Verba and Norman H. Nie, *Participation in America* (New York, Harper & Row, 1972), pp. 31 and 354.

36. Ibid., p. 31. Almond and Verba, *The Civic Culture,* pp. 30 and 33; Robert A. Dahl, *Who Governs?* (New Haven, Yale University Press, 1961), pp. 155-156.

37. *Codebook, The SRC 1968 American National Election Survey* (Ann Arbor, Survey Research Center, University of Michigan, 1968), p. 18.

38. Of the respondents, 13.8 percent that they approved, 38.8 percent said that it depended on the circumstances, and 47.3 percent said that they disapproved. *Codebook, The CPS 1970 American National Election Study* (Ann Arbor, Survey Research Center, University of Michigan, 1971), p. 84.

39. Indeed, in a major book that has not yet been properly absorbed into political science theory, Mancur Olson contends that a desire to have an impact on policy is an insufficient explanation for membership in large group activity, for an individual cannot rationally believe that his or her membership or participation will have any impact. Olson interprets mass participation in groups largely as the product of other forces: coercion (as in membership in trade unions or the American Medical Association), side benefits (as one may join the American Political Science Association to obtain the journal), a desire to make business or social contacts, peer pressure, or the like. *The Logic of Collective Action* (Cambridge, Mass., Harvard University Press, 1965).

40. Dahl, *Who Governs?,* pp. 155-156.

41. Ibid., pp. 156-157.

42. Verba and Nie, *Participation in America,* p. 50.

### 5. Party Saturation in the Soviet Union

1. Austin Ranney, *The Governing of Men,* rev. ed. (New York, Holt, Rinehart, and Winston, 1966), p. 358. For other references, see T. H. Rigby, *Communist Party Membership in the U.S.S.R. 1917-1967* (Princeton, N. J., Princeton University Press, 1968), p. 412, n. 1.

2. For the same argument, see Rigby, *Communist Party Membership,* p. 412.

2. T. B. Bottomore, *Elites and Society* (New York, Basic Books, 1964), p. 8.

4. George K. Schueller, "The Politburo," in Harold D. Lasswell and Daniel Lerner, eds., *World Revolutionary Elites* (Cambridge, Mass., MIT Press, 1965), pp. 97-178.

5. Alfred G. Meyer, *The Soviet Political System* (New York, Random House, 1965), p. 136.

6. This concept is developed in Rigby, *Communist Party Membership.* See also Zbigniew Brzezinski and Samuel P. Huntington, *Political Power USA/USSR* (New York, Viking Press, 1964), p. 100, and Mervyn Matthews, *Class and Society in Soviet Russia* (London, Allen Lane, Penguin Press, 1972), pp. 217-225.

7. For 1973 party membership, see *Partiinaia zhizn',* no. 14 (July 1973), p.

10; for 1973 population, see *Narodnoe khoziaistvo SSSR v 1972 g.* (Moscow, Statistika, 1973), p. 34. A new collection of party statistics was published in 1976. *Partiinaia zhizn'*, no. 10 (May) 1976, pp. 13-23. However, for the first time in recent years statistics on the age distribution of members were not included, and hence most of the calculations of this chapter cannot be updated.

8. See, for example, Ranney, *The Governing of Men*, p. 358. Philip S. Gillette, "Models and Analogies," (letter), *Problems of Communism*, vol. 21, no. 6 (November-December 1972), p. 90.

9. This approach is used, for example, in Rigby, *Communist Party Membership*, p. 449. The age distribution of the population for 1973 is found in *Narodnoe khoziaistvo SSSR v 1972 g.*, p. 34. Since the age groupings in the census do not correspond to the groupings required for the analysis of party membership, extrapolations were required both here and in later analyses of saturation by age group. It was simply assumed, for example, that in the 15-19 age group listed in the census, two-fifths were aged 18 and 19. The result is not exact because of irregularities in the birth rates from year to year, but the errors should not be serious for our purposes.

10. *Pravda*, March 31, 1971, p. 9.

11. *Voprosy istorii KPSS*, no. 8 (August 1976), p. 27.

12. The biographies of the deputies, including their year of birth and of Party admission, can be found in the volumes of *Deputaty Verkhovnogo Soveta* published by the Izvestiia Publishing House (Moscow) shortly after the 1958, 1962, 1966, and 1970 elections to the Supreme Soviet. By my count, 742 deputies joined the party after 1946, and they form the basis for my calculations.

13. *Partiinaia zhizn'*, no. 14 (July) 1973, p. 19; *Narodnoe khoziaistvo v 1972 g.*, p. 34.

14. *Partiinaia zhizn'*, no. 14 (July) 1973, p. 18.

15. *Narodnoe khoziaistvo v 1972 g.*, p. 34.

16. *Partiinaia zhizn'*, no. 14 (July) 1973, p. 14.

17. *Itogi vsesoiuznoi perepisi naseleniia 1970 goda* (Moscow, Statistika, 1972), III, 6-7.

18. The urban-rural distribution of party membership is rarely discussed, but a recent book reports the number of Communists "who work in rural raiony". In 1959: 3,510,613 (42.6 percent of the total); 1961: 3,809,470 (41.1 percent); 1966: 4,694,984 (38.0 percent); 1971: 5, 409, 905 (37.6 percent). V. I. Strukov, compiler, *Kommunisticheskaia partiia Sovetskogo Soiuza, Nagliadnoe posobie po partiinomu stroitel'stvu* (Moscow, Polizdat, 1973), p. 126. These figures are well beyond the estimates of T. H. Rigby (*Communist Party Membership*, pp. 486-491), and the 1947 statistic cited by Strukov (2,449,983) is much above the 1,714,000 rural Communists that *Bolshevik* reported at the time. (Quoted in ibid., p. 488). Part of the problem may be the difference between working and living in rural areas, but the major problem is whether to count Communists in small rural towns as urban or rural, and at what size of town or village to draw the borderline.

19. *Partiinaia zhizn'*, no. 14 (July) 1973, p. 16; *Narodnoe khoziaistvo v 1972 g.*, p. 38.

20. Calculated from *Itogi vsesoiuznoi perepisi naseleniia 1970 goda*, III, 6-7.

21. In 1970, only 28.9 percent of the men in the 20-24 age group were married, but this figure rose to 77.2 percent in the 25-29 group. Ibid., II, 263.

22. Rigby, *Communist Party Membership*, p. 491.

23. See, for example, Darrell P. Hammer, "The Dilemma of Party Growth," *Problems of Communism,* 20 (July-August 1970), pp. 16-21.

24. *Spravochnik partiinogo rabotnika,* 6th ed. (Moscow, Politizdat, 1966), pp. 383-386.

25. *Partiinaia zhizn',* no. 14 (July 1973), p. 12.

26. The number of registered voters was 140,000,000 in 1963 and 146,075,945 in 1967, and the calculation assumes 143,000,000 in 1965. (*Pravda,* March 7, 1963, p. 1; March 21, 1963, p. 1; March 26, 1967, p. 1.) There were said to be 156,507,828 registered voters in 1973 (ibid., June 23, 1973, p. 1), but the 1973 figure is out of line with registration figures of other years and there must have been an undercount that year. (There were 161,724,222 persons registered to vote in 1974. *Izvestiia,* June 19, 1974, p. 1) I have adopted the figure of 159 million for 1973 as the one most consistent with all the data, but if one took the official 1973 registration figures, the rise in the adult population would be 9.4 percent.

27. *Itogi vsesoiuznoi perepisi naseleniia 1970 goda,* II, 12-13.

28. Ibid., II, 12-13.

29. Ibid., VI, 172.

30. In 1971 and 1972 29.0 percent of the new candidates were women. The figure given for the 1971-1975 period as a whole is 29.5 percent, implying that women comprised closer to 30 percent of the candidates between 1973 and 1975. *Partiinaia zhizn',* no. 10 (May) 1976, p. 14.

31. *Narodnoe khoziastvo SSSR v 1964 g.* (Moscow, Statistika, 1964), p. 33; *Narodnoe khoziaistvo SSSR v 1972 g.,* p. 38.

32. This figure is calculated by subtracting the 1971 and 1972 admissions (see note 25) from those given by the 1971-1975 period as a whole. *Partiinaia zhizn',* no. 10 (May) 1976, p. 13.

33. Ibid., no. 19 (October) 1976, pp. 9-11. While calling for a maintenance of high standards of admission, the decision specifically criticized the Kirghiz Party organization for not admitting enough workers and livestock peasants.

34. See, for example, *Pravda,* July 4, 1973, p. 2.

## 6. The Impact of Participation:
### Women and the Women's Issue in Soviet Policy Debates

1. The percentage of women among the members of the Auditing Commission of the Central Committee is higher: 14.1 percent. (In 1971, 2.5 percent of the voting members of the Central Committee, 5.2 percent of the candidate members of the Central Committee, and 11.1 percent of the members of the Auditing Commission were women.) For information on the percentage of women in these bodies in earlier years, see Gail Warshofsky Lapidus, "Political Mobilization, Participation, and Leadership: Women in Soviet Politics," *Comparative Politics,* 8 (October 1975), p. 110.

2. The number of deputy department heads and section heads of the Central Committee apparatus must be obtained through an identification of these officials in the press, but the given total should be fairly accurate. The unidentified party officials are primarily in the heavy industry and defense industry areas and are unlikely to include women.

3. The number of deputy ministers and deputy chairmen can be obtained by following the appointments and removals of these officials as announced in *Pos-*

*tanovleniia Soveta Ministrov SSSR* and their deaths as announced in the press. A few changes may be missed by this method, but the error should be small. The seven women deputy ministers as of April 1975 were Z. M. Kruglova (Ministry of Culture), A. T. Lavrenteva (Ministry of Light Industry), Ia. S. Nasridinnova (Ministry of the Building Materials Industry), E. Ch. Novikova (Ministry of Health, the deputy minister for women's and children's care), M. L. Riabova (Ministry of Finance, apparently the deputy minister for education-culture-health financing), A. P. Shaposhnikova (Ministry of Higher and Specialized Secondary Education), and M. I. Zhuravleva (Ministry of Education). In the fall of 1975, however, Z. M. Kruglova was removed as Deputy Minister of Culture to replace N. V. Popova as Chairman of the Union of Soviet Societies of Friendship and Cultural Ties with Foreign Countries, and her replacement is not known.

4. Calculated through an identification of the bureau members listed in the various republican newspapers at the conclusion of the respective republican Party congresses in January and February 1976. Actually, 2.6 percent of the full members of the republican bureaus were women, 7.4 percent of the candidate members. In 1972, a total of 2.2 percent of the members and candidate members were women, compared with the 3.8 percent figure of 1976. The 1972 figure is calculated on the basis of the identifications found in Grey Hodnett and Val Ogaroff, *Leaders of the Soviet Republics, 1955-1972* (Canberra, Australian National University, 1973).

5. Joel Moses, "Indoctrination as a Female Political Role in the Soviet Union," in Dorothy Atkinson, Alexander Dallin, and Gail Warshofsky Lapidus, *Women in Russia: Changing Realities and Changing Perspectives* Stanford, Calif., Stanford University Press, 1977).

6. These figures are based on data for 56 of the 71 oblasts, krais, and autonomous republics, and for 34 large cities in the RSFSR.

7. *Deputaty Verkhovnogo Soveta SSSR, Deviatyi sozyv* (Moscow, Izdlatel'stvo lzvestii, 1974), p. 3; *Isvestiia,* June 21, 1975, pp. 1-2.

8. *Partiinaia zhizn',* no. 10 (May 1976), p. 20.

9. These figures are based on an actual count of participants in the debates, but do not include the official reporters and coreporters. The sample of regional committee sessions was based largely on the accident of Russian alphabetical order. Midway through what was to be a comprehensive survey of the meetings of the first four months of 1965, the regional press was taken from the Lenin Library preparatory to the move to the new newspaper Library in Khimki. Here, as elsewhere, those speakers whose sex could not be determined by their name or accompanying verb endings were excluded from the calculation.

10. Committee (commission) sessions are reported regularly in *Vedomosti Verkhovnogo Soveta* and sometimes in the press as well. However, the names of the speakers are listed in only a portion of the cases. The figure given is calculated on the basis of 234 names of speakers listed in *Vedomosti Verkhovnogo Soveta SSSR* during these years. (Sessions of the Foreign affairs committees are excluded from the figures on the assumption that they have little relationship to the policy making process.)

11. Figures are based on 60 of 71 oblasts, krais, and autonomous republics.

12. These figures were calculated from the clippings files on soviets in the Institute of State and Law library.

13. *Molodoi kommunist,* no. 7 (July 1975), p. 8.

14. *Politicheskoe samoobrazovanie,* no. 7, 1975, p. 26.

15. Both figures are by actual count. For the selection of the oblast confer-ences, see note 9.

16. *Politicheskoe samoobrazovanie,* no. 7, 1975, p. 26.

17. In the first place, indoctrination is not a word normally used in discussions of policy areas in the West, and consequently its use may not contribute to the development of empirical comparative analysis. In the second place, there are fewer women in posts that most clearly seem to involve propaganda or indoctrina-tion than in the areas that are more purely health, education, and welfare. As table 6.2 indicates, there was not a single woman in a key republican media or indoctrination post in 1975, and in the entire 1955-75 period only 3 percent of the heads of the agitation-propaganda departments of the republican central committees, 4 percent of the chairmen of the state committees for television and radio, and 4 percent of the chairmen of the state publishing committee—two, one, and one persons respectively—have been women. In the RSFSR oblasts, krais, and autonomous republics, the proportion of women among the identified heads of propaganda-agitation departments of the regional party committees stands at 8 percent (N = 72), among the chairmen of the regional TV-radio com-mittees at 7 percent (N = 81), among the heads of the publishing departments at 7 percent (N = 75), and among the regional newspaper editors at 0 percent (N = 116). For the opposite point of view, see Moses, ''Indoctrination as a Female Political Role.''

18. The leading officials in each of the categories were identified in a number of central and regional sources and should constitute a reasonably unbiased sam-ple. (Indeed, in those cases with an N of over 100, some 80-90 percent of all occu-pants of the posts have been identified.) The journal *Sotsial'noe obespechenie* has carried the names of many deputy heads of regional social security depart-ments in recent years, and if this policy area is typical, the proportion of women may well be higher among the deputy heads than among the heads of the depart-ments in these realms. (33 percent of the 55 deputy heads of social security depart-ments that were identified were women.)

19. Norton Dodge, ''The Role of Soviet Women in the Professions,'' in At-kinson et al., *Women in Russia.*

20. *Itogi vsesoiuznoi peripisi naseleniia 1970 goda* (Moscow, Statistika, 1973), VI, 167-169.

21. *Vedomosti Verkhovnogo Soveta RSFSR* regularly publishes lists of certain categories of officials who received an award on their 50th and 60th birthday. Lower officials of the Central Committee apparatus are one of the categories, and it seems that every official in the category who reaches the appropriate age receives an award. In the period from 1970 to mid-1975, 18 percent of the ''responsible officials'' and ''instructors'' of the Central Committee to receive an award were women. (The percentage was higher among ''nonresponsible'' employees and associates, presumably often clerical personnel.) From other evidence it is clear that most of the responsible officials are also instructors, but a few are heads of sections (particularly in sensitive departments such as the international depart-ment). Since the section heads are almost all men, the number of women among other responsible officials aged 50 and 60 should be above 18 percent. However, this figure is probably too high for the Central Committee apparatus, for the

majority of instructors are below the age of 50, and many move back to the state apparatus after a short period of work in the Central Committee. The members of this group on whom we have data are predominantly men, and hence the true figure for the entire apparatus is probably in the 10-15 percent range.

22. See, for example, I. M. Slepenkov and B. V. Kniazov, *Molodezh' sela segodnia* (Moscow, Molodaia Gvardiia, 1972), p. 115.

23. *VLKSM, Nagliadnoe posobie* (Moscow, Molodaia Gvardiia, 1975), pp. 26 and 86.

24. In some areas there are public organizations which are overtly female in nature. For example, Volgograd oblast has a commission for work among women (*Volgogradskaia pravda,* March 8, 1975, p. 1), and Voronezh has a city women's council (*Kommuna,* March 8, 1975, p. 1). Moscow on the other hand seems devoid of such organizations. Most are concentrated in the Central Asian and Transcaucasian republics and in the autonomous republics. For a discussion of women's councils in Tashkent oblast and in Turkmenia, see *Politicheskoe samoobrazovanie,* no. 3, 1966, p. 106, and no. 3, 1968, p. 114.

25. Gail Warshofsky Lapidus, *Women in Soviet Society* (Berkeley, Calif., University of California Press, 1977).

26. *Sovetskaia zhenshchina,* no. 2, 1975, p. 35.

27. *Pravda,* September 5, 1975, p. 2.

28. Ibid., January 31, 1975, p. 3.

29. *Novyi mir,* no. 11 (November) 1969, pp. 23-55.

30. For one of the best such articles on the learning of sex roles in the early socialization process, see *Sovetskaia kultura,* February 4, 1975.

31. Ibid., December 5, 1974, and December 17, 1974; *Pravda,* December 12, 1974, December 14, 1974, December 24, 1974, and December 26, 1974.

32. This interview was distributed by Novosti, and like an Associated Press dispatch, could be published by any editor who thought it worthwhile. One place of publication was *Leninskaia pravda* (Karela), April 18, 1975.

33. For this debate, see *Sovetskaia kultura,* December 17, 1974, January 7, 1975, and January 14, 1975.

34. See Jerry F. Hough, "The Brezhnev Era: The Man and the Regime," *Problems of Communism,* 25 (March-April 1976), 11-13.

35. The correlation does not reflect any overlap in the 1971 data. The 1967-71 figures on women's participation include only soviet sessions held prior to June 1971, while the 1971-75 figures include only sessions held in June or later.

36. Soviet specialists adopting quantitative methods—and, indeed, many political scientists of other specialties—have had a tendency to limit their statistical work to general correlational or regression analysis. The statistics cited are just one of the examples that illustrate the need for a more detailed examination of the data that underlies overall coefficients.

### 7. Centralization and Decentralization in the Soviet Administrative System

1. See, for example, N. S. Koval, ed., *Planirovanie narodnogo khoziaistva SSSR* (Moscow, Vysshaia shkola, 1973), p. 422.

2. This is an awkward essay for which to provide notes. It is based primarily on statistics from 18 annual editions of *Narodnoe khoziaistvo RSFSR* (Moscow, Statistika), and it does not seem worthwhile to indicate at inordinate length pre-

cisely what pages in which handbooks were utilized for each calculation, all the more so because those pages provide no more than the raw materials for what would be a time-consuming effort to verify the calculations. The statistical year-books are organized along similar lines, and any reader who would like to test out or expand the calculations really needs little more than the following general guidelines to find the needed raw materials: the total population and the per-centage of urban population in each oblast can be found in the opening pages of the yearbooks, the rate of industrial growth in the opening pages of the section on industry, the total retail trade in each oblast early in the section on trade (the per captia figure must be calculated by dividing this figure by the oblast's total popu-lation), and the number of hospital beds at the beginning of the section on health (again, the per capita figure—or one for beds per 10,000 population—must be calculated through the use of the total population data). The only unexpected feature of the yearbooks is that the January 1st figures are usually found in the statistical handbooks of the previous year; for example, January 1, 1974 figures in *Narodnoe khoziaistvo RSFSR v 1973 g.*

3. Magadan oblast is excluded from this and succeeding analyses because, particularly in the past, it had an extremely high number of beds per capita and might distort the analysis.

4. See the discussion in William Taubman, *Governing Soviet Cities* (New York, Praeger, 1973), pp. 73-80.

5. Information on the oblast sessions was obtained by examining clippings from the oblast press found in the library of the Institute of State and Law in Mos-cow. A few of the oblasts were not included in the Institute's files, and the auton-omous republics were excluded from this calculation because their soviets met only twice a year in contrast with four times a year for the oblasts and they almost never discussed health questions.

6. Information on tenure of oblispolkom chairman is not available in 3 cases.

7. For analysis of the variation in the amount of per capita housing available in the oblast centers, see Jerry F. Hough, "Soviet Urban Politics and Comparative Urban Theory," *Journal of Comparative Administration* 4 (November 1972), 316-317.

### 8. Inputs and Responsiveness in American Political Science

1. Alex Inkeles, *Public Opinion in Soviet Russia* (Cambridge, Mass., Harvard University Press, 1950), p. 202.

2. Alfred G. Meyer, "The Comparative Study of Communist Political Sys-tems," *Slavic Review,* 26 (March 1967), p. 11.

3. Austin Ranney, *The Governing of Men,* revised edition (New York, Holt, Rinehart, and Winston, Inc., 1966), pp. 207 and 230.

4. Ibid., pp. 230-231.

5. Ibid., pp. 207 and 230.

6. William Mitchell, *The American Polity* (New York, The Free Press, 1963), p. 408, n. 36.

7. See the discussion of "false consciousness" in Nelson Polsby, *Community Power and Political Theory* (New Haven, Yale University Press, 1963), p. 23.

8. Carl. J. Friedrich and Zbigniew Brzezinski, *Totalitarian Dictatorship and Autocracy,* 2nd ed. (Cambridge, Mass., Harvard University Press, 1965), pp. 26-27 and 147. Although the title page indicates a joint authorship, Friedrich stated

that he alone undertook the 1965 revision.

9. David Easton, *A Systems Analysis of Political Life* (New York, John Wiley & Sons, 1965), pp. 38, 80-81, and 39.

10. Ibid., p. 88.

11. Ibid., pp. 88 and 93.

12. James Oliver, "Citizen Demands and the Soviet Political System," *The American Political Science Review,* 63 (June 1969), pp. 465-475.

13. Easton, *A Systems Analysis of Political Life,* p. 93.

14. Ibid., p. 140.

15. Oliver, "Citizen Demands," p. 467.

16. Gabriel Almond and G. Bingham Powell, *Comparative Politics: A Developmental Approach* (Boston, Little, Brown and Co., 1966), p. 73.

17. Ibid., pp. 277-279.

18. Ibid., pp. 79, 276-277, and 312-313.

19. Zbigniew Brzezinski and Samuel P. Huntington, *Political Power USA/USSR* (New York, Viking Press, 1964), pp. 104-121 and 195-196.

20. Ibid., p. 196.

21. Ibid., p. 93.

22. Ibid., pp. 88-89.

23. Ibid., pp. 203-204.

24. C. D. Garson, "On the Origins of Interest-Group Theory: A Critique of a Process," *American Political Science Review,* 68 (December 1974), 1505-1509.

25. A. Lawrence Lowell, *Public Opinion and Popular Government* (New York, Longmans, Green, and Co., 1914), pp. 61-62.

26. Brzezinski and Huntington, *Political Power USA/USSR,* p. 43.

27. Robert A. Dahl and Charles E. Lindblom, *Politics, Economics, and Welfare* (New York, Harper & Row, 1953), p. 86.

28. Charles E. Lindblom, "The Science of 'Muddling Through'," *Public Administration Review,* 19 (Spring 1959), 79-88.

29. Dahl and Lindblom, *Politics, Economics, and Welfare,* pp. 82-88. See also Charles E. Lindblom, *The Policy-Making Process* (Englewood Cliffs, N. J., Prentice-Hall, Inc., 1968), pp. 21-27.

30. David Easton, *The Political System* (New York, Alfred A. Knopf, 1953) pp. 266-306.

31. V. O. Key, Jr., *Politics, Parties, and Pressure Groups,* 4th ed. (New York, Thomas Y. Crowell Company, 1958), p. 24.

32. The most famous depiction of this process is C. Wright Mills' "Power Elite," later embodied in broader form in the term "military-industrial complex." Earlier, however, Ernest Griffith had insisted that this phenomenon (which he called "government by whirlpool") was general in federal government and not to be deplored. Ernest S. Griffith, *The American System of Government,* 4th ed. (New York, Frederick A. Praeger, 1965), pp. 102-103. For a critical survey of this literature, see Theodore Lowi, *The End of Liberalism* (New York, Norton, 1969).

33. Robert A. Dahl, *A Preface to Democratic Theory* (Chicago, University of Chicago Press, 1956), pp. 27-28, 133, and 146.

34. H. L. Childs, "Pressure Groups and Propaganda," in E. B. Logan, ed., *The American Political System* (New York, Harper & Row, 1936), p. 225. Quoted in Wilfred E. Binkley and Malcolm C. Moos, *A Grammar of American*

*Politics* (New York, Alfred A. Knopf, 1949), p. 8.

35. See, for example, the long criticism of the concept in Easton, *The Political System,* pp. 266-306.

36. Gabriel Almond and Sidney Verba, *The Civic Culture* (Boston, Little, Brown and Co., 1963).

37. Karl W. Deutsch, *The Nerves of Government* (New York, The Free Press, 1963), p. 88.

38. Easton, *A Systems Analysis of Political Life,* pp. 433-434.

39. Gabriel A. Almond, *Political Development* (Boston, Little, Brown and Co., 1970), p. 190.

40. Almond and Powell, *Comparative Politics,* pp. 28, 116, and 201.

41. The analysis of this section also applies to such similar theoretical constructs as David Apter's "reconciliation system." David Apter, *The Politics of Modernization* (Chicago, University of Chicago Press, 1969).

42. Almond and Powell, *Comparative Politics,* p. 201.

43. The metaphor is used by Earl Latham in *The Group Basis of Politics* (Ithaca, N. Y., Cornell University Press, 1952), p. 37. However, it describes a role that Latham believes is *not* played by the legislature with respect to the group struggle.

44. Dahl, *A Preface to Democratic Theory,* p. 133.

45. Seymour Martin Lipset, "The Changing Class Structure and Contemporary European Politics," *Daedalus,* 93 (Winter 1964), p. 296.

46. See, for example, Talcott Parsons, *Politics and Social Structure* (New York, The Free Press, 1969), pp. 199-203 and 352-404.

47. C. B. Macpherson, *The Real World of Democracy* (New York, Oxford University Press. 1966).

### 9. Communications and Persuasion in the Analysis of Inputs

1. December was selected out of a desire for comparability with a study of the Soviet press of late 1947 conducted by Alex Inkeles and Kent Geiger, "Critical Letters to the Soviet Press," *American Sociological Review,* 17 (December 1952), pp. 694-703, and 18 (February 1953), pp. 12-23. A month late in the Stalin period was wanted, and December 1951 was chosen over December 1952 out of a fear that the later date would be atypical because of the just-concluded Nineteenth Party Congress. December 1971 was chosen simply because a 20-year interval was a round number. In practice, both months seem quite typical.

2. *XXIII s'ezd kommunisticheskoi partii sovetskogo soiuza, Stenograficheskii otchet* (Moscow, Gospolizdat, 1966), I, 422.

3. *Pravda,* December 10, 1951, p. 2; December 26, 1951, p. 2; *Izvestiia,* December 11, 1951, p. 2.

4. *Pravda,* December 21, 1951, p. 2; *Izvestiia,* December 30, 1951, p. 2; December 22, 1951, p. 2; December 12, 1951, p. 2; *Pravda,* December 12, 1951, p. 2; December 8, 1951, p. 2; *Izvestiia,* December 29, 1951, p. 2.

5. In 1951 both *Pravda* and *Izvestiia* were four pages in length, and criticism of performance and expression of policy proposals were generally limited to a small part of the second page. By 1971, *Pravda* had been expanded to six pages three times a week. In both years *Pravda* was a daily, and *Izvestiia* was published six days a week.

6. Only 33 items were formally listed as letters, but another 21 (which appeared under the headings of "Comments and Replies" or "Leaflets of the

People's Control") were indistinguishable from the letters and will be counted with them.

7. It would be too time-consuming to check the typicality of the month in all respects, but it was possible to count the number of letters in the 100 issues of each newspaper both before and after the month studied. In the 1951 case, the rate was almost identical (.47 letters per issue compared with .52 letters). In 1971, however, only 1.1 letters per issue were found in the 100 issues prior to December (compared with the 1.5 letters in December), and 1.6 letters afterwards.

Inkeles and Geiger, who studied all letters and not just those with a demand, report a smaller number of letters in 1947—.23 letters an issue. However, the fall of 1947 was an abnormal period for *Pravda* and *Izvestiia*. Elections to the local soviets in December received enormous attention, and (probably because of the first enunciation of the "two-camps" image of foreign relations at this time), an unusual amount of coverage was devoted to foreign affairs. From September 1, 1947 to January 7, 1948 (a total of 228 issues), I could find only 16 critical letters printed in the two newspapers, .07 letters per issue. However, in the 100 issues prior to September 1, *Pravda* and *Izvestiia* published an average of .48 letters per issue, and in the 100 issues subsequent to January 8th, .45 letters per issue— almost identical to the 1951-1952 figures.

8. Zbigniew Brzezinski and Samuel P. Huntington, *Political Power USA/ USSR* (New York, Viking Press, 1964), p. 196.

9. *Pravda,* December 1, 1971, p. 2.

10. *Izvestiia,* December 21, 1971, p. 5.

11. *Kommunist* (Erevan), January 23, 1975, p. 3.

12. See *Sovetskaia Kirgiziia,* November 18, 1970, p. 2; November 21, 1970, p. 2; January 5, 1971, p. 2; April 16, 1971, p. 3.

13. *Sovetskaia Moldaviia,* January 29, 1975, p. 2.

14. See note 12.

15. *Sovetskaia Moldaviia,* January 29, 1975, p. 2.

16. Ibid., p. 2.

17. V. V. Kravchenko, *Dobrovol'nye obshchestva v SSSR i ikh pravovoe polozhenie* (Moscow, Iuridicheskaia literatura, 1964), p. 7.

18. These points are discussed in greater length in Merle Fainsod and Jerry F. Hough, *How Russia Is Ruled,* 3rd ed. (Cambridge, Mass., Harvard University Press, forthcoming), chap. 9.

19. A few journals (for example, those of the police bureaucracies) are totally restricted to the professionals for whom they are intended, but they are exceptions.

### 10. The Soviet Experience and the Measurement of Power

1. Robert A. Dahl, "The Concept of Power," *Behavioral Science,* 2 (July 1957), 202-203.

2. V. O. Key, Jr., *Politics, Parties, and Pressure Groups,* 4th ed. (New York, Thomas Y. Crowell Co., 1958), pp. 4-5.

3. Ibid., p. 5.

4. This is, of course, the central criticism made by Dahl and his associates of the assertions of their adversaries. A recent one is Raymond E. Wolfinger's "Non-decisions and the Study of Local Politics," *The American Political Science Review,* 65 (December 1971), 1063-1080. Michael Parenti in turn has contended that Dahl's assertions about the indirect influence of the electorate are not really

supported by hard data. "Power and Pluralism: A View from the Bottom," *Journal of Politics*, 32 (August 1970), 506.

5. See Carl J. Friedrich's discussion of "Influence and the Rule of Anticipated Reactions" in *Man and His Government* (New York, McGraw-Hill, 1963), pp. 199-215.

6. Peter F. Drucker, Delbert C. Miller, and Robert A. Dahl, *Power and Democracy in America*, edited by William V. D'Antonio and Howard J. Ehrlich (Notre Dame, Ind., University of Notre Dame Press, 1961), p. 80.

7. Robert A. Dahl, "A Critique of the Ruling Elite Model," *The American Political Science Review*, 52 (June 1958), 466.

8. Nelson Polsby, *Community Power and Political Theory* (New Haven, Yale University Press, 1963), pp. 8-11, 90, and 93.

9. Robert A Dahl, *Who Governs?* (New Haven, Yale University Press, 1961), p. 86.

10. Drucker et al., *Power and Democracy in America*, p. 78.

11. Polsby, *Community Power and Political Theory*, p. 112.

12. Drucker et al., *Power and Democracy in America*, p. 75. The italics are Dahl's.

13. The attack began with Peter Bachrach and Morton S. Baratz, "Two Faces of Power," *The American Political Science Review*, 56 (December 1962), 947-952. Further bibliography can found in a recent addition to the debate—the exchange between Raymond E. Wolfinger and Frederick W. Frey in ibid., 65 (December 1971), 1063-1104.

The methodological difficulties are well illustrated in Bachrach and Baratz's book, *Power and Poverty* (New York, Oxford University Press, 1970). This book comes very close to stating that the entry of upper-stratum blacks into the political process of Baltimore means the end of nondecision making there—an extraordinary statement.

14. Consider, for example, the image of the Soviet political system that emerges from Zbigniew Brzezinski and Samuel P. Huntington, *Political Power USA/USSR* (New York, Viking Press, 1964), "The political system is monolithic not because few people participate in it, but because the resources which can be employed in the political struggle are very limited. The key resource is control of the party organization . . . Insofar as there are limits on the power of the top leader in the Soviet Union, they stem from his sharing control of the apparat with a small number of colleagues . . . The principal bargainers are very much alike. They are all (or almost all) products of the Party apparatus . . . There should be a high degree of consensus among them . . . All or almost all . . . have the 'Presidial perspective' . . . Only one group—the political professionals of the Party apparat —can be said to 'control' the policy makers, in the sense that the policy-makers are recruited from them and wield power through them." (pp. 195, 197, and 199).

15. In fact, Brzezinski and Huntington suggest that on certain key issues the political leadership makes alliance with the lower status citizen against those of higher status. "While there are greater differences in power between leaders and populace in the Soviet Union there may well be greater differences in attitude between leaders and populace in the United States. The Soviet regime mobilizes the masses against dissenters or deviants from the Party line . . . In the United States the civic associations are a means through which those of higher social-economic standing participate in and limit the political system. In the Soviet

Union, on the other hand, social mobilization encourages lower-class participation to strengthen the political system." Ibid., pp. 102 and 104.

16. Jerzy F. Karcz, "From Stalin to Brezhnev: Soviet Agricultural Policy in Historical Perspective," in James R. Millar, *The Soviet Rural Community* (Urbana, Ill., University of Illinois Press, 1971), p. 54.

17. Barrington Moore, *Soviet Politics—The Dilemma of Power* (Cambridge, Mass., Harvard University Press, 1950).

18. *The Great Retreat* (New York, E. P. Dutton and Company, Inc., 1946).

19. See the discussion in Andrew S. McFarland, *Power and Leadership in Pluralist Systems* (Standford, Calif., Stanford University Press, 1969), pp. 61-63.

20. Two articles that conduct such a survey and conclude that the evidence requires a more pluralistic image of the Soviet political system are by Joel Schwartz and William R. Keech, "Group Influence on the Policy Process in the Soviet Union," *The American Political Science Review*, 62 (September 1968), 840-851, and Philip D. Stewart, "Soviet Interest Groups and the Policy Process: The Repeal of Production Education," *World Politics*, 22 (October 1969), 29-50.

21. Jerry F. Hough, "Soviet Urban Politics and Comparative Urban Theory," *Journal of Comparative Administration*, 4 (November 1972), 324-327.

22. Dahl, "A Critique of the Ruling Elite Model," p. 464; Polsby, *Community Power and Political Theory*, p. 10.

23. Merle Fainsod, *How Russia Is Ruled*, 2nd ed. (Cambridge, Mass., Harvard University Press, 1963), pp. 104-109.

24. Jeremy R. Azrael, *Managerial Power and Soviet Politics* (Cambridge, Mass., Harvard University Press, 1966), pp. 90-98.

25. Arthur F. Bentley, *The Process of Government* (Chicago, The University of Chicago Press, 1908), pp. 314-315.

26. Indeed, Polsby cites Hunter's assertions about such power of blacks in Atlanta in the early 1950s. *Community Power and Political Theory*, pp. 53-54.

27. McFarland, *Power and Leadership in Pluralist Systems*, pp. 53-92.

28. McFarland simply stresses that "most would agree that an analysis of the Soviet system as pluralist is a case of spurious complexity, spurious pluralism . . . If Soviet administration is pluralist, then our conception of "pluralism" is too general to be useful, unless our ideas concerning "unity of education and doctrine" imposed by the Communist Party are totally incorrect." Ibid., pp. 61 and 69. He never explores how such assertions should be verified, particularly in his analysis of power relationships above the level of the industrial plant. If, indeed, his central piece of evidence is the "unity of education and doctrine imposed by the Communist Party," then he is talking about "fundamental issues" of the same type that C. Wright Mills did.

29. Obviously it is not hard to demonstrate that political leaders sometimes shape their actions with an eye on the next election. However, in comparative terms this evidence is hardly convincing. If a regressive tax system based on a property tax that must be paid even when one is unemployed or retired induces the lower and middle strata to be very conservative in their preferences for community services, should political responsiveness to these preferences be cited as evidence of the power of lower and middle strata? The point takes on special force when these same strata prefer high levels of governmental expenditures at the federal level, where the income tax is more progressive.

30. In the construction of a Lorenz curve, the population is ranked by income, and the percentage of national income earned by each percentile of the popula-

tion is then determined. It might be discovered, for example, that the bottom 20 percent of the population receives 5 percent of the income, the bottom 40 percent 20 percent of it, and so forth. Then on a graph on which the vertical axis is the percentile of income and the horizontal axis is the percentile of population, one draws a line connecting the various percentile intersects. If income distribution is perfectly egalitarian (that is, the bottom 10 percent receives 10 percent of the income, the bottom 25 percent receives 25 percent, and so forth), the resulting line is a perfectly straight one which stretches from the lower left corner to the upper right one. The more the actual line deviates from this straight diagonal, the more inegalitarian is the distribution of income. The Gini index, usually employed to summarize this data in short statistical form, is a measurement of the relative area of the graph lying between the real line and hypothetical straight-line diagonal.

31. An attempt to arrive at "field position" by an examination of preferences is extremely difficult. Probably the best hope would be a longitudinal study of elite and mass attitudes on a series of policy issues, so designed that one could look at the changes in values over time as well as policy outcomes in the particular areas. For all the debate about a "Power Elite," it is striking how little we know about the actual values and policy preferences of this group or any similar one.

32. Polsby, *Community Power and Political Theory*, p. 132.

33. Robert A. Dahl, *Polyarchy* (New Haven, Yale University Press, 1971), pp. 82-86.

34. The argument is not that the money may be utilized to achieve political ends, although there is, of course, some possibility of that. Rather, it is that the distribution of income may well be an indicator of the balance of power in the past, however that power may have been "exercised" (including through the processes of anticipated reactions, both political and economic).

35. For a different interpretation of the power of doctors in American society, see Wolfinger, "Nondecisions and the Study of Local Politics," p. 107.

36. Polsby, *Community Power and Political Theory*, pp. 23 and 116-117.

37. For example, an analysis of party membership data in conjunction with census data reveals the following percentages of party membership among the various education groups: 4 percent of those with 8th grade education or less, 11 percent of those with incomplete secondary education, 18 percent of those with complete secondary education, approximately 22 percent of those with incomplete higher education, 31 percent of those with complete higher education, 46 percent of those with a postgraduate degree. In all cases, the percentages refer only to those 25 years of age and older. The party data is extrapolated from *Partiinaia zhizn'*, no. 14 (July 1973), 16 and 19. The number of persons with a postgraduate degree (candidate or doctor of science) is found in *Narodnoe obrazovanie, nauka, i kultura v SSSR: Statisticheskii sbornik* (Moscow, Statistika, 1971), p. 246. The other census data is taken from *Itogi vsesoiuznoi perepisi naseleniia 1970 goda* (Moscow, Statistika, 1972), II, 6-7.

38. For the argument that the Brezhnev era may have been characterized by a considerable amount of change in this direction, see "The Soviet System: Petrification or Pluralism?" in this volume, as well as Jerry F. Hough, "The Brezhnev Era: The Man and the Regime," *Problems of Communism* 25 (March-April 1976), 1-17.

39. This point has also been suggested in William H. Riker, "Some Ambiguities in the Notion of Power," *The American Political Science Review*, 58 (June 1964), 348.

## 11. The Comparative Approach and the Study of the Soviet Union

1. Gabriel Almond and G. Bingham Powell, *Comparative Politics* (Boston, Little, Brown and Co., 1966), pp. 19-21.

2. Ibid., pp. 168-169.

3. Horace M. Miner, "Community-society continua," *International Encyclopedia of the Social Sciences* (New York, Macmillan Co., and Free Press, 1968), III, 174.

4. Max Weber, *The Methodology of the Social Sciences* (Glencoe, Ill., The Free Press of Glencoe, 1949), p. 93. The quotation is cited in an illuminating discussion by Abraham Kaplan in *The Conduct of Inquiry* (San Francisco, Chandler Publishing Company, 1964), pp. 82-83. See also his discussion of the problems of models; pp. 258-293.

5. Almond and Powell, *Comparative Politics,* p. 28.

6. Richard R. Fagen, *Politics and Communication* (Boston, Little, Brown and Co., 1966), p. 65.

7. Erik P. Hoffmann, "Social Science and Soviet Administrative Behavior," *World Politics,* 24 (April 1972), 444, 469.

8. Ibid., pp. 444, 449, and 471.

9. As one reads James Watson's *The Double Helix,* one wonders how he would have phrased his test of hypothesis on a research grant application.

10. Jerry F. Hough, *The Soviet Prefects* (Cambridge, Mass., Harvard University Press, 1969).

11. Not only did the leading Western textbooks on the Soviet Union say little about a coordinating role at that time, but even that very knowledgeable expert on the CPSU, Nikita S. Khrushchev, indicated little belief in its importance when he bifurcated the party apparatus into urban and rural components in 1962—a year after the completion of the dissertation upon which the book was based.

12. Thomas S. Kuhn, *The Structure of Scientific Revolution,* 2nd enlarged ed., (Chicago, University of Chicago Press, 1970).

13. J. D. Watson, "The Cancer Conquerors," *The New Republic,* 166 (February 26, 1972), 18-19.

14. For an elaboration of this argument in the realm of comparative urban theory, see Jerry F. Hough, "Soviet Urban Politics and Comparative Urban Theory," *Journal of Comparative Administration,* 4 (November 1972), 312-314.

15. Such reading need not be limited to formal social science theory. In the case of *The Soviet Prefects,* some of the most fruitful reading from a theoretical point of view involved the prescriptive literature on American business management. The enormous attention given to the phenomenon of delegation of authority, the great difficulty in defining the way in which this was to be accomplished without permitting subordinates unwanted leeway, the evident ambiguity and variability in actual delegation of authority—all of these suggested that the same problems must exist in the Soviet Union and that they must be discussed in the literature. Once this proposition was accepted, many statements in party-state theory took on quite a different meaning than they had previously.

16. Alfred G. Meyer, "USSR Incorporated," *Slavic Review,* 20 (October 1961), 369-376 and *The Soviet Political System* (New York, Random House, 1965); Allen Kassof, "The Administered Society: Totalitarianism without Terror," *World Politics,* 16 (July 1964), 558-575; T. H. Rigby, "Traditional, Market, and Organizational Societies and the U.S.S.R.," ibid., pp. 539-557.

17. For example, *The Soviet Prefects* is organized as an administrative study, but it contains a great deal of material on the central issue of community power

studies—namely, the relationship of the economic elite to urban political authorities. Although the book was published eight years ago, I have yet to see a reference to it in that literature or to meet a specialist on non-Communist urban political questions who has read it.

18. Edward R. Tufte, "Improving Data Analysis in Political Science," *World
Politics,* 21 (July 1969), pp. 641-654. Gudmund R. Iversen, "Social Science and
Statistics," ibid., 25 (October 1972), pp. 145-154.

19. It is possible that "support" questions must be asked more precisely
before they ever can be very useful. In discussing stability and instability in general
and mechanisms of control in specific, are we talking about the maintenance of
the basic institutional structure, of the political dominance of the party leader or
leadership (or, indeed, of his or its role vis-à-vis "society"), of the general rules of
the political process, or of the position of a broadly-defined elite (the New Class)?
What developments should be accepted as evidence of change? Does the very
sharp influx of technically trained personnel into the party apparatus mean that
"the party" (however defined) has been able to strengthen its control over the
economy or does it mean that (in a pattern analogous to that which often takes
place in the West) the regulated have been able to "take over" the regulatory
agency? At the most basic level, should we think of the Soviet Union as having
had a relatively stable political system over time, in which case our central task is
explaining the stability? Or should we agree with Robert Tucker that "what we
carelessly call 'the Soviet political system' is best seen and analyzed as an historical
succession of political systems," in which case our central task is explaining the
instability. Robert C. Tucker, "The Question of Totalitarianism," *Slavic Review,*
20 (October 1961), 381.

20. For a survey of this literature, see Richard I. Hofferbert, "State and Community Policy Studies: A Review of Comparative Input-Output Analyses," in
James A. Robinson, ed., *Political Science, III* (Indianapolis, Bobbs-Merrill,
1972), pp. 3-72.

# Index

Afanasev, V. G., 68
All-people's state, 110-112
Almond, Gabriel A., 173, 177-178, 184, 203, 225-228
Andropov, Iu. V., 26
Apparatchiki, definition of, 51-56, 71-73. *See also* Central Committee; Gorkom; Ideological party officials; Local party organs; Obkom; Raikom; Republican Central Committee
Armstrong, John A., 65
Aspaturian, Vernon V., 52
Autonomy of input structures, 203
Azrael, Jeremy R., 20, 212

Bachrach, Peter, 214
Baranskaia, Nataliia, 149
Baratz, Morton S., 214
Bell, David, 197
Bentley, Arthur F., 71-72, 212
Berliner, Joseph, 65, 83
Blau, Peter M., 57
Bottomore, T. B., 197-198
Boundaries in systems theory, 225-227
Brezhnev, Leonid I., changes initiated by, 11-12, 25-40, 43, 109-119, 133-134, 159-165, 169-170
Brzezinski, Zbigniew, 3, 64, 182, 197; on groups, 178-180, 268n15; on the party apparatus, 51-52, 71, 88-89, 268n14; on the permanent purge, 28; on petrification and the government of clerks, 20-21, 46, 49-53, 56
Burlatsky, Fedeor, 112
Burnham, James, 49

Censorship, 25-27, 191-202. *See also* Debates, freedom of
Central Committee: background of mem-

bers, 28-29, 34, 35, 36, 45; background and role of secretaries and department heads, 29, 36, 73-78, 97, 104, 141
Childs, H. L., 183
Chubar, V. Ia., 31
Churchward, L. G., 67
Circular flow of power theory, 44-46
Communist Party, membership in, 5, 6-7, 113, 117, 125-139. *See also* Apparatchiki; Central Committee
Comparison of the Soviet Union and the United States, 1-2, 8-9, 40-42, 68-70, 120-124, 178-181, 217-221, 222-228. *See also* United States
Council of Ministers, background of members, 28-29, 53, 67
Crozier, Michel, 64, 67
Cyert, Richard M., 68-69

Dahl, Robert A., 9, 23, 188, 204-217
Dalton, Melville, 57
Daniels, Robert V., 22, 44, 47, 69
Day care centers, 153, 155-158
Debates, freedom of, 25-26, 143, 149-152, 190-196, 198-199
Deutsch, Karl W., 183-184, 202
Directed society models, 3, 19-20, 25, 31, 69-70, 119-120
Dissenters, 25, 27
Djilas, Milovan, 21
Doctors, 5
Dodge, Norton, 147
Downs, Anthony, 59, 64
Druzhinniki (auxiliary police), 112, 113, 148

Easton, David, 68, 173, 176-177, 183-184, 202, 237
Education: of population, 118; of party

members, 129-133, 136-139
Elite theory, 209-211, 215
Equilibrium theory, 182-184, 188

Fagen, Richard R., 228
Fainsod, Merle, 66, 100
Fesler, James, 214
Fischer, George, 57
Friedrich, Carl J., 21, 175
Fromm, Erich, 48
Furtseva, E. A., 141
Future of the Soviet system, 43-48, 67, 104, 135

Galbraith, John Kenneth, 60
General Secretary: power of, 43-47, 91-92; relationship to Central Committee apparatus, 103-104
Gorkom (party city committee), background of first secretaries, 36, 38, 41, 74
Granick, David, 64-66
Grechko, A. A., 54
Griffith, Ernest, 11
Grishin, V. V., 30
Groups, see Interest group theory

Heavy industrial-military complex, 242n10
Hoffmann, Erik P., 228-229
Hospital beds, 160-169
Hunter, Floyd, 205
Huntington, Samuel P., 3, 51, 64, 71, 88-89, 178-179, 182

Ideal-type analysis, 227-228
Ideological party officials, 67, 93-94, 97, 144-147
Ikramov, A., 31
Industrial managers: background of, 54-55, 90; role of, 64-66
Inkeles, Alex, 24, 69, 173
Institutional pluralism, 10-11, 22-24, 33, 43-46, 69-79
Interest group theory, 8, 22, 71-73, 104-108, 179, 181-183, 203, 210

Johnson, Lyndon B., 40-41

Kassof, Allen, 3, 50
Key, V. O., 175, 182, 204

KGB, 26
Khodzhaev, F., 31
Khrushchev, N. S., 11, 19; degree of freedom under, 27, 118-119, 244n28; personnel turnover, 28-29; political participation, 109-110, 114-115, 117, 119, 134-135
Kolkhoz Council, 112
Komsomol, 5-6, 11, 90-91, 113, 147
Korotkov, B. F., 52-53
Kossior, S. V., 31
Kovrigina, M. D., 141
Kuhn, Thomas, 231
Kunaev, D. A., 30

LaPalombara, Joseph, 1
Laski, Harold, 60
Lindblom, Charles E., 10
Local party organs, 3-4, 32, 82-85, 88, 230, 243n37. See also Gorkom; Obkom; Raikom; Republican central committee
Lowell, A. Lawrence, 182
Lowi, Theodore, 9

McFarland, Andrew S., 214
Macpherson, C. B., 189
Mannheim, Karl, 20
March, James G., 68-69
Marcuse, Herbert, 19
Matskevich, V. V., 54
Membership in the party, see Communist Party
Meyer, Alfred E., 1-2, 19, 22, 174, 234
Michels, Robert, 62
Mills, C. Wright, 204, 210, 217, 265n32
Mirzoian, L. I., 31
Mitchell, William, 175
Moore, Barrington, Jr., 19, 45-50
Moynihan, Daniel Patrick, 60

New Class, 21, 33
New Haven, 121-123, 182, 207, 210, 217
Nomenklatura, 56
Novocherkassk, 87

Obkom (regional party committee), background of first secretaries, 28-30, 36, 41, 44, 74-75, 78
Oliver, James, 177
Olson, Mancur, 258n39

Parsons, Talcott, 224
Participation in the Soviet Union: 8, 109-124, 141-152. *See also* Communist Party; Debates; Interest group theory; Khrushchev; Komsomol; Trade unions
Pel'she, A. I., 30
People's Control Committee, 113
Pluralism, 8-10, 14, 24. *See also* Institutional pluralism
Politburo, background of members, 4, 28-30, 36, 46, 67
Polsbȳ, Nelson, 205-210, 214-217
Powell, G. Bingham, 178, 225-228
Power distribution in the Soviet Union, 10-14, 22-23, 69-70, 119-124, 157-158, 169-170
Pravo kontrolia, 112, 115
PTA (Parent-Teachers' Association), 121-122
Pysin, K. G., 80-81

Raikom (district party committee), background of first secretaries, 36, 38
Ranney, Austin, 174-175
Republican central committee, background of officials, 29-31, 36-38, 78
Responsiveness, 183-189
Rigby, T. H., 3, 50
Romanov, G. V., 30
Rush, Myron, 44-45

"Saturation," 125-126
Schapiro, Leonard, 21
Shcherbitsky, V. V., 30
Sinitsyn, I. F., 54
Skilling, H. Gordon, 23, 52
Smolensk, 66
Soviets: number and background of deputies, 113, 117, 142-143; background of officials, 55, 142, 145-147, 167-168; work of the oblast soviet, 142-144, 153-158, 167-170. *See also* Standing committees; Supreme Soviet
Stalin, J., 12, 82, 116, 173, 175, 190-196, 208-209
Standing committees of soviets, 116, 123, 142-143, 146-147
Sudnitsyn, Iu. G., 116
Supreme Soviet, background of deputies, 126, 142
Systems theory, 183-185, 225, 227, 272n19

Tarasov, N. N., 55
Taubman, William, 4
Temir-Tau, 87
Timasheff, N. S., 209
Trade unions, 11, 113, 143
Trotsky, Leon, 48-51

United States: average age of officials, 41; bureaucracy, 58-64; debates and access, 202; interest groups, 105-107; pluralism, 9; political participation, 121-123; power of masses, 204-207. *See also* Comparison of the Soviet Union and the United States

Volkov, Iu. E., 116

Wages, 39-40, 150, 152-154
Watson, James, 231
Weber, Max, 49, 57, 58, 60, 62, 65, 224, 234
Wildavsky, Aaron, 65
Wiles, Peter, 13
"Whirlpool" theory, 11

# Russian Research Center Studies

1. *Public Opinion in Soviet Russia: A Study in Mass Persuasion*, by Alex Inkeles
2. *Soviet Politics—The Dilemma of Power: The Role of Ideas in Social Change*, by Barrington Moore, Jr.*
3. *Justice in the U.S.S.R.: An Interpretation of Soviet Law*, by Harold J. Berman*
4. *Chinese Communism and the Rise of Mao*, by Benjamin I. Schwartz
5. *Titoism and the Cominform*, by Adam B. Ulam*
6. *A Documentary History of Chinese Communism*, by Conrad Brandt, Benjamin Schwartz, and John K. Fairbank*
7. *The New Man in Soviet Psychology*, by Raymond A. Bauer
8. *Soviet Opposition to Stalin: A Case Study in World War II*, by George Fischer*
9. *Minerals: A Key to Soviet Power*, by Demitri B. Shimkin*
10. *Soviet Law in Action: The Recollected Cases of a Soviet Lawyer*, by Boris A. Konstantinovsky; edited by Harold J. Berman*
11. *How Russia Is Ruled*, by Merle Fainsod. Revised edition
12. *Terror and Progress—USSR: Some Sources of Change and Stability in the Soviet Dictatorship*, by Barrington Moore, Jr.
13. *The Formation of the Soviet Union: Communism and Nationalism, 1917-1923*, by Richard Pipes. Revised edition*
14. *Marxism: The Unity of Theory and Practice—A Critical Essay*, by Alfred G. Meyer. Reissued with a new introduction*
15. *Soviet Industrial Production, 1928-1951*, by Donald R. Hodgman*
16. *Soviet Taxation: The Fiscal and Monetary Problems of a Planned Economy*, by Franklyn D. Holzman*
17. *Soviet Military Law and Administration*, by Harold J. Berman and Miroslav Kerner*
18. *Documents on Soviet Military Law and Administration*, edited and translated by Harold J. Berman and Miroslav Kerner*
19. *The Russian Marxists and the Origins of Bolshevism*, by Leopold H. Haimson*
20. *The Permanent Purge: Politics in Soviet Totalitarianism*, by Zbigniew K. Brzezinski*
21. *Belorussia: The Making of a Nation—A Case Study*, by Nicholas P. Vakar*

22.  *A Bibliographical Guide to Belorussia,* by Nicholas P. Vakar*
23.  *The Balkans in Our Time,* by Robert Lee Wolff (also American Foreign Policy Library)
24.  *How the Soviet System Works: Cultural, Psychological, and Social Themes,* by Raymond A. Bauer, Alex Inkeles, and Clyde Kluckhohn†*
25.  *The Economics of Soviet Steel,* by M. Gardner Clark*
26.  *Leninism,* by Alfred G. Meyer*
27.  *Factory and Manager in the USSR,* by Joseph S. Berliner†*
28.  *Soviet Transportation Policy,* by Holland Hunter*
29.  *Doctor and Patient in Soviet Russia,* by Mark G. Field†*
30.  *Russian Liberalism: From Gentry to Intelligentsia,* by George Fischer*
31.  *Stalin's Failure in China, 1924-1927,* by Conrad Brandt*
32.  *The Communist Party of Poland: An Outline of History,* by M. K. Dziewanowski. Second edition
33.  *Karamzin's Memoir on Ancient and Modern Russia: A Translation and Analysis,* by Richard Pipes*
34.  *A Memoir on Ancient and Modern Russia,* by N. M. Karamzin, the Russian text edited by Richard Pipes*
35.  *The Soviet Citizen: Daily Life in a Totalitarian Society,* by Alex Inkeles and Raymond A. Bauer†*
36.  *Pan-Turkism and Islam in Russia,* by Serge A. Zenkovsky
37.  *The Soviet Bloc: Unity and Conflict,* by Zbigniew K. Brzezinski. (Sponsored jointly with the Center for International Affairs, Harvard University.) Revised and enlarged edition. Also in Harvard Paperbacks.
38.  *National Consciousness in Eighteenth-Century Russia,* by Hans Rogger
39.  *Alexander Herzen and the Birth of Russian Socialism, 1812-1855,* by Martin Malia*
40.  *The Conscience of the Revolution: Communist Opposition in Soviet Russia,* by Robert Vincent Daniels*
41.  *The Soviet Industrialization Debate, 1924-1928,* by Alexander Erlich*
42.  *The Third Section: Police and Society in Russia under Nicholas I,* by Sidney Monas*
43.  *Dilemmas of Progress in Tsarist Russia: Legal Marxism and Legal Populism,* by Arthur P. Mendel*
44.  *Political Control of Literature in the USSR, 1946-1959,* by Harold Swayze
45.  *Accounting in Soviet Planning and Management,* by Robert W. Campbell*
46.  *Social Democracy and the St. Petersburg Labor Movement, 1885-1897,* by Richard Pipes*
47.  *The New Face of Soviet Totalitarianism,* by Adam B. Ulam*
48.  *Stalin's Foreign Policy Reappraised,* by Marshall D. Shulman*
49.  *The Soviet Youth Program: Regimentation and Rebellion,* by Allen Kassof*
50.  *Soviet Criminal Law and Procedure: The RSFSR Codes,* translated by Harold J. Berman and James W. Spindler; introduction and analysis by Harold J. Berman. Second edition

51. *Poland's Politics: Idealism vs. Realism*, by Adam Bromke

52. *Managerial Power and Soviet Politics*, by Jeremy R. Azrael

53. *Danilevsky: A Russian Totalitarian Philosopher*, by Robert E. Mac-Master*

54. *Russia's Protectorates in Central Asia: Bukhara and Khiva, 1865-1924*, by Seymour Becker

55. *Revolutionary Russia*, edited by Richard Pipes

56. *The Family in Soviet Russia*, by H. Kent Geiger

57. *Social Change in Soviet Russia*, by Alex Inkeles

58. *The Soviet Prefects: The Local Party Organs in Industrial Decision-making*, by Jerry F. Hough

59. *Soviet-Polish Relations, 1917-1921*, by Piotr S. Wandycz

60. *One Hundred Thousand Tractors: The MTS and the Development of Controls in Soviet Agriculture*, by Robert F. Miller

61. *The Lysenko Affair*, by David Joravsky

62. *Icon and Swastika: The Russian Orthodox Church under Nazi and Soviet Control*, by Harvey Fireside

63. *A Century of Russian Agriculture: From Alexander II to Khrushchev*, by Lazar Volin

64. *Struve: Liberal on the Left, 1870-1905*, by Richard Pipes*

65. *Nikolai Strakhov*, by Linda Gerstein

66. *The Kurbskii-Groznyi Apocrypha: The Seventeenth-Century Genesis of the "Correspondence" Attributed to Prince A. M. Kurbskii and Tsar Ivan IV*, by Edward L. Keenan

67. *Chernyshevskii: The Man and the Journalist*, by William F. Woehrlin

68. *European and Muscovite: Ivan Kiereevsky and the Origins of Slavophil-ism*, by Abbott Gleason

69. *Newton and Russia: The Early Influence, 1698-1796*, by Valentin Boss

70. *Pavel Axelrod and the Development of Menshevism*, by Abraham Ascher

71. *The Service Sector in Soviet Economic Growth: A Comparative Study*, by Gur Ofer (also Harvard Economic Studies)

72. *The Classroom and the Chancellery: State Educational Reform in Russia under Count Dmitry Tolstoi*, by Allen Sinel

73. *Foreign Trade under Central Planning*, by Franklyn D. Holzman

74. *Soviet Policy toward India: Ideology and Strategy*, by Robert H. Donaldson

75. *The End of Serfdom: Nobility and Bureaucracy in Russia, 1855-1861*, by Daniel Field

76. *The Dynamics of Soviet Politics*, edited by Paul Cocks, Robert V. Daniels, and Nancy Whittier Heer

77. *The Soviet Union and Social Science Theory*, by Jerry F. Hough

78. *The Russian Levites: Parish Clergy in the Eighteenth Century*, by Gregory L. Freeze

*Out of print.

†Publications of the Harvard Project on the Soviet Social System.